Marketing: The One-Semester Introduction

Marketing: The One-Semester Introduction

Geoff Lancaster and Paul Reynolds

BUTTERWORTH
HEINEMANN

OXFORD AUCKLAND BOSTON JOHANNESBURG MELBOURNE NEW DELHI

Butterworth-Heinemann
Linacre House, Jordan Hill, Oxford OX2 8DP
225 Wildwood Avenue, Woburn, MA 01801-2041
A division of Reed Educational and Professional Publishing Ltd

A member of the Reed Elsevier plc group

First published 2002

British Library Cataloguing in Publication Data
Lancaster, Geoffrey A.
   Marketing: the one-semester introduction
   1. Marketing
   I. Title   II. Reynolds, Paul
   658.8

Library of Congress Cataloguing in Publication Data
A catalogue record for this book is available from the Library of Congress

ISBN 0 7506 4381 1

For information on all Butterworth-Heinemann publications visit
our website at: www.bh.com

Composition by Genesis Typesetting, Laser Quay, Rochester, Kent
Printed and bound in Great Britain by MPG Books Ltd, Bodmin, Cornwall

FOR EVERY TITLE THAT WE PUBLISH, BUTTERWORTH-HEINEMANN
WILL PAY FOR BTCV TO PLANT AND CARE FOR A TREE.

Contents

1   Introduction to marketing   1

2   The marketing-orientated organisation   14

3   The marketing environment   28

4   The functions of marketing   49

5   Market segmentation, targeting and positioning of marketing   68

6   Buyer behaviour   89

7   Marketing communications I   119

8   Marketing communications II – personal selling   153

9   Channels of distribution   176

10 Physical distribution management   191

11 Pricing   209

12 Product policy   233

13 Marketing research   257

14 Sales forecasting   285

15 International marketing   310

16 Societal marketing   333

17 Marketing strategy, planning and control   355

18 The use of Internet technology in marketing   380

19 Customer care and customer relationship management   414

Index   431

v

Introduction to marketing

1

1.1 Introduction

We begin by examining the basic idea of marketing as a business discipline. The *concept of marketing* is not particularly complicated or even original. Sayings such as 'the customer comes first' or 'the customer is always right' have been used by forward-thinking merchants and entrepreneurs ever since the Industrial Revolution. Marketing is a more formal business orientation, based on a simple principle of consumer sovereignty that has developed into a management discipline over the years. The subject of marketing as a management discipline originated in the USA in the 1950s, but its origins go back much further. As William J. Stanton of the University of Colorado has stated, 'the foundations of marketing in *America* were laid in colonial times when the early settlers traded amongst themselves and also with the Indians' (Stanton *et al.*, 1991). It is generally accepted that America gave birth to modern marketing as we know it now, but in terms of its earliest practice it was applied much earlier in Europe. At one time the carpenter, tailor, saddler and stonemason knew their customers personally, and they were in a position to discuss their individual needs of size, colour, shape and design. To gain repeat business craftsmen appreciated that they had to provide satisfactory service to individual customers, and so the notion of caring for customers became apparent. With the Industrial Revolution and large-scale manufacturing, this personal contact ended. With mass production came mass markets and mass distribution, and manufacturers were no longer able to offer a personalised service to their customers, so it could be argued that inadvertently the Industrial Revolution was the birthplace of modern marketing.

There is no unified definition of the subject of marketing; in fact, there is often considerable confusion over the precise meaning of the term among marketing academics and practitioners. The way in which the term is understood conditions people's perceptions of the value of marketing and the contribution it can make both to the success of an individual organisation and to the competitive health of the economy as a whole. As a student of marketing, it is of great importance that you appreciate that the term 'marketing' can, and often does, mean different things to different people. We shall be examining the subject from these different viewpoints later in this chapter.

Definition
The subject of marketing as a management discipline originated in the USA in the 1950s, but its origins go back much further.

Key point
There is no unified definition of the subject of marketing; in fact, there is often considerable confusion over the precise meaning of the term among marketing academics and practitioners.

Definition
Marketing is based on the premise that the customer is the most important person to the organisation.

Marketing is based on the premise that the customer is the most important person to the organisation. Most people think of the term *customer* in the context of a profit-making facility. Whilst it is true that the marketing concept has been more widely adopted and practised in the profit-making sectors of the economy, the fundamental principles of marketing are equally applicable in the not-for-profit sectors; a fact that is often overlooked.

Marketing as an organisational philosophy and activity is applicable to almost all types of organisation, whether profit making or not-for-profit. Throughout this chapter you are encouraged to comprehend the term 'customer' in this wider context, and not just as someone who interacts with a profit-centred business.

Examination candidates tend to be better at discussing marketing as a functional area of management than as an overall business philosophy. When properly understood, it will be appreciated that marketing is not necessarily narrowly confined to a particular office or department, and indeed one of the most frequent problems that companies have is in the vision by other departments (and sometimes even the marketing department itself) that somebody 'does' marketing in the process sense. In its widest sense, marketing is really an attitude of mind or an approach to business problems that should be adopted by the whole organisation. It is only when the discipline is understood in this wider context that the student and practitioner alike can properly appreciate the role of marketing and its value to an organisation. At higher levels examination questions tend to be more about marketing philosophy, whereas at less advanced levels the functional elements of marketing tend to attract more questions.

1.2 The importance of the consumer

As far back as 1776, during the Industrial Revolution, Adam Smith, widely regarded to be the founding father of modern economics, wrote the following in his classic work *The Wealth of Nations*:

> Consumption is the sole end and purpose of all production and the interests of the producer ought to be attended to only so far as it may be necessary for promoting that of the consumer.

Definition
It is the identification and satisfaction of consumer requirements that forms the basis of the modern concept of marketing.

In essence, it does not matter how good a firm may think its product to be or how well organised it is in processing its orders; unless it has customers, there is no business to conduct. In the statement above, Adam Smith has given the essence of the central guiding theme of the subject of marketing. The key word is *consumer*, as it is the identification and satisfaction of consumer requirements that forms the basis of the modern concept of marketing.

Interestingly, Smith went on after the above statement to say:

> The maxim is so perfectly self-evident that it would be absurd to attempt to prove it. But in the mercantile system, the interest of the consumer is almost constantly sacrificed to that of producers who seem to consider production, and not consumption, as the ultimate end and object of all industry and commerce.

What he was saying is that producers make what they deem the market needs. What he did through this classic statement was to point out the parameters of business orientation: the first part describes *marketing orientation* and the second part of the statement describes *production orientation*.

Vignette 1.1

Cunard Cruise Line Corporation markets the magic of a bygone age

The grand tradition of the classic ocean voyage is very much alive today aboard the luxury liners of Cunard, pioneers of luxury ocean-going travel. For more than a century Cunard has provided its customers with a superior travel experience at sea. Sophisticated travellers discovered the world in a world of luxury as they sailed on ships that were dramatic and fascinating.

Since 1840 the Cunard Line has provided the experience of luxury travel from a golden age. The company pioneered the marketing of luxury ocean travel, and even today they use their heritage and reputation to market its modern travel services and products. When you venture onto a Cunard Ocean Liner, you immediately step back into a golden age of ocean travel. The classic traditions of the grand ocean voyage are still retained aboard the modern luxurious liners of Cunard such as the *Queen Elizabeth 2* or the *Caronia*. The 'good life' is still here for the passengers that can afford it.

Cunard was the first company to take passengers on regularly scheduled services (*Britannia*, 1840), the first to introduce electricity on a ship (*Servia*, 1881) and the first to develop steam turbine engines on a liner (*Carmania*, 1905). The company was the first to put a gymnasium on a liner (*Franconai*, 1911), and the first to introduce an indoor swimming pool on a ship (*Aquitania*, 1914). This list of pioneering firsts is not exhaustive, but merely serves to show how the company was dedicated to innovation and product improvement. Cunard was and still is a truly customer-driven and marketing-orientated company.

In order for a profit-making enterprise to prosper, or even to survive, its management must work hard to retain its existing markets against competition and must continually strive to counter technical obsolescence and changes in consumer tastes by attempting to secure new and profitable customers. Not-for-profit organisations must continually justify their existence in terms of their usefulness to society. They have to answer to interested parties who may well withdraw their financial support if the goods or services they offer to the community do not match the requirements of the community. The marketing concept, which puts the emphasis on customers and the identification and satisfaction of customer requirements, results in the customer or consumer becoming the central focus of an organisation's activities.

Some people view the subject of marketing as a branch of applied economics. Other writers and practitioners have worked for a number of years in a specialised field of marketing such as advertising, brand management or marketing research. It is understandable that such people often regard their particular speciality as the most important facet of marketing. Some people take a rather myopic view of the subject and see marketing merely as a

Definition
The marketing concept, which puts the emphasis on customers and the identification and satisfaction of customer requirements, results in the customer or consumer becoming the central focus of an organisation's activities.

collection of well-developed management techniques, which, when combined, constitute a functional area of the organisation's management operations. More enlightened practitioners and theorists view the subject as an overriding business philosophy which guides the organisation in everything it does. Students approaching the subject for the first time might become confused because of the absence of a unified definition of the subject. It can rightly be regarded as somewhat ill-defined, with any definition coloured by the way the subject is approached. Marketing is often viewed as:

1 *A social process*: At a macro level, marketing is viewed as a social process by which individuals and groups obtain what they need and want by creating and exchanging things of value.

2 *A distributive system*: Marketing is viewed as a process whereby in a democratic society, operating within a free market or mixed economy, there evolves a system of distribution that facilitates transactions resulting in exchange and consumption.

3 *A functional area of management*: Marketing is seen as a functional area of management, usually based in a particular location within the organisation, which uses a collection of techniques, e.g. advertising, public relations, sales promotion and packaging, to achieve specific objectives.

Definition
Many successful firms see marketing as the keystone of their business.

4 *An overall business philosophy*: Many successful firms see marketing as the keystone of their business. Marketing in such firms is viewed not as a separate function, but rather as a profit-orientated approach to business that permeates not just the marketing department but the entire business. The central mission of the entire organisation is seen as the satisfaction of customer requirements at a profit (or, in not-for-profit sectors, at a maximum level of efficiency or minimum level of cost). This is achieved by focusing the attention of the entire organisation on the importance of the customer and the needs of the market-place.

5 *A targeting or allocative system*: Marketing is perceived as the way any organisation or individual matches its own capabilities to the needs and wants of its customers. From an organisational point of view, marketing is seen as the primary management function that organises and targets the activities of the entire organisation in order to convert consumer purchasing power into effective demand. Its objective is to move the product or service to the final consumer or user in order to achieve company profit (or optimum cost efficiency).

Vignette 1.2

The Gallup Organisation, Princeton, USA, created by George Gallup, pioneer of commercial data collection

Information is the 'lifeblood' of successful marketing, and George Gallup pioneered the collection and analysis of social science data for use by commercial firms. George Gallup was born in Iowa,

USA, in 1901 and studied journalism at the University of Iowa. He was interested in finding out why people read particular publications and how satisfied they were with the content and presentation of commercial publications such as newspapers and magazines. He began to try and measure these things whilst still a student. His PhD thesis was in psychology, and was entitled 'An Objective Method for determining Reader Interest in the Content of a Newspaper'.

Gallup used scientific methodology drawn from the universities for social science research. Much of this methodology was developed at such august institutions as the London School of Economics and Political Science, and at Harvard University in Cambridge, Massachusetts. Gallup pioneered the use of sample surveys using scientifically constructed sampling techniques. His work at the University of Iowa started a career that would last the rest of his life.

Gallup was offered a job by Raymond Rubicam, another pioneer working in the advertising field and who created the advertising firm Young and Rubicam. Gallup employed his newly developed techniques to research advertising effectiveness. This work was extended to other areas of the marketing mix, and the Gallup Organisation provided a fully developed marketing research service. George Gallup was very interested in politics, and created the Gallup Poll to carry out scientific political surveys into voters' intentions. It is for this side of his work that he is perhaps best remembered.

George Gallup did a great service to the marketing industry, and many of his techniques are still used today in commercial marketing research. Gallup understood the sort of information marketing companies needed, how to get it, what to do with it, and how to turn the findings of his research into commercially valuable recommendations for future marketing actions.

1.3 Definitions of marketing

As a student of marketing, you are likely to have to sit examinations set by a European examining body. The generally accepted European definition of marketing is that given by the Chartered Institute of Marketing (CIM). It might be wise to commit this particular definition to memory (whilst not forgetting that marketing is a very wide-ranging subject which can be looked at from many different points-of-view):

> Marketing is the management process responsible for identifying, anticipating and satisfying customer requirements profitably.

Definition
Marketing is a very wide-ranging subject which can be looked at from many different points-of-view.

Some writers use the terms 'needs' and 'wants' rather than customers 'requirements'. Philip Kotler of Northwestern University, USA, one of the world's leading academics in the field of marketing, defines a 'need' as a basic requirement such as food, shelter, self esteem etc. (Kotler, 1991). He defines a 'want' as a particular way of satisfying a 'need'. For example, a person may need food, but he or she may not necessarily want spaghetti bolognaise!

A more technical definition is given for marketing by the American Marketing Association:

> Marketing is the process of planning and executing the conception, pricing, promotion and distribution of ideas, goods and services to create exchanges that satisfy individual and organisational objectives.

Although this definition is not as succinct as that provided by the Chartered Institute of Marketing it is perhaps more correct, as the CIM definition highlights the 'profitability' criterion whereas, as we have already discussed, marketing principles are also applicable in not-for-profit organisations.

1.4 Historical development

Definition
Marketing is principally concerned with exchange or trade.

Marketing is principally concerned with exchange or trade. Trade in its most basic form has existed ever since mankind has been capable of producing a surplus. Historically this surplus was usually agricultural produce, which was often traded for manufactured goods such as textiles or earthenware. Exchange brought into existence places that facilitated trade, such as village fairs and local markets. The emergence of trade allowed people to specialise in producing particular goods and services, which could be exchanged in markets for other goods they needed.

Vignette 1.3

The East India Company: a pioneer in international marketing logistics

A Royal Charter of Queen Elizabeth I founded the East India Company in 1600. The company was one of the single most powerful commercial forces that the world had ever seen. It was based in London, but its influence reached out to the whole world. The company basically created British India, and founded the British colonies of Hong Kong (now part of China) and Singapore (now independent). Its administration was recognised as superb throughout the world, and it still forms the basis of Indian administrative processes. The company introduced tea to Britain, woollen garments to Japan, opium to China and porcelain to Russia.

Today the company is a modern, dynamic commercial enterprise with experience and contacts throughout the world. The Company is forging partnerships in many parts of the world. It offers international marketing and distribution services and advice to many countries, and provides an authoritative port of call for many businesses looking to expand their operations overseas.

1.4.1 The Industrial Revolution

The period 1760–1830 saw the United Kingdom economy transformed, losing its dependence on agriculture and undergoing a dramatic increase in industrial production. Before the Industrial Revolution, the production and distribution of goods tended to be on a small scale. Industrialisation resulted in dramatic gains in productivity, mainly due to the development of machines. Production became more geographically concentrated, and was carried out in purpose-built mills or factories. Enterprises became larger, production runs longer and products more standardised. Firms produced in volume, not only for a local market but for a national and even an international market.

Although production expanded dramatically during this period, it brought with it many social problems. The simultaneous development of machines, communications, improved transport, agricultural improvements and advances in commercial practices transformed the UK economy, resulting in the growth of the 'factory system'. This caused the migration of the population from the countryside to the new and rapidly expanding industrial towns.

1.4.2 The dispersal of markets

Because of developments during the period of the Industrial Revolution, firms could produce more in terms of volume than the local economy could absorb. Consumption therefore became dispersed over greater geographical distances, and producers no longer had immediate contact with their markets. To overcome this problem, many forward-thinking entrepreneurs of the time started to plan their business operations in a 'marketing-orientated' manner, although the terms 'marketing and 'marketing orientation' were not formally used to describe this process until well into the twentieth century.

> **Key point**
> Producers no longer had immediate contact with their markets.

In order for producers to be able to manufacture goods and services that would appeal and sell in widely dispersed markets, it became necessary for them carefully to analyse and interpret the needs and wants of customers, and to manufacture products that would 'fit in' with those needs and wants.

Prior to examining marketing as an entrepreneurial function, it is appropriate to discuss the principal types of production:

> **Key point**
> In order for producers to be able to manufacture goods and services that would appeal and sell in widely dispersed markets, it became necessary for them carefully to analyse and interpret the needs and wants of customers.

- *Project* or *job production* is effectively 'one-off' production, where every aspect of construction (project) or manufacture (job) is done as a separate activity from the design to the completion stage. Skilled personnel are needed during the design and manufacturing processes. An example of a project is the construction of a hospital, and for job production it is the construction of a ship. Naturally, this means that the manufacturing process is a relatively skilled and expensive procedure.

- *Batch production* is where the numbers produced are more than one, but the skills required and the means of production are similar to job production, and the reality is that batches produced are usually in single figures. Such production is more appropriate to manufacturing than construction.

The two types of production just described applied in manufacturing activity until 1913. This is when Henry Ford set up the first ever continuous flow line production assembly plant in Detroit, USA, to manufacture the Model 'T' car. The Model 'T' Ford was in fact developed in 1908 and was initially constructed using batch production principles, and it was not until 1913 that Henry Ford brought in the first ever moving production line that was based upon the principles of the division of labour. Workers no longer assembled much of the car but instead did one task repeatedly, and hence the task was completed better and faster. Another principle he established was that all components should be strictly interchangeable and precisely identical to the next. The result was that he was able to produce and sell his Model 'T' cars at US$550 each, or 35 per cent less than when they were initially introduced in 1908. Moreover, the car remained in production, largely unchanged, for 19 years, and by 1925 production line refinements meant that the price was down to US$260.

● *Flow (or flow-line) production* as just described is where all aspects of the manufacturing process are broken down into their simplest components of assembly. Less skilled, relatively inexpensive labour can be used. The whole process is a quicker and more cost-effective method of production. End prices are lower, and the implication of such mass production is that all products are basically the same and there is a need for a mass market.

1.4.3 Marketing implications in the UK in respect of developments in production line technology

Flow-line production technology did not receive widespread acclaim and application in the United Kingdom following the introduction of Henry Ford's revolutionary process in the USA in 1913. This was largely owing to the fact that UK society was then divided into a small number of 'haves', who owned most of the wealth, and a huge number of 'have nots', who could only afford the base necessities of life, plus a small number of middle class. This was unlike the USA, which was a more equal society, so the circumstances were right in the USA to expand car production in the knowledge that there was a huge middle class ready to purchase these cheaper mass-produced automobiles.

In the UK, the upper classes would certainly not want anything that was mass produced and the middle classes were a relatively small market, whereas the large numbers of working class would not have been able to afford to run a car even if it was given free. Ford did, however, produce a number of Model 'T' cars at Trafford Park, Manchester, but these were not principally for UK consumption.

The Second World War in 1939 was the trigger for the widespread adoption of flow production in the UK because as men were called up for war service it meant that women were drafted into factories which had switched over to the manufacture of war products. As women were basically unskilled and war products were needed desperately, flow-line production technology was the ideal solution.

The war ended in 1945, but rationing did not end until 1954, so flow production was seen as the most effective way to fulfil demand.

A radical post-war Labour Government under Clement Atlee set about a programme designed to remove the inequality between rich and poor and redistribute wealth. The Government nationalised much of the country's infrastructure and increased death duties and personal taxes, so that the base rate was 33 per cent, moving up in 5 per cent bands to 83 per cent. Investment income commanded an extra slice of 15 per cent on top of the top slice of tax, so effectively some people paid tax at 98 per cent. In fact it was not until 1979, when Margaret Thatcher came into power, that this top band of 83 per cent was reduced to 60 per cent, and then to 40 per cent in 1988.

The effect of all of this was a redistribution of wealth from the upper classes to the lower classes. In terms of its effect on marketing, this was profound. The implication was that goods hitherto classed as luxury products became utility products and were necessary in order to live a modern lifestyle. An example is the telephone, which post-war was a luxury item but is now a virtual necessity; even mobile 'phones are rapidly becoming a utility product. It is, therefore, a fact that people nowadays need a greater 'raft' of goods to lead a modern lifestyle and indeed the number of individual products needed is also greater. For instance, after the war, in working class households it was unusual to possess more than two pairs of shoes. This of course is very unlike today, where multiple pairs of shoes are generally the rule. Therefore, not only do customers need a greater range of products to live a modern lifestyle, but they also need more of individual products as well.

The implications just outlined often form questions on marketing papers along the lines of:

- Marketing is the delivery of a higher standard of living. Discuss.

- Marketing is the creation of unnecessary wants and desires. Discuss.

- Marketing is the creation of unnecessary goods and services. Discuss.

Key point
Not only do customers need a greater range of products to live a modern lifestyle, but they also need more of individual products as well.

Vignette 1.4

Henry Ford, pioneer of mass production and mass marketing of motor vehicles

Henry Ford was born in 1863 and was the first of six children. He was brought up on a farm in Michigan, USA, and showed an early interest in mechanical things. At 16 Henry went to work as a machinist in Detroit, and after serving his apprenticeship worked repairing farm implements and steam engines. Ford got a job with the Edison Illuminating Company in Detroit, rising to become chief engineer. During this time he experimented with the internal combustion engine, and even built his own early motor car – more of a four-wheeled 'cycle' really – known as the Quadricycle. Although Henry Ford was not the first to build a self-propelled vehicle with a petrol engine, he was one of the several automotive pioneers who facilitated the mass production and mass ownership of motor cars.

After two unsuccessful attempts, Henry Ford eventually set up the Ford Motor Company. To start with this was a small-scale operation, with the company only producing two or three cars per day. Ford realised that if he could bring the price of a motor car down sufficiently, everyone in the USA would aspire to own one. To bring the price down he had to first bring the cost of production down. Henry Ford combined precision manufacturing, standardised and interchangeable parts, a division of labour and a continuously moving assembly line.

The introduction of the moving assembly line revolutionised automobile production by significantly reducing the assembly time per vehicle. This lowered costs to a level where even Ford's own assembly workers were able to buy the company's cars.

1.4.4 Marketing as an entrepreneurial function

The process of matching the resources of a firm to the needs and wants of the market place is called *entrepreneurship*. Men such as Josiah Wedgwood

Definition
The process of matching the resources of a firm to the needs and wants of the market place is called *entrepreneurship*.

(1730–1795) came to epitomise the traditional entrepreneur, with their ability to 'sense' what the market wanted in terms of design, quality and price, and then to organise production and distribution to satisfy effective demand at a profit. The early entrepreneurs were practising an early, albeit rule-of-thumb, form of marketing activity, although it was not called marketing as such.

Indeed it was not until 1908, when a Frenchman, Henri Fayol, investigated manufacturing practice and came up with a division of labour, that the first theoretical foundations were laid for the discipline of business. Theory in business is unlike, say, chemistry, where theory is first hypothesised in a laboratory situation and then applied in practice. In business, practice takes place prior to the establishment of any theoretical guidelines. Many mistakes are made without any guidelines for pointers to best practice, and it is only by observing practice that theories can then be established.

1.4.5 The effect of job specialisation

A craftsman, such as a blacksmith or potter, develops a high degree of skill in a particular activity. These craft industries were in fact based on an early form of division of labour, which resulted in specialisation and greater productivity. Industrialisation took the processes of specialisation and division of labour a stage further. Specialisation resulted in greater productivity, which in turn reduced costs and hence the selling price of products. However, the rise in job specialisation that was principally brought about by the development of flow production techniques also increased the need for exchange. Larger-scale production meant that marketing channels had to be created to facilitate the distribution of goods to enable the effective demand from the much larger market to be met. This development laid the foundations of the modern industrial economy, which is still based on the fundamental concept of trade or exchange.

Sellers establish customers requirements and then develop products to satisfy their needs. As Doyle states (Doyle, 1994):

'If potential customers buy, then money is exchanged for the products.

During the first half of the nineteenth century, Britain (England, Scotland and Wales) was the dominant force in the world economy. The main factor underlying industrial growth was the development in international trade. Britain was first and foremost a trading nation that had secured supplies of raw materials and held a virtual monopoly in the supply of manufactured goods to, and the receipt of produce from, the relatively underdeveloped countries which collectively made up the British Empire.

The first half of the twentieth century saw the emergence of Germany and the United States as competing industrial powers. Although Britain faced fierce competition from the economically emerging nations in the areas of textiles, coal and steel, the British economy continued along a path of industrial expansion in the period up to the First World War. The incomes generated in other countries resulted in a world-wide increase in

Jo Coleman

Information Update Service

Butterworth-Heinemann

FREEPOST SCE 5435

Oxford

Oxon

OX2 8BR

UK

Keep up-to-date with the latest books in your field.

Visit our website and register now for our FREE e-mail update service, or join our mailing list and enter our monthly prize draw to win £100 worth of books. Just complete the form below and return it to us now! (FREEPOST if you are based in the UK)

www.bh.com

Please Complete in Block Capitals

Title of book you have purchased: ....

Subject area of interest: ....

....

Name: ....

Job title: ....

Business sector (if relevant): ....

Street: ....

Town: .... County: ....

Country: .... Postcode: ....

Email: ....

Telephone: ....

How would you prefer to be contacted: Post ☐   e-mail ☐   Both ☐

Signature: .... Date: ....

☐ Please arrange for me to be kept informed of other books and information on services on this and related subjects (✔) box if not required). This information is being collected on behalf of Reed Elsevier plc group and may be used to supply information about products by companies within the group.

FOR OFFICE USE ONLY

A member of the Reed Elsevier plc group

Butterworth-Heinemann,
a division of Reed Educational
& Professional Publishing Limited.
Registered office: 25 Victoria Street,
London SW1H 0EX.
Registered in England 3099304,
VAT number GB: 663 3472 30.

total effective demand for goods and services. The total value of Britain's trade increased, even though its share of international trade started to decline.

Today, we have a situation where a large number of producers compete for a share of a finite world market. Modern industry is based on mass production, which necessitates mass consumption. In order for many sophisticated products (e.g. home computers, motor cars, and consumer durables such as washing machines) to be commercially successful, they must be produced in a volume sufficient to bring unit costs down to a competitive level. It is no longer enough to produce a good product, as it was in time of shortages or rationing when producers enjoyed a 'sellers market'. Today, for producers to achieve a sufficient level of effective demand, they must produce goods and services that the market perceives as 'valuable' and, more importantly, that the customers will actually buy in sufficient volume. The final customer's needs and wants not only have to be taken into account, but the identification and satisfaction of these needs and wants has become the most important factor in the long-term survival of a firm.

Key point
The identification and satisfaction of the final customer's needs and wants has become the most important factor in the long-term survival of a firm.

1.5 Summary

✓ Commercial enterprises today are much larger and more complex than they were in the nineteenth century. In a modern organisation, the entrepreneurial function is rarely carried out by one individual, as was often the case earlier. This entrepreneurial function has been developed into the managerial function and overall business philosophy that we now term *marketing*.

✓ It is really only since the end of the Second World War that marketing has developed as a formalised business concept with a codified philosophy and set of techniques. Marketing was on the curriculum of major American business schools such as Harvard, Stanford, and the Wharton School at the University of Pennsylvania from the very early part of this century. Consequently, many of the techniques of marketing were developed and applied first in the USA. It was not until the early 1960s that marketing was taken seriously by leading UK and European companies. The subject of teaching business management at degree level in the UK was generally left to the non-University sector, principally the ex-Polytechnics. In fact, it was not until 1969 that the first joint Honours first degree in marketing was introduced in the UK through the then Huddersfield Polytechnic's BA (Honours) Textile Marketing programme.

✓ Many commentators feel that the UK still has a long way to go in order to become as marketing-orientated as the Americans, and some blame many of the UK's economic ills of the 1980s on the relatively poor marketing performance of much of its industry and commerce. Even today, there are many firms who only pay scant attention to the marketing concept.

Key point
This entrepreneurial function has been developed into the managerial function and overall business philosophy that we now term *marketing*.

Questions

1 Distinguish between a 'need' and a 'want'. Give specific examples.

2 In what way is the marketing concept relevant to non-profit making organisations?

3 Define your organisation's products and/or services in terms of (a) customer needs; (b) customer wants.

4 Why should the customer be *the* most important person that any organisation has to deal with?

5 What do people mean when they say that marketing should be viewed as an 'overall business philosophy'?

References

Doyle, P. (1994). *Marketing Management and Strategy*, p. 37. Prentice Hall International (UK) Limited.

Kotler, P. (1991). *Marketing Management: Analysis, Planning, Implementation and Control*, 7th edn, pp. 4–5. Prentice Hall.

Smith, A. (1776). *An Enquiry into the Nature and Causes of the Wealth of Nations*.

Stanton, W. J., Etzel, M. J. and Walker, B. J. (1991). *Fundamentals of Marketing*, 9th edn, p. 6. McGraw Hill.

Further reading

Armstrong, G. and Kotler, P. (2000). Understanding marketing and the marketing management process. *Marketing: An Introduction*, 5th edn, Chapter 1. Prentice Hall.

Blythe, J. (2001). What do marketers do? *Essentials of Marketing*, Chapter 1. Person Educational Ltd.

Cateora, P. R. and Ghauri, P. N. (2000). The scope and challenge of international marketing. *International Marketing: European Edition*, Chapter 1. McGraw Hill.

Cowell, D. (1984). *The Marketing of Services*. Butterworth-Heinemann.

Davies, M. (1998) Introduction to marketing. *Understanding Marketing*, Chapter 1. Prentice Hall.

Ivanovic, A. and Collins, P. H. (1989). *Dictionary of Marketing*. Peter Collins Publishing.

Keegan, W. J. and Green, M. S. (2000). Introduction to global marketing. *Global Marketing*, 2nd edn, Chapter 1. Prentice Hall.

Lancaster, G. and Massingham, L. (1999). *Essentials of Marketing*, 3rd edn. McGraw-Hill.

Lancaster, G. A. and Reynolds, P. L. (1998) Development of the marketing concept. *Marketing*, Chapter 1. Macmillan Press.

Lancaster, G. A. and Reynolds, P. L. (1999). Marketing defined. *Introduction to Marketing: A Step by Step Guide to All The Tools of Marketing*, Chapter 1. Kogan Page Ltd.

Piercy, N. (1997). *Market-Led Strategic Change*, second edition. Butterworth-Heinemann.

Plamer, A. (2000) What is marketing? *Principles of Marketing*, Chapter 1. Oxford University Press.

The marketing-orientated organisation

2

2.1 Introduction

Marketing maturity does not happen at a stroke. It tends to be a gradual developmental process. Many firms who have reached a full marketing orientation have done so by evolving through secondary stages of development.

Definition
There are three basic types of business orientation: production orientation, sales orientation and marketing orientation.

Generally speaking, there are three basic types of business orientation: production orientation, sales orientation and marketing orientation. These can be viewed as being hierarchical, and usually sequential, stages of development. Many basically production-orientated firms develop greater sales awareness and begin to place much greater importance on moving products on to the consumer through the use of sales push programmes and techniques, rather than through producing objects and expecting them to sell automatically. Eventually, enlightened firms begin to appreciate that selling itself plays but a single part in the overall operation of moving goods from the factory to the consumer. The customer becomes much more than someone who is there merely to sell to. The satisfaction of consumers' needs and wants becomes the rationale for everything the company does. Such companies have progressed to a marketing orientation. Of all the stakeholders in a business enterprise, the customer is by far the most important. It is through the concentration upon the satisfaction of customer needs, and the profits that result from so doing, that all other stakeholder needs are satisfied.

Key point
The satisfaction of consumers' needs and wants becomes the rationale for everything the company does.

2.2 Different types of business orientation

An understanding of the lower levels of business orientation is necessary for a full appreciation of how a marketing-orientated organisation is superior to other forms of business thinking. Each type of orientation will now be examined.

2.2.1 Production orientation

In the nineteenth and most of the twentieth centuries, the primary purpose of all business and industrial activity was thought to be production. The

14

production manager was the key figure within the organisation, and it was normally through production that managers reached the most senior positions in the management hierarchy.

Manufacturers were in a 'supplier's market', and were faced with a virtually insatiable demand for all that could be produced. Firms concentrated on improving production efficiency in an attempt to bring down costs. Generally, firms produced whatever they could produce well, expecting effective demand for their goods and services to present itself automatically. An understanding of customers' requirements was of secondary importance. A famous production-orientated statement reflected this thinking:

> Build a better mousetrap and the world will beat a path to your door.

Henry Ford also made a classic production-orientated statement that is often repeated today, in relation to his Model 'T' Ford that was introduced in 1913:

> You can have any colour you want; as long as it is black!

This production-orientated philosophy was feasible as long as a sellers' market pertained. The economic recession that particularly hit the USA but the UK as well in the 1920s and 1930s concentrated the collective minds of business people. To simply produce was no longer good enough, as warehouses were full of unsold goods and thousands of bankrupt businesses testified to the folly of this philosophy. The lesson to be learned from this experience was that firms that focused all their attention on existing products and existing markets without paying attention to the changing needs of the market place ran the risk of being overtaken by events and becoming obsolete.

Many firms still have this antiquated attitude. They feel that if they produce excellent products and consumers fail to buy them, there can be only two possible reasons: either the consumer does not appreciate the good quality of the product, or the sales force is inept. It is true that many firms produce excellent products, but not necessarily items of the type of or design that potential customers want to purchase. The British motorcycle industry produced many fine machines in the 1950s and early 1960s, but lost their markets to the Japanese on points of styling, design and choice.

Under a production-orientated philosophy, the salesperson's role is a relatively minor one. The salesperson is there to sell what the firm has produced. Such a firm is likely to be organised in the manner outlined in Figure 2.1.

2.2.2 Sales orientation

Gradually, business people began to appreciate that in a highly competitive environment it was simply not enough to produce goods as efficiently as possible. They also had to be sold. The sales concept affirms that effective demand has to be created through the art of persuasion using sales techniques. The sales department was anticipated to hold the key to the firm's prosperity and survival. Scant attention was paid to the genuine needs and requirements of the final consumer, but at least it was understood that goods and services did not necessarily sell themselves without some kind of effort.

Definition
The sales concept affirms that effective demand has to be created through the art of persuasion using sales techniques.

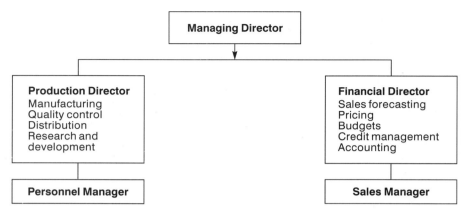

Figure 2.1 Typical organisation of a production-orientated firm.

Even today, many firms think of marketing as a modern term for selling. Many simply change the name of their sales office to 'Marketing Department' to keep up with the times. In fact selling, although important, is but one of several functions for which a true marketing department is responsible.

Peter Drucker explained the relationship between selling and marketing in an eloquent manner, when he stated (Drucker, 1954):

> There will always, one can assume, be a need for some selling. But the aim of marketing is to make selling superfluous. The aim of marketing is to know and understand the customer so well that the product or service fits him and sells itself. Ideally, marketing should result in a customer who is ready to buy!

Definition
The aim of marketing is to make selling superfluous.

In a sales-orientated firm, sales volume is the success criterion. Planning horizons tend to be relatively short-term, with the actual customer and how they perceive the value of the goods being sold being of secondary importance. The implicit premises of a sales orientation are that:

Definition
In a sales-orientated firm, sales volume is the success criterion.

1 The firm's main task is to establish a good sales team

2 Consumers naturally resist purchasing, and it is the salesperson's role to overcome this resistance

3 Sales techniques are needed to induce consumers to buy more.

In the United Kingdom, sales orientation was the generally accepted philosophy during the 1960s. In the late 1950s and early 1960s, World War Two shortages began to be filled and the first reaction on the part of management to a slowing down in sales was to import 'hard sell' techniques from the USA. There was very little consumer protection around then, so many consumers fell prey to such techniques with no redress to the law. Sales techniques like 'putting the customers in a position where they cannot say "no"' flourished (i.e. putting questions such that they will receive assenting answers). After having said 'Yes' so many times, it is then difficult to say 'No' when asked for the order. However, this kind of activity was relatively minor in terms of dishonest practice. Many sales and advertising techniques that

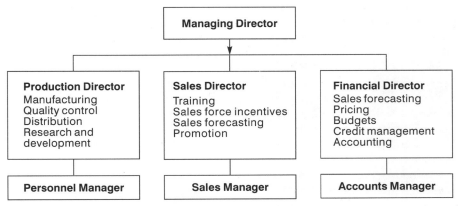

Figure 2.2 The organisation of a sales-orientated firm.

were openly practised then now come under the criminal code (e.g. pyramid selling and inertia selling). It was during the 1970s that the UK government reacted to assist consumers, and much legislation was introduced to protect consumers in this era of what is termed 'consumerism'. In fact, it is often argued that this era of sales orientation, which lasted in the UK and Europe approximately for the decade of the 1960s, is what gave marketing a bad image in the eyes of the public, and this negative image still persists to the present day. There is nothing inherently immoral in production orientation, for it gives customers the opportunity to say 'No'. As we go on to discuss in the next section, marketing orientation is the natural development that follows sales orientation.

In a sales-orientated firm, selling is a major management function, and is often given status equal to that of production and finance. This type of organisation is illustrated in Figure 2.2.

Definition
Marketing orientation is the natural development that follows sales orientation.

Vignette 2.1

The Millennium Dome, London, fails to excite the public imagination

The Millennium Dome at Greenwich in London, UK, was billed as the most exciting visitor experience of the twenty-first century. In fact it turned out to be rather costly, over £800 million, £600 million of which was lottery money. It was rather cold and a rather boring 'damp squib' that by any standard of business calculation was a total commercial failure. The Dome is now about to be sold, although the most attractive commercial prospect for its site seems to be to demolish totally the actual Dome structure, which is already dirty, discoloured and showing signs of wear, and redevelop the site from scratch. The Dome was supposed to have had a 'millennium theme'; the trouble was no one was really sure what the millennium theme was. It ended up as a 'hotch-potch' of rather 'tacky' and unrelated attractions, many of which failed to work properly.

The disposal of the Dome is also being carried out with embarrassing inefficiency. Many of the 'tacky' props have been sold off in public auction for knockdown prices. The complete disposal process could take up to 18 months to complete. Basically, the Dome is an embarrassment that will not go away for the British Government.

What went wrong? The Dome was run by a collection of people, mainly civil servants who had no experience at all in running a visitor attraction. The original Dome chief executive, Jenny Page, was dismissed, and other members of the team had to resign. The management team planning the Dome had not carried out adequate marketing research. They had no idea at all what potential visitors wanted. Where it had been carried out, results were at best questionable. For example, the business plan for the Dome was based on a revenue stream, which in turn was calculated from totally inaccurate and unrealistic projected visitor numbers. The pricing of Dome entry tickets was also something of a mess. Many schoolchildren were let in for nothing, which was a good thing but did nothing for the revenue projections budgeted for, and even those visitors who paid were often supplied with promotional, discounted tickets.

The contents of the Dome were always a cause for disagreement amongst the Dome organisers. Some people wanted the Dome experience to be a 'fun' day out, along the lines of a Disney MAGIC KINGDOM® experience. Others thought the content of the Dome should be higher minded, with a stronger educational content. In the end, the compromise that was eventually reached meant that the Dome contents did not seem to mean anything to anyone. The attraction was difficult to get to. The location was out of the way even for people who lived near London, and an enormous journey for people who lived in the North of the UK. The Dome was basically a large tent, and as such had limited heating. Some of the exhibits were very popular, but the queues for these exhibits were unacceptable; meanwhile, other parts of the attraction had hardly any visitors. Food was of limited quality and over-priced.

Pierre-Yves Gerbeau was brought in from Disneyland Paris to turn the attraction around. He made significant progress, and was certainly more in tune with the market and the intricacies of consumer behaviour than the civil servants he took over from. However, even M Gerbeau's considerable talents were not enough to save the Dome as an ongoing visitor attraction. The Millennium Dome lacked a proper customer focus from day one of the planning stage. No real attempt was made to understand the needs of the market. This lack of proper marketing orientation has resulted in one of the biggest commercial failures in history.

2.2.3 Marketing orientation

Definition
The market concept assumes that in order to survive in the long term, an organisation must ascertain the needs and wants of specifically defined target markets.

The market concept assumes that in order to survive in the long term, an organisation must ascertain the needs and wants of specifically defined target markets. It must then produce goods and/or services that satisfy customer requirements profitably. Under the marketing concept, it is the customer who becomes the centre of business attention. The organisation no longer sees production or sales as the key to prosperity, growth and survival, and these are simply tools of the business. Marketing orientation acknowledges that what is required is the identification and satisfaction of customers' needs and wants. The marketing concept is shown schematically in Figure 2.3.

The main difference between production and marketing orientation is that company management in a production-orientated firm focuses its attention on existing products, paying scant attention to the changing needs and wants of

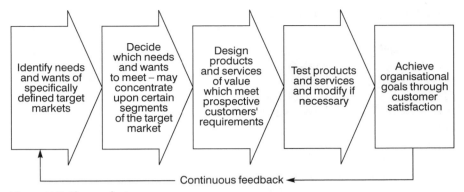

Figure 2.3 The marketing concept.

the market place. The marketing-orientated firm produces goods and services, which it has ascertained the prospective customer actually wants to purchase.

The main difference between sales and marketing orientation has been very well summed up by Theodore Levitt (Levitt, 1960):

> Selling focuses on the needs of the seller; marketing on the needs of the buyer. Selling is preoccupied with the seller's need to convert his product into cash; marketing with the idea of satisfying the needs of the customer by means of the product and the whole cluster of things associated with creating, delivering and finally consuming it.

Sales-orientated firms tend to use shorter-run production methods and are preoccupied with achieving current sales targets, and this philosophy extends down to individual members of the field sales force because of the way that their commission and earnings are structured through the sales quota and target system. In such a company, customer considerations and dealings with individual customers are often restricted to the sales department. In a marketing-orientated organisation, the entire firm appreciates the central importance of the customer and realises that without satisfied customers there will be no business. To be able to progress from a 'sales' to a 'marketing' orientation, senior management in the organisation must work to cultivate a company-wide approach to the satisfaction of customer requirements.

The main problem facing a sales-orientated firm in progressing to a marketing orientation is the management of organisational change. The marketing department is likely to require proportionally more influence and authority over other departments in order to bring about an integrated and cohesive organisation in which all departments pull in the same direction for the benefit of customers. Unless the philosophy of marketing permeates the entire organisation from top to bottom, it will never achieve its full potential.

It is quite natural for departments like sales and production to experience a sense of anxiety that can be brought about by major organisational change,

Definition
The marketing-orientated firm produces goods and services, which it has ascertained the prospective customer actually wants to purchase.

Definition
Sales-orientated firms tend to use shorter-run production methods and are preoccupied with achieving current sales targets.

Definition
In a marketing-orientated organisation, the entire firm appreciates the central importance of the customer.

Table 2.1 Departmental philosophical differences

Other department	Other department's priorities	Marketing department's priorities
Finance and Accountancy	'Cost plus' pricing; rigid budgetary control; standard commercial transactions	Marketing-orientated pricing; flexible budgeting; special terms and discounts
Purchasing	Standard purchasing procedures; bulk orders; narrow product line; standard parts	Flexible purchasing procedures; smaller orders if necessary; wide product line; non-standard products
Production	Long production lead time; long runs; limited range of models; supplier-specified products	Short production lead time; short runs; extensive range of models; customised orders
Sales	Time horizon – short term; success criterion – sales; 'one department'-orientated; short-term sales	Time horizon – long term; success criterion – customer satisfaction; whole organisation-orientated; long-term profits

and they may even resent having to adjust their activities in line with marketing requirements. The human implications of such a change need to be taken into consideration. The reallocation of power within a company can be an uncomfortable experience for those with a vested interest in keeping the *status quo*. The main departmental differences and possible organisational conflicts between marketing and other areas of the firm are summarised in Table 2.1.

In a marketing-orientated company, it is quite probable that the Managing Director will come from a marketing background. This marketing philosophy is not confined to the Marketing Director or to the marketing department, but it permeates the whole company.

Key point
In a marketing-orientated company, it is quite probable that the Managing Director will come from a marketing background.

Vignette 2.2

The Sheraton Safari Hotel, Lake Buena Vista, Florida, exemplifies the application of the marketing concept

The Sheraton Safari Hotel can be found on Apopka-Vinland Road, Lake Buena Vista, on the outskirts of Orlando, Florida, USA. The hotel is very popular and very successful. Many of its clients come back to the hotel again and again. The hotel gives its customers exactly what they want, and management strives not only to meet the expectations of their customers but also to exceed them. Judging by the amount of repeat business the hotel gets, they are obviously doing the right thing.

The Sheraton Safari Hotel is located just 1/8 of a mile from the WALT DISNEY WORLD® resort, 10 miles from downtown Orlando and 15 miles from Orlando International Airport. When you enter the hotel, you enter a world all its own – lush jungle vegetation throughout the property, a lobby brimming with African artefacts and native décor, and a pair of brilliantly coloured macaws perched on a branch, lovingly preening each other. The Sheraton Safari Hotel creates a mood of adventure, intrigue and African sophistication. The excitement of a safari permeates the hotel.

The mission of the Sheraton Safari Hotel is to be an outpost for Disney and Orlando fun, in fact a family 'funscape'. You can play golf at one of the nearby championship courses and go shopping at area outlet malls. The hotel provides complimentary transportation to the MAGIC KINGDOM® Park, Disney-MGM Studios, Epcot®, Disney's Animal Kingdom™ Theme Park and the Downtown Disney area. Sea World® and Universal Studios Escape® are located a few minutes away. The options for family fun are virtually endless. There are hundreds of hotels in the Orlando area, but the Sheraton Safari offers customers something different.

The hotel is not cheap, but offers good value for money. Customers can get a two-room suite overlooking the swimming pool for around $125 per night if they take advantage of advanced booking promotions. An ordinary single family room would cost about $85 per night. There are Disney 'theme' hotels available in the 'Disney area', but not everyone holidaying in Orlando wants to have Disney in front of their face night and day. The Sheraton Safari offers a compromise. It's cheaper than the Disney-owned hotels, it's very close to all the 'Disney' action, it has its own African theme that children find exciting and intriguing, and it gives the opportunity for adults to leave the Disney experience behind after a day going around the parks, allowing them to relax over good food and drinks at reasonable prices, take a swim, go for a walk or even go to the gym. The Sheraton Safari Hotel exemplifies the application of the marketing concept. It is a very customer-focused organisation, is fully aware of what the competition is offering, and gives the customer something different. It offers a really good holiday experience for both adults and children, and does so at a reasonable price. The levels of service at the hotel are second to none.

The adoption of a proper organisational structure is a necessary condition for marketing orientation, but is not the sole condition. A change of management labels and titles is purely cosmetic, and such changes will not bring about the necessary shift in company attitudes. A marketing-orientated firm is typically organised as outlined in Figure 2.4.

Marketing organisational issues arise quite frequently in examinations. The important thing is not to become 'carried away' by the finer points of an organisation chart. Putting personalities and departments in the right boxes is necessary, but you must appreciate that on its own this is not enough. When addressing such questions, always emphasise that it is the adoption of the marketing concept as a business philosophy, rather than the adoption of a particular organisational structure, that is really important. It is the company's whole approach to the business situation that is the key issue. It is again reiterated that it is the adoption of a business philosophy that puts customer

Key point
The adoption of a proper organisational structure is a necessary condition for marketing orientation, but is not the sole condition.

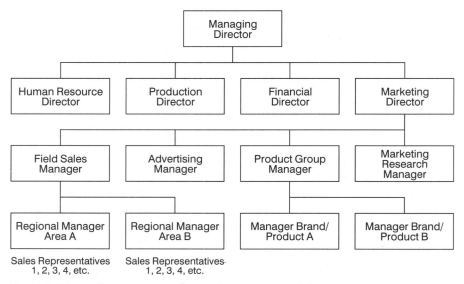

Figure 2.4 Typical organisation of a marketing-orientated firm.

satisfaction at the very centre of management thinking throughout the organisation, and this is what distinguishes a marketing-orientated firm from a production- or sales-orientated organisation.

Vignette 2.3

Virgin Atlantic Airlines has grown to a world-class company through marketing orientation

The well-known entrepreneur, Richard Branson, created Virgin Atlantic Airlines in the early 1980s. Richard Branson was already running the highly successful Virgin group when in 1984 he received a telephone call from a colleague asking him if he might be interested in running a passenger jet service from London to New York. This was just the sort of challenge that appealed to Richard Branson's risk-taking, entrepreneurial nature. He believed that business was fundamentally simple. He left the technical aspects such as accounting to others, but believed he had the marketing skill to beat the competition by offering a better product and service offering. The key to business success was giving customers what they wanted more efficiently than the competition. Richard Branson decided that this philosophy could be applied to any business, whether finance or pop records. He decided to have an attempt at applying it to the airline business.

Although Richard Branson himself was extremely exited and enthusiastic about the prospect of running a Trans-Atlantic airline, the rest of the Virgin Group directors were not and tried to dissuade him. However, being a risk-taking entrepreneur with an eye to a good marketing opportunity, Richard Branson went ahead.

The airline was born, and the first aircraft 'took off' within three months of the original telephone call. Richard Branson managed to find a suitable aircraft and got all the licences and other administrative procedures out of the way, and that was it. The first aeroplane took off on 22 June 1984 to Newark airport in New Jersey. Virgin Atlantic offered a highly competitive price. Although the original aircraft were rather old, the service offered to passengers was superb. Richard Branson took a personal role in selecting chefs to design the imaginative menus, he selected the in-house videos, and contributed to the design of the aircraft's livery and corporate work-wear. Customers voted Virgin Atlantic their favourite airline.

Today, Virgin Atlantic is the second largest British long-haul international airline operating services out of London's Heathrow, Gatwick and Manchester Airports to 18 different destinations all over the world. In December 1999, Richard Branson sold 49 per cent of Virgin Atlantic to Singapore Airlines to form a global partnership. This deal valued Virgin Atlantic at £1.225 billion. The company has always been very customer focused and marketing orientated. It pioneered the application of relationship marketing principles in building repeat business and long-term relationships with its customers. Marketing orientation has helped to propel Virgin Atlantic from a one-aeroplane firm to a global airline.

2.3 Marketing as a business philosophy

Students approaching the subject of marketing for the first time might be confused because they see it as a rather complex phenomenon, drawing its theories from a disparate number of sources. The main source of confusion is the combination in marketing of the philosophy of business and its practice. These are two separate yet interrelated areas: a basic way of thinking about business that focuses on customers' needs and wants, and a functional area of management that uses a set of techniques. As Peter Doyle explains (Doyle, 1994):

> The Marketing Concept is not a theory of marketing but a philosophy of business. It affirms that the key to meeting the objectives of stakeholders is to satisfy customers. In competitive markets this means that success goes to those firms that are best at meeting the needs of customers.

Definition
The Marketing Concept is not a theory of marketing but a philosophy of business.

Because this is such a source of confusion, a separate section is devoted to these issues. If the points that follow are not fully understood at this stage, then you are likely to become confused when studying later chapters.

Vignette 2.4

The Kwik-Fit Group gives motorists what they want by applying the marketing concept

The first Kwik-Fit Centre was opened in Edinburgh in 1971 by Sir Tom Farmer, the Group's present Chairman and Chief Executive. By 1980, the Kwik-Fit Group was operating through over 200 centres nationwide. Today the Kwik-Fit group is one of the largest automotive parts repair and replacement specialists in the world. The company has been so successful because it puts the customer firmly at the centre of everything it does. The reason the company exists is to make a profit through the identification and satisfaction of customers needs and wants more efficiently than the competition.

Since the creation of the Kwik-Fit concept there have been many 'me too' imitations. Despite this competition, Kwik-Fit has been able to retain its leading position in the market by paying close attention to what its customers think. Information is the very lifeblood of the Kwik-Fit business. Management is very pro-active in soliciting the views and opinions of customers in every part of the firms operations, whether these are ordinary retail customers or business-to-business customers.

The company offers a range of services to its retail customers. These include the supply and fitting of tyres at competitive prices and at a high level of customer service. They also supply and fit brakes, exhausts and shock absorbers, and carry out oil changes. They offer guarantees for their products and for their work. They also offer finance facilities with interest-free credit and a charge card option to allow customers to spread the cost of car maintenance and to get their cars fixed when they need to be fixed, not having to wait until they have the cash.

Kwik-Fit entered the 1980s as market leader in the UK. The Kwik-Fit 'Code of Practice' was introduced in 1981, and set down the standards that every customer has a right to expect from the company. Everyone in the company does everything possible to adhere to the Code of Practice and exceed customer expectations in terms of service and quality. Also in 1981, the company acquired 17 centres in Holland. Kwik-Fit Fleet was set up in 1986 to look after corporate clients. In 1987, the firm was awarded the British Midland 'Diamond Service Award'; the company also gained the AA Seal of Approval. Further centres were acquired in Ireland and again in Holland. Turnover reached £193.4 million by 1989. In the 1990s the firm went from strength to strength and received many other awards, including the Institute of Management Award for Excellence, a National Training Award, and the Fleet News Award for 'Best Service Company'.

The Kwik-Fit Group has progressed substantially since it was started in 1974. It is now a world leader in the automotive parts repair and replacement sector. It is customer focused and highly marketing-orientated. It places great emphasis on staff training and delivering 100 per cent customer satisfaction. The awards it has received are testimony to the fact that proper application of the marketing philosophy throughout the entire organisation can result in a first-class business enterprise.

2.3.1 Taking a holistic view

To look at the subject of marketing as an overall business philosophy is to take a holistic view of the discipline. This approach is explained by Peter Drucker, who has contributed so much to the development of marketing management as a serious discipline (Drucker, 1954):

Definition
Marketing is not only much broader than selling, it is *not* a specialised activity at all. It encompasses the entire business.

Marketing is not only much broader than selling, it is *not* a specialised activity at all. It encompasses the entire business. It is the whole business seen from the point of view of its final result, that is, from the customer's point of view. Concern and responsibility for marketing must, therefore, permeate all areas of the enterprise.

Marketing cannot exist in a vacuum. An integrated approach is needed, not just the creation of a marketing department. Such an approach to business propels the marketing-orientated firm towards embracing new opportunities, and away from the narrow preoccupation with selling existing products to existing customers.

2.3.2 Distinguishing features of marketing

Because of the difficulty of incorporating all the various facets of marketing into a single definition, let us look instead at the distinguishing features of the subject in summary form:

1 Marketing is dynamic and operational, requiring action as well as planning.

2 Marketing requires an improved form of business organisation, although this on its own is not enough.

3 Marketing is an important functional area of management, often based in a single physical location. More importantly, it is an overall business philosophy that should be adopted by everybody in the entire organisation.

4 The marketing concept states that the identification, satisfaction and retention of customers is the key to long-term survival and prosperity.

5 Marketing involves planning and control.

6 The principle of marketing states that all business decisions should be made with careful consideration of customer requirements.

7 Marketing focuses attention from production towards the needs and wants of the market place.

8 Marketing is concerned with obtaining value from the market by offering items of value to the market. It does this by producing goods and services that satisfy the genuine needs and wants of specifically defined target markets.

9 The distinguishing feature of a marketing-orientated organisation is the way in which it strives to provide customer satisfaction as a way of achieving its own business objectives.

2.4 Summary

✓ In this chapter, we have described and attempted to clarify what the subject of marketing encompasses. Marketing is seen as both a functional area of management that utilises a set of management techniques, and an overall business philosophy. The functions of marketing are examined as a whole in Chapter 4, then in more detail in specialised chapters throughout the rest of the book.

✓ We have also shown that the marketing-orientated firm achieves its business objectives by identifying and anticipating the changing needs and wants of specifically defined target markets. The subject of targeting is addressed in Chapter 5. The range of techniques used for identifying customer requirements is termed marketing research, and this is discussed in Chapter 13.

✓ As mentioned at the beginning of the chapter, the fundamental principles of marketing are equally applicable to not-for-profit organisations, where efficiency or minimum cost criteria can be substituted for profit objectives. These issues, along with a number of specific examples, are discussed in Chapter 16.

Questions

1 Outline and discuss those factors that you believe have given rise to the need for modern companies to be marketing-orientated.

2 Discuss the contention that successful marketing stems more from the adoption of a sound organisational philosophy than from the application of functional skills.

3 Many companies are still confused about the distinction between marketing and selling. As a newly appointed marketing manager, how would you explain to your managing director the differences between the two?

4 'The marketing concept has failed to live up to the high expectations of its early protagonists'. Using your own experience of companies and products with which you are familiar, critically evaluate this statement.

5 What characteristics would distinguish a truly marketing-orientated organisation from a production- or sales-orientated organisation?

References

Drucker, P. (1954). *The Practice of Management*, p. 65. Harper and Row.
Levitt, T. (1960). Marketing myopia. *Harvard Business Review*, **Jul–Aug**, 45–6.
Doyle, P. (1994). *Marketing Management and Strategy*, p. 57. Prentice Hall International (UK) Ltd.

Further reading

Adcock, D. (2000). Customers, company capabilities and competitors. *Marketing Strategies for Competitive Advantage*, Chapter 2. John Wiley.

Armstrong, G. and Kotler, P. (2000) Marketing in a changing world: creating customer value and satisfaction. *Marketing: An Introduction*, 5th edn, Chapter 1. Prentice Hall.

Blythe, J. (2001). What do marketers do? *Essentials of Marketing*, Chapter 1. Person Educational Ltd.

Cateora, P. R. and Ghauri, P. N. (2000). The scope and challenge of international marketing. *International Marketing: European Edition*, Chapter 1. McGraw Hill.

Davies, M. (1998). Introduction to marketing. *Understanding Marketing*, Chapter 1. Prentice Hall.

Drucker, P. F. (1999). *Management Tasks, Responsibilities, Practices*. Butterworth-Heinemann.

Frain, J. (1981). *Introduction to Marketing*. MacDonald and Evans.

Keegan, W. J. and Green, M. S. (2000). Introduction to global marketing. *Global Marketing*, 2nd edn, Chapter 1. Prentice Hall.

Kotler, P. (1997). *Marketing Management: Analysis Planning, Implementation and Control*, 9th edn. Prentice Hall.

Lancaster, G. A. and Massingham, L. C. (1999). Marketing – origins and development. *Essentials of Marketing: Text and Cases*, 3rd edn, Chapter 1. McGraw-Hill.

Lancaster, G. A. and Reynolds, P. L. (1998). Development of the marketing concept. *Marketing*, Chapter 1. Macmillan Press.

Lancaster, G. A. and Reynolds, P. L. (1999). Marketing defined. *Introduction to Marketing: A Step by Step Guide to All the Tools of Marketing*, Chapter 1. Kogan Page Ltd.

Oliver, G. (1980). *Marketing Today*. Prentice Hall.

Piercy, N. (1997). *Market-led Strategic Change*, second edition. Butterworth-Heinemann.

Plamer, A. (2000). What is marketing? *Principles of Marketing*, Chapter 1. Oxford University Press.

The marketing environment

3

3.1 Introduction

The marketing firm operates within a complex and dynamic external environment. It is the task of the marketing-orientated company to link the resources of the organisation to the requirements of customers. This is done within the framework of opportunities and threats present in the external environment. Change is an unequivocal fact of life, and organisations have to adapt. Sometimes change occurs very slowly – indeed, almost imperceptibly. At other times it occurs quickly and, although it is obvious to everybody at the time, it can be so rapid that organisations might find it difficult to react quickly enough.

Charles Darwin, author of the classical work *Origin of the Species*, put forward a theory that is widely accepted – that living organisms have been able to survive in a constantly changing and potentially hostile world because of their ability to adapt to changing environmental conditions. Firms operate in an ever-changing business environment. They too, in order to survive, need to take account of and adapt to changing economic and technological conditions.

In the previous chapter we discussed the importance of the customer as the essence of the business philosophy we call 'marketing'. Although a clear understanding of customer requirements is of paramount importance in putting such a business philosophy into practice, this alone is not enough. Firms must monitor not only the changing needs and wants of target markets, but also changes in the wider, external or 'macro' environment. This is necessary if the organisation is to be able to prepare to adapt to changing conditions.

3.2 Monitoring the external environment

3.2.1 Capitalising on environmental change

With environmental change organisations should, if possible, capitalise on it rather than merely react to it in a purely defensive manner. Firms can very rarely control their macro-environment, but they can understand and, to a certain extent, anticipate it.

The ability of companies to understand and react to environmental forces is of vital importance to marketing success. In fact an individual organisation's new technology may be the external environmental force of technology that is affecting other organisations! Zeithaml and Zeithaml (1984) give examples of environmental management strategies that firms can use to influence the largely uncontrollable environment.

The general marketing environment is made up of all factors and forces that affect or influence the marketing function. These include interdepartmental relationships (referred to here as the *intra-firm environment*) and all other external factors (the *macro-environment*).

Definition
The general marketing environment is made up of all factors and forces that affect or influence the marketing function.

The macro-environment can, in turn, be broken down into two broad categories:

1 The marketing company's immediate environment is the marketing function itself, consisting of the 'Four Ps' plus an extra People 'P', the latter being those who are there to ensure the smooth operation of the marketing function. This leads to the 'intra-firm' environment, consisting of other departments in the company such as finance, production, human resource management, and research, design and development. The next layer is called the 'micro-environment', and this consists of suppliers, customers, competitors, distributors and marketing intermediaries like advertising agencies and marketing research companies.

2 The wider external environment is termed the 'macro-environment', and this includes political, economic, socio-cultural and technological factors (remembered through the well-known acronym 'PEST'). Lately, 'legal' factors have been isolated from 'political' factors, making the acronym 'SLEPT'. More recently still the acronym has become 'PESTLE', with the extra 'E' standing for 'environmental'. Its latest incarnation is now 'STEEPLE', with yet another 'E' standing for 'ecological'. As a student of marketing it is important that you know these various acronyms, because they are quite often referred to in these shorthand terms in marketing strategy examination papers.

Definition
The wider external environment is termed the 'macro-environment', and this includes political, economic, socio-cultural and technological factors (remembered through the well-known acronym 'PEST').

In order for organisations to be in a position to adapt successfully to changing conditions, their management requires an appreciation of the many factors and forces influencing such changes. Firms would like to be in the position of being able to adapt to changes as they occur. Ideally, management would like to be able to adapt in advance of change by anticipating events. By identifying environmental trends early enough, management should be able to anticipate the likely outcome of such trends.

Unless firms are able to identify and react to changes quickly, they run the risk of being dictated to by circumstances beyond their control; firms are then forced into being 'market followers' rather than playing a part in the changes occurring, influencing events and 'leading' the market.

3.2.2 Speed of response

In terms of speed of response and an ability to react to changing conditions, we can identify three types of organisation:

1 Companies that make things happen! Such organisations identify and understand the forces and conditions that bring about change. They continually strive to adapt, and stay 'ahead of the game'. To a certain extent, such companies may themselves play some part in influencing the rate and direction of change.

2 Companies that watch things happen! These organisations fail to adapt to changes early enough to actually become part of that change. Such firms have little opportunity of actually influencing events, but are usually forced to make changes in order to survive. Such changes are always 'reactive' rather than planned, and are often instigated as part of a defensive 'crisis management' programme.

3 Companies that wonder what happened! Companies in this final category are those that are blind and impervious to change. Such firms sometimes even fail to realise that circumstances have altered. Even when this change is acknowledged by company management, the management team often refuses to adapt to an ever-changing environment. Such firms are unlikely to survive in the long term.

3.2.3 The need constantly to monitor environmental factors

In mixed economies, like those of Europe and North America, companies are allowed a great deal of autonomy in the management of their business affairs. Company management has control over how it chooses to organise and integrate functions and responsibilities within the organisation. Generally, management is free to decide what to produce and the methods of manufacture, and to make decisions concerning distribution, pricing, packaging and communications. Providing management operates within the law of the country, it is relatively free to conduct its business affairs as it chooses.

Definition
The business variables that are the responsibility of the marketing function, such as price, advertising, new product development, packaging and the customers to whom the products are marketed, are collectively referred to as the *marketing mix*.

The business variables that are the responsibility of the marketing function, such as price, advertising, new product development, packaging and the customers to whom the products are marketed, are collectively referred to as the *marketing mix*. The functions of marketing and the concept of the marketing mix are discussed in greater detail in Chapter 4.

Although marketing-orientated firms have direct control over their mix elements, they do not formulate plans and strategies in a vacuum.

As we have already discussed, organisations are influenced by a plethora of environmental factors largely outside their control. Environmental change poses both opportunities and threats to the marketing firm. The success of the firm in meeting the challenge posed by change will depend on the ability of management and individual managerial skills in carrying out the following tasks:

● Monitoring the external environment and anticipating significant changes

● Evaluating the likely effect of change or potential change on the business activities of the firm

- Drawing up short-, medium- and long-term plans to deal with the new environmental scenario; this includes the formulation of contingency plans

- Using the controllable variables at management's command and control (the marketing mix elements) to adapt successfully to changes in the external environment

- Monitoring the ability of plans and strategies to cope successfully with, and ideally capitalise on, the changed conditions, and to undertake corrective action where necessary.

3.3 The general marketing environment

The general marketing environment is made up of a number of separate but interrelated elements. From a conceptual point of view, it is perhaps easier to think of these individual elements as 'sub-environments'. Marketing management is primarily concerned with anticipating and reacting to perceived changes occurring outside the organisation itself. This external environment, as has already been mentioned, is referred to as the *macro-environment*.

The term 'general marketing environment' is often used to refer to all factors and forces that impinge upon marketing management's ability to conduct its affairs successfully. This also includes interdepartmental factors and influences. In Chapter 2 it was explained that the marketing concept is a customer-orientated philosophy that should permeate the whole organisation. A distinction was also made between marketing as an overall concept or philosophy, and the more narrowly held view of marketing as a specific functional area of management. As a functional area of management, marketing invariably has to both compete and co-operate with other departments within the firm. Again, as has been stated earlier, we term this 'micro' area of the general marketing environment the *intra-firm environment*, and this is all part of the company's *micro-environment*. These terms are reiterated here because they often appear as a part of marketing examination questions.

Definition
The general marketing environment is made up of a number of separate but interrelated elements.

Definition
The term 'general marketing environment' is often used to refer to all factors and forces that impinge upon marketing management's ability to conduct its affairs successfully.

3.4 The intra-firm environment

Companies have a finite amount of money and other resources, and the marketing function often has to compete with other management functions to secure that share of the firm's overall budget that it requires in order to carry out its tasks effectively. Marketing needs a revenue budget to spend on advertising, exhibitions, direct mail, sales personnel, marketing research and other activities that form part of the process of winning orders. It also needs a capital budget in order to purchase equipment like computers.

Other management departments such as production, finance and human resource management feel that they too provide important services, and hence deserve an equal share of the company's budget.

The marketing department not only has to 'compete' with other departments for financial resources, but it also has to work in co-operation with these other functions. For example, marketing research may identify a 'gap' in an existing market that the firm can commercially exploit. In order to produce products or services that might fill this gap the marketing department will have to call upon the services of other departments, such as finance, research, design and development, production, and the legal department. Hence, marketing tasks cannot be achieved in isolation, but need the full co-operation of many other departments.

When considering the overall environment in which marketing operates, it is important to appreciate that although the marketing function is the process through which the organisation adapts to changes in external conditions, it also has to take note of internal factors. Marketing managers make decisions that directly affect other functional areas of the firm. Likewise, decisions made elsewhere within the organisation affect marketing's ability to carry out its job effectively. When addressing the environmental problems facing the marketing department, students often fail to appreciate the importance of understanding the degree of conflict and co-operation inherent in the interaction between marketing and other functional areas of the firm.

Key point
Marketing tasks cannot be achieved in isolation, but need the full co-operation of many other departments.

3.5 The macro-environment

Although departmental rivalries and conflicts that present themselves within the company's intra-firm environment are often a problem, they are to a certain extent within the control of the organisation's management. It is generally uncontrollable forces in the external macro-environment that pose the most important sources of opportunities and threats to the company.

The term *macro-environment* denotes all forces and agencies external to the marketing firm itself. Some of these forces and agencies will be closer to the operation of the firm than others, e.g. a company's suppliers, agents, distributors and other distributive intermediaries and competing firms. These 'closer' external factors are often collectively referred to as the firm's *proximate macro-environment* to distinguish them from the wider external forces found, for example, in the legal, cultural, economic and technological sub-environments.

Definition
The term *macro-environment* denotes all forces and agencies external to the marketing firm itself.

3.6 The proximate macro-environment

The proximate macro-environment consists of people, organisations and forces within the firm's immediate external environment. Of particular importance to marketing firms are the sub-environments of suppliers, competitors and distributors (intermediaries). These sub-environments can each have a significant effect upon the marketing firm.

3.6.1 The supplier environment

Suppliers are generally other business firms, although they can also be individuals (e.g. a marketing consultant supplying advice). Suppliers provide the marketing firm with raw materials, product constituents (parts), services or, in the case of retailing firms, possibly the finished goods themselves. For example, motor vehicle manufacturers (e.g. Ford) must obtain sheet steel, windscreens, interior fabric and the many other components from which they produce their vehicles. Such components are often produced by specialist manufacturers. Some of these suppliers can be companies as large and almost as well known as the vehicle manufacturer itself (e.g. Lucas Industries, Dunlop, Pilkington Brothers and Unipart), and others may be small firms dependent on the motor industry for their survival, supplying components such as engine gaskets and industrial fasteners.

Large retailers such as Marks & Spencer purchase clothing and other textile products from a wide range of suppliers. Many suppliers to large retailers supply finished goods rather than intermediate constituent product parts.

Companies, whether these are manufacturers or retailers, often depend on numerous suppliers. However, it is not a case of one-way dependence; supplying firms also depend on the future prosperity of the buying firm for future orders. The buyer/supplier relationship is one of mutual economic interdependence, both parties relying on the other for their commercial well-being. Changes in the terms of the relationship can have a significant effect on both parties, and any such changes are usually the result of careful negotiation rather than unilateral action. Both parties seek a degree of security and stability from their commercial relationship that is increasingly viewed as being long term. This is borne out by relatively recent development of the *'just-in-time'* manufacturing technique, which was developed by the Japanese Toyota Company but is now becoming increasingly adopted by companies throughout the world. This philosophy of management demands absolute reliability from suppliers to deliver goods that are never sub-standard ('zero defects' is the term used), so that any inspection at the customer's works before they are committed to the production line is eliminated. This philosophy also demands that goods and components be delivered exactly when they are required (so the ordering company does not effectively have to hold any stocks).

Although both parties to a commercial contract are seeking stability and security, it would be wrong to believe that factors in the supplier environment are not subject to change. Suppliers may be affected by industrial disputes that might affect delivery of materials to the buying company. Other changes (e.g. a sudden increase in raw material prices) may force suppliers to raise their prices. They may even be compelled to go into liquidation owing to financial difficulties. Whatever the product or service being purchased by the marketing firm, unexpected developments in the supplier environment can have an immediate and serious effect on the firm's commercial operations. Because of this, marketing management, by means of its market intelligence system, should continually monitor changes and potential changes in the supplier environment and have contingency plans ready to deal with potentially adverse developments.

Definition
Suppliers are generally other business firms, although they can also be individuals (e.g. a marketing consultant supplying advice).

Vignette 3.1

The supplier environment: BSE in France impacts on Carrefour's share price

Many retailers depend on the quality assurances of their suppliers, and can end up in serious trouble if the supplier lets them down. This is illustrated well by the case of the Carrefour retail chain, which experienced serious quality problems with some of its meat supplied by one of its trusted and regular suppliers. France is experiencing an increase in the incidence of BSE in cattle. Some commentators claim that French beef is considerably less safe than British beef, which is still banned in France despite the EU's ruling that it is safe. British farmers are calling for a full ban on French beef in the UK in retaliation for the intransigence of the French government in supporting the ban against British beef. French concerns about BSE increased in October 2000 when Carrefour, the biggest retailer in Europe, announced that it had been seriously let down by one of its trusted suppliers, and accidentally sold about a ton of beef from 11 animals infected with mad cow disease.

Once the company realised what had happened it tried to recall the beef, but for many people it was too late as it had already been eaten. Public knowledge of the problem only came to light because of a public prosecution brought against a particular herd's dealer by the French Ministry of Agriculture. The meat had been on sale in Northern France at around 40 outlets. The company destroyed all remaining meat, but not before the shares fell significantly on the stock market. Because of the sensitivity of the French people to the BSE problem, the incident could have further long-term implications of Carrefour's share price and profits. The case illustrates how important the buyer–supplier relationship is, and how a mistake by a supplier can impact on the commercial health of the marketing firm.

3.6.2 The competitive environment

Key point
Factors in the competitive environment can affect the commercial prosperity of any company.

Factors in the competitive environment can affect the commercial prosperity of any company. Management must be alert to the potential threat of other companies marketing product substitutes. Many United Kingdom manufacturers in industries like steel and textiles have experienced intense competition from imported foreign products.

For example, the UK carpet industry has traditionally had a reputation for producing excellent quality Axminster and Wilton woven carpets. Much of this production is still carried out in the textile town of Kidderminster in the Midlands, which has been traditionally acknowledged as the 'carpet centre of the world'. Over recent years the market has changed, with cheaper 'tufted' carpets (not woven, but with the yarn punched into a backing material) becoming more popular. Since people have become increasingly mobile and inclined to move home more often, many are reluctant to invest in a top-quality woven carpet that may well last 20 years or more, especially when it is recognised that it is often impractical to take up a fitted carpet when moving home. A further reason for the increase in popularity of tufted carpets is that not only are they significantly cheaper than traditional woven carpets, but also the quality and visual appearance of synthetic fibres has dramatically improved. To a certain extent, the UK carpet industry failed to react fast enough to changes in consumer tastes and to the changes in technology required to produce tufted synthetic carpet.

Nowadays, much of this type of carpet is imported into the UK from Belgium and the USA. The UK carpet industry is much smaller today than it was 20 years ago, and many manufacturers of traditional woven carpets have been forced into liquidation.

In some industries, as in the carpet industry, there may be numerous manufacturers worldwide posing a potential competitive threat. In other industries, such as aerospace or motor vehicle manufacture, there may only be a few. Whatever the type, size and composition of the industry in question, it is essential that marketing management has a full understanding of competitive forces. Because of the globalisation of the market place for many products, some firms are forming strategic alliances; for example, Louis Kraar discusses the case of Ford and Volkswagen setting up a joint company in Brazil (Kraar, 1989). Companies need to establish exactly who their competitors are, and the benefits they are offering to the marketplace. Armed with this knowledge, the company will have a greater opportunity to compete effectively (see Reynolds and Day, 1995, 1996; Reynolds *et al.*, 1998).

Key point
Whatever the type, size and composition of the industry in question, it is essential that marketing management has a full understanding of competitive forces.

Vignette 3.2

The competitive environment: the competition closes in on AstraZeneca as patents run out on its leading drug Losec®

Maybe it's a sign of the times, but one of the most common medical complaints in the Western world is stomach ulcer-related problems. First we had Glaxo's 'Zantac®', a very successful drug in the field of ulcer prevention. This was overshadowed by AstraZeneca's wonder-drug Losec®, which is even more effective and is the most frequently prescribed drug in the world. However, October 2000 was something of a turning point in the fortunes of AstraZeneca. Britain's second largest drugs company has warned that the world's top selling prescription medicine is not selling as well as expected in the most important, and hence most ulcerated, market of all, the USA. Although forecasting growth in the sales of Losec® in double digits for the year ending October 2000, only 8 per cent annual growth in sales was actually realised in the USA.

Losec® was developed in Astra's Gothenburg laboratories in the early 1970s before the merger with Zeneca, and has been a huge success by any industry standard. However the markets are concerned that AstraZeneca has 'too many eggs in one basket', and when profits from Losec® fall profits for the company as a whole are bound to suffer. The company has developed a new product to succeed Losec®, to be marketed as Nexium®, but experts say that the product improvements are very marginal. They feel most doctors are more likely to prescribe the plethora of generic substitutes for Losec® that are likely to come onto the market once the patents protecting the drug's market position come to an end. The company denies this, and still claims to be able to meet forecasted profit targets. The markets however took a different view, and news of the poor US sales resulted in a significant fall in share price, reducing the market value of the Anglo-Swedish firm by £1.5 billion.

Competitors continue to put pressure on AstraZeneca by using aggressive price reductions of similar, albeit less effective, ulcer remedies. The firm is trying to buy time by having lawyers attempt to get the patents on Losec® extended until new products can be developed to take its place in their product portfolio. As well as the next generation of ulcer drug, Nexium®, the company is also in advanced stages of developing a new heart drug called ZD4522, at present in clinical trials. However the competition is moving in ahead of the end of patent protection on Losec®, and the company seems to have significantly underestimated the power of competitive actions, particularly in relation to price cuts but also product development.

3.6.3 The distributive environment

Many firms rely on marketing intermediaries to ensure that their products reach the final consumer. Some firms supply directly to a retailer, whilst others use a more complex 'chain' including intermediaries such as wholesalers, factors, agents and distributors. The use of intermediaries is more common in the distribution of consumer goods that are usually targeted at a mass market. Firms manufacturing industrial products, particularly where these are custom made, or buyer specified rather than supplier specified, are more inclined to deliver their products direct to the final customer. However, this is a generalisation, as a number of industrial marketing firms make use of factors, distributors and other intermediaries.

It may seem that the conventional method of distribution in any particular industry is relatively static. To a certain extent this is true, although distribution channels are subject to evolutionary change, just like any other facet of business.

The rate of change in the distributive environment has often been likened to the hour hand of a watch. The hand of the watch is always moving, although each individual movement is so small as to be imperceptible. Taken over time, the cumulative movement is, of course, very significant.

Key point
Because changes in the distributive environment occur relatively slowly, there is a danger of marketing firms failing to appreciate the commercial significance of cumulative change.

Because changes in the distributive environment occur relatively slowly, there is a danger of marketing firms failing to appreciate the commercial significance of cumulative change. Existing channels may be declining in popularity over time, whilst new channels may be developing unnoticed by the marketing firm. An obvious recent example has been the advances that have been made in this direction by e-commerce companies.

The subject of distribution, and in particular the factors and forces influencing change, is discussed in greater detail in Chapter 8. At this early stage, it is sufficient to appreciate that the distributive environment, like any other environmental factor, is likely to be subject to change.

3.7 The wider macro-environment

In the previous section we examined a number of factors present in the *proximate* macro-environment, which are the macro-environmental forces closest to the marketing firm (i.e. suppliers, competitors and marketing intermediaries). Changes in the wider macro-environment may not be as immediate to the marketing firm's day-to-day operations, but are just as important. The main factors making up these wider macro-environmental forces fall into four groups:

1 Political (and legal) factors

2 Economic factors

3 Social (and cultural) factors

4 Technological factors.

As mentioned in Chapter 2, these are remembered through the acronym 'PEST', and this definition has expanded to include additional factors that go to make up the acronym 'STEEPLE'. However, the view is taken that excessive subdivisions make for detail of complexity. Such finite divisions are only appropriate in circumstances when, say, the final ecological 'E' in 'STEEPLE' has a great bearing on the company's operations – for example, if it is operating in an environment where ecological issues might be particularly sensitive (e.g. drilling for oil). For our purposes, the subdivisions under the acronym 'PEST' are quite appropriate for the discussion that follows.

Changes in these sub-environments affect not only the marketing firm, but also those organisations and individuals that make up the proximate macro-environment. The two parts of the overall macro-environment (the proximate and wider macro-environments) are therefore very closely related. A change in the supplier or competitive environment may, for example, have its basic cause in wider changes taking place in the technological or political arenas.

In Figure 3.1 we have shown the organisation's inner proximate marketing environment surrounded by its wider macro-environmental influences, and we now examine each of these wider macro-environmental influences in more detail.

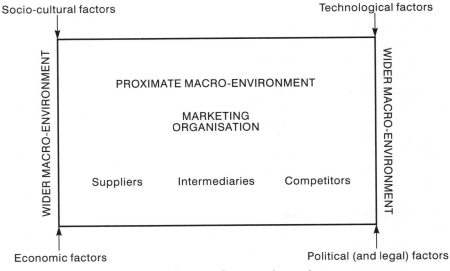

Figure 3.1 Macro-environmental factors influencing the marketing organisation.

3.7.1 The economic environment

Economic factors are of concern to marketing firms because they are likely to influence, among other things, demand, costs, prices and profits. The business pages of the quality press are principally concerned with the country's level of industrial output; the level of retail buying, inflation and unemployment; the balance of payments; and exchange rates. These economic factors are largely outside the control of the individual firm, but their effects on individual enterprises can be profound. One of the weaknesses of economics as a social science is the relatively poor predictability of economic variables. Not even the 'experts', such as Sylvia Nasar in the USA, have produced anything like accurate long-range economic forecasts for economic conditions throughout the 1990s. The problem too with such forecasts is that they tend to assume a spurious accuracy in the minds of people who apply them in business settings. Of course, how accurate such forecasts will turn out to be is a matter that only the passage of time will tell.

Key point
Political and economic forces are often strongly related.

Political and economic forces are often strongly related. For example, the Middle East War in Autumn 1973, which was a political and military conflict between Israel and its Arab neighbours, produced economic shock waves throughout the Western world that probably had greater economic implications for the world than the Second World War. Indirectly, the conflict resulted in the Arab nations dramatically increasing crude oil prices, a commodity upon which the economies of advanced Western nations were principally dependent. This contributed significantly to a world economic recession, which lasted for more than a decade. Increased oil prices meant increased energy costs (hence increased transportation, power and heating and lighting costs), as well as increases in the cost of many oil-based raw materials such as plastics and synthetic fibres.

The 'oil crisis', as this period of world economic history has become known, demonstrated to the world that any state or confederation of states possessing prime resources has far more economic, and therefore political, power than had hitherto been realised. This oil crisis demonstrates clearly how dramatic economic change can upset the traditional structures and balances in the world business environment.

Another economic development that has had a significant effect on individual United Kingdom enterprises was joining what was then called the European Economic Community, or EEC (now the European Union, or EU), on 1 January 1973. The EU, or 'Common Market', was initially set up as a customs union. This implies that all tariffs between member states on all goods and services should be abolished and that a uniform tariff be adopted for all goods and services imported into the customs union area from non-member countries. However, as we have seen, the EU has expanded beyond its original customs union remit and is now a political union; this was particularly evidenced when the words 'Economic' and 'Community' were dropped from the original EEC nomenclature to become 'Union'. The issue of the EU is dealt with in more detail later in Chapter 15, when the subject of international marketing is examined.

As has been already demonstrated, changes in world economic forces are potentially highly significant to marketing firms, particularly those engaged in international marketing. However, an understanding of economic changes and forces in the domestic economy is also of vital importance, as these forces have the most immediate impact.

A factor that has persistently troubled the UK economy over the past 15 years, in spite of a relatively impressive economic performance, has been (until only relatively recently) the high level of unemployment. This level of domestic unemployment has consistently decreased the effective demand for many luxury consumer goods, which in turn has adversely affected the demand for the industrial machinery required to produce such goods. In some regions of the UK, particularly in those that have switched from 'old' industries like coal production to newer 'high-tech' industries, the local economy, and in particular the retail and other service sectors that served it, has been devastated by the blight of persistent long-term unemployment.

Other domestic economic variables are the rate of inflation and the level of domestic interest rates (i.e. the variable that determines the cost of borrowing). These can of course be significantly influenced by world economic factors. High levels of inflation, and the high levels of interest rates used to combat inflation, affect the potential return from new investments and can inhibit the adoption and diffusion of new technologies. Governments of every persuasion attempt to encourage economic growth through various policy measures. Tax concessions, government grants, employment subsidies and capital depreciation allowances are simply some of the measures that have been used to stimulate growth.

The examples used in this section all demonstrate the importance to marketing firms of continually monitoring the economic environment at both domestic and world levels. The complex interaction of economic forces, and the political responses made by individual governments in an attempt to influence and manage their national economies, can have dramatic effects on individual firms' business operations. Economic changes pose a set of opportunities and threats to the marketing organisation. By understanding and carefully monitoring the economic environment, firms should be in a position to guard against potential threats and capitalise on the opportunities.

Key point
Economic changes pose a set of opportunities and threats to the marketing organisation.

3.7.2 The technological environment

Technology is a major macro-environmental variable that affects not only the marketing firm but also all the elements in the company's proximate macro-environment, including its customers. The rate of technological change is accelerating. Marketing firms themselves play a part in technological progress, either through having their own research departments or through the sponsorship of applied research. Organisations must make use of current technology and play a part in innovating new developments and new applications.

Technology has influenced the development of many of the products that we take for granted today – for example, television, calculators, aerosol sprays, compact disc players, video recorders and home computers. In the advanced industrial nations, more mature 'smoke-stack' industries such as steel making are in relative decline. New 'sunrise' industries such as biotechnology, electronics and information technology have developed, and it is to these new industries that advanced industrial nations should look for manufacturing and trading opportunities.

Of the 'sunrise' industries, the development of information technology (IT) has had particularly wide-reaching effects on marketing organisations. The development and large-scale production of the microprocessor has enabled the development of new products (e.g. calculators and digital watches). It has also revolutionised the collection, processing and dissemination of information, which has in turn affected the whole spectrum of marketing activity. The area of marketing research provides a good illustration of change in practice resulting from the adoption of the new technology. Questionnaires can now be designed and coded by computer, and data collected from respondents can go directly back to the computer via optical readers. 'Computed-aided telephone interviewing' (CATI) provides sophisticated screen presentations and enormous capacity in terms of the complexity, scope and sample size of the respondents to be interviewed. Response speed and fast data-processing turnaround time are the principal advantages of this system.

Sales forecasting is another example of an important marketing activity revolutionised by advances in information technology. Before the advent of computers, sales forecasts were usually subjective 'educated guesses'. Computers, and the software packages that go with them, have given even the smallest organisation access to powerful, sophisticated, quantitative forecasting techniques.

Vast amounts of data can now be stored, and the numerous, complex equations inherent in sophisticated quantitative methods can be solved and updated automatically by the computer. Routine sales forecasting can now largely be left to a computer, leaving the manager free to tackle more important, non-routine activities.

The impact of technological change on marketing activities can also be seen at the retail level. Electronic point of sale (EPOS) data capture is now being applied by retail multiples. The 'laser checkout' reads a bar code on the product being purchased and stores this information. It is then used to analyse sales and re-order stock, as well as giving customers a printed readout of what they have purchased and the price charged. Such a system obviates the tedious task of marking every item with the retail price and the need for the checkout person to key the price of each item into the till machine. Manufacturers of fast-moving consumer goods (FMCGs), particularly packaged grocery products, have been compelled to respond to these technological innovations by incorporating bar codes on their product labels or packaging.

Developments in communications have been particularly striking. Further developments in fibre optics and high-definition television (HDTV) have made remarkable advances over the past decade. Stanton, Etzel and Walker provide a particularly good discussion in relation to this area (Stanton *et al.*, 1991).

Key point
Technological change, like all other factors in the macro-environment, poses both threats and opportunities to the marketing firm.

The examples that have been provided in support of this section illustrate how changes in the technological environment can affect the products and services that firms produce, and the way in which firms carry out their business operations. Technological change, like all other factors in the macro-environment, poses both threats and opportunities to the marketing firm.

Vignette 3.3

The technological environment: Bayer trials compound derived from human genome

The German chemicals and drugs firm Bayer announced that it would start clinical trials on a new compound derived from the Human Genome Project. The compound will be used to help fight the war against cancer, and Bayer will be the first pharmaceutical company to register a drug based on the work of the Human Genome Project. The new product development project is a result of a strategic alliance with an American biotechnology firm, Millennium Pharmaceuticals, who specialise in finding new uses and new markets for pharmaceutical compounds. The firm is considered to be a leading 'light' in this area by experts in the industry. The Human Genome Project is at the very leading edge of biotechnological research, and those firms who are exploiting the new technology quickly are likely to remain major players in this market once it expands.

Genomic research has advanced considerably over the last few years, especially in the last year, when the project has neared full completion. Bayer is very proactive in seizing the opportunity to develop major drugs based on this research. However, although they have moved fast they are not alone, and many other major pharmaceutical companies are on their heels in the development of new drug products. A number of firms have registered genes and proteins, although there has been some public outcry about the whole concept of registering such items. However the Franco-German firm Aventis and the British firm SmithKline Beecham are said to be close to starting trials on compounds based on genomic research. A number of other firms are not very far behind. As in Bayer's trials, these firms are developing products based on small molecule drugs rather than the genes and proteins themselves.

The decoding of the human genome is one of the greatest scientific achievements of the twentieth century, and provides unprecedented commercial opportunities for pharmaceutical companies that can capitalise on the new knowledge speedily. Once the leading company in pharmaceuticals in the world, Bayer has declined to become around the fifteenth most important firm in this sector over the last 20 years or so. The firm is hoping to regain poll position by being the first in the market and investing heavily in genomic-related product development. Bayer, in collaboration with Millennium Pharmaceuticals, has already identified 70 target areas for new drugs produced with the new technology, and as a result of the success of the Human Genome Project this number is likely to turn into thousands over the next 10 years.

3.7.3 The political and legal environment

For clarity, we have been examining the factors present in the firm's macro-environment in isolation. In reality these factors are very much interrelated, and this is particularly true when considering political factors. The political environment cannot be examined in a vacuum, as it simply becomes academic. Politics may be intellectually interesting, but has no substance until translated from theory into practice (or from rhetoric into action).

The outcomes of political decisions are manifest in the legislation of government. Changes in the legal environment are of necessity preceded by political debate and decisions. This is why political and legal forces are grouped together here, but in the context of 'PEST' the 'legal' part of 'P' is often subsumed under 'political' when it appears on its own in many question papers.

Many of the legal, economic and social developments in society are the direct result of political decisions put into practice. The government of the United Kingdom, for example, has followed a basically 'free market' philosophy since the late 1970s. This started with the privatisation of many previously nationalised state industries in 1979.

Key point
The government of the United Kingdom, for example, has followed a basically 'free market' philosophy since the late 1970s.

There is a belief amongst the major UK political parties that business enterprise should be in the hands of private shareholders rather than being controlled by the state.

The central guiding objective of government economic strategy is the control of inflation. To this end, great significance is attached to controlling the monetary supply, reducing and attempting to eliminate the public sector borrowing requirements (PSBR), and keeping public expenditure to a level commensurate with a balanced budget. Entrepreneurship, self-help, private ownership and a reasonable level of profit with the lowest possible level of taxation are viewed by Government as being vital to the country's prosperity. These matters have been introduced to illustrate the important fact that many aspects of the economy are directly influenced by the political climate of the day.

To many companies, domestic political considerations are likely to be of prime concern. However, firms involved in international operations are faced with the additional dimension of international political developments. Many firms export, and may have joint ventures or subsidiary companies abroad. In many developing countries, the domestic political and economic situation is less stable than in the UK. Change is often sought by force, rather than through the democratic process. Marketing firms operating in such volatile conditions clearly have to monitor the local political situation very carefully.

Whatever industry the marketing firm is involved in, changes in the political and legal environments at both the domestic and international levels can affect the company and its implications, and therefore need to be fully understood.

Vignette 3.4

The political environment: Deutsche Bank positions itself to capitalise on the enlarged European Union

As European integration becomes ever more strong, and with the imminent possibility of huge expansion of the European Union with many former Soviet block countries joining under the policy of 'enlargement', many of Europe's firms are seeking a truly pan-European position. Many are taking the long view, and want to be in a position to take advantage of the enormous potential market eventual enlargement will bring. A case in point is the German financial organisation Deutsche Bank, a dynamic organisation that is showing a strong interest in Europe's wealthy potential customers.

The board of Deutsche Bank is considering using the retail division of the organisation, the largest bank in Germany, as a base for marketing a range of financial products throughout the enlarged European Union. There is a large segment of affluent consumers within Europe who will be interested in the wide range of sophisticated financial products the bank plans to offer, including, amongst other things, mutual and investment funds. Deutsche Bank has already consolidated retail-banking operations in Germany and seven other European countries. It now wants to expand this operation in Belgium, Poland and France under its existing successful 'Deutsche 24' brand. The bank currently has approximately seven million customers in Germany and just over a million in other European countries, mainly Italy, where it is the largest foreign bank, and Spain. It aims to increase its customer base significantly on a pan-European basis in the near future.

Europe's affluent segment is likely to continue to grow with enlargement and the increased economic opportunities such a policy is likely to bring to entrepreneurs, and indeed Europe's population as a whole. Such a segment appreciates the sophistication of the bank's products and services, and offers the organisation good potential profit margins. Deutsche Bank is a good case of a pro-active marketing organisation scanning the wider political environment and attempting to capitalise on the changes such dramatic European policies are likely to bring.

3.7.4 The social and cultural environment

Of all the elements making up the marketing macro-environment, perhaps socio-cultural factors are the most difficult to evaluate, and hence pose the greatest challenge to the marketing firm. Social and cultural change manifests itself in changing tastes, purchasing behaviour and priorities. The type of goods and services demanded by consumers is a function of their social conditioning and their consequent attitudes and beliefs.

In essence a society's culture is a distinctive way of life of a people, which is not biologically transmitted but is a learned behaviour that is evolving and changing over time. Cultural influences give each society its particular attributes. Although the norms and values within a society are the result of many years of cultural conditioning, they are not static. It is the cause and effects of cultural change and the resulting revised norms and values within a society that are of particular interest to marketing firms.

The UK culture was greatly influenced during the late nineteenth century by the Victorian Protestant work ethic, which prescribed hard work, self-help and the accumulation of material wealth. Other industrial societies are also materialistically orientated. Cultural values do, of course, change over time, and such change is particularly evident amongst the young. Evidence suggests that many young people today question the desirability of a culture with core values based upon materialism.

Core cultural values are those that are firmly established within a society and difficult to change. Such beliefs and values are perpetuated through the family, religion, education, the government, and other institutions within society. As a result, core cultural values act as relatively fixed parameters within which marketing firms are compelled to operate.

Secondary cultural values tend to be less strong and thus more likely to undergo change. Social and cultural influences are so interrelated that it is

Definition
In essence a society's culture is a distinctive way of life of a people, which is not biologically transmitted but is a learned behaviour that is evolving and changing over time.

difficult to evaluate the effects of each in isolation. Generally, social change is preceded by changes over time in a society's secondary cultural values. The following are examples of changes in the secondary cultural values of UK society that have caused quite dramatic social changes in the United Kingdom, and in the Western world in general.

Changes in social attitudes towards credit

As recently as the 1960s, credit (or hire purchase as it was more commonly called then) was generally frowned upon. It was more acceptable to finance major purchases such as cars and houses on credit, although even these financial arrangements were rarely discussed openly, even among friends, as they are nowadays. There tended to be a stigma attached to buying goods on credit. Credit was often referred to in derisory terms such as 'on tick' or the 'never-never'.

Today, offering instant credit has become an integral part of marketing activity. Many people have credit accounts at garages and stores, and many use credit and charge cards such as Access, Visa and American Express. Credit transactions are now conducted openly in stores and elsewhere without any hint of social stigma. Credit transactions are so prevalent nowadays that it is the person who never finances purchases on credit who is unusual.

For many people today it is often the availability and terms of credit offered that are the major factors in deciding to purchase a particular product. Credit has lost its stigma and is an accepted part of everyday life. Indeed, it is demanded by many customers, for without it the purchase would probably never take place. Marketing companies' response to this change in attitude can be seen in the large number of credit schemes on offer today.

Key point
For many people today it is often the availability and terms of credit offered that are the major factors in deciding to purchase a particular product.

Changes in attitude towards health

People are more concerned about their health than they were a few decades ago. They question the desirability of including artificial preservatives, colourings and other chemicals in the food they eat. In the early 1980s, people who ate special 'health' foods and who took regular exercise like jogging were considered to be rather odd. Today, eating wholesome foods and taking sensible, regular exercise is an important part of many people's lives. Marketing firms have responded to this increase in general health awareness amongst the population. Today, many food products are advertised as being 'natural' or 'additive-free', and food producers have to specify the ingredients on the package. Sports equipment and sportswear marketing is now aimed at all sectors of society, irrespective of age, sex or social class. The concern of what were the 'eccentric few' has grown into a multi-million pound industry. This has resulted in increased business opportunities for firms who can provide goods and services that can satisfy the requirements of a health-conscious population.

Smoking, which was thought to be the height of sophistication a few decades ago, is now accepted as being detrimental to health, and is generally regarded as being antisocial. Many people today never start smoking, and many who do, attempt to stop. It is now the norm to have to look for smoking sections in public places rather than for non-smoking sections. This is a classic example of how changes in social attitudes have posed a significant threat, in this case, to the tobacco industry. Tobacco manufacturers are diversifying out of these products into new areas of growth in an attempt to counteract the general decline in their traditional markets.

Changes in attitudes towards working women

The old cliché that 'a woman's place is in the home' reflects the chauvinistic attitude held by many people (including women) a few decades ago. In the UK today, social attitudes are more enlightened and a high proportion of economically active people are women. Approximately 60 per cent of all working women are married, and combine running a home with the demands of a job or career.

Marketing firms have reacted to these changes. The fact that many women now have less time for traditional 'housekeeping' has doubtless contributed to the proliferation and acceptance of convenience foods as a normal part of everyday life. To a certain extent, the development of convenience foods raises conflict between this development and health awareness – a conflict that is being resolved by food manufacturers now producing ranges of 'healthy', additive-free convenience foods.

This high proportion of working women has also contributed to the development of 'one-stop shopping'. When both partners are working, leisure time is at a premium. The large hypermarket allows people to do most of their shopping under one roof. Today it is common for couples to make one major shopping expedition to a hypermarket, travelling by car and purchasing a week's or even a month's worth of major supplies. Freezers and timesaving devices such as food processors and microwave ovens have all increased in popularity. Meals can be pre-cooked, stored in the freezer, and rapidly defrosted and cooked when required.

Changes in moral attitudes

The period of the 1960s and early 1970s has been described by social commentators as being the era of the 'social revolution'. The 1960s is recognised to have seen the birth of the so-called 'permissive society'. Throughout the 1960s, society's values went through a period of dramatic change. Attitudes towards marriage, divorce, sexual relationships, drugs, religion, family, economic and social institutions, and towards authority in general, underwent considerable change. Many members of the 'older generation' were shocked to see how value and beliefs, which had been held for many generations, were cast aside or totally ignored by younger people. Generally, people became more responsive to change. This was the period of 'individualism', where behaviour considered socially unacceptable a few years previously became tolerated and even accepted as being typical.

Since the 1990s, society has experienced something of a reversal in moral attitudes among the young. Young people have witnessed periods of economic recession and high unemployment, a dramatic increase in the divorce rate and the number of single parent families, and the consequences of drug abuse,

Definition
The period of the 1960s and early 1970s has been described by social commentators as being the era of the 'social revolution'.

sexual permissiveness and the advent of AIDS. Today, there is a tendency amongst younger people to place a greater emphasis on health, economic security and more stable relationships.

3.7.5 Other macro-environmental factors

Key point
In a number of countries the religious environment may pose an important source of threats and opportunities for firms.

The macro-environmental factors discussed so far are not intended to form an exhaustive list, but merely demonstrate the main areas of environmental change. Other sub-environments may be important to marketing management. For example, in a number of countries the religious environment may pose an important source of threats and opportunities for firms.

In the UK, demographic changes are viewed as being important by many companies. The UK population has been stable at approximately 56 million for a number of years, but the birth rate is falling and people are living longer. Companies that produce goods and services suitable for babies and small children (e.g. Mothercare) have seen their traditional markets remain static or decline slightly. Such companies have tended to diversify, offering products targeted at older age groups. A larger older sector of the population offers opportunities for companies to produce goods and services to satisfy their particular needs. Special products and services such as holidays and pension-related financial services are being marketed to meet the needs and wants of this relatively affluent sector, the over-55s, who have more disposable income available than any other age group. This group is the modern marketer's dream, as many people have retired early on generous occupational incomes. A company called SAGA specifically set itself up to target this age group, offering a range of products including holidays and insurance provision.

Some of the environmental variables discussed in this chapter are covered later in greater depth in Chapter 8, which covers marketing intermediaries, particularly the forces influencing change in the structure of retail distribution.

Technological advances in the field of marketing practice itself are discussed further in Chapter 13 in the context of marketing research, in Chapter 14 in the context of planning and control, and in Chapter 17, which deals with sales forecasting.

Culture and cultural change is discussed further in relation to the arena of international marketing in Chapter 15. Marketing intermediaries are also examined further in Chapter 15, with particular reference to overseas agents and distributors.

Questions

1 *Definition*
What do you understand by the term 'macro-environment'? Use examples to illustrate the importance of this macro-environment to the marketing management of an organisation with which you are familiar.

2 *Monitoring*

The Chartered Institute of Marketing's definition of marketing includes the following: 'Marketing . . . is responsible for identifying, anticipating and satisfying customer requirements profitably'.

To what extent can the monitoring of the technological, economic and social environments contribute to anticipating customer requirements? Illustrate your answer with examples drawn from your own knowledge and experience.

3 *Supplier environment*

'Whatever the product or service being purchased by the marketing firm, developments in the supplier environment can have an immediate and possibly serious effect on the company's commercial operations.'
Critically evaluate this statement using examples to illustrate the points made.

4 *Supplier environment*

Under what circumstances might it be possible for a firm to exert influence over its distributors and intermediaries? What kind of influence may be exerted, and how can this be achieved?

5 *Social environment*

Give examples of how the changing roles of men and women in society have affected marketing practice over the past 25 years. How do you envisage developments over the next 25 years, and how do you feel this might affect the practice of marketing?

6 *Analysis*

Explain the term PEST analysis. Describe, using specific examples, what type of analytical information marketing management might be interested in and why, under each of the PEST headings.

7 *Supplier environment*

'Whatever the product or service being purchased by the marketing firm, developments in the supplier environment can have an immediate and possibly serious effect on the firm's commercial operations' (Lancaster and Reynolds, 1995, p. 40).
Critically evaluate the above statement, and use specific examples to illustrate the points made.

8 *Environmental elements*

List and discuss the main elements in (i) the micro-environment or proximate environment; (ii) the wider general macro marketing environment.

References

Kraar, L. (1989). Your rivals can be your allies. *Fortune*, **27 Mar**, 66.

Lancaster, G. A. and Reynolds, P. L. (1995) *Marketing*. Butterworth-Heinemann.

Reynolds, P. L. and Day, J. (1995) The marketing of public sector professional building services in a compulsory competitive tendering environment. In: *Proceedings of the 1995 Marketing Education Group Conference, University of Bradford, 5–7 July*, MEG/ University of Bradford.

Reynolds, P. L. and Day, J. (1996). The Marketing of Public Sector Professional Building Services in a Compulsory Competitive Tendering Environment – Entrepreneurial Behaviour in the Public Sector. Paper presented at the UIC/AMA Research Symposia on Marketing and Entrepreneurship, University of Illinois at Chicago and the American Marketing Association, San Diego, USA, 2–3 August.

Reynolds, P. L., Day, J. and Lancaster, G. A. (1998). A marketing strategy for public sector organisations compelled to operate in a compulsory competitive tendering environment. *International Journal of Public Sector Management*, **11(7)**, 583–95.

Stanton, W. J., Etzel, M. J. and Walker, B. J. (1991). Super television: the high promise – and high risks – of high definition TV. In: *Fundamentals of Marketing*, 9th edn. McGraw-Hill.

Zeithaml, C. P. and Zeithaml, V. A. (1984). Environmental management: revisiting a marketing perspective. *Journal of Marketing*, **Spring**, 46–53.

Further reading

Adcock, D. (2000). Analysing external markets and internal assets for strategic decisions. *Marketing Strategies for Competitive Advantage*, Chapter 3. John Wiley & Sons.

Armstrong, G. and Kotler, P. (2000). The global marketing environment. *Marketing: An Introduction*, 5th edn, Chapter 3. Prentice Hall.

Blythe, J. (2001). The marketing environment. *Essentials of Marketing*, Chapter 2. Person Educational Ltd.

Davies, M. (1998). Marketing planning, the environment and competitive strategy. *Understanding Marketing*, Chapter 2. Prentice Hall.

Kotler, P., Bowen, J. and Makens, J. (1996). The marketing environment. *Marketing for Hospitality and Tourism*, Chapter 5. Prentice Hall.

Lancaster, G. A. and Massingham, L. C. (1999). The marketing environment. *Essentials of Marketing: Text and cases*, 3rd edn, Chapter 2. McGraw-Hill.

Lancaster, G. A. and Reynolds, P. L. (1998). Marketing and the macro-environment. *Marketing*, Chapter 2. Macmillan Press.

Lancaster, G. A. and Reynolds, P. L. (1999). Marketing defined. *Introduction to Marketing: A Step by Step Guide to All The Tools of Marketing*, Chapter 1. Kogan Page.

Nasar, S. (1988). Preparing for a new economy. *Fortune*, **26 Sep**, 86.

Nickels, W. and Burk-Wood, M. (1997). Environmental analysis, ethics and social responsibility. *Marketing, Relationships, Quality, Value*, Chapter 3. Worth Publishers.

Plamer, A. (2000). The marketing environment. *Principles of Marketing*, Chapter 2. Oxford University Press.

Soloman, M. and Stuart, E. (1997). Decision-making in the new era or marketing: enriching the marketing environment. *Marketing, Real People, Real Choices*, Chapter 3. Prentice Hall.

The functions of marketing

4

4.1 Introduction

In Chapter 2, marketing was described as a conceptually based business philosophy that has as its primary objective the realisation of profit through customer satisfaction. This philosophy is implemented through the various functions that make up marketing.

It is a common error to think of marketing as a limited set of activities, notably advertising, sales promotion and market research. A truly marketing-orientated company should ensure that the marketing concept is uppermost in the thoughts and actions of all its departments and personnel.

It is true that marketing specialists are the people most directly concerned with implementing the marketing concept and most closely associated with the customer. Individual marketing specialisms are known as marketing's functions. The role of the functional specialists is to identify the needs of the market, to interpret these, to bring products and services to the market place in a manner that is appealing, and to ensure lasting customer satisfaction.

4.2 Marketing in practice: the mix

Marketing strategy can be likened to a recipe, where the ingredients are the various marketing functions. Just as recipes vary according to the dish being prepared, so different marketing strategies require differing levels and combinations of functional ingredients. Even if a relatively minor ingredient is calculated incorrectly or forgotten, a recipe will not be successful. The same is true of marketing strategy, where all functional ingredients depend on each other for success.

The idea of the *'Four Ps'* – *product, price, promotion* and *place* (distribution) – was first suggested by E. Jerome McCarthy (1960). These are the key elements of the marketing function. Each of these mix elements possesses a number of variables (see Figure 4.1) whose emphasis can be varied according to a chosen strategy. Inherent in any marketing strategy is a series of inter-mix variables as well as several intra-functional variables. These functional aspects of the marketing mix which include the 'Four Ps' in addition to customer

PRICE	PROMOTION
Level	Advertising
Discrimination	Sales promotion
Discount	Personal selling
PRODUCT	**PLACE**
Design	Warehousing
Packaging	Transportation
Display	Service
Brand	Stockholding

Figure 4.1 The marketing mix – available marketing tools to target customers.

Key point
A marketing strategy takes the tools of the marketing mix and ascribes to them varying degrees of emphasis that marketing considers appropriate to a given situation.

segmentation, targeting and positioning are referred to as the *marketing mix –* a term coined by Neil Borden (1964). These marketing mix variables are directly controlled by marketing, and the manipulation of the Four Ps is how the company reaches its target segments.

Figure 4.2 gives a diagrammatic representation of how the marketing mix can be utilised. A marketing strategy takes the tools of the marketing mix and ascribes to them varying degrees of emphasis that marketing considers appropriate to a given situation. This placing of emphasis is described as marketing effort. The marketing effort has human resource allocation as one of its components. Considered in financial terms, the use of the marketing mix concept allows management to arrive at a total budget for marketing strategy, and then allows for this budget to be allocated at various levels across the mix and within each element of the mix.

Remembering that the marketing mix is composed of closely interrelated elements, it is necessary to examine each of these functions in turn to be clear about their respective roles. As each function has at least a chapter devoted to it, the purpose here is to examine these functions at an introductory level and to put them in perspective relative to one another.

PRICE	PROMOTION
Level	Advertising
Discrimination	Sales promotion
Discount	Personal selling
PRODUCT	**PLACE**
Design	Warehousing
Packaging	Transportation
Display	Service
Brand	Stockholding

Figure 4.2 A hypothetical marketing strategy.

Markets are dynamic in nature and can be affected by a wide range of environmental, uncontrollable variables. The task of marketing is to devise strategies that take account of these variables using available marketing tools. These tools of the marketing mix are controllable variables to be applied to a given situation with creativity and imagination. The only constraint on creativity is the level of financial support that the company can give to its marketing effort. Each of the functions of marketing is now considered.

4.3 Product (or service)

The marketing mix is a combination of many factors, but consumers tend to view the whole of marketing effort in more tangible terms of the product (or service). It is important for marketers to recognise that much of the 'want-satisfying' nature of the product is derived from consumer perceptions of the product. The true nature of the product is always what the consumer perceives it to be, and not what the company thinks it is or would like it to be. Marketing management is responsible for finding out what perceptions will contribute to consumer satisfaction, and then manipulating the marketing mix to ensure that the product embodies these perceptions.

Definition
The marketing mix is a combination of many factors.

The product (or service) is the cornerstone of the marketing mix and should be considered as the starting point for marketing strategy, because without it there is nothing to promote, price or distribute.

Marketing strategies have a variety of options available in their design. These vary in their levels of sophistication and long-term impact. Figure 4.3 illustrates the very popular strategy bases that can be derived from a simple matrix, whatever individual strategic path is taken by the company.

Companies who make 2/2 decisions (concentrating on existing products in existing markets) lack imagination and run the risk of becoming outmoded; 2/1 decision makers (existing products into new markets) represent attempts to extend the *product life cycle* (see Chapter 12); and 1/1 and 1/2 decisions are

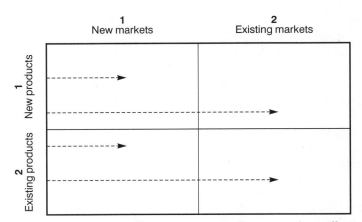

Figure 4.3 Strategic options (Ansoff's matrix). (Originally proposed Ansoff, 1957).

more adventurous and risky. In the longer term, however, new product (or service) development is the principal means of survival for the company.

The key aspects of the product as a marketing function can be summarised as follows:

1 Product planning
   a. Product/market decisions – to whom, where and in what quantity?
   b. New product decisions, research and development programmes, marketing research studies.

2 Product management
   a. Organisational decisions relating to human accountability for the success of the product
   b. Marketing decisions relating to the numbers and types of product on offer. These are product line and product mix elements.

3 The physical product
   a. Design decisions
   b. Quality/image decisions
   c. Packaging decisions.

In service industries, it should be recognised that the service is, in effect, the product, and marketing practitioners often refer to their individual services as 'products' (e.g. banking and insurance). This point is dealt with more fully in Chapter 12.

Vignette 4.1

Lack of marketing focus on the company's core products makes The Lego Corporation lose direction and money

Lego®, the Danish toy firm, had a good year in 1999. The company enjoyed healthy sales, especially for its traditional building brick toy products. The sales for the year were so good in fact that the company decided to diversify into other related products in a big way. This strategy has not been so successful, and the company seems to have lost its marketing focus and competitive edge.

Other large toy firms have had a hard time in the year up to March 2001, with Mattel and Hasbro also announcing losses for the year. Lego's chief executive and main shareholder of the family-owned firm blamed lack of market focus for the company's poor profit performance. The company's core competence is creating toys that allow children to use their imagination and creative talents. The famous Lego brick products exemplify this core competency. However, Lego has moved away from this core stance into a wide range of products such as clothing, watches and other Lego branded goods.

The healthy sales of 1999 gave them motivation to move into these other areas, but the firm has had to pay the price. The firm is now moving back into its core products, where it sees plenty of growth potential.

Not all of its moves have been unsuccessful. The Legoland theme parks continue to be successful, although the firm has no plans to expand in this area. Their move into robotic toys has also shown progress. The Lego case shows the importance of keeping a keen market focus and giving customers what they want and expect from the company's product range.

4.4 Price

Price is a particularly potent element of the marketing mix because of its direct impact on the customer, the company and the economy. To the consumer, price is a major indication of quality and an important factor in the decision-making process. For the company, the price at which a product or service is sold represents the sole means of recouping costs and making a profit.

The price that customers are prepared to pay for a product determines the level of demand for that product, which will affect the overall prosperity of the marketing company and may have a bearing on the company's competitive position in the market place. Price levels in general have far-reaching implications for the national economy. They influence wages, interest rates and government policy.

Sales people sometimes claim that price is the only factor of importance in their particular market. It is true that in some commodity markets, various companies have achieved similar levels of service, product quality and promotional support so that price has become the major method of product differentiation. However, we should not overlook the major marketing efforts that these companies have made in order to reach such a state of similarity. We should also be aware that if one company is able to differentiate its product on a non-price basis or, conversely, if a company fails to maintain the standards of its competitors, then price will decrease in importance as the major determinant of product choice. Certainly price must be regarded as important, but never all-important.

Marketing management faces a particular problem when attempting to arrive at a specific price level. The problem is complicated because price is difficult to define. Whilst it is possible to think of the price of a product as the monetary value given in exchange, this definition is simplistic if we wish to consider price in relation to the other elements of the marketing mix.

The buyer and seller have different views of the price of an item. Whatever the buyer's actual motive for purchasing, the economic consideration of price as an opportunity cost cannot be ignored. As levels of affluence continue to rise, it remains true that the decision to spend a certain amount of money on one product leaves the purchaser with less to spend on other products or services. Whilst price is often thought of as an indicator of quality and prestige in the minds of consumers, it is also a negative aspect of the product. If the quality of two products is perceived to be equal, buyers will naturally tend to choose the one that bears the cheaper price. Whilst there is ample scope for product differentiation by the seller, price remains an important, albeit imperfect, yardstick that buyers use in reaching a purchase decision.

Key point
Sales people sometimes claim that price is the only factor of importance in their particular market.

Key point
Certainly price must be regarded as important, but never all-important.

Initially, the seller considers price as the mechanism for making profit. There is often a close relationship between the selling price of a product and the cost of production. The marketer does not, however, view price as being something that is 'attached' to the product after all the other components (tangible and intangible) have been assembled. Rather, the marketing-orientated seller hopes that price will be considered as a product feature, viewed by the buyer in conjunction with a variety of other product attributes. In this way, the marketer never loses sight of the reality that price is but one, albeit very important, element of overall marketing effort.

The pricing decision is further complicated by the fact that it can create conflict within the firm, within marketing channels and within the competitive environment. Marketing management may arrive at a price that fits perfectly with total marketing effort and at a price they believe will be considered to be optimal by the customer. The application of this price may be frustrated by other members of management who consider it to be impractical in terms of the immediate rate of return. Distributive intermediaries may consider the price to be unfair, or disagree with the manufacturer's pricing policy. Finally, the most effective pricing strategy can be disrupted by competitive action; this point is discussed further in Chapter 11, along with the options available to companies who are faced with competitive pricing pressures.

If any element of the marketing mix strategy is mismanaged or ill-conceived, the consequences for the company can be grave. Where errors of judgement occur outside the realm of pricing, the company can face major setbacks.

Key point
The financial or survival implications associated with pricing strategy make this functional area one of key importance that must be approached with caution.

Although the cost (not just the financial cost) to the company can be severe, remedial action can usually be taken. Where pricing is concerned, the effects of misjudgement are more immediately apparent in terms of their influence on the financial well-being of the organisation. It is a simple economic reality that companies cannot survive unless the value of sales is in excess of costs. A price that is pitched too high may destroy the effectiveness of an otherwise well conceived marketing mix strategy. If a price is set too low and the volume of sales cannot offset this disparity, it is unlikely that a subsequent increase in price will be readily acceptable to the marketplace. The financial or survival implications associated with pricing strategy make this functional area one of key importance that must be approached with caution.

Vignette 4.2

Price discrimination in the European car market, with British customers being the losers

The British car trade has always had a reputation for giving its customers a poor deal when it comes to price. Car prices in Britain are significantly higher than in other European countries, and have been for many years. This has lead to many potential customers sourcing their cars overseas and importing them into the UK with significant savings. If customers are buying a British car they can order and pay for it in, say, Spain, and the vehicle is delivered to their door from a UK factory. UK driving specification is no trouble at all, and the delivered vehicle has never been out of the country.

Many commentators say the price differentials are because of the relatively high £ sterling and the fact that the UK is not one of the 'Euro Zone' single currency countries. Prices in Euros for a number of models have fallen in the UK. In fact retail prices overall in the UK have fallen by about 10 per cent in the last year, but this has had little effect on the yawning gap between car prices in the UK and in many other countries on the continent. Compared with Denmark, for example, UK car prices are up to 50 per cent higher. In the UK, a Volkswagen Passat costs 49 per cent more than in Portugal. In many other countries the differentials may not be so dramatic but they are still significant.

The European Commission is looking into the matter and states that it can find no good reason why car price differentials should be more than 12 per cent, even taking into account the different taxation regimes in different parts of the EU, which very often clouds the true post-tax price. Despite a damning European Commission report and orders by the British Government for car firms to look at UK prices and increase competition, the British car buyer still seems to be getting a poor deal compared with buyers on the Continent.

4.5 Promotion

The promotion of a product is perhaps the element of the marketing mix that is most subject to variation according to the type of product or service on offer. For some products, promotion may only play a minimal role in the marketing effort; for others, marketing strategy may be almost solely based on this mix element.

No product can be sold if the target market is unaware of its existence. It is also undeniable that no amount of promotion will help to sell a product that is not acceptable to the market. This is a major defensive argument against critics who claim that advertising is over-persuasive and over-pervasive.

Key point
No product can be sold if the target market is unaware of its existence.

In consumer markets particularly, promotion often has the highest budget allocation of all mix elements, especially after the product has been launched. For this reason promotion receives a great deal of attention as a marketing function. However, the effects of promotional expenditure are particularly difficult to measure, and although recognised procedures exist for measuring its effectiveness, the task remains complex.

Lord Leverhulme, of washing detergent fame, is quoted as saying: 'Half the money I spend on advertising is wasted. The problem is I don't know which half!'.

One of the main reasons why promotion is so difficult to evaluate is that promotional expenditure does not create immediately tangible success. Correctly viewed, promotion is an investment, but problems often arise when fixing a company's promotional budget. Unlike the purchase of machinery, the recruitment of extra staff or improved warehousing facilities, the promotional budget provides nothing that can be readily perceived as 'value for money'. This is a recurrent source of dispute and confusion in companies where budgets are allocated by managers who are not altogether convinced about the value of 'promotion'. This can be overcome by ensuring that promotional strategy is preceded by the setting of clear, well-defined objectives. By so doing, it is possible to attempt to make judgements about a strategy's effectiveness.

Definition
The term 'promotion'
traditionally covers
four basic activities:
advertising, personal
selling, public
relations, and
specialised sales
promotion techniques.

The term 'promotion' traditionally covers four basic activities: advertising, personal selling, public relations, and specialised sales promotion techniques. An element of overlap occurs, but there are definitions that help to clarify the respective roles of each area:

1 Advertising is concerned with communicating messages to selected segments of the public in order to inform and influence them in a manner that leads them to perceive favourably those items that the advertising features. *Advertising* is always clearly identifiable in terms of the product being promoted. It is also a commercial transaction between the advertiser and the management of the chosen media.

2 Whilst advertising tends to be aimed at a group, *personal selling* (as the description implies) tends to be tailored towards individuals. The seller may convey the same basic messages that are included in advertising, but the presentation can be modified where necessary to suit specific situations and potential customers.

3 *Public relations* includes a broad set of communicational activities through which an organisation creates or maintains a favourable image with its various 'publics'. These publics range from customers and company employees to shareholders, and even the government. Public relations thus has its major role as a marketing activity, but it also extends to other aspects of an organisation.

4 *Sales promotion* involves those activities and elements of promotion not already mentioned. Temporary price reductions, displays, coupons and free sample distributions are only a few of the many sales promotional techniques available.

Key point
The purpose of
promotion is to create
and stimulate demand.

The purpose of promotion is to create and stimulate demand. Most promotional strategies are likely to involve all four of the activities discussed, and how they are 'blended' together is referred to as the *promotional mix* or, more correctly, the *communications mix*. Just as the basic marketing functions go to make up the overall marketing mix, communications functions can be employed to form an intra-functional mix. Again, integration is the key word: sales are made easier when consumers are informed and made interested by prior advertising. The effectiveness of advertising is in turn increased when it is co-ordinated with specific sales promotional techniques.

The other elements of the marketing mix – price, product and place – are all indispensable. In contrast, advertising, public relations and sales promotion, although not personal selling, are more abstract activities that can sometimes be omitted from a marketing programme without any immediate detrimental effects. Harm would occur over a period of time, either sooner or later, depending on the nature of the product being marketing (e.g. branded foodstuffs would be more quickly affected than quality furniture because of the former's shorter purchasing cycle). Management who are not marketing-orientated have a tendency to treat advertising, public relations and sales promotion as the 'poor relations' among the marketing mix elements. In times of entrenchment, these are the areas that are more readily cut back.

While the assessment of advertising effectiveness can be difficult, it is also well established that a good product, an efficient distributive system and an appropriate price are insufficient to provide overall success without the aid of promotion. A marketing mix without advertising and sales promotion might appear dull when compared to the efforts of competitors, and such a strategy would be vulnerable to competition.

The importance of promotion is made clear when we consider that its task is to stimulate demand by constant communication, which, if effective, should convince buyers that the featured products are 'right' for their particular needs. Chapter 6 identifies the stages in the purchasing process, and it is seen that communication at every stage is vital. Even when the buying decision has been made, promotional communication is necessary to convince the buyer that the correct decision has been made, so that positive attitudes are reinforced and repeat purchases are made.

Definition
Promotion is a communication process whose basic objectives are to modify behaviour, inform, persuade and remind.

Promotion is a communication process whose basic objectives are to modify behaviour, inform, persuade and remind. Chapter 7 deals more thoroughly with the overall and specific aims of promotion.

4.6 Place

This function is concerned with all those activities needed to move the product or service from the seller to the buyer, and its origin is in the word 'placement'. To understand *place* (usually referred to as distribution) as a function in itself and as part of the marketing mix, we must divide the function into two categories:

1 A structure or network through which transactions can be completed so that the product is made available and accessible to the final user. This structure is referred to as a *distribution channel*.

2 Once the channels of distribution have been established, the company must turn its attention to the problem of how its products are to be physically moved through the distributive system. This is called *physical distribution management (PDM)*, or *logistics*.

4.6.1 Distribution channels

Although changes in retail trends during the past 30 years have increased the number of goods that flow directly from manufacturers to retailers (in the form of super- and hyper-markets), the use of intermediaries still remains quite significant for the movement of many goods. Manufacturers themselves feature in the channel system, as they are the recipients of goods (raw materials and components) from their own suppliers.

The use of intermediaries in a channel system has a number of advantages:

1 The sheer number of transactions that must be made is dramatically reduced when sales are effected through intermediaries or middlemen. Instead of a manufacturer selling to numerous retail outlets or other manufacturers, distributors or wholesalers can assume this task, reducing the manufacturer's transactions to more easily manageable proportions.

2 Middlemen relieve some of the financial burden that manufacturers need to bear when marketing directly to the end user.

3 The manufacturer's costs of transport, storage and stock levels are reduced, as these are 'broken up' (the wholesaler's function is technically known as 'breaking bulk') and shared throughout the channel network.

4 Channel members possess skills and knowledge of their localised markets that it would be impractical for the producer to possess.

5 Middlemen also market a variety of related (and sometimes competing) products and have established contacts and means of entry into local markets that the producer might find difficult to approach if acting independently. They may promote the product and employ a sales force with an intimate knowledge of the local market. Only the very largest manufacturers would be able to field a sales force equivalent in both number and knowledge to the combined sales teams of a group of middlemen.

The advantages of the channel system can be summarised by describing the utilities that channels create:

1 *Time utility*: distribution is co-ordinated so products reach the user or consumer when they are demanded.

2 *Place utility*: this describes the physical movement of goods from one place to another.

3 *Possession utility*: intermediaries ensure that possession is facilitated. The financial risks and burdens are reduced with the changes of *title* (ownership) that occur as goods move down the channel towards the ultimate consumer.

4 *Form utility*: goods are progressively changed into a more usable form as they proceed downwards along the chain of distribution.

Key point
Ideally, the channel structure should operate to the mutual satisfaction of all members.

While the benefits of channel systems are clear, these cannot be enjoyed without an element of cost. When responsibilities are shared or passed on, the company must pay a cost in terms of loss of control. Ideally, the channel structure should operate to the mutual satisfaction of all members. In reality, there is always a tendency for the behavioural dimensions of the channel to cause power struggles and conflict. Channel members may attempt to disrupt the *status quo* if they perceive that the actions of others are working to the detriment of their own interests. To protect themselves from such action channel members might attempt to establish positions of power to regain control over their products, which was lost when responsibility was delegated.

The main sources of power are financial strength and strong brand leadership. For example, the Kellogg Company has successfully retained power over the supermarket chains by refusing to supply 'own label' products. The Kellogg brands are strong enough for the company to control its distribution and production, as indicated by one of their consistent advertising themes: 'We do not make cereals for anyone else'. Channel power is further developed in Chapter 9.

4.6.2 Physical distribution management

Physical distribution management (PDM) is concerned with transporting finished goods to the customer, stock control, warehouse management, and order processing. It is also referred to as *logistics*. The key task of this element of the place function is to ascertain the level of service that the customer requires, then to ensure that this is adhered to and that the product arrives with the customer in an acceptable condition. Physical distribution, like promotion, represents a financial cost to the company. The art of PDM is to achieve a pre-ordained level of service at a cost that is acceptable to the profit objectives of the company. This is a critical area of marketing, because failure to deliver on time not only negates the rest of the marketing effort but can also irrevocably lose customers. PDM is important in two other ways:

Definition
Physical distribution management (PDM) is concerned with transporting finished goods to the customer, stock control, warehouse management, and order processing.

1 Depending on the nature of the product, physical distribution costs can represent as much as 30 per cent of the cost of sales (mostly the cost of transportation). Clearly, if distribution savings can be effected, the company can have a competitive advantage in terms of pricing.

2 If a company is able to offer a particularly efficient service to its customers, this can reduce the customer's sensitivity to price.

Distribution is, therefore, a most valuable weapon for those companies whose strategy is one of *non-price competition*.

The usual measure of a company's distribution efficiency is in the order cycle or lead time, i.e. the length of time that elapses between receipt of an order and delivery of the goods. Although always a critical factor, this lead time has increased in importance over the past 25 years as economic pressures have forced companies to reduce stock levels in order to save on working capital, which helps to finance stockholding. In most industries, the onus of stockholding is placed on the supplier. Automotive manufacturers have now taken this practice to such an extreme that in some cases they only take receipt of goods literally hours before they are required. Such manufacturers operate a production technique known as *'just-in-time'* manufacturing (JIT). The technique is more correctly termed *'lean manufacturing'*. The theory is that components are offloaded from transport and directly marshalled to the production line. Sophisticated statistical techniques are employed in order to arrive at optimum order quantities and to ensure logistical co-ordination between raw material supply, production and distribution.

Management is faced with two particular problems when dealing with physical distribution:

1 It must ensure that the efforts of all concerned are optimised. This means that effort and efficiency should be judged upon the end result and not upon the individual results of separate departments.

2 The other consideration is known as the total cost approach to distribution. If a lead-time of five days is the distributive objective, this might involve maintaining high stock levels or using an expensive transport mode. Other managers in the company may strive to reduce costs in their own areas of activity, but it must be ensured that these efforts are not detrimental to achieving the overall distribution objectives that end customers have been promised.

It is sufficient at this stage to suggest the following guidelines for PDM:

1 Managers must decide the level of service that the company wishes to achieve, using the overall distribution mix strategy

2 When the service level has been decided, the company can examine the most economic method of achieving this

3 The costs involved must be realistic, but at no time should the service objective be sacrificed in the interest of cost saving.

We can draw the conclusion that it is not possible to both maximise service and minimise costs.

Vignette 4.3

Eddie Stobart Ltd, the UK's favourite logistics company, uses a dial-in solution to keep track of warehouse stock

Founded in 1970, Eddie Stobart Ltd is one of the UK's leading transport and warehousing organisations. A private company with headquarters in Carlisle, UK, Eddie Stobart Ltd is in fact the UK's largest transport and logistics company. Chairman and Chief Executive Edward Stobart, the son of 'Eddie', believes the Cumbrian location has been central to the firm's success. The firm's strategic position is next to the M6 motorway linking Scotland with the rest of the UK's motorway network, obviously very important for the sort of warehousing and distribution services the company offers its customers.

From 100 vehicles in 1991, itself a remarkable achievement, the company now has 800. The company has 20 depots nationally, and over three million square feet of warehousing. It is to the subject of warehousing and in particular the tracking and management of warehouse stock that this vignette now turns. The company was looking for a 'dial-in' solution to keep track of warehouse stock that would allow its customers' suppliers to check warehouse stock levels held by the company. One of Eddie Stobart's biggest customers needed to provide its suppliers with dial-in access to warehouse information, for the purpose of monitoring stock levels held in the Eddie

Stobart warehousing system. Eddie Stobart Ltd saw the potential of developing and making available such a system to all of its customers.

The company chose a Perle 833AS Remote Access Server to meet its multiple requirements. Customers can now use dial-in services as part of a package so that they can keep track of their stock in Eddie Stobart warehouses. The service is very secure and very fast. It will allow customer's suppliers to see at a glance the amount of inventory held in the Eddie Stobart warehousing system. It will also show users how long it has been there for stock rotation purposes, the amount in transit at any one time, where the stock is going to, and when it will be delivered. The Eddie Stobart scenario is another good example of a total integrated physical distribution system, as well as illustrating the increased use of computer-based information within the logistics industry.

4.7 Personal selling

Personal selling has already been described in its context as a function of the promotional or communications mix. Selling is, however, important enough to be considered as a function of marketing in its own right, even though it is not included separately as one of the 'Four Ps' of the marketing mix. In its promotional role, selling contributes to the overall effectiveness of the marketing effort; however, it also has a more fundamental role to play, in that the act of selling is the end result of all marketing activity.

Whatever functional aspects of marketing an individual may be involved in, it is important never to lose sight of the fact that the process of making sales is the means of perpetuating the life of the company.

Sales personnel are frequently (and quite properly) requested to perform marketing tasks in addition to those of selling. These may include gathering marketing information or carrying out public relations activity. These are valuable duties, but they should never detract from the primary role of the salesperson: that of selling the company's products or services.

Selling is a process of communication. Companies promote a particular image. This may be one of a small family firm whose strong point is personal service. Others may wish to emphasise their size and ability to provide expert service. A company's philosophy of business and its particular merits combine to form a company message, and it is the job of the salesperson to communicate this message to customers. Buyers usually require more than the physical product when they consider potential suppliers; at the same time, the salesperson is helped by being able to talk about the company in addition to the products on offer. As well as considering their selling skills, it is important when recruiting sales personnel that companies take into account how well the applicant 'fits in' with the desired company image and how well the company image will be transmitted.

Definition
Selling is a process of communication.

The salesperson relies heavily upon the company for basic support in meeting delivery times or providing satisfactory levels of quality. The company's marketing effort may only go part of the way in reaching the customer. The efficient projection of the company message provides a 'backcloth' in front of which the salesperson can carry out his or her role.

Between the company and customer, a 'communication gap' might exist. This can be filled to a limited extent by advertising, but this is not an easy form of two-way communication. Personal selling fills the gap and completes the company's marketing efforts, reinforcing the company message by providing an interpretation that is personally and specifically tailored to the customer.

Key point
In addition to the communication process, the salesperson's role requires physical sales to be made.

In addition to the communication process, the salesperson's role requires physical sales to be made. The salesperson must utilise communication as a means to 'persuade' customers that the company's products can offer something that is superior to competitive products. Buyers arrange their needs and requirements according to a scale of preference that is linked (consciously or subconsciously) to a budget. Where this scale already includes the products a particular salesperson is offering (as is usually the case), the selling task requires that a competitive preference scale that is not merely one of financial negotiation be considered. The word 'persuasion' should be interpreted with caution. It does not imply that to sell is to encourage buyers to purchase items that they do not really want or which offer no advantage; rather, persuasion implies that the buyer should be convinced of the advantages that the proposed product can provide.

Sales personnel are employed to further the communications process, but the level of direct persuasion required varies according to the particular sales task. During the process leading up to a sale (which can vary from minutes to weeks, months or even years) the salesperson is likely to be required to adopt different approaches according to the stage in the buying process that has been reached, or the type of customer being canvassed.

The typical caricature of the 'salesman' usually refers to the cold canvasser or lead seller. The prominence of such salespersons has declined because of changing retail structures, but has re-emerged with the advent of products and services such as double glazing, cavity-wall insulation, prefabricated home extensions and life insurance policies that are 'one-off' purchases. The seller, in many such circumstances, has little or no prior knowledge of his or her customers and relies heavily upon persuasion. This mode of selling is unsuitable in industrial situations. Lead selling is similar, but in this case the seller is supplied with lists of customers who have expressed at least a potential interest in the product. Such lists might be compiled from replies to advertisements or names that have been gathered as a result of a 'survey' purporting to be a market research survey. The real intention of many such 'surveys' is to gain names and addresses as 'leads' for potential canvassing (this practice is called 'sugging', which is short for 'selling under the guise of market research').

'Canned selling' is a method by which the salesperson is allowed very little deviation from an 'approved presentation' that has been based on careful research of customer reactions, needs and objections, and is a method of presentation that has been proved to be effective in certain situations. Whenever a customer objection is voiced, the 'canned sales' approach attempts to overcome this by a rote-learned presentation of an answer to the objection. In addition, salespersons are trained to ask questions that will produce assenting answers, so it will then be more difficult for the customer to say 'No' at the end. This method is often used when selling goods direct to the public in the retail or home environments. The level of creativity required of the individual salesperson is low, although his or her personality is important in ensuring success.

The types of selling discussed represent the negative image of selling, which has done much to diminish the importance and standing of selling as a profession and as an essential element of marketing. The vast majority of salespersons are employed selling on a business-to-business or development sales basis. They are involved in competitive selling. A high degree of product knowledge is required, as well as skill in the techniques of selling. The salesperson is attempting to achieve a sale in the face of direct competition with other products. Much emphasis is placed on building up a basis for co-operation and trust. The persuasion element is concerned with convincing the buyer that the correct company has been chosen with which to make the business development. The missionary salesperson performs a similar function to that just described, except that whereas development sales are usually concerned with established products, missionary selling is more concerned with communicating the company and product message in new markets than in securing actual sales. The salesperson in this context visits customers to inform and influence rather than to sell; such selling will then be the task of a competitive seller. Many large companies employ different personnel to perform development, missionary and competitive selling, and indeed it is easy to see that each task requires a different personality type. In fact, missionary salespeople have sometimes been dubbed 'commando salesmen'. In industrial markets it is common for the sales force to carry out all of these tasks, and a variety of skills and extensive product knowledge is required.

Key point
The salesperson is attempting to achieve a sale in the face of direct competition with other products.

Vignette 4.4

Avon Products Inc., the direct selling company for women

Avon Products Inc. is the world's largest direct seller of beauty and related products. Avon can be found in 139 countries on six continents. The latest countries to receive the Avon treatment are Bulgaria, Latvia, Lithuania, Slovenia and Hong Kong. In fact there is tremendous profit potential in all of the developing countries. As emerging economies develop, the population has greater disposable income and a larger middle-class segment comes into being. People in this segment, particularly women, are prepared to spend a large amount of their disposable income on personal grooming and on beauty products in particular. There are parts of the developing world where the use of cosmetics by women is discouraged for cultural and religious reasons, but otherwise developing nations hold out wonderful future prospects for the firm as Avon moves towards becoming a truly global organisation.

As the world's leading direct seller of beauty and related products, with $5.7 billion in annual revenues, Avon also markets an extensive range of fashion jewellery, apparel, gifts and collectibles. Avon's international management team looks after business operations in 51 different markets. The company uses a network of three million independent representatives, and handles over a billion customer transactions a year.

Traditional representatives make direct contact with customers, often friends and relatives. Using network-marketing principles, representatives are also rewarded for introducing other representatives and get financial rewards based on downstream commissions earned. It is also possible to be an e-commerce representative for the company. Most of these positions can be run on a part-time basis, although there are opportunities to join Avon on a full-time basis as part of its management team.

The vision of the company is to be the organisation that best understands and satisfies the product, service and self-fulfilment needs of women globally. It is not only Avon products that the company offers women, but also health, fitness, self-empowerment and financial independence.

4.8 Marketing information

From the customer's point of view, the information process is the least visible of all marketing functions. It is, nevertheless, fundamental to all marketing activity. If the product is the cornerstone of marketing, then it must be remembered that good products accurately reflect the needs and wants of customers, which can only be ascertained by gathering information. Information provides the means for a company to fulfil the marketing concept.

Key point
Information provides the means for a company to fulfil the marketing concept.

Figure 4.4 illustrates how the information process works. To be of value, it should be a constant process. First, market requirements are established and then translated into products and action. The reaction of the market is then assessed. This provides feedback and guidance as to whether customer needs have been correctly interpreted, and suggests any remedial action that may be required.

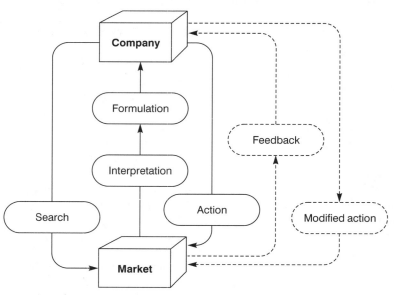

Figure 4.4 The information process.

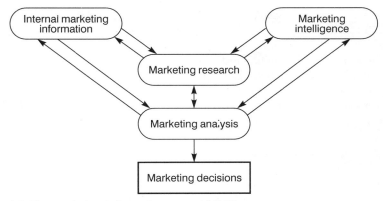

Figure 4.5 The marketing information system (MkIS).

The primary need of any company is to assess the requirements of the market and then act accordingly. In order to function efficiently, a company must augment its information requirements beyond this basic need.

Looking at Figure 4.4, we should interpret 'market' in a much wider sense than simply consumers or customer needs. An examination of the market should encompass the macro-, competitive and public environments. The company should also address itself to information that can be made available from its internal management systems. The sum of all such information and activity is grouped together to constitute a formal system designed to collect, process and report, and this is known as a *marketing information system (MkIS)*. The components of the MkIS are shown in Figure 4.5, which shows that the information sources are fed into an analytical process that guides decision-making and provides feedback which can then suggest modifications to the original course of action.

Marketing research is the best-known function of the information process. It is directly concerned with discovering the needs of customers, and subsequent testing to ensure these needs have been correctly interpreted. Techniques exist for pre- and post-testing specific elements of the marketing mix, such as advertising research and sales research. The pre-testing of products and the prediction of their penetration into the market also come under these headings. The activities mentioned so far are categorised as consumer research. This is in contrast to market research, which focuses on the marketplace itself, including market size and market share analysis. These are but some elements that come under the broader description of marketing research. Marketers should view the research process as a continuous and comprehensive activity that involves fact-finding, monitoring and problem solving.

Market intelligence is concerned with wider issues that affect the company, as well as monitoring a particular market. The monitoring of environmental factors discussed in Chapter 3 is the responsibility of the intelligence system. Its role is to provide information that precedes action, and also to forewarn management of any tendencies that might significantly alter the market.

Definition

The sum of all such information and activity is grouped together to constitute a formal system designed to collect, process and report, and this is known as a *marketing information system (MkIS)*.

Definition

Market intelligence is concerned with wider issues that affect the company, as well as monitoring a particular market.

Key point
A lot of marketing
information exists
within the organisation
itself.

A lot of marketing information exists within the organisation itself. Utilising such information depends on liaison between the various company departments so that information is presented in a useful form for the purposes of marketing analysis. Financial and sales data form the basis for customer and profit analysis. Analysis of the performance of individual products builds up a picture of company performance and provides an indication of market trends. Such information can also provide the basis for desk research, and this is dealt with in detail in Chapter 13.

The various information functions have been described separately, but are indivisible in terms of managerial reliance on them in the decision-making process. Information does not make the decisions; it provides the basis for making them. The most comprehensive MkIS cannot guarantee that the correct decisions will be made and that successful marketing action will result.

4.9 Summary

✓ Marketing functions combine together to form a single strategy. Functional specialists provide a convenient and practical method for operating the marketing mix, but this does not detract from the integral nature of marketing mix management.

✓ It is one of the functions of senior management to ensure that this integration takes place. *Synergy* is a word that is sometimes used to describe the value and the total effect of the marketing mix. Synergy implies that the combined value of a group of activities is greater than the sum of their individual values.

✓ Most people develop a specific interest in a particular marketing function. The aim of this chapter has been to ensure that specialisms are always approached in the context of the total marketing mix.

Questions

1 *Marketing concept*
   (a) 'Marketing is satisfying customer needs at a profit.'
   (b) 'Marketing is the process of creating unnecessary needs and wants.'
       Discuss the issues to which the above two statements give rise.

2 *Marketing mix*
   Consider which of the marketing mix variables is most important in:
   (a) Consumer goods marketing
   (b) Industrial goods marketing.

3 *Product*
Product is generally regarded as being the most important of the 'Four Ps'. Why is this?

4 *Promotion*
Does the fact that selling is included as part of the promotional mix weaken its role as a sub-element of marketing?

5 *Place*
Do you feel that channels of distribution and physical distribution management are sufficiently linked to warrant their combined grouping under 'place'?

6 *Marketing information*
Why are companies increasingly seeking to establish marketing information systems, when in the past marketing research has been sufficient for a company's information needs?

References

Ansoff, I. (1957). Strategies for diversification. *Harvard Business Review,* **Sep**.

Borden, N. (1964). The concept of the marketing mix. *Journal of Advertising Research*, June, pp. 2–7.

McCarthy, E. J. (1960). Basic Marketng: a Managerial Approach. Irwin, p. 48.

Further reading

Armstrong, G. and Kotler, P. (2000). Developing marketing strategy and the marketing mix. *Marketing: An Introduction*, 5th edn, Part 3. Prentice Hall.

Blythe, J. (2001). What marketers do. *Essentials of Marketing*, Chapter 1. Person Educational Ltd.

Cateora, P. R. and Ghauri, P. N. (2000). The scope and challenge of international marketing. *International Marketing: European Edition*, Chapter 1. McGraw Hill.

Davies, M. (!998). Introduction to marketing. *Understanding Marketing*, Chapter 1. Prentice Hall.

Keegan, W. J. and Green, M. S. (2000). The global marketing mix. *Global Marketing*, 2nd edn, Part 4. Prentice Hall.

Lancaster, G. A. and Reynolds, P. L. (1999). Marketing defined. *Introduction to Marketing: A Step by Step Guide to All The Tools of Marketing*, Chapter 1. Kogan Page.

Plamer, A. (2000). Developing the market mix. *Principles of Marketing*, Part 3. Oxford University Press.

Market segmentation, targeting and positioning of marketing

5

5.1 Introduction

Now that we have a better understanding of the nature of marketing, we can examine the subject in more detail. A logical starting point is an examination of customers, and this is the theme of this chapter, along with the next chapter, which deals with their purchasing behaviour.

Market segmentation can be defined as:

> The process of breaking down the total market for a product or service into distinct sub-groups or segments, where each segment may conceivably represent a distinct target market to be reached with a distinctive marketing mix.

Marketers realise that, to improve their opportunities for success in a competitive market environment, they must focus marketing effort on clearly defined market targets. The intention is to select those groups of customers that the company is best able to serve in such a way that pressure from competition is minimised. The sequential steps in this process are *segmentation*, *targeting* and *positioning*. In this chapter we examine each of these steps, showing how they can be used to improve the effectiveness of marketing decision-making.

There are increasingly more segmentation bases available, which means that targeting and positioning strategies are becoming more meaningful.

5.2 The need for segmentation

We have seen that the essence of the marketing concept is the idea of placing customer needs at the centre of the organisation's decision-making. It has also been said that the need to adopt this approach stems from a number of factors, including increased competition, better informed and educated consumers, and, perhaps most importantly, changing patterns of demand. Primarily it is this change in patterns of demand that has given rise to the need to segment markets.

Reflect on the products and services that you purchase. Do you purchase exactly the same kinds of products as your friends, or are your purchasing requirements slightly different? Your friends may have different tastes in clothes or in the type of holidays they take. Perhaps they purchase different brands of toothpaste or breakfast cereals. This obvious example shows that market segmentation and the subsequent strategies of targeting and positioning start by recognising that increasingly, within the total demand/market for a product, specific tastes, needs and amounts demanded may differ.

We refer to a market that is characterised by differing specific preferences as being heterogeneous. Market segmentation is disaggregative in nature – in other words, it breaks down the total differently behaving market for a product or service into distinct subsets or segments, with customers who share similar demand preferences being grouped together with each segment. This is illustrated in Table 5.1.

Effective segmentation is achieved when customers sharing similar patterns of demand are grouped together and where each segment differs in the pattern of demand from other segments in the market (i.e. where the clustering gives rise to *homogeneous* demand within each segment and *heterogeneous* amongst all of the segments). Most markets for consumer and industrial products can be segmented on some kind of basis.

Definition
We refer to a market that is characterised by differing specific preferences as being heterogeneous.

5.3 Targeted marketing efforts

The fact that most markets are made up of heterogeneous demand segments means that companies have to decide which segments to serve. Most companies recognise that they cannot effectively serve all segments in a market. They must instead target their marketing efforts.

Imagine that you are a part of a team developing a new car. Should the proposed new model be a two-, four- or five-seated model? Should it have a 1000, 2000 or 3000cc engine? Should it have leather, fabric or plastic seats? The developer has to address these and many other questions. In deciding these issues, the overriding factor is customer demand – i.e. what are customer needs? Some customers (segments) may want a five-seated 2000cc model with leather upholstery, whilst others may prefer a four-seated model with a 1000cc engine and fabric seats. One solution would be to compromise and produce a four-seated 1500cc model with leather seats and fabric trim. Clearly, such a model would go some way to meeting the requirements of both groups of buyers. The danger is that, because the needs of neither market segment are precisely met, most potential customers might purchase from other suppliers who are prepared to cater for their specific requirements.

In short, varied patterns of demand require that marketers develop specific marketing mixes (i.e. product, price, promotional and channels appeals) aimed or targeted at specific market segments. Marketing writers liken this targeting versus mass marketing approach to using a *rifle approach* as opposed to using a *shotgun approach*.

This idea of how companies target their marketing efforts was put forward by D. F. Abell (1980) when he suggested targeting strategies based upon customer group concentrations, or customer need concentrations, or a combination of each. Table 5.1 illustrates how the idea works in practice.

Table 5.1 Customer wants/groups

Customer wants	*Customer groups*		
	Group 1	*Group 2*	*Group 3*
Want 1			
Want 2			
Want 3			

Table 5.2 shows a marketing strategy of complete coverage. This is termed *undifferentiated* marketing, and an appropriate example here might be a popular brand of washing powder/liquid.

Table 5.2 Complete coverage

Customer wants	*Customer groups*		
	Group 1	*Group 2*	*Group 3*
Want 1	X	X	X
Want 2	X	X	X
Want 3	X	X	X

Table 5.3 shows a strategy that concentrates on a specialist want or wants that cover different customer groups. This is a *differentiated* marketing strategy. An example here would be an adhesives manufacturer who supplies the engineering, textiles, schools, office supplies and 'do-it-yourself' markets.

Table 5.3 Want satisfaction specialisation

Customer wants	Customer groups		
	Group 1	*Group 2*	*Group 3*
Want 1			
Want 2	X	X	X
Want 3			

Table 5.4 shows a strategy that concentrates on supplying a variety of wants to a specific customer group, for example, a mining machinery manufacturer supplying the coal industry. This is also a *differentiated* marketing strategy.

Table 5.4 Customer group specialisation

Customer wants	Customer groups		
	Group 1	*Group 2*	*Group 3*
Want 1			X
Want 2			X
Want 3			X

Table 5.5 shows a strategy of specialist supply where the company serves customer groups 2 and 3 with wants 1 and 3 respectively. An example is a spinner of carpet yarns who supplies carpet manufacturers, but who also manufactures and sells needle punch carpets to the motor trade. This is known as a *concentrated* market strategy.

A number of factors affect the choice of targeting strategy. For example, smaller companies with fewer resources often have to specialise in certain segments of the market in order to be competitive, so they must pursue a concentrated strategy. Competition will also affect the choice of strategy. In the final analysis, choosing a targeting strategy is a matter of striking the optimum balance between the costs and benefits of each approach in the particular situation.

Table 5.5 Selective specialisation

Customer wants	Customer groups		
	Group 1	Group 2	Group 3
Want 1		X	
Want 2			
Want 3			X

Specifically, the advantages of target marketing are:

1 Marketing opportunities and 'gaps' in a market may be more accurately identified and appraised

2 Product and market appeals (through the marketing mix) can be more finely tuned to the needs of the potential customer

3 Marketing effort can be focused on the market segment(s) which offer the greatest potential for the company to achieve its objectives.

Vignette 5.1

Segmentation: UK banks reluctantly target 'lost' financially excluded segment

Literally millions of people in the UK have a poor financial history. County Court Judgements (CCJs), credit defaults (usually the result of non-payment of credit card debts) and late payment histories (again on credit cards and other hire purchase agreements, including rental agreements) affect many households. People with such histories are usually recorded on the files of credit reference companies. The biggest credit reference companies in the UK are Experian and Equifax. Mortgage arrears and default records are kept separately by the building societies.

Traditionally people with such poor financial histories have been of little interest to the high-street banks, which have regarded them as a bad risk. However, the government wants to end the financial exclusion of these people and give them the opportunity to have a bank account, cash card and standing order and direct debit facilities. Such people often miss out on the opportunity to purchase many goods and services because they cannot pay by standing order or direct debit.

Conventional current accounts are regarded as a 'cash cow' by the banks. They generate deposits, and income from overdraft charges, and give the bank the opportunity to 'cross-sell' other products such as loans, insurance, mortgages and pensions. The government wants the banks to open 'basic accounts', with no overdraft facilities or chequebooks, but including standing order, direct debit and cash card facilities. In the short term the banks will operate these accounts at a loss, but they hope to make money eventually as the account holders get their financial affairs in order and become regular account holders. Undischarged bankrupts will still be denied even one of the basic accounts; otherwise, such accounts will be open to all regardless of credit history and the state of their credit reference files.

Although the banks are entering into the spirit of the government's wishes, there is some debate as to whether they are demonstrating the degree of enthusiasm the government had hoped them to have for the new scheme. They have given the government their commitment to set up such accounts, but do not seem to be going out of their way to attract new account holders. Barclays and Lloyds TSB launched such accounts throughout the UK in the third week of October 2000, and Lloyds TSB piloted the scheme in Scotland for eight months before that. NatWest set up similar facilities for 'blacklisted' customers at the beginning of October 2000, and HSBC followed suit. Such moves represent an interesting targeting of a relatively unexploited market segment, which could result in profitable business in the long term – although the banks themselves do not seem particularly optimistic about the viability of such a segment.

5.4 Effective segmentation

Ideally, the base(s) used for segmentation should lead to segments that are:

1 *Measurable/identifiable.* The base(s) should ideally lead to ease of identification (who is in each segment?) and measurement (how many potential customers are in each segment?)

2 *Accessible.* The base(s) used should ideally lead to the marketer being able to reach selected market targets through marketing efforts

3 *Substantial.* The base(s) used should ideally lead to segments that are sufficiently large to be worthwhile serving as distinct market targets

4 *Meaningful.* The base(s) used should lead to segments that have different preferences/needs, and show clear variations in market behaviour/response to specialised marketing efforts.

Of the four requirements for effective segmentation, the last, that segments are meaningful, is very important. It is an essential prerequisite in identifying and selecting market targets.

Before we examine each of the steps involved in segmentation, targeting and positioning in more detail, we need to understand and appreciate further what market segmentation means, and how this relates to our criteria for effective segmentation. A simple illustration of this idea is shown in Figure 5.1. Here, the country (England) is broken down into five distinct selling regions, each served by a regional sales representative.

Remember that in segmentation, targeting and positioning, we are seeking to identify distinct subsets of customers in the total market for a product where any subset might eventually be selected as a market target and for which a distinctive marketing mix will be developed. For instance, taking the

Key point
Remember that in segmentation, targeting and positioning, we are seeking to identify distinct subsets of customers in the total market for a product where any subset might eventually be selected as a market target and for which a distinctive marketing mix will be developed.

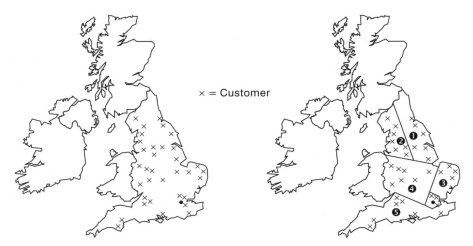

Figure 5.1 Market segmentation for a machine tools manufacturer.

geographical segmentation example in Figure 5.1, on examining the northwest region it is broken up into an 'assisted region' and a 'non-assisted region', as shown in Figure 5.2.

An 'assisted region' attracts various grants and benefits from the government and the European Union. An industrial goods supplier selling certain types of capital equipment (machine tools in this illustration) will target firms to whom it sells in an assisted region with a different message (perhaps emphasising grants available) to that it uses for those firms it sells to in a non-assisted region.

In this hypothetical example we are assuming that buyers in assisted regions will be more prone to the cost-savings motive (through grants), whereas those in

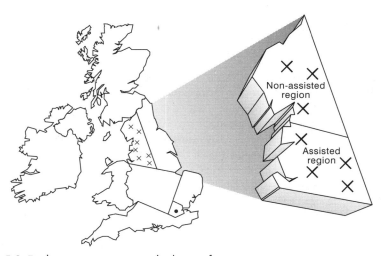

Figure 5.2 Further segmentation on the basis of assistance status.

non-assisted regions will react more to general commercial criteria like reliability, price and service. The important element to note is that the bases selected for segmentation (geography and assistance status) are meaningful ones. Remember that it only makes sense to continue to subdivide markets in this way as long as the resulting segments are worthwhile serving as distinct market targets with distinct marketing mixes. There are some markets where complete segmentation (i.e. tailoring the marketing mix to individual customers) is not only desirable, but also essential. In shipbuilding each customer may be treated as a separate market, but for most consumer product markets such customising of the marketing effort would be totally impractical.

The following represents the sequential steps in conducting a segmentation, targeting and positioning exercise for any given product market:

1 Select bases(s) for segmentation and identify segments

2 Evaluate and appraise the market segments resulting from step 1

3 Select an overall targeting strategy

4 Select specific target segments in line with step 3

5 Develop 'product positioning' strategies for each target segment

6 Develop appropriate marketing mixes for each target segment in order to support positioning strategies.

These steps will each now be dealt with individually.

The machine tools example used the bases of geography and benefits to segment the market. There is no prescribed way to segment a market; different bases and combinations of bases, particularly innovative ones, should be sought by the marketer. There are, however, a number of relatively common bases frequently used by marketers.

Key point
There is no prescribed way to segment a market; different bases and combinations of bases, particularly innovative ones, should be sought by the marketer.

5.5 Segmentation bases in consumer product markets

5.5.1 Geographic segmentation

In international marketing, different countries may be deemed to constitute different market segments. Within a country, a market may be segmented into regions that normally represent an individual salesperson's territory.

5.5.2 Demographic segmentation

This approach consists of a wide variety of bases, and some of the more common ones are age, income, sex, education, nationality, family size, family life cycle, social class/occupation, and type of neighbourhood.

Demographic bases constitute the most popular bases for segmentation in consumer product markets (see Reynolds and El-Adley, 1995, 1997). The reason for this is that they are often associated with differences in consumer demand (i.e. they are meaningful).

Family life cycle segmentation is based on the idea that typically consumers pass through a series of quite distinct phases in their lives. Each phase gives rise to, or is associated with, different purchasing patterns and needs. For example, the unmarried person living at home will probably have very different purchasing patterns to someone of the same age who has left home and recently married. Similarly, it is recognised that purchasing patterns of adults often change as they approach and then move into retirement. The subject is given fuller treatment in Chapter 6, but the stages are defined as:

1 Young

2 Young single, no children

3 Young couple, youngest child under 6 (Full Nest I)

4 Young couple, youngest child 6+ (Full Nest II)

5 Older couple with children 18+ at home (Full Nest III)

6 Older couple, family head in work, no children at home (Empty Nest I)

7 Older couple, family head retired, no children at home (Empty Nest II)

8 Older alone (in work)

9 Older alone (retired).

A further development in the application of family life cycle has been developed by Research Services and termed 'SAGACITY'. This combines life cycle with income and occupation in order to delineate different consumer groups. Consumers are divided into one of four life cycle groups:

1 *Dependent*: adults 15–34 who are not heads of household or housewives, unless they are childless students in full-time education

2 *Pre-family*: adults 15–34 who are heads of household but childless

3 *Family*: adults under 65 who are heads of household or housewives in households with one or more children under 21 years of age

4 *Late*: all other adults whose children have already left home or who are 35 or over and childless.

These four major life cycle groups are then broken down further by a combination of occupation and/or income to produce 12 major SAGACITY groupings:

		Approx. % of UK population
(DW)	Dependent white collar	6
(DB)	Dependent blue collar	9
(PFW)	Pre-family white collar	4
(PFB)	Pre-family blue collar	4
(FW+)	Family, better-off white collar	6
(FB+)	Family, better-off blue collar	9
(FW−)	Family, worse-off white collar	8

(FB–)	Family, worse-off blue collar	14
(LW+)	Late, better-off white collar	5
(LB+)	Late, better-off blue collar	7
(LW–)	Late, worse-off white collar	9
(LW–)	Late, worse-off blue collar	19

Occupation and *social class* are linked because in most developed economies official socio-economic group (social class) categorisations are based on occupation. Of all the demographic bases for segmenting markets, social class is probably the most widely used basis for segmenting consumer product markets.

Social class scores highly against other segmentation criteria in being identifiable and accessible. It is easy to classify individuals on the basis of occupation, and to reach different social classes according to different media and shopping habits. The social class grading system used in the UK, together with a broad indication of the type of occupation associated with each, is:

Social class grading	Type of occupation	Approx. % of UK population
A	Higher managerial	4
B	Intermediate management	11
C1	Supervisory, clerical, administrative	26
C2	Skilled manual	30
D	Semi-skilled/unskilled	25
E	Pensioner (no supplementary income) Casual and lowest grade workers	4

Although still widely used in marketing, doubt is sometimes expressed about social class being a meaningful basis for segmenting markets. For example, it is often the case that the skilled manual group (C2) can earn higher incomes than their counterparts in supervisory or even intermediate management (C1 or B). They are often able to purchase products and services that were traditionally the prerogative of the upper social grades.

Education might also be said to be related to social class, because the better educated tend to get the higher paid jobs. Education is usually expressed as terminal education age (TEA). This classification is open to criticism because of an increase in the provision of part-time and distance learning education, which means that although a person's TEA might be low, education might have been enhanced through later part-time higher qualifications.

Partly because of the diminishing meaningfulness of social class/occupation as a basis of segmentation, new forms of social classification have begun to emerge which take into account a wider range of factors than the single index of occupation on which more conventional social grading systems are based. An example is the *type of neighbourhood/dwelling – the ACORN system* (**A** **C**lassification **O**f **R**esidential **N**eighbourhoods). This system takes dwellings, rather than individuals, as a basis for segmentation. It is based upon the 10-yearly return made by the householder in the census enumeration district within which the house is situated. This census of population takes place in every year that ends in one (i.e. the last one was in 2001), and householders must complete their return by law. There is also a 10 per cent sample taken in every year that ends in six. In the United Kingdom, there are around 125 000 such census districts, and the ACORN system has classified each of these into one of 11 major groups. Each of these major groups is further subdivided to yield a total of 36 specific neighbourhood types. The 11 major groups, and some examples of how Group A is further subdivided into neighbourhood types, are given below:

A   agricultural areas
A1   agricultural villages
A2   areas of forms and smallholdings
B   modern family housing, higher incomes
C   older housing of intermediate status
D   poor quality, older terraced housing
E   better-off council estates
F   less well-off council estates
G   poorest council estates
H   multi-racial areas
I   high-status non-family areas
J   affluent suburban housing
K   better-off retirement areas
U   unclassified

Essentially, the ACORN system is based on the idea that the type of area and housing in which an individual lives is a good indicator of his or her possible patterns of purchasing, including the types of products and brands that might be purchased. There is evidence to suggest that this is the case. In other words, the ACORN system goes some way to fulfilling the 'meaningfulness' criterion for a segmentation basis.

ACORN was developed at the research firm Consolidated Analysis Centres Inc. (CACI). 'Sample Plan', for instance, is a service that can be used for marketing research using a computer program to select ACORN areas. Individual addresses can then be chosen that provide a truly representative sampling frame for survey work.

The effectiveness of census data in providing segmentation bases has been further refined. *Pinpoint (PIN)* analysis is based on census data, and it claims 104 census variables to delineate 60 neighbourhood types that are clustered into 12 main types.

MOSAIC is another approach based on census data. It has added data on the financial circumstances of potential target customers living within each district by relating it to Royal Mail postcodes. Each postcode represents on average between eight and twelve individual homes of a similar type, and each is ascribed an individual MOSAIC categorisation. For example, M1 is 'High status retirement areas with many single pensioners'; M17 is 'Older terraces, young families in very crowded conditions'; M34 is 'Better council estates but with financial problems'; and M55 is 'Pretty rural villages with wealthy long-distance commuters'. It is called 'MOSAIC' because if each of the 58 different MOSAIC categorisations ascribed to postal codes was represented as a different colour and then superimposed onto a map of the UK, it would resemble a mosaic pattern.

This classification is a very powerful database for direct mail, because individual householders can be personally targeted according to the type of MOSAIC categorisation of their home, and in the specific geographical area in which their home is situated. For instance, it is possible to specify that a personal letter go out to all residents in South-East Huddersfield (HD8) who fall in the M46 'Post-1981 housing in areas of highest income and status' MOSAIC category.

5.5.3 Lifestyle segmentation

This is referred to as *psychographic segmentation*. It is based on the idea that individuals have characteristic modes and patterns of living that may be reflected in the products and brands they purchase. For example, some individuals prefer a 'homely' lifestyle, whereas others may have a 'sophisticated' lifestyle.

Young and Rubicam, the advertising agency, put forward a formal lifestyle classification called '4Cs', where 'C' stands for 'customer type'. Consumers are put into one of the following categories:

- Mainstreamers (the largest group, containing in excess of 40 per cent of the population)

- Aspirers

- Succeeders

- Reformers.

5.5.4 Direct or behavioural segmentation

All the approaches to consumer market segmentation described so far have been examples of *associative segmentation* – that is, they are used where it is felt that differences in customer needs and purchasing behaviour may be associated with them. For example, if we use age to segment a market, we are assuming that purchasing behaviour in respect of a certain product is a function of age. Most of the problems that arise from using associative bases are concerned with the extent to which the bases are truly associated with a reflection of actual purchasing behaviour.

Because of the problems of associative segmentation, many marketers believe that it is better to use direct bases for segmenting markets. Such bases take actual consumer behaviour as the starting point for identifying different segments, and they are therefore referred to as behavioural segmentation bases. These divide into three categories:

1 *Occasions for purchase*. Segments are identified on the basis of differences in the occasions for purchasing the product in question. In the market for men's ties, the 'occasion for purchase' might include gift-giving, subscription to clubs or societies, and purchasing a new shirt or suit.

Key point
Because of the problems of associative segmentation, many marketers believe that it is better to use direct bases for segmenting markets.

2 *User/usage status.* A distinction may be made between 'heavy', 'light' and 'non-user' segments for a product.

3 *Benefits sought.* This is certainly one of the most meaningful ways to segment a market. The total market for a product or service is broken down into segments that are distinguished by the principal benefit(s) sought by that segment. For example, the household liquid detergent market might include the following benefit segments: economy, mildness to hands, cleansing power and germ protection.

5.5.5 Loyalty status

A direct approach to segmenting markets is the extent to which different customers are loyal to certain brands (brand loyalty) or retail outlets (store loyalty). Identifying segments with different degrees of loyalty may enable a company to determine which, if any, of its prospective customers may be brand-loyalty prone. Such a market segment is clearly a very attractive one on which to concentrate any future marketing effort. Once convinced of the relative merits of a brand/supplier, such customers are unlikely to switch brands. Understandably, where existing brand loyalty is already strong in a market, the would-be new entrant is faced with a particularly difficult marketing problem. In this situation it may be advisable or necessary to identify and target segments with low brand loyalty.

It is suggested by a number of marketing writers that consumers fall into one of four categories as far as loyalty status is concerned:

1 *Hard core loyals*, who have absolute loyalty to a single brand (e.g. brands AAAAAA)

2 *Soft core loyals*, who divide their loyalty between two, or sometimes more brands (e.g. brands AABABBA)

3 *Shifting loyals*, who *brand-switch*, spending some time on one brand and then moving to another (e.g. brands AAABBB)

4 *Switchers*, who show no brand loyalty, often purchasing products that are lowest in price or have a special offer (e.g. brands BCBAACD).

Vignette 5.2

Segmentation: British Airways wants a long-term replacement for Concorde to service the supersonic business class segment

You only have to travel to Times Square in New York City at 42nd Street and Broadway and look at the British Airways advertising on the hoardings. At the most important crossroads in the world, in the centre of the worlds 'capital', along with the almost full-size replica of Concorde in BA livery, you realise that Concorde is the most important 'brand icon' the firm possesses. The Concorde disaster at Charles De Gaulle airport near Paris in July 2000 left the future of the aircraft in grave doubt. However, British Airways is taking the long-term view on one of its most important and prestigious market segments, and is asking aircraft designers and manufacturers to develop a long-term replacement for the aircraft, whether or not Concorde is allowed to re-enter service in the near future.

Expensive modifications will have to be made to the plane if it is ever going to be allowed to fly again. BA is pushing the original manufacturers, European Aeronautic Space and Defence and BAE Systems, to try and get the modification in place by the end of 2000 to allow the plane to re-enter service around September 2001 – a very ambitious time horizon. If the present Concorde fleet is allowed to resume service in 2001, then BA intends to keep them flying until around 2015 but is eager to find an even better aircraft to replace the by-then ageing icon of sophisticated business travel.

Major aircraft manufacturers such as Boeing see little future in scheduled flight supersonic air travel. They are not convinced that there are sufficient customers out there willing to pay the sort of ticket prices necessary to make the economics of developing and manufacturing such an aircraft add up. They see the demand for smaller 'Lear' and 'Gulfstream' type supersonic business jets rather than for the more 'mass market' type Concorde replacement craft. British Airways is looking forward to getting Concorde back into service not only because it wants to satisfy demand from one of their most prestigious market segments, but also because it regards Concorde as one of its most effective marketing tools. The marketing effects of having a Concorde fleet in operation to key destinations around the world impacts positively on all BA's services. Whether BA has misread the future market for such a service remains to be seen. Many in the business jet and supersonic military jet markets do not believe a replacement for Concorde will turn out to be financially viable, even given the different economic circumstance that might exist 15 years down the line.

5.6 Segmentation bases in industrial product markets

The concept of segmentation, targeting and positioning is the same between consumer and industrial markets. Segmenting industrial product markets suggest a number of additional bases and precludes others that are used for consumer markets.

The most frequently encountered bases for segmentation of industrial product markets are:

Key point
The concept of segmentation, targeting and positioning is the same between consumer and industrial markets.

- *Geographic*, e.g. northwest and southeast, Germany and Denmark

- *Type of application/end use*, e.g. nylon for clothing or that used for parachutes

- *Product/technology*, e.g. plastic containers and steel containers

- *Type of customer*, e.g. manufacturing industry versus public authority

- *Customer size*, e.g. by customer turnover or by the average value of orders placed with the company

- *Loyalty of customer*

- *Usage rate*, e.g. heavy or light

- *Purchasing procedures*, e.g. centralised or decentralised, the extent of specification buying, tender versus non-tender procedures

- *Benefits sought*, based on the product needs that customers require from their purchase – e.g. a car might be needed for the company's representatives, for hiring out, or as the managing director's personal car.

Shapiro and Bonoma (1984) have suggested a 'nested' approach to industrial market segmentation. They identified five general segmentation bases arranged in a nested hierarchy, as shown in Figure 5.3:

1 *Demographic* variables give a broad description of the segments and relate to general customer needs and usage patterns

2 *Operating* variables enable a more precise identification of existing and potential customers within demographic categories

3 *Purchasing approaches* looks at customers' purchasing practices (e.g. centralised or decentralised purchasing); it also includes purchasing policies/criteria and the nature of the buyer/seller relationship

4 *Situational factors* consider the tactical role of the purchasing situation, requiring a greater or less detailed knowledge of the individual buyer

5 Personal characteristics relate to people who make purchasing decisions.

As with consumer markets, industrial market segmentation may be on an indirect (associative) or a direct (behavioural) basis. Again, a variety of bases may be used together in order to obtain successively smaller sub-segments of the market. The criteria given for bases of consumer market segmentation – being identifiable, accessible, substantial and, most important, meaningful – are equally applicable to industrial market segmentation.

Key point
The criteria given for bases of consumer market segmentation – being identifiable, accessible, substantial and, most important, meaningful – are equally applicable to industrial market segmentation.

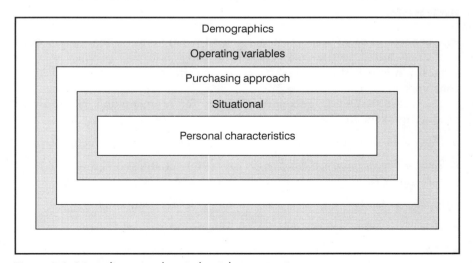

Figure 5.3 'Nested' approach to industrial segmentation.

5.7 Evaluating and appraising market segments

Having decided on a basis for segmentation and identified market segments, the marketer must then evaluate the various market segments that have been identified. Overall, segments should be appraised with respect to sales and profit potential or, in the case of a not-for-profit organisation, the potential to contribute to overall organisational objectives. This in turn requires that each segment be appraised with respect to factors such as overall size, projected growth, extent of existing and potential competition, nature of competitive strategies, and customer requirements.

Vignette 5.3

Segmentation: Merck and Co. Inc. targets USA's bald males

Merck and Co. Inc., the American pharmaceutical company, has found a potentially very profitable commercial use for its existing drug Finasteride®. The drug has been used to treat prostate medical complains for some years. In a lower dose (1 mg), the drug has been successful in trials treating male-pattern baldness (androgenic alopecia). The drug will be marketed under the brand name 'Propecia®' in the USA. The product is in the form of a pill, which patients have to take once a day. It is the only treatment for male-pattern hair loss in pill form, and is available from pharmacists on a prescription basis only. However, a number of Internet companies are already marketing the product and will supply customers without the need of a doctor's prescription. Obviously taking the drug without first consulting a doctor or at least some other health professional has certain risks. However, many people are prepared to take the risk, and Internet suppliers and customers are on the increase.

The United States Food and Drug Administration granted a marketing licence to Merck on December 22, 1997. The marketing clearance of Propecia® is based on a double-blind, placebo-controlled, multicentre trial involving 1879 men. Eighty-three per cent of men in the Propecia® group reported reduction in hair loss or increase in hair growth. This was verified scientifically by hair counts. Seventy-two per cent of the people in the placebo group were found to have progressive hair loss over the same time period (24 months). Propecia® is targeted at men only; it is not safe for use by women; in fact, women must not even handle the drug whilst pregnant as it can cause foetal abnormalities. The tablets have a coating that prevents contact with the active ingredients in normal situations, but there is always a risk of tablets being crushed, exposing the active ingredients. Treatment causes loss of sexual function in some males, although this is usually temporary and very limited. The treatment needs to be taken every day. When the treatment is stopped, hair loss reverts to the pre-treatment level.

A licence to market the product has been granted in the UK to Merck, Sharp and Dohme of Hertfordshire, but at the time of writing (July 2001) the company has no release date for a UK launch. Much has been written about Propecia®, and much scientific information is available on the Internet. Those suffering hair loss problems in Britain are waiting anxiously for the drug's release. There is a huge market all over the world, worth £ billions, for any scientifically proven product for the treatment of andogenic alopecia. The only comparable product to Propecia® is minoxidil, marketed by Phamacia and Upjohn as 'Regain®' (Rogaine® in the USA). Minoxidil is available without a doctor's prescription over-the-counter in pharmacies. Many websites offer minioxidil as well as Finasteride®.

Minoxidil is administered as a lotion, topically. It is sold in regular and extra strength solutions. The drug minoxidil was originally developed for treatment in high blood pressure patients, who were also observed to grow more hair when taking the medicine. A perfect candidate for minoxidil is a young male who is just starting to bald in the vertex/crown of the scalp. It is also suitable for women, although not in the extra strength version. Propecia® is likely to be more popular than Regaine®, as it is in tablet form and therefore much more convenient to take. However, it is not suitable for women.

5.8 Selecting specific target markets

This step concerns organisations that decide to pursue a concentrated or differentiated targeting strategy. The company must decide which of the segments in the market it is best able and willing to serve. This decision must be based on some of the factors outlined, including company resources, competition, segment potential and company objectives. Four characteristics will make a market segment particularly attractive:

1 The segment has sufficient current sales and profit potential to meet company objectives

2 The segment has the potential for future growth

3 The segment is not over-competitive

4 The segment has some relatively unsatisfied needs that the company can serve particularly well.

5.9 Developing product positioning strategies

Definition
Product positioning relates to the task of ensuring that a particular company's products or services occupy a predetermined place in selected target markets, relative to competition in that market.

For each segment in which a company chooses to operate, it must determine a product positioning strategy. Product positioning relates to the task of ensuring that a particular company's products or services occupy a predetermined place in selected target markets, relative to competition in that market. This process is also called 'perceptual mapping' or 'brand mapping'. The idea of product/brand positioning is applicable to both industrial and consumer markets. The key aspects of this approach are based on a number of assumptions, which are now explained. All products and brands have both objective and subjective attributes that they possess to a greater or lesser extent.

Examples of objective attributes include:

Size	Large ⇔ Small
Weight	Heavy ⇔ Light
Strength	Strong ⇔ Weak

Examples of subjective attributes include:

Value for money	Good value ⇔ Poor value
Fashion	Very fashionable ⇔ Old fashioned
Reliability	Very reliable ⇔ Very unreliable

Customers consider one or more of these attributes in choosing between products and/or brands in a given segment.

Customers have their own ideas about how the various competitive offerings of products or brands rate for each of these attributes; i.e. positioning takes place in the mind of the customer.

Using these criteria, it is then possible to establish:

- important attributes in choosing between competitive offerings

- customer perceptions of the position of competitive market offerings with respect to these attributes

- the most advantageous position for the company within this segment of the market.

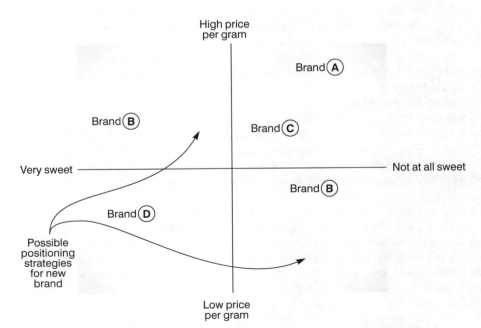

Figure 5.4 A hypothetical product positioning map for the 'instant' breakfast food market.

An example best serves to illustrate this process. Imagine a company is proposing to enter the market for 'instant' breakfast foods, in which there are already five competitors – A, B, C, D and E. The company should first establish what customers believe to be the salient attributes in choosing between brands in this market. In addition, the perceived position of existing competitors with respect to these attributes should also be investigated. If the important attributes have been found to be 'price' and 'taste', a possible positioning map might be drawn as shown in Figure 5.4.

Using this information, the company must now decide where to position its product within the market. One possibility is to position the new brand in the medium-price, medium-taste part of the market; another, to position it at the low-price, less sweet taste area (these possibilities are plotted on the position map, Figure 5.4). Both of these strategies would give the new brand distinctiveness, as opposed to positioning the brand next to one of the established brands, which would mean intense competition for market share.

Vignette 5.4

Segmentation: Deutsche Post, Germany's largest postal company, targets Europe's small investors

The German government has decided to float off 25 per cent of Germany's most successful postal and logistics organisation, the state-run Deutsche Post. Like Britain, Germany has a share-owning culture, thanks mainly to the release of the first issue of Deutsche Telekom shares in 1996, from which a number of small investors did very well. The government wants at least 50 per cent of the share issue of Deutsche Post to go to the millions of potential small investors around Europe. In reality it is expected that the majority of investors will come from inside Germany, or at least that is what the company hopes. Things could go terribly wrong. The government is full of angst. A failure of the issue would not only be a political embarrassment, but also a good deal of money could be lost to the government's coffers.

The company faces a difficult marketing communication problem in persuading Germany's plethora of small investors to take the new issue. One of the main problems is that although the first two tranches of Deutsche Telekom shares were deemed a success by investors, the third tranche was somewhat disappointing and many investors got their fingers burnt. The company is spending serious money in trying to persuade Germany's small investors to make the issue an unqualified success.

The offer, if successful, could raise as much as E7.4 billion for the government, which is obviously supporting Deutsche Post's marketing efforts. As well as extensive advertising, Deutsche Post is planning to offer the shares at the lower end of price expectations to create an attractive 'bargain' – in a sense, a form of promotional pricing. It is also using sales promotions to improve the perceived value of the new issue by offering a E0.5 discount per share if investors subscribe to the offer before a set date. Those who keep their shares until 30 November 2002 will also qualify for an additional free share for every 15 shares held. Overall the package is very attractive, and should overcome any possible investor resistance due to the third tranche of Deutsche Telekom experience.

5.10 Developing appropriate marketing mixes

This is the final step in the appraisal of segmentation, targeting and positioning. It involves the design of marketing programmes that will support the chosen positional strategy in the selected target markets. The company must now determine how to apply the 'Four Ps' of its marketing mix – i.e. what price, product, distribution (place) and promotional strategies will be necessary to achieve the desired position in the market.

5.11 Summary

✓ Used well, the techniques and concepts described in this chapter can contribute significantly to overall company marketing success. Market segmentation, targeting and positioning decisions are strategic rather than tactical. In later chapters these areas will be considered in relation to strategic aspects of marketing planning.

Questions

1 *Bases for segmentation*
The process of market segmentation requires the use of different bases for segmentation strategy to be effective. Outline the most effective bases that might be used to segment industrial markets.

2 *Evaluation of bases*
What are the main criteria used by management to assess the possible effectiveness of any potential segmentation base or variable?

3 *Segmentation, targeting and positioning*
How do you explain the importance now attached to effective market segmentation, targeting and positioning?

4 *Segmentation bases*
Using two consumer goods examples and two industrial goods examples, suggest segmentation bases for each of these.

5 *Targeting*
Explain each of the following types of targeting strategy: (a) undifferentiated marketing; (b) differentiated marketing; (c) concentrated marketing.

6 *Selecting targets*
Discuss the considerations that should be made when selecting specific target markets.

7 Positioning
What do you understand by the term 'product positioning'?

References

Abell, D. F. (1980). Defining the business: the starting point of strategic planning, Chapter 3. Prentice Hall.

Reynolds, P. L. and El-Adley, M. (1995). The changes in the UK financial services environment and its relation to the importance of market segmentation. *Proceedings of the 9th Annual Financial Services Marketing Workshop*, The Manchester School of Management, University of Manchester Institute of Science and Technology (UMIST), 23–24 November.

Reynolds, P. L. and El-Adley, M. (1997). Market segmentation within the UK banking personal loans sector. Presented at the INFORMS Marketing Science Conference, University of California at Berkeley, California, USA, 22–24 March.

Shapiro, B. P. and Bonoma, T. V. (1984). How to segment industrial markets. *Harvard Business Review*, **May–Jun**, 104–10.

Further reading

Adcock, D. (2000) Segmentation as a strategic tool. *Marketing Strategies for Competitive Advantage*, Chapter 6. John Wiley & Sons.

Armstrong, G. and Kotler, P. (2000). Market segmentation, targeting and positioning for competitive advantage. *Marketing: An Introduction*, 5th edn, Chapter 6. Prentice Hall.

Blythe, J. (2001). Segmentation, targeting and positioning. *Essentials of Marketing*, 2nd edn, Chapter 4. Person Educational Ltd.

Davies, M. (1998). Targeting, segmentation and positioning. *Understanding Marketing*, Chapter 4. Prentice Hall.

Day, G. S. and Shocker, A. D. (1976). *Identifying Competitive Product Market Boundaries – Strategic and Analytical Issues*. Marketing Science Institute.

Kotler, P., Bowen, J. and Makens, J. (1996). Marketing segmentation, targeting and positioning. *Marketing for Hospitality and Tourism*, Chapter 9. Prentice Hall.

Lancaster, G. A. and Reynolds, P. L. (1998). Customers and marketing. *Marketing*, Chapter 3. Macmillan Press.

Lancaster, G. A. and Reynolds, P. L. (1999). Segmentation, target marketing and positioning. *Introduction to Marketing: A Step by Step Guide to All The Tools of Marketing*, Chapter 2. Kogan Page.

Nickels, W. and Burk-Wood, M. (1997). Market segmentation, targeting and positioning. *Marketing, Relationships, Quality, Value*, Chapter 8. Worth Publishers.

Plamer, A. (2000). Segmentation and targeting. *Principles of Marketing*, Chapter 3. Oxford University Press.

Wells, W. D. and Gubar, G. (1996). Life cycle concepts in marketing research. *Journal of Marketing Research*, **13**, 355–63.

Buyer behaviour

6

6.1 Introduction

It is interesting to think back five or ten years and compare ourselves then with the way we are (or think we are) now. Have our attitudes towards the world around us changed or remained the same? Do we still like and dislike the same things? As consumers, we are continually exposed to new experiences and different influences throughout our lives. Whilst it is true that some of us are more susceptible to change and influences than others, nobody goes through life remaining the same as at birth. Some of our responses to our environment are the results of our inherent psychological makeup. As our situations change, opportunities often emerge as we are subject to a wider range of influences to which we may consciously or subconsciously respond in a positive or negative manner. Changes in circumstances may arouse inherent needs or promote completely new needs and wants in our consumption patterns.

The task of marketing is to identify these needs and wants accurately, then to develop products and services that will satisfy them. The role of marketing is not to 'create' wants, but to fulfil them. Chapter 2, which discussed the marketing concept, provided some explanation of what this means in terms of business practice.

Definition
The role of marketing is not to 'create' wants, but to fulfil them.

For marketing to be successful, it is not sufficient simply to discover what customers require. It is infinitely more valuable to find out why it is required. Only by gaining a deep and comprehensive understanding of buyer behaviour can marketing's goals be realised. Such an understanding works to the mutual advantage of the consumer and the marketer. By understanding consumers, marketing should become better equipped to satisfy their needs efficiently. This, in turn, should lead to a company being able to establish a loyal group of customers with positive attitudes towards its products.

6.2 Definitions

Consumer behaviour can be formally defined as:

> The acts of individuals directly involved in obtaining and using economic goods and services, including the decision processes that precede and determine these acts.

The underlying concepts of this chapter form a system in which the individual consumer is the core, surrounded by an immediate and a wider environment that influences his or her goals. Such goals are satisfied by consumers passing through a number of problem-solving stages, eventually leading to purchasing decisions.

The study and practice of marketing draws on many sources that contribute theory, information, inspiration and advice. Pricing, for example, uses economics to provide a framework for price determination and the associated pricing strategy. In the past, the main input to the theory of consumer behaviour has come from psychology. More recently, the interdisciplinary importance of consumer behaviour has increased such that sociology, anthropology, economics and mathematics also contribute.

Vignette 6.1

The Black Sheep Brewery tickles the fancy of the discerning beer drinker

In general terms, the consumer behaviour within the UK in relation to the consumption of beer has been changing for some time – 40 years or more. Since the 1960s there has been a move away from the heavier beers towards a preference for lighter beers such as lager. Amongst the younger segments there has been a preference for 'designer label' beers and lagers. Even when considering the consumption of more traditional beers, the British consumer has become much more discerning and is prepared to seek out and pay more for quality beers and something out of the ordinary. The Black Sheep Brewery produces fine beers using traditional methods. Their beers are of superb quality and unusual in both taste and the range of alcoholic strength.

The Black Sheep Brewery was set up in 1992 in Masham UK by Paul Theakston, the fifth generation of the famous Theakston brewing family. Paul had plenty of experience of brewing really good beer. The ingredients used to brew Black Sheep beers are Yorkshire Dales water from the company's own well, malted barley, crystal malt, wheat and English whole hops. After mashing and boiling, the wort is pumped from the company's brewhouse to be cooled down and then on to the fermenting vessels.

Once in the fermenting vessels the beer ferments for six days in what are known in the brewing trade as 'Yorkshire Stone Squares', which are actually fermenting vessels made from Welsh slate but extensively used to make beer in the Yorkshire region. The yeast that is then added to the brew is composed of strains developed over the years especially for use with the 'Yorkshire Squares' method. This old-fashioned method of brewing beer produces a product that is high in alcoholic strength and has a very distinctive flavour. For example, 'Black Sheep Special' is a draft beer of 4.4 per cent strength alcohol by volume. 'Yorkshire Square Ale' has a very distinctive Yorkshire ale taste, and is 5.0 per cent strength.

Key point
If a company does not understand the culture in which the market operates, it cannot develop products and market them successfully.

6.3 Cultural and social influences

If a company does not understand the culture in which the market operates, it cannot develop products and market them successfully. Marketers should recognise how culture shapes and influences behaviour. Culture can be defined as a group of complex symbols and artefacts created by humans and handed down through generations as determinants and regulators of human behaviour in a given society. These symbols and artefacts include attitudes, beliefs, values, language and religion. They also include art and music, food, housing and product preferences. Culture is 'learned' behaviour that has been passed down over time. It is reinforced in our daily lives through the family unit and educational religious institutions. Cultural influences are powerful, and cannot be easily classified because they concern unwritten laws about what is socially acceptable or appropriate in a given society. A comparison of Far Eastern culture with that of Western Europe provides us with an example of two opposing cultures. Even within Western Europe distinct cultures exist – for example, in differences in social etiquette and sense of humour. Such generally accepted norms of behaviour are called *social mores*. The importance of culture is more appropriate to international marketing, and this is discussed further in Chapter 15.

Definition
Culture can be defined as a group of complex symbols and artefacts created by humans and handed down through generations as determinants and regulators of human behaviour in a given society.

Much of our life is directed by *customs*. Similar to mores in the way they have developed, customs can be deeply rooted in society. Customs associated with birth celebrations, marriages and funerals have changed very little over centuries. Many customs are so deeply rooted in society that they have not changed or 'evolved' to reflect the existing cultural climate.

Laws relating to Sunday trading and the licensing of alcohol consumption in the UK are examples of laws that have been changed to catch up with the liberalising demands of changing attitudes within society. Marriage remains an important custom, but this has been challenged in the UK over the past 25 years. When couples began to set up home together and raise families outside of marriage, society, for the most part, adopted an attitude of condemnation. Today, society has adopted a more relaxed attitude to those who ignore the convention.

Changes in attitudes usually reflect changes in culture. It is important to recognise that culture, although powerful, is not fixed forever. Changes in culture are slow, and are often not fully assimilated until more than a generation has passed.

The twentieth century has witnessed significant cultural change; for example, changing attitudes towards work and pleasure. The idea that it work is 'good for the soul' has faded since the Victorian era. It is no longer accepted that work should be difficult or injurious to mind or body. Many employers make great efforts to ensure that the workplace is a pleasant environment, realising that this might increase productivity. Employees more frequently regard work as a means to an end, rather than a *raison d'être*.

If people have worked to earn money, it is now more socially acceptable to reward themselves by spending this on goods or services that give them pleasure. Many products and services whose function is to provide enjoyment now rank alongside, in terms of purchasing necessity, those that provide the necessities of life.

Increased leisure time follows from this changed attitude to work, as the working week is shorter and paid holiday time has increased. At home, labour-saving devices release more time to be spent on enjoyment. The amount of leisure time available influences how, when and what consumers purchase.

A major cultural change in this century that has accelerated since the 1950s and 1960s is the role of women in society. Working women in particular have helped to the alter traditional stereotypes that society has applied to women. Increased independence and economic power have not only changed the lives of women, but also influenced society's and women's own perception of their socio-economic role.

Society has also witnessed profound changes in family structure. In sociological terms, we have moved away from the extended family base towards the 'nuclear family'. Increased mobility of labour has produced a migrant mentality, with family units tending to move away from their native regions and close relations. Increased affluence and better transport communications have increased mobility within regions, creating large suburbs and less-populated inner urban areas. Average family size is becoming smaller, and couples are waiting longer before having children.

Key point
In many societies, when considering culture we must also consider subcultures.

In many societies, when considering culture we must also consider subcultures. Immigrant communities have become large enough in many countries to form a significant proportion of the population of that country. Just as society itself cannot ignore subcultures, marketers must consider them because of their interactive influence on society and because, in some cases, they constitute sufficiently large individual market segments for certain product areas. Subcultures are often identified on a racial basis, but this is a limited view. Subcultures can exist within the same racial groups sharing common nationality, and such bases may be geographical, religious or linguistic.

Vignette 6.2

Flat-pack office aims to capitalise on the changing pattern of work

Launched at the Daily Mail Ideal Home Show, the Ardis 450 costs around £7000. The product is basically a flat-pack executive office that can be constructed as a stand-alone office facility in the garden, or as a 'lean to' type extension to the house. It can be erected within a day, and comes with all necessary fittings and fixtures. It may seem a lot of money for what might look rather like a shed in the garden. However, people are prepared to pay such a price if they are self-employed and working from home. Firms are also prepared to purchase such a product for their staff who work from home.

More and more people are working from home, either all or part of the time. It is no longer enough to have a space at the kitchen table or in a spare bedroom. Earning a living is a serious business, and it required serious facilities. The government has estimated that 50 per cent of the workforce is going to be working from home in 10 years time. It will be necessary to have the right facilities and an appropriate working environment.

The Ardis 450 comes fully fitted with a desk and cabinets, carpet, double glazing, central heating and executive lighting. The product illustrates the fact that work patterns and people's purchasing behaviour regarding work-related products have changed radically over the last 20 years. Companies such as Staples plc and other specialist designer office providers have also capitalised on the same phenomenon.

6.4 Specific social influences

6.4.1 Social class

Social class is perhaps the most easily recognised social influence. It is noted in Chapter 13 that marketing research often uses social class as the main criterion in identifying market segments, because such a classification reveals a lot about likely behaviour. Traditionally, one of the chief determinants of social class was income. Although income can provide a broad indication of the social class to which an individual is likely to belong, salary structures have altered a lot during the past 30 years.

Classification of consumers on the basis of *'lifestyle'* is perhaps more meaningful. If a group of consumers with approximately the same income is considered, their behavioural patterns and lifestyles are likely to vary markedly because these will reflect the social class to which each belongs.

Social class is an indicator of lifestyle, and its existence exerts a strong influence on individual consumers and their behaviour. Whatever income level a consumer reaches during a lifetime, there is evidence to suggest that basic attitudes and preferences do not change radically. It would, however, be reasonable to expect the 'level of consumption' to rise in line with income. As consumers, we usually identify with a particular class or group. Often it is not the actual social class that is revealing, but that to which the consumer aspires. People who 'cross' social class barriers usually begin when they are young. Income and/or education allow younger people to adopt lifestyles that are different to those of their parents. Young consumers tend to absorb the influences of the group to which they aspire, and gradually reject the lifestyles of their parents and their parents' friends and relations. For this reason, 'occupation' is a useful pointer to social class.

'Eating out' and drinking wine were once pleasures only enjoyed regularly by the upper echelons of society. Today, wine marketers address a wide variety of consumers, although a different marketing mix strategy is designed for each identifiable group of consumers.

A study of social class (like all marketing topics) should be approached without preconceptions. It is important that the marketer does not associate social class or social stratification with any derogatory interpretation of the term. Marketing does not make value judgements in its distinctions of social class; a 'lower' or 'higher' social grouping does not imply any inferiority or superiority. Such a classification is merely an aid to the identification of market segments and how they should be approached. The marketer should make decisions on the basis of information revealed by objectively designed research, at this is the only way that changes in behaviour can be identified.

Definition
Social class is an indicator of lifestyle, and its existence exerts a strong influence on individual consumers and their behaviour.

6.4.2 Reference groups

A reference group has a more intimate role to play in influencing the consumer. The reference group is a group of people whose standards of behaviour influence a person's attitudes, opinions and values. In general, people will tend to imitate and seek advice from those closest to them.

Definition
The reference group is a group of people whose standards of behaviour influence a person's attitudes, opinions and values.

Reference groups can be quite small; for instance, the family group. The frame of reference can also be large; for instance, a person involved in a certain occupation is likely to behave in the manner expected and accepted by his or her immediate colleagues and the wider occupational group. Reference groups are also found in a person's social life. He or she may be a member of a club or organisation concerned with a particular hobby or interest. In order to foster a sense of 'belonging', such individuals are unlikely to deviate too far from the behavioural norms laid down by the group, whether these be formal or informal behavioural norms.

Secondary school children provide an example of how reference groups influence the individual. Although children are strongly influenced by their family group, they are also keen to 'fit in' with their peers, and it is never long before a new hairstyle, fashion or other fad has spread through the classrooms.

Not all individuals imitate those in their reference group. Reference group theory does not suggest that individualism does not exist, but it does suggest that even individualists will be aware of what is considered 'normal' within their group.

Key point
The smaller and more intimate a reference group, the stronger its influence is likely to be.

The smaller and more intimate a reference group, the stronger its influence is likely to be. Within a small social circle, or within the family, the advice and opinions of those who are respected as knowledgeable and experienced will be highly influential. Such persons are termed *opinion leaders*. There can also be influences from outside the group. 'Snob appeal' is often due to the existence of opinion leaders outside the immediate reference group, who are emulated by opinion followers. Some companies make a direct appeal to this 'snob' instinct. A marketing strategy can be based on the assumption that if a company can make its products acceptable to social leaders and high-income groups, then other sectors of the population will follow them. Another variation is deliberately to segment markets by appealing to snobbery. Credit and charge cards are frequently marketed in this manner. The strategy is to create an aura of exclusivity around the target group, whilst effectively intimidating and isolating those not targeted. For a number of charge cards, this strategy is reinforced by income requirements set down for applicants. American Express provides an example of such a marketing strategy, and this company also makes appeals within reference groups (i.e. cardholders) encouraging them to enlist new members.

While snobbery 'between' reference groups is a basis for approaching the consumer, this is not viable for all products. Snobbery within the reference group – for example, the syndrome of 'keeping up with the Jones's – can also be used. Snobbery apart, influence and information flow on a 'horizontal' basis within the reference group is of greatest value to the marketer.

6.4.3 The family

Of all the different types of reference group, the family merits particular attention, as it is the most intimate group. The nature of the family can be identified by considering the *family life cycle*. Eight stages of the life cycle are identified, although many texts quote different divisions:

1 *Unmarried.* This carries with it the 'young, free and single' label. Financial and other responsibilities are low, whilst relative disposable income is high. Young, unmarried consumers tend to be leisure-orientated, and are opinion leaders in fashion. As such, they constitute a very important market segment for a wide range of products.

2 *Newly-married couples – no children.* This group does not have the responsibilities of children. Members concentrate expenditure on those items considered necessary for setting up a home, and have been dubbed 'DINKIES' ('double income, no kids').

3 *Young married couples with youngest child under 6 (Full nest I).* Here, expenditure is child-orientated. Although spending is high, there is little 'spare' money for luxury items. Much recreational activity takes place in the home. Such consumers are eager for information and receptive to new product ideas, but are particularly economy-minded.

4 *Married couples with youngest child 6 or over (Full nest II).* Children are still dependent, but expenditure has switched to more durable items for children, such as bicycles and computers. Fashion clothes purchases for children become important, and a lot of recreational activity tends to take place away from the home.

5 *Older married couples still with children at home (Full nest III).* The amount of disposable income may have increased. Often both parents are working, and children are relatively independent and perhaps working part-time or full-time. Parents too are likely to be more independent, with more time for their own leisure activities. Often consumer durables are replaced at this stage. Furniture purchase may have an increased aesthetic, rather than functional, orientation.

6 *Older married couples with no children living with them (Empty nest I).* At this stage, the family unit has been transformed. Income is likely to be at a peak. These consumers are, however, likely to be conservative in their purchasing patterns. Thus, whilst spending power is high, marketers may experience difficulty in changing existing attitudes and preferences. They have been dubbed 'WOOPIES', meaning 'well-off older persons'.

7 *Older retired couples (Empty nest II).* The family unit has made most of its major purchases in terms of consumer durables. The thrust of fast-moving consumer goods (FMCG) marketing is not directly aimed at this group, as their consumption is relatively low and buying patterns are firmly established. In demographic terms, the number of older and retired consumers is increasing rapidly and marketers are paying increasing attention to this group. Although income has probably reduced significantly, many retire with an occupational pension, which allows them to lead full and active lives. The tourist industry, in particular, is increasingly addressing itself to these consumers.

8 *Solitary survivor.* Solitary survivors used to be typified by the pensioner whose spouse had died, but increasingly this category includes divorced people. This latter category is a group to whom marketing appeals can be

made on the basis of their particular circumstances. Many, having come to terms with their new 'single' status, seek a more fulfilling life through the pursuit of educational, social and leisure activities, and they often like to entertain at home and be entertained.

Within the family unit, the marketer should be conscious of the need to identify the principal decision-maker and to ascertain the level of influence exerted on him or her by other family members. Traditional thinking holds that the male takes responsibility for car, garden and DIY purchases, and that the female makes decisions on furnishing and kitchen-related purchases. Social changes over recent years have affected such traditional precepts. Marketers should not approach a market with preconceptions; their strategies should be based on careful enquiry and research into purchasing motivations.

6.5 The consumer as an individual

We have considered consumers as occupants of a wider environment whose behaviour is influenced by cultural and social structures. Specific influences such as reference groups and the family unit affect consumer behaviour. We now consider the individual principally from an 'inner' or psychological point of view. This will help us to understand how consumers respond to external influences.

As the consumer is a physical being, it is not difficult to define characteristics that may provide explanations for some of those actions described collectively as 'behaviour'. Consumers are male or female; some live in towns, some in the country; they are tall, small, young or old. The psychological state of the consumer, on the other hand, is more difficult to determine. The consumer as an individual absorbs information and develops attitudes and perceptions. A personality also develops. This will affect the needs that person has, as well as the methods chosen to satisfy them. Any need-satisfying action is preceded by a motive. Although each human being is physically and psychologically unique, marketing must attempt to identify patterns of behaviour that are predictable under given conditions. This increases the marketer's ability to satisfy human needs, which is the essential aim of marketing.

Key point
The psychology of human behaviour is highly complex.

The psychology of human behaviour is highly complex. We now focus on five psychological concepts that are generally recognised as being most important in understanding buyer behaviour: personality and the self-concept, motivation, perception, attitudes, and learned behaviour.

6.5.1 The self-concept and personality

The 'self-concept' or 'self-image' is an important determinant of individual behaviour because it is concerned with how we see ourselves and, more importantly, how we think other people see us. It is logical to suppose that individuals wish to create a picture of themselves that will project an image that is acceptable to their reference groups.

This 'inner picture' of the self is communicated to the outside world by behaviour. The behaviour that interests marketers is that relating to the consumption of goods, such as the choice of clothes, type of house, choice of furniture and decoration and the type of car. The sum of this behaviour is a 'statement' about 'self' and the person's lifestyle. Consumption is a non-verbal form of communication about the self. The individual will also reinforce his or her image through verbal statements that express attitudes, feelings and opinions. Individuals express their self-image in a way that relates to their inner 'ideal', and this promotes acceptance within a group. The self-statement can also be an expression of rejection. For example, the music, fashion and values adopted by the so-called 'punk' movement of the early 1980s showed a reference group process in action. The 'punk' movement also rejected much within society that was considered to be 'normal' amongst other reference groups.

Marketing can make direct appeals to 'self-image' particularly through advertising. Many car advertisements appeal to the 'executive' whose 'self-image' is one of confidence, success and sophistication.

Advertisements for Marlboro cigarettes have 'macho' connotations. The advertising theme for Guinness is esoteric. Advertising propositions are changed regularly, but the implication is that Guinness drinkers are set apart from the 'masses' and are unorthodox in a mysterious way. Guinness had to do this because the success of their earlier advertising, with the theme of 'Guinness is good for you' and the implication that 'Guinness gives you strength', meant that its consumers were typically middle-aged to older men. What Guinness wanted was to attract younger consumers without alienating traditional consumers. Hence they introduced 'extra-cool Guinness', which is the traditional product but served at a colder temperature, as well as difficult-to-interpret advertising themes, which started in the early 1990s with the 'mysterious man' who was meant to personify a glass of Guinness.

Self-image is influenced by social interaction, and people will make purchases that are consistent with their self-concept in order to protect and enhance it. We also know that we are subjected to a changing environment and changing personal situations, so individuals are involved in a constant process of evaluating and modifying their self-concept.

Personality has a strong influence on buyer behaviour. It is one of the components of self-concept. This much is universally accepted, but attempts to define personality further are less clear cut and more difficult to bring together. Certainly it is overly simplistic to define personality merely as an expression of the self-concept, but we do know that certain purchase decisions are likely to reflect personality. We would expect the owner of an ostentatious sports car to have a confident, outgoing personality, but there is nothing conclusive to provide us with a specific rule. Such as assumption could be entirely misplaced. Marketing must consider personality, because of its close connection with 'self'.

Marketers can, however, learn from psychoanalytical theories of personality, pioneered by Sigmund Freud. These suggest that we are born with instinctive desires that cannot be gratified in a socially acceptable manner and are thus repressed. Indirect methods of satisfying such desires are sought by individuals attempting to find an outlet for repressed urges through socially acceptable

Definition
Consumption is a non-verbal form of communication about the self.

Key point
Personality has a strong influence on buyer behaviour.

channels. The implication for marketing is that a consumer's real motive for taking certain actions or buying certain products may be hidden in the subconscious. The stated motive may be an acceptable translation or substitution of the inner desire. The task of marketing is to appeal to inner needs, whilst providing products that enable these needs to be satisfied in a socially acceptable way.

6.5.2 Motivation

Motivation can be defined as goal-related behaviour. Marketers are interested in motives when goals are related to purchasing activity. Marketers are interested in why consumers make certain purchases. We know that in order for a motive to exist there must be a corresponding need. Motives and needs can be generated and classified in a variety of ways. Some motives, like hunger, thirst, warmth and shelter, are physiological; others, such as approval, success and prestige, are psychological.

Having made this distinction, we can now distinguish between instinctive motives such as survival and learned motives such as cleanliness, tidiness and efficiency. Still further, we can distinguish between rational economic motives and emotional ones. However, this last distinction is imprecise, as many purchase decisions are compromises due to economic restrictions.

Motivation is a complex psychological issue. Most marketers accept a classification of motives, based on a *hierarchy of needs*. Although this classification has been refined, the most convenient reference model is that developed by A. H. Maslow in the 1940s (Figure 6.1). He suggests that an individual's basic (or lower-order) needs must be relatively well satisfied before higher needs can begin to influence behaviour. As lower-order needs are satisfied to an increasing degree, so the individual will have time and interest to devote to higher needs. Once the basic physiological needs (e.g. hunger, thirst) are satisfied, the individual will concentrate on acquiring products and services which increase social acceptability (e.g. love, sense of belonging) and status (e.g.. esteem, recognition). Maslow describes the ultimate need as one of *self-actualisation*. When somebody has reached a stage in life when basic

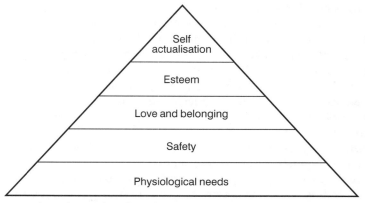

Figure 6.1 Maslow's hierarchy of needs (Maslow, 1943).

needs, love and status have been achieved, then the overriding motivation is one of acquiring products and carrying out activities that permit self-expression. This may take the form of hobbies or a series of new purchases that have been desired for a long period, but have been relegated until those needs that are lower in the hierarchy have been satisfied.

Within this hierarchy, marketers should appreciate that enormous differences exist between individuals. Goals differ widely, so that in the short term an element of hierarchy stage 'hopping' is likely. Moreover, a product that represents self-actualisation for one person may only satisfy a lesser need for another. So complex is the question of motivation that it is impractical to devise marketing strategies based on the hierarchy theory alone. *Motivation research* has developed considerably in recent years, although this is more directly related to specific consumer and product problems. The hierarchy of needs has general value in that it suggests that marketers of consumer products should understand and direct their effort at the higher needs of their customers. The theory also provides a useful starting point when attempting to explain the basic nature of consumer behaviour.

6.5.3 Perception

Whilst motivation is an indication of willingness to act or respond to a stimulus, perception concerns the meaning that the individual assigns to that particular stimulus. Marketers are concerned with influencing a buyer's perception of their products in relation to factors like price, quality and risk. The product image is only as good as the consumer's perception of it. The product only exists (in commercial terms) if the consumer perceives that it is capable of satisfying a need.

Any stimulus is received through the five senses (sight, hearing, smell, taste and touch). The perception of the stimulus is therefore affected by its physical nature, by the environment of the individual, and by his or her psychological condition. Before any form of perception can take place, it is necessary that the stimulus (in this case the product) receives attention.

Definition
Any stimulus is received through the five senses (sight, hearing, smell, taste and touch).

An individual is exposed to thousands of stimuli, most of which receive little or no attention. Advertisers and promotional experts face a challenge in attempting to ensure that their particular stimuli receive the individual consumer's attention. Having gained that attention, the marketer must then attempt to ensure that it is retained. At this point the task becomes even more difficult, because perception is constantly selective. Consumers are only exposed to a limited proportion of all the marketing stimuli that are available – they do not read all newspapers and magazines, nor do they visit every part of a store. Even when a medium of communication has our attention (e.g. a magazine or television), we do not read or watch every advertisement that appears. Individuals have many sources of stimuli competing for their attention. Thus, an advertisement may only be partially read and easily forgotten; consumers can only act on information that is retained in the mind. Marketers cannot provide unlimited or 'blanket' exposure for their products, so they attempt to place their stimuli where they think they are most likely to be well received. This is the basis of media selection. The practical aspects of media selection are covered in detail in Chapter 7.

It is a well-known cliché that 'beauty is in the eye of the beholder'. Although marketers may succeed in gaining maximum attention, perhaps because the consumer has identified a problem and is actively involved in the search process, there is no guarantee that a consumer's perception of a particular product will be the interpretation that the marketer desires. Previous experience of a similar product may influence perception, either favourably or unfavourably. Experience, environment, the immediate circumstances, aspirations and many other psychological factors combine together to shape, alter and reshape consumer perceptions.

6.5.4 Attitudes

Attitudes can be defined as a set of perceptions that an individual has of an object. In this context, the 'object' could be a person, product or brand, or a company. For example, our attitude towards imported goods is likely to be influenced by our feelings about the country of origin, and possibly by our interpretation of the domestic economic climate. Similarly, our attitudes towards a certain store or company are likely to be favourable if the staff are particularly helpful, or if we know that some profits are donated to a worthwhile cause. As discussed earlier, the influence of reference groups on the individual tends to be strongly emphasised. Social interaction plays a major part in attitude formation. Attitudes may be learned from others. In particular, many of our attitudes are due to the influence of the family group; some of the attitudes developed in our formative years remain with us throughout our lives.

Attitudes can be positive, negative or neutral. In general, attitudes can be firmly held by individuals, who tend to resist attacks made on such attitudes. This is not to say that attitudes never change or cannot be changed. A bad experience can rapidly alter an attitude from positive to negative, while a small product modification may generate a favourable attitude when the previous attitude to the product was neutral or negative. Marketers must be aware of the importance of generating a favourable attitude towards their companies and products. Once established in the mind of the consumer, attitudes are difficult to alter. In a competitive environment, such a process can work both for and against a producer or retailer. An attractive promotion or advertisement may appeal to the consumer's emotions and temporarily change patterns of action, but will not necessarily result in a change of the basic attitude.

6.5.5 Learned behaviour

Learning results from 'experience'. This is an important element in the study of behaviour because it has the power to change attitudes and perceptions. Learning not only provokes change, but is also able to reinforce a change in behaviour. A consumer may 'learn' that certain products are more acceptable than others to their family or reference group. In an attempt to promote this acceptability, the purchaser might reinforce the acceptable purchase with similar repeat purchases. As marketers realise, a prime objective of the marketing effort is to influence consumers sufficiently so that they make a first purchase. The ultimate success of that marketing effort depends on a succession of repeat purchases.

Such learning by 'trial and error principles' is referred to as 'conditioned learning'. Each time a satisfactory purchase is made, the consumer becomes less and less likely to deviate from this conditional behaviour. This type of learning results in *brand loyalty*, which, once established, is difficult to alter.

Learning also occurs as a result of information received. The information source may be a reference group, or a direct approach to the consumer through advertising, publicity or promotion. From the marketer's viewpoint, learning for the sake of stored or accumulated information is of little value. For learning to have an effect on motives or attitudes, the marketing effort of a particular company should attempt to direct these changes towards products or services that are offered for sale.

It has been shown that at any given moment the consumer is subject to the combined and continuous influences of the socio-economic and socio-cultural environments as well as to more proximate social interaction and psychological influences. Having discussed some of the complex issues that make up consumer behaviour, it is worthwhile to reflect on the consumer's fundamental goal. When consumers buy products, their aim is to achieve satisfaction. This might appear obvious, but it has two important implications:

1 Those companies who provide most satisfaction will enjoy the greatest success (the basis of the marketing concept)

2 Because consumers are constantly engaged in a search for satisfaction, competition will always have potential appeal.

It is not, therefore, sufficient to provide satisfaction. Companies must strive to maintain and improve the level of satisfaction that they provide. Complacency is the worst enemy of the marketer.

Key point
Complacency is the worst enemy of the marketer.

For the majority of consumers, it is unlikely that total satisfaction in relation to 'all needs and wants' will ever be achieved. It is possible that marketing has the theoretical wherewithal to supply satisfaction, but we must be realistic enough to admit that satisfaction depends, to a high degree, on the financial status of the consumer. Throughout their lives, consumers will be subject to a variety of competing demands that are made on limited financial resources. The family life cycle discussed in Chapter 5 provides a good example of changing circumstances. Of necessity, satisfaction may only be partial and is a compromise. Of course, we should be careful not to judge satisfaction purely as a function of 'spending power', which is a materialistic interpretation. It is, however, realistic to suggest that freedom from financial worries helps us to achieve material satisfaction, which in turn contributes to complete satisfaction. Marketers should always remember that consumer goals have an aesthetic component that concerns quality of life rather than simply the quantity of products that money can buy.

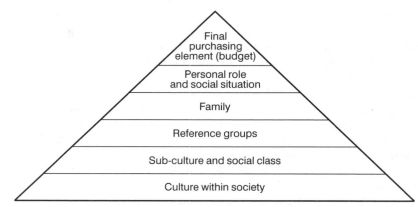

Figure 6.2 Purchasing influences on individual consumers.

6.5.6 Pyramid of influences

In order to summarise the various elements that affect consumer choice, a hierarchy is suggested in Figure 6.2 that indicates how purchasing behaviour is affected from a general cultural level to an individual purchasing level. It is suggested that each subsequent stage in the hierarchy might have a more poignant effect on the purchase decision than the preceding stage.

6.6 Models of consumer buying behaviour

So far we have examined the consumer as an individual in terms of psychological influences relating to the workings of the mind. We have also considered wider forces that influence consumer behaviour. We should consider them as a whole, or as a series or group of influences that exert themselves simultaneously and continually on the consumer. Models of consumer behaviour attempt to do this. They relate to the total buyer decision process, and to the important issue of new product adoption. Consumer behaviour is a complex subject, and behavioural models attempt to reduce this complexity. Much literature is available on the subject of consumer behaviour. Our aim is to bring together a series of simple models that attempt to explain buying or decision processes in relation to relevant variables.

Key point
Consumer behaviour is a complex subject, and behavioural models attempt to reduce this complexity.

6.6.1 The buyer decision process

Chapter 12 examines in detail how products are classified according to the degree of complexity that their purchase demands, but an example here suffices to explain the process.

We recognise that the purchase of shower gel (a 'fast-moving consumer good' – FMCG) is less complex for the consumer than purchasing a new car. Whatever the buying task and associated degree of complexity confronting the consumer, it is important to consider the steps leading to a purchase as a problem-solving process. Figure 6.3 is a simple model of the mental states that the buyer passes through during the buyer decision process.

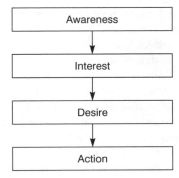

Figure 6.3 Mental states of buying.

'Awareness' is considered in the next section, which relates to new product adoption. The consumer is aware of many products, but does not necessarily experience a desire to purchase them. This state of awareness becomes important when a product is perceived as being capable of solving a problem. For this reason, Figure 6.4, first put forward by Robinson *et al.* (1967), is a more useful model of the buyer decision process, because it describes the activities involved.

Key point
The consumer is aware of many products, but does not necessarily experience a desire to purchase them.

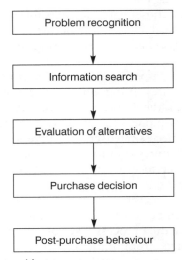

Figure 6.4 Steps in the buyer/decision process.

Our daily lives are made up of constant processes of problem recognition and need satisfaction. We need to buy food to satisfy hunger. Our problem is in deciding what kind of food, and which brand to purchase from which store. We may be invited to a special function and want to buy a new outfit. Again, we must go through the stages of the buyer decision process. By identifying or feeling a need or want, we then recognise a problem.

If, for example, a person moves from an apartment to a house with a garden, then he or she will recognise the need to mow the lawn. Although the person will be aware that lawnmowers exist, this basic knowledge may constitute the full extent of awareness at that point in time.

The next move towards purchase involves information search. A lawnmower might be a relatively expensive purchase and the potential consumer knows little about the product, so in this case the search process will be extensive (in contrast to the almost routine search activity carried out for everyday shopping items). Information sources may include the family, neighbours, colleagues, and the marketing activity of lawnmower manufacturers. The degree of influence each source has on the consumer will depend on the nature of the product and on the individual making the purchase. We know that reference groups, in particular the family, exert a powerful influence. In this lawnmower example, the consumer is likely to turn to parents and older relatives and friends for information and advice. Marketing provides information through advertising and displays. Magazines and newspapers may feature articles and advertisements for selected products from time to time. By the time that the search period nears completion, the consumer will already have rejected certain lawnmowers as being unsuitable in some way – perhaps too expensive or too heavy. A 'prefer British' attitude might have ruled out foreign machines. A mental short-list of possible alternatives will remain.

This short-list allows the consumer to move to the next buying stage – that of evaluation of alternatives. The relative merits of each potential product must be assessed so that the chosen product maximises (or at least optimises) satisfaction. Often an ideal choice will be arrived at relatively easily, but financial limitations may oblige another alternative to be the product finally chosen.

In the information search period the short-list is usually easy to establish, and basic product features bring about attraction or rejection in the consumer's mind. When the range of choices has been narrowed down, evaluating alternatives is more difficult. This is particularly true when the potential purchase has necessitated an extensive search process. Here, the differences in product features or attributes are likely to be more subtle and difficult for the consumer to evaluate. For FMCGs, the brand and brand image are major influences.

Looking at the buyer decision process from the marketer's viewpoint, segmentation strategy can be considered most influential during the information search stage. Thus a dual process takes place, and the consumer quickly eliminates some products from those on offer because they are clearly unsuitable. By segmenting the market a company is eliminating some consumers from the total population of potential purchasers, and concentrates its efforts on segments more likely to short-list its products. As well as segmenting the market, the marketer's task is to ensure that, because of certain attributes, products receive high rankings in the consumer's mind during the evaluation stage. The creation of product attributes is, therefore, the 'fine tuning' of a segmentation strategy. This can only be achieved after detailed marketing research.

Finally, the actual *purchase decision* must be made. When making a choice, the consumer is not only seeking satisfaction, but is also aiming to reduce risk

Key point
The degree of influence each source has on the consumer will depend on the nature of the product and on the individual making the purchase.

as much as possible. This is especially true when a product is costly and where the purchase decision will be accompanied by some anxiety. This anxiety relates to making the right choice from the chosen product group, and also concerns the wisdom of actually having made the purchase in the first place. In the lawnmower example, there will be a wide range of demands on the consumer's limited resources – perhaps it would have been more sensible to pay a gardener, and purchase a new carpet or washing machine instead?

Immediately prior to purchase, the consumer is still susceptible to 'influence'. A decision not to purchase may be the result of influence from any of the motivations discussed. Conflicting influences only serve to confuse and make the purchaser's task more difficult.

The salesperson can be highly influential at this stage. 'Forcing' a sale at this delicate stage might help the salesperson's commission, but from a marketing standpoint it does not give the kind of satisfaction that will lead to repeat purchases. Often a *hard sell* will only reinforce anxiety, or what is termed *cognitive dissonance*. Marketing strategies should concentrate on reducing anxiety and perceived risk.

It might be assumed that post-purchase behaviour is beyond marketing's control. The last paragraph concluded that control can be exercised if the product is marketed skilfully and thoughtfully before the purchase is made. Marketers must be aware of post-purchase behaviour, because this directly affects repeat sales. Quite simply, consumers can be either satisfied or dissatisfied with their purchase. If the consumer is satisfied then all is well, provided that the company does not reduce its standards in some way. Advertising must take care not to build consumer expectations too high, as this might lead to dissatisfaction. Post-purchase dissonance, or cognitive dissonance, is a feeling of dissatisfaction or unease that consumers sometimes feel following a major purchase. The product itself may be perfectly acceptable, yet the consumer may feel that the purchase was not as good as it could have been. Despite these feelings of unease, consumers frequently rationalise and reinforce their purchase decision. In other words, they will not wish to voice their dissatisfaction and thus appear to be poor decision-makers in the eyes of their reference group. They prefer to feel positive in their own minds about their actions and actively seek information that justifies their purchase, tending to ignore any doubts they might still have.

> **Key point**
> Marketers must be aware of post-purchase behaviour, because this directly affects repeat sales.

If consumers publicise their dissatisfaction, marketers face a problem because of the power and influence attached to word-of-mouth communication. Clearly, if a product is faulty, or does not perform as claimed, the marketer is at fault, but marketers should be aware of the negative effects of dissonance that can occur when there is nothing wrong with the product. Whilst actions to reduce potential dissonance can be taken before the purchase is made, marketers can do much to instil confidence and security after the sale. Companies should attach as much importance to after-sales service as they do to making the sale in the first place. This reduces dissonance in the case of genuine complaints. In addition, companies can follow up sales by some form of communication with customers. This builds the customer's confidence in having made the 'right' decision, and some advertising campaigns are expressly designed with this purpose in mind. The term that is attached to this kind of after-sale follow-up is 'customer care'.

> **Key point**
> Companies should attach as much importance to after-sales service as they do to making the sale in the first place.

Key point
The more complicated the buying process, the more important it is that companies assist consumers in the problem-solving process, and reassure them that their choices have been made wisely.

The importance of each stage of the buyer decision process varies according to the type of product under consideration. For some product groups the whole process is simple routine, whilst for others each stage involves long and careful consideration by the consumer. Understanding how the buyer decision process works is vital to the success of any marketing strategy. Where purchases are routine, the task of marketing is to break that routine in favour of the company's own products. The more complicated the buying process, the more important it is that companies assist consumers in the problem-solving process, and reassure them that their choices have been made wisely.

6.6.2 The adoption process

As marketers we are interested in consumer behaviour as it relates to new products. Figure 6.4 shows a sequential model of the buyer decision process. It refers to general situations for existing products or services, and focuses initially on problem solving and search. Figure 6.5 depicts the adoption process for an innovatory new product. The key difference between the two models is that the adoption model begins with awareness. It is the task of the marketer to create awareness, and then to guide the consumer through subsequent stages of the process. Without awareness of the new product, consumers cannot even consider it as a solution to need-related problems. To be worthwhile, innovative products should always be problem-solving in nature as far as the consumer is concerned.

Key point
It is the task of the marketer to create awareness, and then to guide the consumer through subsequent stages of the process.

Awareness can come about by word-of-mouth communication, or from the marketing effort of the firm. The individual is exposed to the innovation and becomes aware of its existence. If the product has initial appeal, further

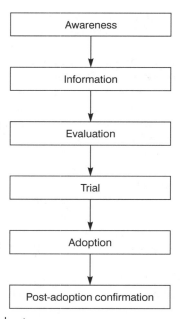

Figure 6.5 Stages in the adoption process.

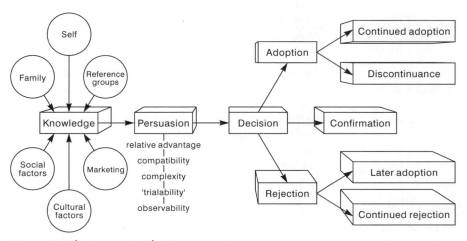

Figure 6.6 The innovation decision process.

information is sought. At the *evaluation* stage, the consumer 'weighs' the relative advantages of the new product against those of existing products (and perhaps against directly competing products if these have been launched).

The consumer might make a 'temporary' adoption by obtaining a sample to *trial*. A lot of new FMCG products are produced in a 'trial size', and companies distribute free samples. It may be possible to borrow a friend or relative's product for trial purposes. If a trial cannot be made, the likelihood of adoption decreases.

Key point
If a trial cannot be made, the likelihood of adoption decreases.

At the *adoption* stage, the decision is made whether or not to 'adopt' (buy or begin to use) the product – either singly or, in the case of industrial purchases, on a full-scale basis. *Post-adoption confirmation* is when the product has been adopted and the consumer might be seeking assurance and reassurance (unconsciously perhaps) that the correct decision has been made. New information has been accepted and prior information rejected. Often, after an important purchase, cognitive dissonance is present. As stated earlier, it is important that such dissonance is countered by providing some kind of follow-up using appropriate marketing means at the company's disposal.

Figure 6.6 expands the adoption process model. At the beginning of the process it is useful to regard the circles shown as a series of 'inputs' that flow into the 'melting pot', creating knowledge. It is important to remember that the 'self' input includes the psychological concepts of attitudes, perception, learning and motivation. Like the other inputs, they set the scene for knowledge to be translated into a favourable condition of awareness. Figure 6.6 also shows that persuasion, and hence the rate of adoption, is affected by the product's:

● relative advantage (over other products on the market)

● compatibility (with the needs of the consumer)

● complexity

● trialability or trial opportunity

- observability (e.g. a new car purchase is easily observed, whereas an insurance policy is more difficult to comprehend in the 'observability' context).

The model allows for reviewed action after the decision stage. At this point, consumers are highly sensitive to the influence of information sources including reference groups.

The rate of adoption for an innovation also depends on the type of consumer to whom the product is marketed. Chapter 12 deals with product policy issues, and in particular with the product adoption process. It details how consumers can be divided into groups, or adopter categories, and the rate that these adoptions are taken up. Some adopters are receptive and readily adopt innovations, whilst others are slow to adopt new products. This 'diffusion of innovation' process suggests that certain groups of consumers are highly influential, and that this influence will 'diffuse' through to subsequent consumer groups. In this context of consumer buying behaviour, we see how each of these groups possesses distinct characteristics.

Key point
The rate of adoption for an innovation also depends on the type of consumer to whom the product is marketed.

1 *Innovators* are likely to be younger, better educated, and relatively affluent with a higher social status. In terms of personal characteristics, they are likely to be broader-minded, receptive people with a wide range of social relationships. Their product knowledge relies more on their own efforts to gather objective information than on company literature or salespeople.

2 *Early adopters*, whilst possessing many of the characteristics of the innovators, tend to belong to more 'local' systems. Although their social relationships are less broadly based, they tend to be opinion leaders and are highly influential within their particular group. As such, they are a major target for marketers, whose aim is to get their product accepted as quickly as possible.

3 *The early majority* is a group that is slightly above average in socio-economic terms. Members rely heavily on the marketing effort for information, and are clearly influenced by the opinion leaders of the early-adopter category. They adopt new products before the average consumer.

4 *Late majority* adopters are more likely to adopt innovations because they have become accepted by previous groups. Social pressure or economic considerations are, therefore, more influential in this group than innate personal characteristics.

5 *Laggards* make up the cautious group. They tend to be older, with relatively lower socio-economic status. The innovator group may already be considering another, newer product before laggards have adopted the original innovation.

The theory of the diffusion of innovations is useful in relation to the study of consumer behaviour. This theory can also be applied to industrial marketing if a relevant profile of the industrial customer base is prepared. We should, however, be aware that consumers who exhibit particular adopter characteristics for one category of product may behave quite differently in the adoption of another product type. It should also be understood that the model refers to innovatory products, and not to repeat purchases.

Vignette 6.3

Political marketing communications: New Labour uses fear to frighten its supporters into the polling booths

Although evidence from the polling organisations indicated that New Labour would win the 2001 General Election in the UK, Labour 'spin doctors' and communications strategists took no chances. They knew that voters' attitudes and behaviour were very fickle and could change dramatically in a short period of time. They planned a communications campaign designed to strike fear into the hearts of any potential Tory voter, particularly those who voted Labour last time around who may have been tempted to switch their allegiance to the Tories. Under the New Labour plans, William Hague, the leader of the Conservative Party, was depicted as a 'son of Satan' character. The character is believed to be modelled on the 1970s horror film 'The Omen'.

Even though the polls indicated that New Labour would win with a large majority, many in the New Labour Party were worried. They were concerned that the foot and mouth crisis, the public's anger over the running and disposal of the Millennium Dome, the spate of serious rail crashes, the BSE debacle, the Peter Mandelson and Geoffrey Robinson 'sleaze' problems and a raft of other problems may cause previous New Labour voters to think again.

The video was handed out free to voters and compared Mr Hague to Damien, the son of the devil in the film. The tape also suggested that Margaret Thatcher was the antichrist, and recalled all of the 'suffering' she brought on the country during her time as Prime Minister of the United Kingdom. The theme was that people think Mrs Thatcher is off the political scene now, but they have 'forgotten her son' William Hague. Viewers were warned of a new threat to the country's economic order. The video uses the psychological message of fear and loss to attempt to influence voters' intentions and behaviour.

6.7 Organisational buying behaviour

It is common for industrial buying to be thought of as being devoid of the psychological and emotional connotations attached to consumer behaviour. After all, industrial purchasers cannot afford the luxury of 'impulse' buying. They are employed to make purchases for a specific reason. They have budgets, and usually a great deal of knowledge about what they purchase. Although there are differences, many parallels can be drawn between industrial and consumer buying.

First, though, note that the heading of this sections is *organisational* buying behaviour, whereas we are now referring to *industrial* buying behaviour. *Organisational buying* is a wider term, used to cover industrial, retail and public authority purchasing. However, the principles of organisational buying are, for our purposes, the same as those for industrial buying. In many marketing textbooks the terms 'organisational buying' and 'industrial buying' are interchanged, although strictly speaking the latter refers to a narrower context.

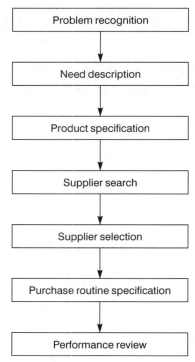

Figure 6.7 The industrial buyer decision process.

The most apparent similarity between organisational and consumer buying is that both activities represent a need-satisfying process. Although these needs may differ, they must be fully understood before any selling approach is made. Figure 6.7 is a model of the industrial buyer decision process, and it closely resembles the model that was used for consumers (Figure 6.4). The approach and reaction to new products is also broadly similar. Diffusion theory can, for example, be applied with equal validity to both types of buying situation. In fact, a 'diffusion of innovations' model was not originally developed by Everett Rogers for consumer markets. Finally, we should remember that organisational buyers are also subjected to influences that affect their decisions: marketing effort influences industrial behaviour; reference groups exist within industrial situations; as individuals, buyers are influenced by their own psychological make-up.

A more sophisticated model was suggested by Wind in 1967, when he proposed the 12 stages detailed in Figure 6.8 (Robinson *et al.*, 1967).

An important question that organisational marketers must ask is: 'Who are the powerful buyers?'. This does not necessarily correlate with rank within the purchasing organisation. Those with little formal power may be able to stop a purchase or hinder its completion.

Five major power bases are highlighted:

1   *Reward*: the ability to provide monetary, social, political or psychological rewards to others for compliance

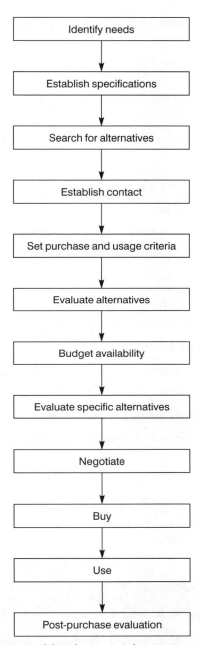

Figure 6.8 Wind's 12-stage model (Robinson *et al.*, 1967).

2 *Coercive*: the ability to provide monetary or other punishments for non-compliance

3 *Attraction*: the ability to elicit compliance from others because they like you

4 *Expert*: the ability to elicit compliance because of technical expertise, either actual or reputed

5 *Status*: compliance through the capacity of a legitimate position of power in a company.

In general, it can be said that organisational markets differ from consumer markets in the following respects:

1 The rationality of buying motives

2 The derived demand

3 The smaller numbers of buyers

4 The larger number of influences on the buyer

5 There is often a multi-person decision-making unit

6 Customers are sometimes in economic competition

7 Industrial customers may have more power than sellers

8 Many products are 'buyer specified'

9 The economic relationship between buyer and seller is often long term

10 The high value of purchases

11 Distribution is more direct

12 Sales are often preceded by lengthy negotiation

13 Company policies may act as a constraint on the buyer

14 There may be 'reciprocal' buying (we buy from you and you buy from us)

15 There is unequal purchasing power amongst customers

16 Often there is geographic concentration.

Such characteristics have to be taken into account when the marketing firm develops its communications strategy.

Vignette 6.4

American importers turn away from European meat for fear of the foot and mouth problem spreading across the Atlantic

Buyer behaviour in the world's meat and livestock markets is starting to show the widespread fear and panic associated with the spread of highly contagious diseases. In this instance they are concerned with foot and mouth disease, which started up in the UK and is now spreading to other European countries.

Meat importers around the world are still worried over the BSE problem, and many are still reluctant to buy British beef. Their concerns are now exacerbated, and have extended to lamb and pork. The USA and Canada announced a complete ban on meat and livestock imports from all EU counties in March 2001 as the foot and mouth problem spread from Britain to France. They were followed by a raft of other countries, including Australia, New Zealand and South Korea, as governments took action to limit the spread of the disease. Some countries have gone even further, and banned imports of all EU grain.

The European Union (EU) is to complain to the World Trade Organisation (WTO) because it is generally thought the bans are excessive and unnecessary, as the disease is usually harmless to humans. However, business is business. If buyers think that products are likely to cause them a problem, then they will not buy them and will source supplies from other markets. Even if the ban were lifted under a WTO directive, it would probably have little effect on the buyer behaviour of importers around the world. Consumers would not buy meat if there were a possibility of it being infected with foot and mouth disease, even if the disease is harmless to humans. The WTO organisation may be able to lift the ban, but it cannot make people buy the meat.

Having made these general observations, we now focus on specific factors that pertain to the organisational buying situation. Most evident is the fact that it is an 'organised' process. Whilst consumer markets attract much of marketing's limelight, it is easy to overlook the magnitude of industrial sales and purchases. Every time a consumer makes a purchase from a retail outlet, a derived demand is created for a series of component parts and materials that make up the finished product. We can add to this complex chain of supply those companies who buy and sell machinery, packaging materials and maintenance equipment. In order to control this constant flow of goods and services, companies must organise their buying activity so that they have:

- a constant supply (in terms of quality and delivery)

- a system of control which monitors performance specifications

- a review policy towards existing and potential suppliers.

The larger the organisation, the more structured should be the methods of buying. A formal process should be established for each of the components that make up organisational purchasing procedure, as outlined in Figure 6.7.

Key point
The larger the organisation, the more structured should be the methods of buying.

For the majority of purchases made by consumers, the negative aspects of an ill-advised purchase are shorter term and can be more easily rectified. In contrast, for a large company whose machinery is in use 24 hours a day, even a small quality or delivery problem from suppliers could cause considerable loss in terms of down-time on the production line. Organisational purchasing must therefore adopt a formal structure because of the responsibility that it bears.

Just as consumer behaviour varies according to product types, industrial purchases demand more or less attention according to their nature. This is not to say that the approach for routine purchases should be any less formal than that for more critical items. A more formal classification of industrial products is given in Chapter 12. The purchasing approach for each type of product bought varies according to the buying situation.

6.7.1 Buying situations

Three major types of organisational buying situation can be identified:

1 *The new task.* This is most challenging for the company's purchasing department. The product item may be a new machine or a new raw material required for a new product. Although buyers will have professional expertise, they will be relatively unfamiliar with the product and must engage in extensive need description, product specification and supplier search.

2 *Straight rebuy purchases.* As the description suggests, these involve little effort and are routine within the current purchasing structure. It is important to appreciate that this 'routine' is only possible because careful buying in the past has established a reliable supply pattern.

3 *The modified rebuy.* Here, for a variety of reasons, the product specification or supplier has to be changed, and a modified rebuy situation arises. In many ways this can be as challenging as the new task situation. Although the basic product may be well known, any change involves risk. Often industrial buyers keep alternative suppliers as minor suppliers, buying a little from them from time to time to test their reliability in preparation for greater participation should the need arise. With the same risk-reducing goal in mind, product modifications are usually introduced gradually so that problems can be resolved before too great a commitment has been made.

Key point
The principal difference between consumer and organisational buying is that the latter usually involves group decision-making.

The principal difference between consumer and organisational buying is that the latter usually involves group decision-making. Here, individuals have different roles in the purchasing process, and this view was first put forward by Frederick E. Webster Jr as his notion of the *buying centre* (Webster and Wind, 1972). The categories described are, however, more commonly referred to as the *decision making unit (DMU)*:

- *Users* are the people who will work with or use the product, and they are sometimes involved in product specification

- *Buyers* have authority to sign orders and make the purchase; they might sometimes help shape the specification, but their principal role is in supplier negotiation and selection

- *Deciders* are people who make the actual buying decision (frequently the decider and the buyer is the same person)

- *Influencers* can affect the buying decision in different ways (e.g. technical people may have helped in a major or minor way to develop the product specification)

- *Gatekeepers* control the flow of information to and from people who buy (e.g. the chief buyer's secretary or even a receptionist).

Organisational buyers' roles vary widely according to the complexity and size of structure of the company. In technical sales situations, the salesperson may hardly meet the buyer until the technical manager is thoroughly satisfied with the salesperson's offering. The buyer then takes over to handle the commercial aspects of the sale. Many companies employ buyers who are skilled in purchasing procedures, but who only have limited technical knowledge of the products being purchased. Other companies employ buyers for specific product areas. Whatever buying structure is in operation, the industrial salesperson should realise that the buyer is not always the final decision-maker. Clearly, the real decision-maker should be the principal target for sales effort.

Key point
Many companies employ buyers who are skilled in purchasing procedures, but who only have limited technical knowledge of the products being purchased.

Purchasing should not only be considered in terms of transactions between buyers and sellers, because the purchase has repercussions on other aspects of the company. Sales and marketing managers are, for example, concerned with product quality and delivery. Technical and production managers are concerned with performance. Marketers should be aware of factors that influence organisational buyers. Although many are beyond the control of the seller, it is essential that problems purchasers face are understood, and marketing and sales strategies designed accordingly. While price is important, it is not the only influence in industrial purchasing decision-making.

Figure 6.9 highlights the main tools available to industrial markets for targeting DMUs.

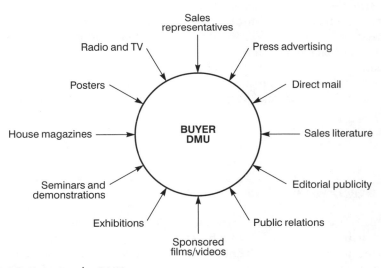

Figure 6.9 Targeting the DMU.

With a move towards companies holding less stock of raw materials and components in the interests of saving working capital, *reliable delivery* is an increasingly vital factor. As mentioned in Chapter 2, in certain flow-production manufacturing situations stockholding is theoretically non-existent, and the system of 'just-in-time' (or lean) manufacturing is being increasingly adopted by mass manufacturers around the world. Buyers require a constant stream of goods with zero defects. Should defects occur, the company's entire production can be stopped, so reliability of supply is of paramount importance. In these situations relationships tend to be long term, and it is just as common for buyers to visit sellers as it is for sellers to visit buyers (the traditional pattern). Indeed, this very notion has now been termed *reverse marketing*, where buyers tend to take the commercial initiative and actively source suppliers who can match up to their criteria of reliability of quality and supply. There is even the notion of *open accounting*, where price does not enter the equation, as buyers are fully aware of the price make-up of the components that are being marketed. In turn, suppliers also know the profit margin of their customers, and buyers and sellers agree a common mark-up. If the supplier then devises a way to make the products more cheaply without compromising quality, then the savings from the new process are divided between the supplier and the customer. Needless to say such agreements imply long-term relationships, from which the phrase *relationship marketing* has been coined.

Key point
It is important to acknowledge that buyers are individuals as well as purchasing professionals.

It is important to acknowledge that buyers are individuals as well as purchasing professionals. In many industrial markets, the levels of service and price are such that there is little to distinguish suppliers. The personal impression that the single buyer or the DMU has of a supplier's image, as well as the personal rapport that the salesperson can achieve, can profoundly influence buying decisions. Just as purchasers of consumer goods are responsive to the actions of sellers, organisational buyers have individual personalities that sellers must take into account. Some buyers may be aggressive, devious or indecisive. The salesperson cannot afford to adopt a 'blanket' approach to customers. The human factor also extends to the buyer's relationships with colleagues within the organisation. Companies themselves have 'personalities', in more abstract terms of attitudes and policies, which can make them more or less susceptible to particular sales and marketing approaches.

6.8 Summary

Key point
Although industrial buyers have a clear rationale for their actions, this is not to say that they are insensitive to psychological influences.

✓ Whilst we can identify factors common to both consumer and industrial buying behaviour, we should be clear that the two markets should be approached differently. The needs of consumers should be ascertained and the marketing response communicated largely through appropriate media. In industrial markets, buyers and sellers do communicate through media, but they also rely heavily on personal communication. Industrial buyers work to obtain satisfaction for the company's 'physical' needs, whereas much consumer behaviour has a psychological basis. Although industrial buyers have a clear rationale for their actions, this is not to say that they are insensitive to psychological influences. This is especially important in a market where the products on the offer are essentially similar.

Questions

1 *Advertising and consumer behaviour*
How far do you agree with the statement that advertising is the biggest single influence on consumer behaviour?

2 Industrial buying
It is common to think of the purchasing decision processes of industrial buyers as being devoid of emotion. How far would you agree with this?

3 *Customer care*
Why is the idea of 'customer care' such a relatively recent one?

4 *Buyer behaviour*
How far do models of buying behaviour go towards providing marketers with better tools for targeting customers?

5 *Organisational buying*
How does organisational buying relate to industrial buying?

6 *DMU*
Do you define the DMU as a committee of people, or something more informal?

References

Maslow, A. H. (1943). A theory of human motivation. *Psychological Review*, **50**, 370–96.

Robinson, P. J., Jarvis, C. W. and Wind, Y. (1967). *Industrial Buying and Creative Marketing*, Allyn & Bacon.

Webster, F. E. and Wind, Y. (1972). *Organisational Buying Behaviour*, pp. 78–80. Prentice Hall.

Further reading

Armstrong, G. and Kotler, P. (2000). Consumer and business buyer behaviour. *Marketing: An Introduction*, 5th edn, Chapter 5. Prentice Hall.

Blythe, J. (2001). Consumer and buyer behaviour. *Essentials of Marketing*, Chapter 3. Person Educational Ltd.

Cateora, P. R. and Ghauri, P. N. (2000). Business customs and practice in international marketing. *International Marketing: European Edition*, Chapter 7. McGraw Hill.

Davies, M. (!998). Consumer and organisational buying behaviour. *Understanding Marketing*, Chapter 5. Prentice Hall.

Keegan, W. J. and Green, M. S. (2000). Social and cultural environments. *Global Marketing*, 2nd edn, Chapter 4. Prentice Hall.

Lancaster, G. A. and Reynolds, P. L. (1998). Buyer behaviour. *Marketing*, Chapter 4. Macmillan Press.

Lancaster, G. A. and Reynolds, P. L. (1999). Consumer and organisational buyer behaviour. *Introduction to Marketing: A Step by Step Guide to All the Tools of Marketing*, Chapter 3. Kogan Page.

Plamer, A. (2000). Buyer behaviour. *Principles of Marketing*, Chapter 7. Oxford University Press.

Marketing communications I

7

7.1 Introduction

The word 'communications' is derived from the Latin word *communis*, meaning 'common'. Communication, then, can be thought of as the *process of establishing a commonality or oneness of thought between a sender and a receiver*. This definition highlights two important ideas. First, communication is a process, and as such has elements and inter-relationships that can be modelled and examined in a structured manner. Secondly, oneness of thought must develop between sender and receiver if true communication is to occur, which implies that a sharing relationship must exist between sender and receiver.

It is a mistake to view the 'sender' (a speaker for instance) as the active member in the relationship and the 'receiver' (a listener) as passive. Consider a person (the sender) speaking to a friend who is not really listening (the intended receiver). It might appear that communication is taking place, but no thought is being shared and there is no communication between these friends. The reason for this lack of communication is the passivity of the intended receiver. Note that we call one of the people the *intended* receiver. Although sound waves are being transmitted, the intended listener is not receiving and sharing thought. A human receiver can be likened to a television set: A television set is continuously bombarded by television (electromagnetic) waves from several stations. However, it will receive only the station to which the channel selector is tuned. Human receivers likewise are bombarded with stimuli from many sources simultaneously, and, like the television example, a person selects one source to be 'tuned to' at any moment in time. Both sender and receiver must be active participants in the communicative relationship in order for thoughts to be shared. Communication is something one does *with* another person, not *to* another person. We will see the relevance of this simple analogy to marketing communications as we proceed through this chapter.

Definition
Communication can be thought of as the process of establishing a commonality or oneness of thought between a sender and a receiver.

Key point
Both sender and receiver must be active participants in the communicative relationship in order for thoughts to be shared.

Figure 7.1 A simple communications model.

7.2 Marketing communications overview

7.2.1 Models of communication

Models of the communications process may be verbal, non-verbal or mathematical. Regardless of form, they share three basic elements: *sender, message* and *receiver.*

In its simplest form, the communications process can be modelled as shown in Figure 7.1. The *sender* (source) is a person or group having a thought to share with some other person or group (the *receiver* or destination). In marketing, receivers are present and prospective consumers of the company's product. The *message* is a symbolic expression of the sender's thoughts. The message may take the form of the printed or the spoken word, a magazine advertisement or television commercial being examples.

Figure 7.2 shows a slightly more complex model. This model introduces *encoding, decoding, channel* and *feedback* elements. *Encoding* is the process of putting thought into symbolic form that is controlled by the sender. Similarly, *decoding* is the process of transforming message symbols back into thought that is controlled by the receiver. Both encoding and decoding are mental processes. The message itself is the manifestation of the encoding process and is the instrument used in sharing thought with a receiver. The *channel* is the path through which the message moves from the sender to the receiver. The *feedback* element recognises the two-way nature of the communications process; in reality, individuals are both senders and receivers and interact with each other continually. Feedback allows the sender of the original message to monitor how accurately the message is being received. Thus, the feedback mechanism gives the sender some measure of control in the communication process. In marketing, it is sometimes acknowledged that an advertising message is not received by customers as originally intended. Based on market feedback, the message can be re-examined and perhaps corrected.

In addition to these graphic representations, there are *verbal* models of the communications process. Harold Lasswell provides us with a useful one by

Definition
Encoding is the process of putting thought into symbolic form that is controlled by the sender.

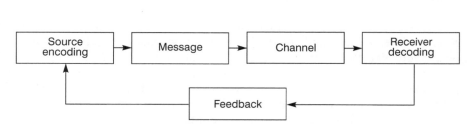

Figure 7.2 A more detailed model of the communication process.

Model	Related area of analysis
Who?	Source analysis
Says what?	Content analysis
In which channel?	Media analysis
To whom?	Audience analysis
With what effect?	Effects analysis

Figure 7.3 Lasswell's verbal model of communication.

posing questions (Lasswell, 1948). Although this describes only the elements of communication, and not their inter-relationships, its real value lies in the area of research. The model identifies five key areas of analysis, as shown in Figure 7.3.

Although this model is useful from the standpoint of posing critical questions for research, most verbal models are of limited use. Generally, they fail to show the dynamic nature of the communication process, partly because of the static nature of words.

Vignette 7.1

Dr Ed Levine offers SkylivecamToday for all the 'Big Apple' fans

If you like New York City, then you will like SkyliveToday from Dr Ed Levine. This is an Internet site that people can subscribe to free of charge. Every day Dr Ed, as he likes to be known, emails you. When you open the email, you get a message from him about the weather conditions in New York City. For example, on 22 March 2001 Dr Ed's message on email was 'Another day of rain and wind . . . with snow in tonight's forecast. Must be March'.

You are also provided with a WWW 'hot link', which takes you into an Internet site www.upscaleNewYork.com/index.htm. This enables you to open a 'Streaming Skylinecam', which is basically a view of mid-town Manhattan, including the Empire State Building, shown in real time.

Dr Ed's email also gives you two more Internet sites, which is basically the rationale for the email in the first place. Dr. Ed Levine operates a business selling discounted hotels in New York, which you can find on http://www.HotelDiscounts.net, and economy travel facilities, which you can find on http://www.EconomyTravel.com. These are arranged for you by http://www.HOTELDISCOUNTS.NET.

Not only does Dr Ed give you real-time pictures of New York, but also a number of still shots taken under different lighting and weather conditions. The site sells hotels and travel, but with a really friendly face. Dr Ed communicates with the site visitor directly. On the http://www.upscaleNewYork site, Dr. Ed has his picture in the right-hand margin along with a number of marketing communications messages. You can email Dr Ed about your travel and hotel requirements, and he will personally answer your email. It's almost like personal selling communications, but over an interesting and enjoyable Internet site. If you are a big New York fan, then you will look forward to receiving the email every day.

7.3 Elements of marketing communications

7.3.1 The marketing communications process

Traditionally, promotion (in its broadest sense of being one of the 'Four Ps' of the marketing mix) has been viewed as being the organisation's communication link with prospective buyers. Today promotion is viewed as only one element of an organisation's overall effort to communicate with consumers, and to view it simply as promotion is to take too narrow a perspective. All marketing mix variables, as well as other company actions, must be seen as part of the total message the company conveys to consumers about its 'offering'.

If we consider the company and the consumer as systems, we see that they share certain characteristics. The company system might be in a position it wishes to improve (or at least maintain). For example, the company may wish to increase profits and market share; enhance its reputation among competitors, the trade, and its consumers; and/or be perceived as an innovator and leader in its field. These desires are usually expressed in the form of company goals. Thus, the company has needs to fulfil. In analogous fashion, consumers perceive their present position and personal goals they wish to attain. They also have needs to fulfil.

The common vehicle that permits each to move towards its goals is the *total product offering*. This is the 'bundle of satisfactions' the company offers to prospective consumers. Consumers do not purchase a product for the product's sake, but for the meanings it has for them and for what it will do for them in both an instrumental and a psychological sense. This is the concept that was developed in Chapter 6.

Thus, the role of the marketing communications function is to share the meaning of the company's total product offering with its consumers in such a way to help consumers attain their goals and at the same time move the company closer to its own goals.

Key point
All marketing mix variables, as well as other company actions, must be seen as part of the total message the company conveys to consumers about its 'offering'.

Definition
The role of the marketing communications function is to share the meaning of the company's total product offering with its consumers in such a way to help consumers attain their goals and at the same time move the company closer to its own goals.

7.3.2 The marketing communications mix

Promotion in its broadest sense means 'to move forward'. However, in business, it refers to the communications activities of *advertising, personal selling, sales promotion* and *publicity*.

Advertising is a visible form of mass communications that is non-personal and paid for by an identified sponsor. *Personal selling* is a form of personal communication in which a seller attempts to persuade prospective buyers to purchase the company's product or service. *Sales promotion* relates to those short-term marketing activities that act as incentives to stimulate quick buyer action, e.g. coupons, premiums, free samples and trading stamps. These three promotional activities are variables over which the company has control. The company generally has little control over the presentation of *publicity*. Like advertising, publicity is a form of non-personal communication to a large group of people, but, unlike advertising, publicity is not paid for by the company. Publicity is usually in the form of news or editorial comment about a company's product or service. However, companies can instigate publicity through the release of news items, thereby exercising some measure of control over the publicity component of promotion (a point discussed later in this chapter, under the heading 'Public relations').

The blend of these promotional activities is referred to as the *promotional mix* or, more correctly, the *communications mix*. The emphasis placed on each element in the communications mix varies according to:

Key point
Publicity is usually in the form of news or editorial comment about a company's product or service.

- product type

- consumer characteristics

- company resources

- producers within the same industry, who will have different promotional mixes depending on size of firm, competitive strengths and weaknesses, managerial strengths and weaknesses, and managerial style and philosophy.

Other communications elements with which promotion must be co-ordinated are the product itself, price, and choice of distribution channels. Components of product communication include brand name, package design, package colour, size, shape, trademark and aspects of the physical product itself. These product 'cues' provide the consumer with subtle messages about the total product offering. *Price* also has important communications value and is often used by sellers to connote quality in the product offering, and can often imply 'snob appeal'.

Retail stores (*place*) in which products are found have significant communications value. Stores, like people, possess 'personalities', which consumers readily perceive and often associate with the merchandise located in the stores. Two stores selling essentially similar products can project different product images to prospective consumers, particularly when the consumers are not familiar with the product category. For example, a camera sold exclusively through specialist camera shops may project an image of higher quality than one sold in a discount department store, even though the cameras may be of comparable quality. If a company has to decide whether to sell its men's cologne through fashionable menswear shops or through drug stores, discount houses and supermarkets, the channel decision must be made in light of the firm's communications objectives.

Promotion is one of several activities in which companies engage to communicate their product offerings. The blend of all these variables as perceived by consumers is the *marketing communications mix*.

Definition
Promotion is one of several activities in which companies engage to communicate their product offerings.

7.3.3 Marketing and marketing communications

Given that the 'Four Ps' are important elements of both concepts, how does marketing differ from marketing communications? Some texts argue that the market mix is really a communications mix in which all activities interact, sometimes in a mutually reinforcing way and sometimes in conflict with one another, to form an image that can be favourable or unfavourable. Other texts differentiate between marketing and marketing communications by considering marketing communications as a later stage in the total marketing process.

Marketing effectiveness depends on effective communication. The market is energised (activated) by information flows. The buyers' perception of the seller's market offering is influenced by the amount and type of information they have about the offering, and their reaction to that information. Marketing, according to this view, relies heavily on information flows between sellers and prospective buyers. Marketing involves decision-making activities, whereas marketing communication is the process of implementing marketing decisions. Implementation of marketing decisions requires enactment of the communications process. The company's message is the combination of product, price, place and promotional stimuli it transmits to the marketplace, and communication takes place when consumers in the market interpret these stimuli.

A good marketing communications system provides for information flows from the consumer to the firm. It is a dialogue between buyer and seller, not simply a monologue from seller to buyer.

Definition
Marketing involves decision-making activities, whereas marketing communication is the process of implementing marketing decisions.

7.4 Definition of marketing communications

So far no formal definition of marketing communications has been given. Instead an attempt has been made to describe what marketing communications is, to convey a 'feel' for the breadth of the area. A 'macro' definition of the process is that marketing communications is the continuing dialogue between buyers and sellers in a marketplace. However, this definition is too general.

A practical alternative definition defines marketing communications as the process of:

1 Presenting an integrated set of stimuli to a market target with the intent of evoking a desired set of responses within that market target

2 Setting up channels to receive, interpret and act on messages from the market to modify present company messages and identify new communications opportunities.

This definition recognises that the company is both a sender and a receiver of market-related messages. As a sender, a firm in a competitive environment must attempt to persuade consumers to buy the company's brands in order to achieve a certain level of profits. As a receiver, the company must attune itself to its market in order to realign its messages to its market targets, adapt its

Key point
As a sender, a firm in a competitive environment must attempt to persuade consumers to buy the company's brands in order to achieve a certain level of profits.

messages to changing market conditions and take advantage of new communications opportunities. This interpretation is in line with the marketing concept.

7.5 Message source

The nature of the source of a message as a component in the communications process can have a great influence on receivers. Some communicators are more persuasive than others, and the degree to which they are more successful depends on how credible or believable the audience perceives them to be. Note the word 'perceives', for it is less important that the source is credible, and more important that the audience *perceives* it to be. Credibility is the sum of the set of perceptions that receivers hold in relation to a source. The audience's set of perceptions might include factors like the source's perceived trustworthiness/honesty, intentions to manipulate, prestige, expertise, power and age.

Definition
Credibility is the sum of the set of perceptions that receivers hold in relation to a source.

If an audience perceives the communicator to be honest, he or she will be more persuasive than if perceived to be dishonest. The perceived degree of honesty or trustworthiness of a source depends on the audience's perception of his or her *intent*. If the audience believes that a communicator has underlying motives, especially ones of personal gain, he or she will be less persuasive than someone they perceive as having nothing to gain. '*Overheard conversation*' has a similar effect in that the receiver believes he or she is not the intended target of the message, and therefore that the communicator has no intent to manipulate, which increases the source's credibility.

In advertising, the consumer is wary of the intentions of the advertiser. It is difficult to eliminate intent to persuade. Some television advertisements attempt to increase credibility by using 'candid' interviews with homemakers. The homemakers are asked to explain why they purchase a particular brand, or asked to 'trade' their usual brand for another, for example, one box of their regular detergent for two boxes of another detergent (and the answer is always 'No'). Another approach is to ask 'consumers' to compare their brand of product with another, both in disguised form. These 'consumers' act surprised when they learn that the sponsor's brand performs better than their regular brand. In these commercials, advertisers are attempting to imply a degree of objectivity to establish credibility for their message.

If the audience perceives the source to be an 'expert' speaker, perhaps one who has appropriate education, information or knowledge on a given subject, the source will be more successful in changing audience opinions pertaining to this area of expertise. Specialised sources of information, particularly the media, are quite often perceived as expert sources. In a study on physician's adoption of a new drug, researchers learned that physicians were more influenced by specialised technical journals than by journals aimed at the entire profession.

The effectiveness of a specialised source is largely due to the fact that its messages are aimed at selected audiences. In advertising, professionals are often used as promoters for brands. For example, Jack Nicklaus is used to advertise a line of golf equipment. However, his effectiveness as an 'expert' source is reduced to the extent that his audience perceives him to benefit personally from the promotion.

Perceived status or prestige of the source affects its credibility. This can relate to a class concept, but also to the 'role' of the source in the particular situation. Everyone has several roles to play. One individual may be a corporate executive, a husband, a father and secretary of the local Chamber of Commerce. Each role carries with it a status or level of prestige. A person usually separates these roles, adopting the one appropriate to a given situation. Generally, the higher the perceived status of a source, the more persuasive it will be. This is particularly true when the source is communicating on a topic related to role position.

When a receiver likes a source, the source will be more persuasive than if disliked. There is evidence that age, sex, dress, mannerisms, accent and voice inflection affect source credibility. These are characteristics that subtly influence an audience's evaluation of the communicator and the message.

Key point
Perceived status or prestige of the source affects its credibility.

7.5.1 The 'sleeper effect'

Sources high in credibility can cause opinion changes in receivers, but does this change endure? Evidence suggests that influence of a credible source dissipates rapidly after initial exposure to a persuasive message. Furthermore, a surprising finding observed in several experiments is that where an audience is initially exposed to a low credibility source, their opinion change *increases* over time in the direction suggested by the source. Figure 7.4 illustrates this phenomenon, referred to as the *sleeper effect*.

There is another facet to the 'sleeper effect'. Evidence suggests that when a high credibility source is reinstated (e.g. by a repeat advertisement), as would be expected, audience agreement with the source is higher after a period of time than if the source had not been reinstated. However, for a low credibility

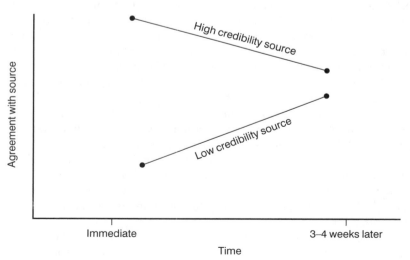

Figure 7.4 The 'sleeper effect'.

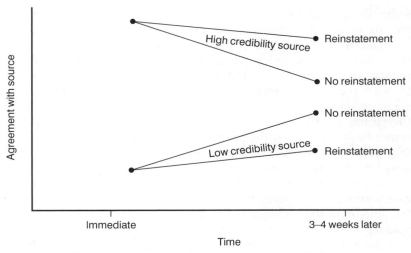

Figure 7.5 The effects of reinstatement of source on source credibility.

source, reinstatement results in less agreement with the source than with no reinstatement – i.e. reinstatement negates 'sleeper effect'. This phenomenon is illustrated in Figure 7.5.

7.6 Advertising

7.6.1 What is advertising?

A feature of advertising is that it is paid for by a sponsor attempting to convey a message to the recipient. A salesperson is paid to convey the employer's (sponsor's) message to a recipient, and this is not regarded as an advertisement. Another distinguishing feature is that the advertisement should be received by a large number of recipients through *mass, paid-for communication*. It is sometimes referred in the advertising industry to an '*above-the-line*' promotion. This simply means that it is advertising that is paid for through the advertising industry commission system, where advertising agencies that are 'recognised' (by their professional body, The Institute of Practitioners in Advertising) receive a commission from the media for the advertising taking place on their clients' behalf. The 'line' is simply the line above which they receive commission. Promotional activity that does not receive such commission is termed '*below-the-line*' promotion, and this activity is dealt with later in this chapter.

> **Definition**
> A feature of advertising is that it is paid for by a sponsor attempting to convey a message to the recipient.

Above-the-line advertising has three main aims:

1 To impart information

2 To develop attitudes

3 To induce action beneficial to the advertiser (generally the purchase of a product or service).

Washing detergent advertisements on television, party political broadcasts and 'situations vacant' advertisements in newspapers are examples of different forms of advertising. They are mass communications directed at an audience rather than at a specific person, paid for by a sponsor (a detergent manufacturer, a political party and an employer) who wishes to achieve some end – here, the sale of detergent, the winning of votes at an election, or the hiring of personnel.

Advertising is rarely able to create sales by itself. Whether or not the customer buys depends on the product itself, the price, packaging, personal selling, after-sales service, financing and other aspects of the marketing process. Advertising is only one element of the communications mix. Advertising performs certain parts of the communicating task with greater economy, speed and volume than can be achieved through other means.

Definition
Advertising is only one element of the communications mix.

The amount of the communication task performed by advertising will vary depending on the nature of the product, the frequency of purchase and the price. Where the product is sold through mail-order catalogue or by direct mail, virtually the whole communication task is achieved by advertising. In contrast, in the case of industrial goods the salesperson will usually close a sale, but the task of selling the company's product is helped by the potential client's awareness of the product achieved in part through company advertising. Here, advertising's purpose is to enhance potential clients' responses to the firm and its products.

The contribution of advertising is likely to be greatest when:

1 Buyer awareness of the company's product is low

2 Industry sales are rising rather than remaining stable or declining

3 The product has features not normally observable to the buyer

4 The opportunities for product differentiation are strong

5 Discretionary incomes are high

6 A new product or new service idea is being introduced.

Vignette 7.2

'Take me to your unglamorous but essential layer of software that enables seamless integration across business processes': 'Big Blue' uses advertising featuring aliens to sell unglamorous software

'Big Blue', as IBM is often called, had quite a marketing communications challenge on its highly technical hands. It needed to advertise the benefits and virtues of its 'middleware', an essential but rather boring layer of software that enables seamless integration across business processes. The company has four main 'middleware' products; these are DB2, Lotus, Tivoli, and WebSphere.

A huge integrated advertising campaign was created by the WPP Group's Ogilvy and Mather Worldwide, New York. The campaign incorporates all four of IBM's middleware products into one integrated campaign. From a marketing communications perspective, it is the most comprehensive and integrated campaign IBM has ever run. Ogilvy and Mather considered the middleware products to be so unglamorous that they failed to find a solution to the communications problem on this Earth; they had to turn to the deepest part of the cosmos and recruit the help of highly intelligent extraterrestrials to help market the products. The initial 'teaser' advertisements show two spacemen from another world, with the caption 'they come in search of better software'. The aliens are known as 'codernauts'.

The creative rationale for the campaign is based on the premise that the science fiction approach appeals to IBM's target audiences, business decision-makers and information technology professionals. These include software engineers, developers, chief information officers and other similar types. The IBM tagline is used in the advertising: 'It's a different kind of world, you need a different kind of software'.

7.7 Advertising models

A number of models have been developed to answer the question, how does advertising work? These models have been drawn from varying disciplines, particularly psychology, as well as from advertising practitioners. The early models relied on the stimulus/response formula, while later ones began to take into account the environment in which the purchasing decision is made.

7.7.1 Starch

One of the oldest models of advertising is that of Daniel Starch, who said in 1925: 'for an advertisement to be successful it must be seen, must be read, must be believed, must be remembered and must be acted upon'. This model is generally not very useful, because it takes little account of the state of mind of the consumer with respect to the product. The advertisement is assumed to be the main influence, and no allowance is made for the combined or multiple effects of advertisements, implying that the effects of single advertisements on consumers are independent of each other. In reality, it is likely that the cumulative impact of repetition of one advertisement or different advertisements in a campaign will have a greater effect on the consumer than a single viewing of one advertisement. However, it is still referred to in the advertising industry, but more in the context of 'Starch ratings' having become a generic term relating to the effectiveness ratings of advertisements. This is a little bit like the ballpoint pen being referred to as a 'Biro', as they were the first manufacturers to introduce this concept of writing instrument.

7.7.2 The DAGMAR philosophy

This model allows for the cumulative impact of advertisements, although not in a quantitative way. *Colley's DAGMAR model (Defining Advertising Goals for*

Measured Advertising Results, Colley, 1961) refers to the sequential states of mind through which it is assumed consumers must pass:

1 From unawareness to awareness

2 To comprehension

3 To conviction

4 To action.

Definition
Advertising is seen as one of a number of marketing tools (the others being promotion, personal selling, publicity, price, packaging and distribution) which, acting singly or in combination, move the consumer through the successive levels of the spectrum.

Colley describes these levels as the *marketing communications spectrum*. Advertising is seen as one of a number of marketing tools (the others being promotion, personal selling, publicity, price, packaging and distribution) which, acting singly or in combination, move the consumer through the successive levels of the spectrum as follows.

1 *Unawareness/awareness*. People who have never heard of the product are at the unawareness level. It is possible that people buy products whose names are unknown to them, but such sales are few. At this level, the advertisement is trying to make the potential customer aware of the product's existence.

2 *Comprehension*. At this level the consumer is not only aware of the product, but also recognises the brand name and the trademark and has some degree of knowledge about the product – what it is and what it does. This knowledge may have been gained from the actual advertisement and/or gained after an information search prompted by the advertisement. For example, a potential hotel guest would by this stage recognise the names of hotels X and Y, and also know that hotel X is a three-star hotel near the airport, while hotel Y is a four-star hotel in the centre of town.

3 *Conviction*. Conviction implies a firm attitude towards the product. In the hotel example, conviction may be illustrated by a consumer who says 'Hotel A is a four-star hotel in city Z where I can get good service for a reasonable price. I intend to stay there next time I visit city Z'. Colley also illustrates the conviction level by the examples of a woman who prefers a particular brand of lipstick and a man who prefers a particular brand of beer, where the preferences are on an emotional rather than a strictly rational basis (Colley, 1961).

4 *Action*. At this stage the consumer has made some overt move toward the purchase of the product. In the hotel example, this will occur when the customer tries to book a hotel room. Inducing an actual purchase may be beyond the power of advertising (the hotel may be fully booked, or the room rate may be considered too expensive), but the advertisement will have been 'acted upon', which is the end point of the Starch model.

The idea that advertisements 'nudge' consumers along a spectrum that extends from complete ignorance of the product to attempting to purchase, rather than individually achieving or failing to achieve results which owe nothing to previous exposures, leads to the concept that the purpose of advertising is to bring about a change in state of mind towards the purchase of a product. Rarely is a single advertisement powerful enough to move a prospect from complete unawareness to action. Advertising effectiveness should be measured in terms of the extent to which it moves people along the spectrum.

Adoption of the DAGMAR model can lead to a clearer statement of advertising objectives, and to valid measurements of success in obtaining these objectives. A study, reported by Majaro in 1970, looked at UK and European companies and tried to answer the following questions:

1 How many companies measure systematically, if at all, the results of their advertising effort?

2 How many companies are able to express in quantitative terms the impact that a specific campaign has achieved?

Questionnaire replies revealed that 70 per cent of firms *claimed* that they formulated advertising objectives. Nearly all consumer goods firms selected objectives for their advertising (or said they did). Only 55 per cent of the sample actually presented their objectives in written form. The study showed that companies formulating advertising objectives fared better in the market-place than those that did not. Only 35 per cent of the total sample reported *increased* market share during a four-year period. Of these 'high fliers', 85 per cent actively pursued an advertising-by-objectives philosophy.

The conclusions of the study promoted the value of adopting a systematic *advertising-by-objectives* process based on a stepwise movement through the communications spectrum, but it did not prove that success (in terms of increased market share or financial performance) is directly related to advertising.

7.7.3 The Lavidge and Steiner model

Another sequential model, similar to DAGMAR, was put forward by Lavidge and Steiner (1962). They proposed a hierarchical sequence of effects resulting from the perception of an advertisement that moves the consumer ever closer to purchase. The six levels are:

1 Awareness

2 Knowledge

3 Liking

4 Preference

5 Conviction

6 Purchase.

The six steps indicate three major functions of advertising: the first two, awareness and knowledge, relate to information or ideas; the second pair to attitudes or feelings toward the product; and the final two steps, conviction and purchase, produce action, or the acquisition of the product. They claimed that these three functions (information, attitudes and action) are directly related to a classic psychological model that divides behaviour into three components or dimensions: cognitive, affective and cognative (or motivational).

'Hierarchy-of-effects' models have been criticised by marketing writers. Joyce (1967) said:

> . . . they are put forward not on the basis of empirical evidence, but on the basis of an appeal to intuition or common sense.

Although these models differ in the number and nature of the stages in the process leading to the buying action, there is general agreement that the buying action is the culminating stage of a sequence of persuasion events. This assumes a predictable one-way relationship between changes in a consumer's knowledge and attitudes towards a product, and changes in his or her buying behaviour towards that product.

7.7.4 Dissonance theory

This indicates that the flow of causality is not unidirectional as proposed by hierarchical models. Most decisions involve the decision-maker in *cognitive dissonance*, or the notion that the chosen option will have some unattractive features, while rejected options will have some attractive features. Therefore it is predicted that after making a decision the decision-maker will actively seek information to reinforce and justify the decision, and will 'filter' information to which he or she is exposed, favourable data being assimilated and unfavourable data being discarded or ignored. Hence there is a two-way relationship, with behaviour influencing attitudes as well as attitudes influencing behaviour.

Key point
The major implication of dissonance theory is that for existing brands in the repeat purchase market, the role of advertising is essentially defensive.

The major implication of dissonance theory is that for existing brands in the repeat purchase market, the role of advertising is essentially defensive. It should seek to maintain the brand within the buyer's choice portfolio, and be aimed at existing users of the brand who are aware of the brand and who have formed positive attitudes towards it. The consumer tends perceptually to select advertisements for brands that are habitually purchased. Repetitive reassurance advertising should, therefore, reinforce the continuation of the buying habit in the face of competition.

7.7.5 Unique selling proposition

Key point
People in advertising who put forward models often have a particular view of advertising they wish to promote.

The models so far discussed have largely been developed by researchers drawing either on research in psychology or on experiments or observations actually made in the marketplace. People in advertising who put forward models often have a particular view of advertising they wish to promote. One of the best-known examples is the theory developed by Rosser Reeves, who reported the principles his agency had worked with for 30 years, embodied in the *Unique Selling Proposition* or *USP* (Reeves, 1961). Reeves stated:

> The consumer tends to remember just one thing from the advertisement – one strong claim, or one strong concept. Each advertisement must make a proposition to the customer. The proposition must be one that competition either cannot, or does not, offer. The proposition must be so strong that it can move the masses (i.e. pull them over to your product).

Reeves is saying that an advertisement works by making a claim for the product that is clearly related to consumer needs and which will be recalled by the consumer and motivate purchasing action at the appropriate time.

7.7.6 The 'brand image' school

Alternative approaches to advertising used to be concerned with the contrast between the 'USP school' and the *'brand-image school'* led by David Ogilvy. The brand-image school concentrated on non-verbal methods of communication, evoking moods and investing a brand with additional favourable connotations that are not necessarily specifically associated with the product's properties in use – for example, connotations of prestige and quality, which Ogilvy claims can 'give a brand a first-class ticket through life' (Ogilvy, 1961). However, while these models are intuitively feasible, there is no direct evidence to validate them.

It must be remembered that an advertisement is the carrier or channel through which the sponsor communicates a message to an audience. In 1982, Aaker and Myers used the diagram shown in Figure 7.6 to illustrate the communication process (note that this diagram is an elaboration of Figure 7.2).

Definition
It must be remembered that an advertisement is the carrier or channel through which the sponsor communicates a message to an audience.

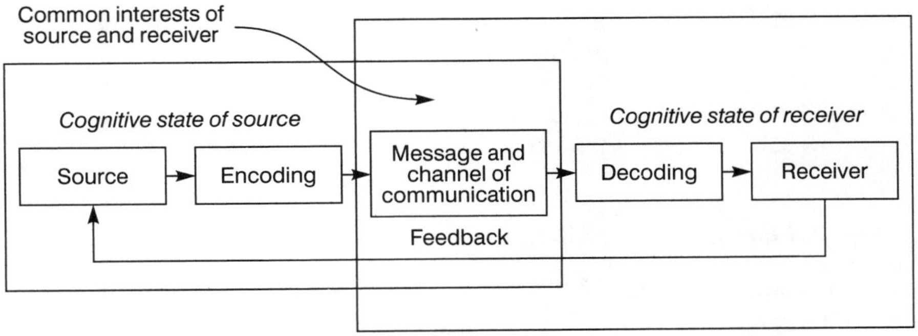

Figure 7.6 Aaker and Myers' model of communication (Aaker and Myers, 1982).

The sponsor's encoded message is transmitted to recipients (by advertising or salespeople), who decode and absorb it, either in whole or in part. The accuracy of communication depends on the 'fidelity' with which the message is transmitted and the correspondence between the meaning assigned to the symbols used by the source and by the receiver.

Good communication requires an area of overlap between the cognitive fields of the sender of a message and the receiver. Anything that distorts the quality of transmission, reducing the effectiveness of a message, is called *noise*. Noise can occur because the receiver does not interpret the message in the way the source intended. This can be caused by differences in the cultural backgrounds of the source and the receiver. A further example of noise is *cognitive dissonance*, which occurs when people's experience (receipt of the message) does not agree with what they previously believed.

The individual receiver may handle dissonance in a number of different ways, by:

1 Rejecting the message

2 Ignoring the message

3 Altering the previous opinion

4 Searching for justifications.

The first two possible reactions are negative effects from the source's point of view. Noise may also act as a message to the source (feedback) that may well change the behaviour of the source, which may either change the message or cease communication if convinced that the particular receiver is not receptive to ideas and that further communication would be wasted.

The view that advertising works by converting people into users of a particular product or brand can be misleading. Advertising may have a positive affect, even if the level of sales is steady (or declining), by preventing loss (or greater loss) of users. In some markets, increasing the loyalty of existing users and increasing the amount they buy may be a better prospect than winning over non-users.

It is contended that advertising situations are so varied it is impossible to generalise how advertising works, and that general model building can be misleading because every advertising campaign is a unique response to a unique situation and should generate its own measure of effectiveness. This supports the idea that any potential advertisers should have an advertising plan that sets out what they are trying to achieve, how they intend to achieve their goal and how they are going to measure the effects of the plan – an approach known as *advertising-by-objectives*.

7.7.7 Advertising by objectives

Modern companies rarely fail to measure the effectiveness of their human resources. Similarly, they analyse plant utilisation to assess the potential returns from this capital investment. But how many companies measure the results of their advertising efforts? Few are able to express, in quantitative terms, the impact of a specific campaign, and give little scientific thought to precisely what they are trying to achieve through advertising.

Clear objectives assist operational decision-making for advertising programmes. Operational decisions for advertising include:

● How much should be spent on a particular campaign?

● What should comprise the content and presentation of the advertisement?

● What are the most appropriate media?

● What should be the frequency of display of advertisements or campaigns?

● Should any special geographical weighting of effort be used?

● What are the best methods of evaluating the effects of the advertising?

According to a classic study by Corkindale and Kennedy in 1978, systematically setting and evaluating objectives for the various elements in an advertising programme provides the following benefits:

1 Marketing management has to consider and define in advance what each element in the programme is expected to accomplish

2 An information system can be set up to monitor ongoing performance, with the nature of information required being clearly defined

3 Marketing management will learn about the system it is operating from the accumulated experience of success (and failure), and can use this knowledge to improve future performance.

Majaro's study on objective setting revealed that although 70 per cent of companies appeared to set objectives, these were mostly crude and tended to be confused with marketing objectives. The question 'What are the actual advertising objectives of your company?' yielded the following in order of frequency of mention:

1 To increase or support sales

2 To create or increase product or brand awareness

3 To improve the image of the company's products

4 To improve the company's image

5 Sales promotion

6 To influence attitudes

7 To inform or educate the consumer

8 To introduce new products.

Most managers saw increasing sales or market share as their main objective, but this is a total marketing objective. Unless advertising was the only element of the marketing mix that is used (as is sometimes the case in direct mail and mail-order businesses), it would not be reasonable to expect advertising alone to achieve this objective.

According to DAGMAR theory, the main objective of advertising is to accomplish clearly defined communication objectives. Thus, advertising succeeds or fails according to how well it communicates predetermined information and attitudes to the right people, at the right time, at the right cost.

Majaro's study found that the following methods of evaluation were *claimed* to be used (in rank order of frequency of mention):

1 'Sort and count techniques' such as consumer mail or coupon response

2 Group interviews or panel discussions

3 Recall tests

4 Comparison of sales results (monthly, quarterly or annually)

5 Psychological 'depth interviews'

Key point
According to DAGMAR theory, the main objective of advertising is to accomplish clearly defined communication objectives.

6 Folder tests

7 Salesmen's monthly reports

8 Annual survey by market research department

9 Reports from dealers

10 Mathematical models.

A common failure reported was that measurement methods did not dovetail with specific objectives. For instance, depth interviews were claimed to be used to measure attitude changes, although the advertising objective given on the questionnaire was 'to inform the public of a product's availability'. The overall conclusion was that relevant measures were not being used. Clear, precise advertising objectives would rectify this situation.

Majaro set out a number of advantages of the *advertising-by-objectives* approach to advertising (Majaro, 1970):

1 It helps to integrate advertising effort with other ingredients of the marketing mix, thus setting a consistent and logical marketing plan

2 It facilitates the task of the advertising agency in preparing and evaluating creative work and recommending the most suitable media

3 It assists in determining advertising budgets

4 It enables marketing executives and top management to appraise the advertising plan realistically

5 It permits meaningful measurement of advertising results.

7.7.8 Setting objectives

It is often the case that many people in a company who influence advertising decisions do not have a common understanding of its purpose, for example:

- the Chairman may be most concerned with building a corporate image

- the Sales Manager may regard advertising solely as a means of getting larger orders from retailers

- the Finance Director deals with advertising as an expense, chargeable to a given fiscal period

- the Advertising Manager or the Agency Account Executive may see it as an investment directed toward building a brand image, and increasing the company's share of the market.

The main difficulty is differentiating between marketing objectives and advertising objectives. The proper sequence is first to define the overall marketing objectives, and then to determine the contribution that advertising can make to each of these. An advertising objective should be one that advertising alone is expected to achieve.

The following should be considered when setting advertising objectives:

1 Advertising objectives should be consistent with broader corporate objectives

2 Objectives should be realistic in terms of internal resources and external opportunities, threats and constraints

3 Objectives should be widely known, so people understand the goals of their work and how they relate to the broader objectives of the firm as a whole

4 Objectives need to be flexible, acknowledging that all business decisions, including advertising decisions, have to be made in circumstances of partial ignorance

5 Objectives should be periodically reconsidered and redefined, not only to take account of changing conditions, but also to ensure that objectives are generally known.

Before any practical work on setting advertising objectives can begin, information on the product, the market and consumers must be available. Of prime importance is a thorough assessment of consumer behaviour and motivation with particular reference to the company's target group of customers. The statement of advertising objectives should then make clear what basic message is intended to be delivered, to what audience and with what intended effects, and the specific criteria that are going to be used to measure success.

Corkindale and Kennedy summarised the main considerations in setting advertising objectives under five key words:

1 *WHAT* role is advertising expected to fulfil in the total marketing effort?

2 *WHY* is it believed that advertising can achieve this role? (What evidence is there and what assumptions are necessary?)

3 *WHO* should be involved in setting objectives; who should be responsible for agreeing the objectives, co-ordinating their implementation and subsequent evaluation? Who is the intended audience?

4 *HOW* are the advertising objectives to be put into practice?

5 *WHEN* are various parts of the programme to be implemented? When can response be expected to each stage of the programme?

7.8 Sales promotion

7.8.1 Introduction

Sales promotion is a dynamic and flexible marketing/sales tool that does not easily lend itself to the confines of a rigorous definition. However, two of the popular definitions are:

- 'The short-term achievement of marketing objectives by schematic means', and

- 'Immediate or delayed incentives to purchase, expressed in cash or in kind'.

Both are accurate, within their limitations, although they are very different. We are concerned with the function of sales promotion (i.e. what it consists of and what it does), so we will not dwell on abstract definitions.

7.8.2 The main elements of sales promotion

Figure 7.7 shows the primary types and their possible uses.

Objective	Self-liquidating premium	On-pack premium	In-pack premium	With-pack premium	Container premium	Continuing premium	Trading stamps / gift coupons / vouchers	Competition	Personalities	Couponing	Sampling	Reduced price pack	Limpet pack	Related items
Product launch or re-launch							×			×	×	×	×	
Induce trial							×	×			×			
Existing product new usage										×	×	×	×	×
Gain new users				×	×	×	×	×	×	×	×	×	×	
Retain existing users				×	×						×	×		
Increase frequency of purchase				×	×									
Upgrade purchase size	×	×		×	×						×			
Increase brand awareness								×		×				
Expand distribution							×	×				×	×	×
Increase trade stocks			×									×	×	×
Reduce trade stocks								×						×
Expand sales 'off season'						×		×				×	×	×
Activate slow-moving lines								×				×	×	×
Gain special featuring in-store	×	×	×	×	×		×					×	×	×
Increase shelf display		×	×										×	×

Figure 7.7 The effective use of consumer promotions showing objectives that certain promotions might achieve.

Other marketing elements that generally come within the realm of sales promotions are:

- display materials (e.g. stands, header boards, shelf strips, 'wobblers')

- packaging (e.g. pack-flashes, coupons, premium offers)

- merchandising (i.e. demonstrations, auxiliary sales forces, display arrangements)

- direct mail (e.g. coupons, competitions, premiums)

- exhibitions.

Generally speaking, the main types of promotions already mentioned are applicable, with due modification, to the industrial sector. However, industrial promotions are more likely to be closer in type to those promotions mounted by manufacturers of consumer goods for their retailers. In essence, they will be designed to gain optimum-sized orders over long periods.

Vignette 7.3

If you want to shop at Sainsbury's, then why don't you BOGOF and use your loyalty card?

J. Sainsbury plc, the large UK-based grocery multiple, has come to be regarded as an innovator and expert in the field of retail sales promotions. Over the last 10 years in particular, the quality of Sainsbury's in-store promotions has dramatically improved. They have become much more creative and imaginative, and hence more interesting to the customer.

A particularly successful promotional initiative has been the use of 'buy-one-get-one-free' (or BOGOF) offers. This gives the customer significant extra value, and such BOGOF offers are very difficult to resist. Such an offer falls within the category of 'immediate incentive to purchase' below-the-line sales promotion. The customer gains immediate value when purchasing the product. Unlike competitions or vouchers, there is no delay in gaining the extra value. This extra value is immediate in terms of extra product.

Sainsbury's also practices a relationship marketing customer retention strategy. The main tool used to achieve high levels of customer retention is the loyalty card. Basically, customers can apply for a Sainsbury's loyalty card, which enables them to earn loyalty points when buying certain products. Customers can save up the points and either have a money reward or have the amount saved subtracted from their grocery bill. Sometimes different products earn extra points, such as 'double points'. Sometimes the BOGOF offers are combined with extra loyalty points to make the perceived value of the purchase even better in the eyes of consumers.

7.8.3 Sales promotion planning

There are a number of stages during the running of a particular promotion. As with any business task, a full plan should be prepared to ensure that each stage is reached. An example of a planned sequence of stages in the context of sales promotion is:

1 Analyse the problem/task

2 Define the objectives

3 Consider and/or set the budget

4 Examine the types of promotion likely to be of use

5 Define the support activities (e.g. advertising, incentives, auxiliaries)

6 Testing (e.g. a limited store or panel test)

7 Decide the measurements required

8 Plan a timetable

9 Present the details to the sales force, retailers, etc.

10 Implement the promotion

11 Evaluate the results.

7.8.4 Advantages and disadvantages of sales promotions

Advantages:

- easily measured response
- quick achievement of the objectives
- flexible application
- it can be relatively cheap
- direct support of sales force.

Disadvantages:

- price-discounting can cheapen the brand image
- short-term advantages only
- it can cause problems with retailers, who might not want to co-operate
- the difficulty in communicating the brand message.

7.8.5 Importance of sales promotion

Key point
The amount spent on sales promotion by companies has been increasing for some time now, which is a recognition of its importance as a tool of marketing communication.

There is much disagreement about which 'marketing' expenditures should be attributed to sales promotion. A free plastic daffodil with every packet of washing powder is certainly a sales promotion, but price reductions can be confusing in that '15% extra free' is a sales promotion, but what about price-discounting by manufacturers?

Sales promotional expenditure data can easily be collected and analysed. The amount spent on sales promotion by companies has been increasing for some time now, which is a recognition of its importance as a tool of marketing communication.

7.9 Public relations (PR)

7.9.1 Definitions

There are a number of definitions of PR, each emphasising a different approach. The difficulty in developing a single definition reflects its complexity and diversity. Two definitions are useful. First, that of the Institute of Public Relations (IPR):

> Public Relations practice is the deliberate, planned and sustained effort to establish and maintain mutual understanding between an organisation and its *publics*.

Note that the definition refers to an organisation's 'publics' in the plural, since PR addresses a number of different audiences.

An alternative definition is provided by Frank Jefkins (1988):

> Public Relations consists of all forms of planned communication, outwards and inwards, between an organisation and its publics for the purpose of achieving *specific objectives* concerning mutual understanding.

This modified version of the IPR definition adds an important element, 'specific objectives', making PR a tangible activity – i.e. it can be measured and evaluated.

Definition
Public Relations practice is the deliberate, planned and sustained effort to establish and maintain mutual understanding between an organisation and its publics.

7.9.2 Communications and PR

Communication is central to PR. The purpose of PR is to establish a two-way communication to resolve conflicts of interest by seeking common ground or areas of mutual interest. If we accept this, then we must also accept its further implications – that PR exists whether an organisation wants it or not. Simply by carrying out its day-to-day operations an organisation necessarily communicates certain messages to those who interact with the organisation, and they will form an opinion about the organisation and its activities. The task of the PR function is to orchestrate those messages in order to help the organisation project a *corporate identity* or *corporate personality*.

7.9.3 Corporate identity

All PR activity should be carried out within the framework of an agreed and understood corporate personality. This personality should reflect the style of top management, since they ultimately control the organisation's policy and activities. A corporate personality can become a tangible asset if it is managed properly and consistently.

It should not be assumed that managers will consciously consider the role of personality when they make decisions. Therefore, the PR executive needs to be placed so that he or she is aware of all issues, policies, attitudes and opinions that exist in the organisation, and have a bearing on how it is perceived by outsiders who form part of the organisation's 'publics'.

Key point
A corporate personality can become a tangible asset if it is managed properly and consistently.

The use of the word 'personality' rather than the more commonly used 'image' is deliberate. An image is a reflection or an impression that may be a little too polished, or a little too 'perfect'. True PR is more than superficial. This is important because, in common journalistic parlance, a 'PR job' implies that somehow the truth is being hidden behind a glossy, even false, facade. Properly conducted, PR emphasises the need for truth and full information. The PR executive, as manager of corporate personality, can only sustain a long-term corporate identity that is based on truth and reality.

Despite the inclusion of 'specific objectives' in the definition of PR, it remains difficult to evaluate because of the abstract nature of 'personality' and the practical implication of the time lag between initial costs and derived benefits.

Definition
Properly conducted, PR emphasises the need for truth and full information.

7.10 Telephone marketing

The telephone derives its power as a marketing medium from its transactional nature (i.e. one human being in a *controlled conversation* with another). What originally began as 'ordering by telephone' soon evolved into *telemarketing*, a concept that can be defined as:

> Any measurable activity that creates and exploits a direct relationship between supplier and customer by the interactive use of the telephone.

The American Telephone and Telegraph Company define it as:

> the marketing of telecommunications technology and *direct marketing* techniques.

7.11 Direct mail

7.11.1 What is direct mail?

Definition
Direct mailing is the use of the postal service to distribute a piece of informative literature or other promotional material to selected prospects.

Direct mail is considered by some to be an advertising medium, but by others to be a quite separate element of the marketing communications mix. Direct mailing is the use of the postal service to distribute a piece of informative literature or other promotional material to selected prospects.

A 'direct mail shot' may consist of anything from a letter to weighty catalogues of product offerings. The most familiar regular users of direct mail techniques in the UK today are probably Readers Digest and the Automobile Association.

Direct mail is a method of communicating a message directly to a particular person, household or firm. As such it falls under the more general heading of *direct marketing*, which includes many other forms of direct communication. To avoid confusion, let us distinguish direct mail from related activities with which it is commonly confused.

Direct mail is *not*:

1 *Direct advertising.* This is one of the oldest methods of reaching the consumer. It consists of printed matter that is sent by the advertiser directly to the prospect. This material is often sent by mail, but it may also be distributed by house-to-house or personal delivery, handed out to passers-by, or even put under the windscreen wipers of parked cars. That portion of direct advertising that is sent through the mail is called *direct mail advertising.* Hence some, but not all, direct advertising is a form of direct mail.

2 *Mail order.* If the object of a direct mail shot is to persuade recipients to order the product or service by return post, the correct term is *mail order* or *mail order advertising.* Deliveries are made through mail, parcel services or by carrier direct from a warehouse or factory, or sometimes through a local agent. Mail order is a special form of direct mail. Mail order seeks to complete the sale entirely by mail, while direct mail is generally supplementary to other forms of advertising and selling. Direct mail is usually a part of a company's general marketing plan, whereas mail order advertising is a complete plan in itself, and companies exist solely to conduct business in this manner. Hence mail order is a type of direct mail, but not all direct mail is mail order.

Definition
Mail order is a special form of direct mail.

3 *Direct response advertising.* Neither direct mail nor mail order should be confused with direct response advertising. This is the strategy of using specially designed advertisements, usually in newspapers and magazines, to invoke a direct response rather than a delayed one. The most familiar type of direct response advertising is the *coupon-response press ad.*, in which a return coupon is provided which the reader may use to order the advertised product or service or to request further information or a sales call. Other variants involve incentives to visit the retail outlet immediately, such as special preview invitations and money-off coupons. Direct mail can also be used for direct response advertising.

Key point
Neither direct mail nor mail order should be confused with direct response advertising.

7.11.2 The growth of direct mail in UK marketing

Post Office statistics show a continuing rise in the annual volume of direct mail and in the number of organisations using it for both business and consumer communication. There are a number of factors that account for this increased usage and acceptance of direct mail as a major communications medium. One of the most significant is the increased fragmentation of media.

● There are now three UK terrestrial commercial television channels, as well as satellite plus cable television being available to subscribers

● In the print media, there has been the rapid growth of 'freesheets' alongside traditional 'paid for' local press, as well as a proliferation of 'special interest' magazines.

This fragmentation has meant that media buyers and advertisers either have to spend more money to make sure they reach as wide an audience as previously, or spread the same amount of money more thinly over a range of media.

Developments within the direct mail industry have removed many difficulties that have previously deterred large advertisers, particularly in respect of the poor quality of large mail shots – hence dubbed 'junk mail'. Information technology advances have made it possible to 'personalise' mail shots, targeting them to individuals by name. Quality has been greatly improved by the increased money and creative intelligence that has been channelled into direct mail.

In order to segment and target their markets effectively and gain best value for money, organisations are increasingly opting for the benefits of direct mail – flexibility, selectivity and personal contact.

7.11.3 Uses of direct mail

The range of products or services that can be sold by direct mail is very wide, as are its uses. To help define it more fully, it is appropriate to deal with direct mail to consumers and that to businesses separately.

Consumer direct mail

The uses of consumer-targeted direct mail are only limited by the scope of marketing imagination. Some of the more common uses are:

1 *Selling direct.* If a company has a convincing sales message, any product or service can be sold by direct mail. Direct mail is a good medium for selling a product directly to the customer without the need for 'middlemen'. The product or service can be described fully, and orders can be sent straight back to the advertising company.

2 *Sales lead generation.* If a product requires a meeting between the customer and a specialised salesperson (e.g. fitted kitchens, central heating and insurance), direct mail can be a useful method of acquiring good, qualified leads for the company's sales people. Sales calls are expensive, so anything that helps improve the call success (sale) rate is welcomed. A well-planned mail shot can act as a preliminary 'sieve', pinpointing the best prospects and ranking others in terms of sales potential. The 'warmer' the leads, the more effective will be the company's sales force, with fewer wasted calls. Responses, indicating potential interest, can be followed up by direct mail, a telephone call or a personal visit by a salesperson. A potential customer can then be placed in a personal selling situation, by issuing an invitation to view the product in a retail outlet or showroom or an exhibition. This is particularly useful for products that sales people cannot take to the 'prospect' for demonstration because of the size or function of such products. Direct mail creates a receptive atmosphere for the company's salespeople through '*cordial contact*' *mailings* that build on the reputation of the company and through the 'impact' or impression created. Well-executed mailing identifies the company in a favourable light to prospects, setting up 'good will' or creating a latent desire that might be triggered into action by a later mailing.

3 *Sales promotion.* Direct mail can send promotional messages – 'money off' vouchers, special offers, etc. to selected targets. This can be a useful way of encouraging people to visit a shop or exhibition.

4 *Clubs.* Book clubs are perhaps the best-known example of the use of direct mail as a convenient medium of communication and transaction between a club and its members. Other items can be marketed by the club system, particularly 'collectibles' such as record 'collections', porcelain and miniatures.

5 *Mail order.* Some mail order companies use direct mail to recruit new customers and local agents, as well as for direct selling.

6 *Fundraising.* One of the advantages of direct mail is the ability to communicate personally with an individual. This makes it a powerful method of raising money (e.g. for charitable organisations). It can carry the 'long copy' often needed to convince a recipient of the worthiness of the charity, and make it more likely that the reader might respond with a donation.

7 *Dealer mailings.* If a product is sold through dealers or agents they can use direct mail to reach prospective customers in their particular catchment area, just as a producer might.

8 *Follow-up mailings.* The company's name can be promoted to the customer by following any kind of sales activity with a mailing – e.g. checking that the customer is satisfied with their purchase, or letting the customer know that perhaps the car bought last year is coming up for its annual service. Customers can be kept informed of new developments, latest products and improved services. 'Exclusive' offers can be made and invitations issued. Using direct mail in this way helps to maintain contact quickly, personally and effectively, and to increase repeat sales.

Business direct mail

Business markets are made up of closely defined, discrete groups of individuals. These groups may not be best reached by mass advertising media. Direct mail can be used to identify different market sectors accurately, and provide messages appropriate to each sector. Some of the more common uses in this context are:

1 *Product launch.* Often the launch of a new industrial product or business service entails getting the message across to a small, but significant, number of people who will influence buying decisions (e.g. catering managers and car fleet managers).

2 *Sales lead generation.* As in consumer markets, direct mail can effectively reach qualified sales leads for a company's sales force.

3 *Dealer support.* Direct mail makes it easy to keep dealers, retail outlets, franchise holders etc. more fully informed of tactical marketing promotions and plans.

4 *Conferences and exhibitions.* Business and trade conferences and exhibitions are well-established means of communicating with potential customers and business colleagues. Direct mail can be used to invite delegates, who may be attracted if the event relates to a specific theme of direct interest to them.

5 *Follow-up mailing using the customer base.* Much business takes the form of repeat sales to the existing customer base. Since these are existing clients it can be worthwhile mailing them regularly, as long as the content of the mail-out relates to something that is new or of specific interest rather than simply 'junk mail'.

6 *Marketing research/product testing.* Direct mail can be used for marketing research, especially amongst existing customers. Questionnaires can be used as part of a regular communication programme, with levels of response being increased by some kind of incentive. Small-scale test mailings can be made to sample a target market. The results can give a quick and accurate picture of market reaction, with minimum risk. A marketing approach that is successful in a 'test mailing' can later be mailed to the full list.

7.11.4 Direct mail as part of the promotional mix

In both consumer and business markets, direct mail must fit in with a company's other promotion efforts. For example, a television or press campaign can reach a broader audience, and raise the level of general awareness of the company and its products. If such a campaign is added to a direct mail campaign aimed specifically at groups of people or companies most likely to buy, or to people particularly wanted as customers, the effectiveness of the overall campaign can be significantly raised.

Lists of respondents to direct response techniques in other media (e.g. 'couponed' press advertisements, or television or radio commercials which give a 'phone-in' number or a contact address) can be used as mailing lists for direct mail approaches.

7.12 Sponsorship

Like most below-the-line activity, this is growing in popularity. In some ways sponsorship achieves many of the functions of exhibitions, especially in terms of audience quality. We have already established that in business-to-business marketing environments, high status decision-making unit members are notoriously difficult to contact on a personal basis. The firm sponsoring an event can invite important members of a prospective customer company's DMU to the event, thereby enabling personal contact to be made in a social setting.

Key point
Sponsorship has a strong PR component to it, and firms can use it in a variety of ways.

Sponsorship has a strong PR component to it, and firms can use it in a variety of ways. Being associated with the arts can give a sense of supporting and being part of the fabric of society. Important clients and other key individuals who form significant groups of 'publics' can be invited to artistic events such as concerts, plays or opera. Afterwards they can mix with artists and directional staff, so in this way the key individuals who have been targeted for such promotion can be contacted and entertained, and long-term relationships built and maintained.

Vignette 7.4

Volvo uses tennis sponsorship with tremendous success to market its range of cars

Volvo, the Swedish car manufacturer, has turned to the sponsorship of tennis to gain greater communication coverage for its range of motor vehicles. Tennis is a very popular sport all over the world, and many of the people who go to tennis matches and watch the sport on television are just the sort of people Volvo are interested in and are trying to target with its tennis sponsorship programme. These people are well educated, reasonably affluent, and are prepared to pay for quality and safety. These are just the product attributes that Volvo cars embody in their product concept. Tennis sponsorship has turned out to be a very effective way of targeting communications at this particular segment.

Volvo estimates that its £2 million investment in tennis sponsorship during 2000 was actually worth the equivalent of spending £15 million on conventional advertising in terms of the positive communications coverage it managed to achieve.

Its advertising logos and corporate flags are displayed at its tournaments, and can been seen by visitors and by those watching the match on television. Volvo advertising usually appears in the tournament literature, such as programmes. The Volvo brand is a central feature of all the advertising for the tennis event, and Volvo cars are usually used in a high profile way at the actual event. Some of the top tennis players are provided with complimentary Volvo cars whilst at the tournament, and some players are actually transported to a particular match in one of the cars in full view of the television cameras.

7.12.1 Sponsorship of sport

Sponsorship of sporting events is of course big business, and nearly everyone is familiar with some form of sponsored sports event – especially Formula One motor racing, football, cricket, snooker and even bowls. Sponsorship of sport brings a high profile to the sponsoring organisation. There is also some 'entertainment' value to the sponsorship of sport in terms of complementary tickets for key customers, using the sponsored event as a reward for key sales staff who have achieved their targets, and so on. Corporate hospitality has become a very big part of the sports sponsorship industry. Hospitality 'tents' are now common at all major sports events, including Royal Ascot, the Royal Henley Regatta and the Wimbledon Tennis Championships. Some of the main reasons for firms becoming involved in the commercial sponsorship of sport include the following (the list is not intended to be exhaustive, but merely indicative):

Key point
Sponsorship of sport brings a high profile to the sponsoring organisation.

● To build awareness of the company name

● To achieve an association with a particular sporting activity, such as Formula One motor racing

- To 'entertain' important clients

- To entertain staff

- To attempt to make an uninteresting product or service more interesting by association

- To relate the product to the success of a particular team

- To gain international recognition

- Because the competition is involved

- Because the Chairman is particularly interested in the sport in question.

7.12.2 Sponsorship of the arts

Most people can intuitively understand why firms get involved in the sponsorship of sport; it is less clear to many, however, why firms get involved in sponsorship of the arts. When we discuss sponsorship of the arts, we interpret the term 'arts' very liberally – basically, as everything that is not sport. The reasons why commercial firms sponsor the arts include the following:

- To obtain personal contact with high status visitors

- So that the firm is seen as a benefactor of society

- To sponsor minority activities and education

- To be seen to be putting something back into the community.

As explained previously, sponsorship falls under the heading of below-the-line activity. Other below-the-line communication activities include exhibitions and public relations, both of which are discussed in this chapter. The key concept is the integrated marketing communications mix, where above-the-line and below-the-line activities are fully integrated, with the one class of activities supporting and augmenting the other.

7.13 Exhibitions

Definition
Exhibitions are another form of below-the-line promotional activity.

In the UK there are hundreds of exhibitions of interest to companies, and if overseas opportunities are taken into account the number extends to thousands. They vary considerably in scope, from a small show with perhaps 20 or 30 modest stands to vast international fairs with a thousand or more exhibitors, covering the entire market for a particular product class or industry. Trade exhibitions appear to have a permanent place in the marketing communications mix of many firms. Exhibitions are another form of below-the-line promotional activity. As with many other below-the-line methods, they are growing in use and popularity. They come in three basic forms:

1 Those aimed at the consumer

2 Those aimed solely at the trade

3 Those aimed at and open to both.

The third category has become the most common. Most exhibitions start off as trade exhibitions and then, after the first week or so, when all of the 'trade' business has been seen to, they are often opened to the general public. The public usually pays an entry fee, which brings in extra cash for the exhibition organiser and helps to pay for the costs of putting on the show. The public may have an actual interest in the products and services being exhibited – for example, Clothes Shows, Motor Shows and Home Exhibitions. Sometimes the products and services are of little direct interest to the general public – that is, they are highly unlikely to buy any of the products on show – but nevertheless attendance at the exhibition can be a 'good day out' (e.g. an agricultural show or an air show), and the public is prepared to pay an entry fee for this opportunity of entertainment.

An essential guide to forming a communications mix is deciding what the various elements of the mix are supposed to accomplish. Setting clear, operationally relevant communications objectives provides the basis for selecting how advertising, sponsorship, direct mail, exhibitions, personal selling and other communications tools will be used in the communications programme. An exhibition is just one medium by which a company may choose to communicate with its target markets. Generally, exhibitions are used to complement other communications media. All the elements in the communications mix reinforce one another, producing a synergistic effect, with each element having its own part to play in the overall scheme of things. Exhibitions tend to draw a high quality group of visitors, and company directors will frequently be present at an important trade exhibition. Such trade exhibitions offer the marketing firm the chance to come in direct contact with high status decision-making unit (DMU) members. There is a significant public relations dimension to exhibitions. Many visitors to trade shows go to view the total industry range of products or services in an economic period of time and in one place. People visiting exhibitions seem to regard them as a 'viewing opportunity' and a chance to obtain technical information. Frequently products are accessible for examination, along with specially designed models of products. There can often be an important 'social' aspect to trade shows, with stands offering refreshments and a chance to interact socially for potential clients. Interacting and networking can be facilitated.

Purchasing agents and other executives involved in the buying process will often have their own preference for various information sources at different stages of the overall buying sequence. An understanding of the stages in the buying decision process is useful in selecting communications objectives and the appropriate communications tools to achieve them. In relation to new products, we can describe the decision-making process by the simple model shown in Figure 7.8.

Choice of target audience will usually include those people who either decide or can influence the buying decision. These individuals will be of varying status and will be situated at varying stages of the decision-making process, so it will be necessary to reach them through different communications channels. Communications tools differ in their cost effectiveness in accomplishing objectives. For example, although industrial marketers will

Key point
An essential guide to forming a communications mix is deciding what the various elements of the mix are supposed to accomplish.

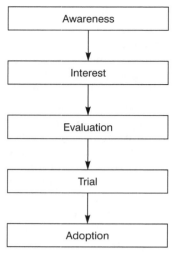

Figure 7.8 Innovation-adoption model.

generally spend far more on personal selling than on advertising, it would be inefficient to use the sales force for all communications purposes.

7.13.1 Exhibition evaluation

In order to evaluate the effectiveness of exhibitions and to plan for future exhibits, certain qualitative and quantitative data must be collected and analysed. As a first step it is necessary to decide what measures of cost effectiveness to use for evaluation. The following proxy measures are often used in practice:

1 Audience size

2 Audience quality

3 Media impact.

Key point
One of the more meaningful measures for evaluation is audience quality, which relates to the status of the visitors to the exhibition.

One of the more meaningful measures of the above is audience quality, which relates to the status of the visitors to the exhibition. Measurement of media impact requires some form of research to establish the effectiveness of the exhibition to both visitors and exhibitors. The most common measure used, simply because very often it is based on the only accurate data available, is audience size. This can be used as a measure of cost effectiveness when broken down into different categories as follows:

1 *Cost per visitor (= total cost of exhibition/total number of visitors)*. This gives an indication of the potential audience size that might be exposed to the firm's promotional activities at the exhibition.

2 *Cost per contact (= total cost of exhibition/total number of visitors to stand)*. This shows the ability of the firm to attract visitors to its stand. It reflects the extent of real interest and the contacts made with potential customers, and is therefore related to one of the objectives of exhibiting.

3 *Cost per enquiry (= total cost of exhibition/total number of enquiries)*. This gives the cost to the firm for each enquiry.

When comparing the cost effectiveness of exhibitions with other media, it would be unfair to argue that the contacts made with 'targets' or 'publics' by different communications media are of similar value. The difficulty in making a comparison indicates that the cost effectiveness of each activity needs to be made in the light of the objectives it is designed to achieve. Some objectives cost more to achieve than others, and this needs to be taken into consideration. Finally, it can be concluded that the role of the exhibition is a very important one; one that offers the marketing firm a unique opportunity in terms of personal contact, meeting high status visitors, the following on opportunities, and creating databases for future marketing exercises to name but a few.

7.14 Summary

✓ The theme of communication (specifically dealt with in this chapter and the next) is linked with most other aspects of the text. In particular, Chapter 2 described marketing orientation. It is principally through above- and below-the-line promotion that marketing orientation is communicated to consumers. Chapter 4 outlined the overall marketing mix of which promotion is a principal component. Chapter 8 covers personal selling. The promotional aspects of communications that have been covered in this chapter are an essential 'back-up' to the selling function.

✓ Effective communication is only possible with an understanding of buyer behaviour, which was the subject of Chapter 6. Communication is one of the more contentious areas of marketing, especially in the light of consumerism and the broader social dimensions of marketing, and these aspects are looked at in Chapter 16.

Questions

1 Explain, using illustrations, what is meant by (a) the 'source effect' and (b) the 'sleeper effect', as the concepts are applied in marketing communications theory.

2 'The evaluation of advertising effectiveness is not worth the effort and cost involved.' Critically evaluate this statement.

3 What are the advantages to an organisation of systematically evaluating the effectiveness of sales promotion expenditure with reference to clearly defined communication objectives?

4 What form would such a marketing communications evaluative procedure take? Outline a scheme for such an evaluation programme.

5 Explain how direct mail can be used to (a) generate sales leads, and (b) 'follow-up' a sales visit.

References

Aaker, D. A. and Myers, J. A. (1982). *Advertising Management*, 2nd edn, pp. 233–6. Prentice-Hall.

Colley, R. H. (1961). *Defining Advertising Goals for Measured Advertising Results.* Association of National Advertisers. New York.

Corkindale, D. R. and Kennedy, S. H. (1978). *The Process of Advertising.* MCB Publications.

Jefkins, F. (1988). *Public Relations*, 3rd edn. Pitman Publishing.

Joyce, P. (1967). *What Do We Know About How Advertising Works?* Advertising Age.

Lasswell, H. D. (1948). *Power and Personality*, p. 104. W. W. Norton.

Lavidge, R. T. and Steiner, G. A. (1962). A model for predictive measurement of advertising effectiveness. *Journal of Marketing*, October, pp. 74–94.

Majaro, S. (1970). Advertising by objectives. *Management Today*, January, p. 98.

Ogilvy, D. (1961). *Confessions of an Advertising Man.* Atheneum.

Reeves, R. (1961). *Reality of Advertising.* A. A. Knopf Inc.

Further reading

Armstrong, G. and Kotler, P. (2000). Integrated marketing communications: advertising and public relations, consumer and business buyer behaviour. *Marketing: An Introduction*, 5th edn, Chapter 12. Prentice Hall.

Blythe, J. (2001). Marketing communications and promotional tools. *Essentials of Marketing*, Chapter 9. Person Educational Ltd.

Broadbent, S. (1983). *Spending Advertising Money.* Business Books.

Cateora, P. R. and Ghauri, P. N. (2000). The international advertising and promotion effect. *International Marketing: European Edition*, Chapter 16. McGraw Hill.

Coulson-Thomas, C. J. (1983). *Marketing Communications.* Heinemann.

Davies, M. (1998). Marketing communications 1: advertising and sales promotion. *Understanding Marketing*, Chapter 9. Prentice Hall.

Hart, N. and O'Connor, J. (1983). *The Practice of Advertising.* Heinemann.

Keegan, W. J. and Green, M. S. (2000). Global marketing communication decisions 1: advertising and public relations. *Global Marketing*, 2nd edn, Chapter 14. Prentice Hall.

Lancaster, G. A. and Reynolds, P. L. (1998). Above and below the line promotions. *Marketing*, Chapter 12. Macmillan Press.

Lancaster, G. A. and Reynolds, P. L. (1999). *Introduction to Marketing: A Step by Step Guide to All The Tools of Marketing*, Chapters 8 and 9. Kogan Page.

McIver, C. (1984). *Case Studies in Marketing, Advertising and Public Relations.* Heinemann.

Plamer, A. (2000). *Principles of Marketing*, Chapters 16–20. Oxford University Press.

Marketing communications II – personal selling

8

8.1 Introduction

The function of selling is to make a sale. This obvious statement remains true despite the recent addition of many ancillary functions. Much of the background task of selling can be done remotely, for instance by direct mail. *Personal selling* is the specific task that involves face-to-face contact on a personal basis. This means that suitably skilled and trained individuals with a professional manner should carry out this function. Selling tasks differ, depending on the type of goods and services involved. Some salespeople are little more than order-takers, whilst others employ the more sophisticated arts of prospecting, negotiating and demonstrating in order to close a sale.

Personal selling is the primary communication vehicle in organisational marketing in general but for industrial marketing in particular (these buying situations were discussed in Chapter 6), where anything up to 80 per cent of the total marketing budget can be spent meeting sales force costs. Personal selling is less important in many retail consumer markets, especially in FMCG markets such as packaged grocery products. Selling to end-users increasingly uses non-personal forms of communication such as packaging, advertising, merchandising and the sales promotional techniques discussed in Chapter 7. It is because personal selling is such an important part of the communications mix that this entire chapter has been devoted to the subject. Communications mix elements are generally not used in isolation; they complement each other.

Definition
Personal selling is the specific task that involves face-to-face contact on a personal basis.

Key point
Communications mix elements are generally not used in isolation; they complement each other.

8.2 The nature of selling

'Everyone lives by selling something', and in essence this is true. Every time we engage in a conversation or discussion, we are exchanging views and ideas. In a sense, when we attempt to get others to accept our point-of-view, we are attempting to 'sell' our ideas. Without selling as a commercial activity, many transactions would simply not take place. Personal selling plays a vital role in the exchange process within any advanced economy.

8.2.1 The importance of personal selling to the individual firm

As already mentioned, the importance of personal selling varies from firm to firm. Goods requiring low-involvement decisions, for example everyday purchases like FMCGs, are usually sold through retail stores on a 'self-service' basis. Salespeople are, however, needed to 'sell' these products in bulk to the retail trade. The degree of selling skill required for this type of task depends on the reputation of the manufacturer and the popularity of the brands involved. It is not really necessary actually to 'sell' well-known brands of grocery products such as Heinz beans, Nescafe coffee or Bovril to the trade; they will stock them because of their popularity with customers. In such situations, the salesperson's role is really one of re-ordering, ensuring stock replenishment and rotation, and merchandising advice and customer liaison. Indeed, when selling to big supermarket chains they monitor this type of activity themselves, and head office central buyers will simply perform a negotiating role with manufacturers' representatives.

With goods and services requiring high-involvement decisions, the role of personal selling is clearer. Negotiating the sale of expensive consumer durables like cars usually requires a personal approach, a high degree of product knowledge and a certain amount of selling skill. Selling in business-to-business situations generally presents the greatest challenge, and requires the highest degree of professional selling skills. Expensive capital equipment, such as machine tools, is purchased only after much negotiation. In such situations involving appraising technical complexity there is a high degree of perceived risk, and therefore the buyer (or people who form the *DMU* who are involved in the purchasing decision process) requires detailed knowledge of the goods or services being considered. The salesperson must identify the prospective customer's key requirements, not only in terms of product performance, but also their price ceiling, delivery, credit and after-sales service requirements.

Key point
The salesperson must identify the prospective customer's key requirements, not only in terms of product performance, but also their price ceiling, delivery, credit and after-sales service requirements.

Vignette 8.1

Kitchens Direct uses personal selling to 'close' the sale

Kitchens Direct Ltd is part of the HomeForm Group of companies. The firm advertises extensively in the newspapers and in particular in the Sunday 'glossy' newspaper supplements, such as those of the *Mail on Sunday*. Kitchens Direct take a fully integrated approach to marketing communications. It is a business-to-consumer marketing company. The advertisements in the Sunday supplements, for example, show a beautifully designed kitchen and the invitation to telephone a Freephone 0800 number in order to secure an extensively informative colour brochure that covers all aspects of the firm's products and services – all aspects, that is, except the price.

The potential customer is sent a very high quality colour brochure, and left in peace to consider the products for about a week. Then the customer receives an outgoing telephone marketing call. This call usually runs along the lines of the company having a kitchen surveyor in the area working on another contract, and it would be no trouble at all to send the surveyor round to actually show a sample of drawer fronts, doors and work surfaces. If the prospect agrees to this, a 'warm up' sales person comes around and shows a sample of the product. He or she is unable to provide an estimate of price, because each case is different and the customer really needs a full survey. A free survey is offered to the prospect, which includes a free computer design service.

The surveyor designs the kitchen, gives a price and tries to 'close the sale'. Often this works and the prospect signs a contract. If this does not work, further outgoing telemarketing calls are made to the prospect over the following weeks. An offer is made for a representative to call to discuss price with the prospect of a reduction.

Kitchen Direct has no showrooms or middlemen, offers free delivery, free design and a low price. The company uses advertising, telephone marketing and brochures extensively in its marketing communications programme. However, the firm still relies heavily on personal selling to actually 'close' the deal with a prospect. All aspects of non-personal and personal forms of communication are integrated into a unified communications strategy, which sells a lot of kitchens in the UK.

8.2.2 The importance of personal selling to the national economy

The United Kingdom is a trading nation, which earns its living in the world by selling goods and services abroad. In terms of the national economy, the most important role of personal selling is its contribution towards promoting the sale of UK-produced products and services overseas. Exports are needed to compensate for goods and services that are imported, and this is all fundamental to the maintenance of a healthy *balance of trade*.

Since the United Kingdom joined the European Economic Community (EEC) in 1973 (now called the European Union, or EU), European markets have become increasingly important to UK firms. As discussed in Chapter 3, the intention of the EU was to create a completely 'free' market. The creation of this genuinely free European market for all member states means that even greater competition faces UK companies. It also provides an exciting business environment. The role of the UK's professional selling capability in this context is of great importance, and the ability of UK organisations to rise to this challenge and capitalise on the opportunities offered by this free market depends largely upon the calibre of the UK selling profession.

Key point
The United Kingdom is a trading nation, which earns its living in the world by selling goods and services abroad.

8.2.3 The cost effectiveness of personal selling

As an individual element of the organisation's marketing communications mix, the relative importance of personal selling really depends on the overall objectives, the type of industry in which the company is involved, and the general conditions of the marketplace. Personal selling can, in many situations, be extremely effective. However, it can also be very expensive, and the salesperson's salary is not the only selling cost. Other 'add-on' costs, like a company car, expense account, extra travelling costs, administrative support and a share of general overheads, often exceed the salary cost of an individual salesperson. Personal selling is usually the most expensive form of

Key point
Personal selling can, in many situations, be extremely effective.

communication available to a company when calculated on a straight cost-per-contact basis. Because of this cost, personal selling should be used sparingly and when it can achieve results more cost effectively than other marketing mix elements such as advertising or direct mail.

8.3 Situations requiring a personal approach

A personal approach is required in a number of selling situations, which will now be discussed.

8.3.1 Situations of high perceived risk

The purchase of products that are radically new, expensive or technically complex is often viewed with a certain amount of perceived risk by prospective buyers. A salesperson uses professional skill to identify the customer's areas of concern, and takes steps to lower the concern or eliminate the perceived problems. Perceived risk is one of the most common barriers to the achievement of a sale. Without a clear understanding of consumer and organisational buying behaviour, the salesperson would lack the necessary psychological tools to be truly effective.

Key point
Perceived risk is one of the most common barriers to the achievement of a sale.

8.3.2 Technically complex products

Products such as new robotic machine tools or a new computer system often confuse potential customers, particularly if they are non-experts. Such products need careful explanation if the potential customer is fully to grasp the capabilities of the product or system being sold. These tasks can only really be carried out in face-to-face situations by salespersons with a high level of product knowledge.

8.3.3 Commercially complex negotiations

Financial arrangements, maintenance contracts, spare-parts availability, responsibility for staff training and many other areas can make the commercial details of many transactions complicated. The commercial complexity of the buying situation contributes to the degree of perceived risk experienced by the potential purchaser and such situations require negotiation and explanation, which are most effectively conducted on a personal basis.

8.3.4 Industrial/organisational markets

It has already been mentioned that up to 80 per cent of the total marketing budget of firms operating in industrial markets can be spent on personal selling. The reason for this is that the goods and services sold are often technically complex, expensive and innovative. They are perceived by prospective purchasers as being potentially risky, so lots of personal reassurance is needed, and this can only be provided on the face-to-face basis that is afforded by personal selling.

Vignette 8.2

Whitegates Estate Agents rely on good sales negotiators to sell houses

Whitegates Estate Agents Ltd is a national chain of UK estate agents offering a full property service to clients. These services include the selling of domestic properties, property leasing and management, mortgages and insurance. Whitegates has been an innovator in providing value-for-money services to house buyers for over 20 years. The company during this time has acquired a huge amount of expertise and know-how from which all of their customers benefit.

Central to the success of the retail sales side of the business is the quality of the firm's property sales negotiators. All other areas of the business are based on the skills of the negotiator. For example, house insurance and mortgages, both of which are very profitable to the firm in terms of the commissions generated on sales, are only realised when a successful sale has been made. The parties concerned may then wish to take advantage of these services in order to facilitate their moving house.

Sales negotiators do not have to be members of the Royal Institution of Chartered Surveyors, although in small practices the partners, who are often qualified valuation surveyors, do their own negotiating. In the larger firms the qualified valuation surveyors are often dealing with the valuation side of the business, leaving trained sales negotiators to deal with individual customers. The firm has an extensive staff development programme, and trains its staff in all areas of negotiation and sales. Negotiating between two parties in a house sale situation requires a lot of diplomacy and negotiating skill. If the individual negotiator fails at any point, then a whole chain of property deals may be lost. Sales negotiation is of paramount importance to the success of any retail property company.

8.4 The expanded role of the modern salesperson

The primary responsibility of any salesperson is to achieve a successful sale. To modern, professional, marketing-orientated salespersons, selling is but one facet of the task. There are many other functions undertaken in the course of customer contact. Job responsibilities in modern selling include servicing, prospecting, information gathering, communicating and allocating.

Key point
The primary responsibility of any salesperson is to achieve a successful sale.

8.4.1 Servicing

The salesperson will often provide various services to customers, such as consultancy, technical advice, arranging after-sales service and finance, and expediting delivery from the factory to the customer's premises.

8.4.2 Prospecting

Although many companies supply their salespeople with qualified 'leads', a certain amount of a salesperson's time must still be devoted to obtaining and developing his or her own leads. Some will result from the salesperson *cold calling*. Existing satisfied customers are a potentially highly productive source of leads, and new prospects can be obtained by asking satisfied customers if they know of anybody who might have a need for the type of goods and services on offer. This technique has been used successfully in industrial selling, but is also applicable to typical cold-calling situations like life assurance.

8.4.3 Information gathering

Salespeople are in the 'front line' in that they are in personal contact with customers and potential customers most working days. They are in an excellent position to collect market information and intelligence. By talking to customers and keeping alert, they should be able to gather information that might be useful to marketing management in a number of areas such as:

- marketing plans – salespeople can make a valuable contribution to marketing plans by offering advice on customer preferences and requirements in such matters as price, credit, discounts, promotions, market segmentation and timing of marketing efforts

- sales forecasting – whereby the *sales force composite method* is an established method of subjective forecasting (a subject that is covered in detail in Chapter 14)

- new product development – existing customers can provide salespeople with ideas for new products or improvements to existing products

- general marketing research – salespeople can provide information about market conditions, competitive developments and customers. Customers may have a multi-sourcing policy and, by probing, the salesperson may be able to gain information about competitors' activities. Chapter 4 outlined the need for a marketing intelligence system, which is a crucial component of the organisation's overall marketing information system.

8.4.4 Communicating

Salespeople use many forms of communication with customers in addition to verbal communications, e.g. reports, charts, models, diagrams, and video, laptop computer and slide presentations. They use these skills when they visit customers and when addressing potential customers at exhibitions and other venues. As Rubin and Brown (1975) explain, the aim of communicating may not specifically be to make a sale; it may be to communicate the message of the company's image.

8.4.5 Allocating

There are times when the salesperson may have to perform an allocating role. During times of product shortage (perhaps resulting from an industrial dispute, shortages of raw materials, production problems or unexpected excessive demand), salespeople may have to evaluate customer loyalty and future sales potential and allocate stocks accordingly.

8.5 The salesperson as a communicator

Whilst the salesperson uses many forms of communications, in the final analysis the most effective form is voice communication. Many elements of sales courses are concerned with what salespeople should say, when they should say it and how they should say it. Effective communication is a two-way process because, important as it is for the salesperson to talk, it is just as important to listen. *Listening skills* should be taught and developed. It is too easy to 'switch off' when someone is talking a lot and think about something else. The hallmark of the professional salesperson is actively to listen to what customers have to say. Listening requires a conscious effort on the part of the listener that can be mentally exhausting.

Key point
The hallmark of the professional salesperson is actively to listen to what customers have to say.

Salespeople often work within one industry, or even for one firm, for a considerable period. Over the years they develop not only selling skills, but also technical expertise. When somebody is an 'expert', it is sometimes difficult to communicate with non-experts. When talking to a fellow expert, a person often skips over elementary points. When a potential customer is discussing something new with a salesperson, there is a temptation for the salesperson to think: 'I wish she would get to the point'. Simple points that the salesperson may have heard from other customers many times are nonetheless new and very important to this potential customer. The professional salesperson should listen attentively and use the extra mental time not needed for comprehension to interpret what is being said and plan his or her reaction.

A salesperson deals with a finite range of products, but often with a large number of customers. Many customers' problems are likely to be similar. To the customer the situation probably appears unique, but the salesperson may well think 'I've heard it all before!'. Many sales situations are similar, but they are rarely exactly the same and such thinking is bad sales practice. During customer contact, the professional salesperson not only makes sure that he or she is listening to everything the customer has to say, but actually shows the customer this through non-verbal forms of communication such as eye contact, facial expressions, hand and head movements and other forms of body language. Such non-verbal cues enable the salesperson to signal understanding or, indeed, non-understanding of what the customer is saying. A salesperson can use non-verbal communication to regulate the speed, depth and detail of the customer's discussion without verbal interruption. Such non-verbal exchange encourages customers to 'open up' and discuss points in greater detail. It also helps to build rapport between the salesperson and the customer, and is an important factor in making the sale.

Attempting to understand a complicated topic takes mental effort and concentration. If the salesperson is not concentrating and simply nods in agreement, this will be counterproductive. The speaker takes non-verbal response as an indication that the listener has understood the problem, and this might subsequently necessitate the embarrassing task of returning to 'clarify' certain points. If the topic being discussed is too technical or complicated, the professional salesperson should be honest and tell the buyer that it is beyond his or her area of knowledge and obtain technical assistance from head office.

8.6 The sales sequence

The most important part of a salesperson's job is the sales interview, but, as already discussed, many other tasks have found their way into the selling itinerary. In addition, a good deal of time is taken up in travelling – often an average of 30 per cent of the working day. Such a diverse range of activities and travelling means that careful planning must be done to ensure that face-to-face contact with customers is maximised. This can be achieved by adopting a general plan for all sales interviews, and a specific tactical plan for individual interviews.

Key point
The general sales sequence should act as a guide, remembering that the key word is *flexibility*.

The general sales plan used for all sales interviews is called the *sales sequence*. It must be flexible and capable of being adapted to suit individual selling/ purchasing situations. The general sales sequence should act as a guide, remembering that the key word is *flexibility*. The role of the professional salesperson is to listen to what the prospect has to say and to interpret non-verbal clues, then adjust the sales message and approach to fit in with the requirements of the particular situation. The following sequence outlines a general plan for this activity:

1 Preparation – the planning of individual interviews.

2 The approach – the way the salesperson meets and greets the customer.

3 The presentation and/or demonstration – often the central part of the sales interview, and the appropriate time for the salesperson to emphasise product benefits.

4 Negotiation – deciding delivery dates, price, credit terms, etc.

5 Closing – the final bringing together of what has been discussed and agreed, and the time when the order, or potential order, can be discussed.

6 After-sales service – the salesperson's task does not finish when the goods have been sold; an important element of good customer relations (and repeat business) is a caring after-sales service, which is not merely the province of a technical service department but part of a customer relations process that includes salespeople.

This sales sequence is a formula. Each stage is now examined in more detail.

8.6.1 Preparation

Company knowledge

This includes knowledge of the company's systems, procedures, price, terms, and general policy on such matters as complaints and returned goods. The salesperson needs to update such information on a regular basis. For example, if the company decides to extend credit terms or alter its quantity discount structure, it is important that the salesperson knows about such changes immediately.

Product knowledge

This includes knowledge of both existing and new products. Inadequate product knowledge can be humiliating to the salesperson in buying situations, and might affect long-term relationships. The limitations of the company's range of products or services should also be known. Making exaggerated claims for a product will lead to customer dissatisfaction. Salespeople paid on a low salary (or no salary) plus commission basis will be more likely to make such exaggerated claims, merely to advance personal remuneration.

Key point
Making exaggerated claims for a product will lead to customer dissatisfaction.

Market knowledge

The salesperson needs an up-to-date understanding of the general state of the market, and must be knowledgeable about new developments in the market. Such knowledge includes the activities of competitors. Chapter 4 emphasised the importance of market intelligence, an intrinsic part of the organisation's overall marketing information system. Salespeople are particularly well placed to act as 'intelligence providers'. For instance, if the salesperson finds out that the competition is giving special trade discounts or some other form of trade incentive, this should immediately be reported to their marketing department.

Customer knowledge

General knowledge is needed about the size of the customer's company, affiliation to other companies, bargaining power, markets they serve, etc.

Specific preparation for individual interviews also includes having as much personal knowledge about customers as possible (even down to personal idiosyncratic behaviour) so that the interview can be conducted at a more personal level. For example, knowledge of the buyer's family circumstances, perhaps picked up at the last sales interview (e.g. a son or daughter getting married), can help to provide a personal touch and show that the salesperson really cares. Preparation for individual interviews is often made easier by using a very straightforward aid traditionally known as a *customer record card*, but now done via the salesperson's laptop computer. The professional salesperson should keep such a file for every live account. Many also keep records for potential customers and lost customers in the hope of winning them over or back in the future. Information on such a record will include:

Key point
The professional salesperson should keep a customer file for every live account.

1 A record of previous purchases (particularly the most recent purchase).

2 Any particular comments of interest made by the prospect, e.g. 'We might be interested in investing in a new machine if and when our new USA venture takes off'. Such a comment, with details of the date it was made, would be most useful to, say, a machine-tool salesperson, especially if American interests have started to develop.

3 Personal details, including basic things as the customer's name (and forename if the buyer likes to operate on a personal rather than a formal basis). The salesperson should make a point of introducing him or herself by forename and surname (both should be on a visiting card), and then let the

buyer choose whether to use a formal or informal style of address. Quite often it will start formally, and when the salesperson has gained the customer's confidence the informal forename might be used. The names of other people in the purchasing or technical departments visited should be similarly logged (Assistant Buyers eventually become Chief Buyers!). Customer family details and special interests are also useful. This provides good background information that can be used to 'break the ice' at the beginning of an interview (e.g. 'Did you manage to reduce your golf handicap after all?').

4 The best and worst days to call (from the customer's point-of-view).

By referring to a record card before making a call, the salesperson can be more adequately prepared. For example, if interest was previously shown in a particular product range, then prices, delivery, discounts, etc. for the possible order can be prepared beforehand and talked about with conviction.

Equipment, samples and sales aids

The following list is indicative, and which are most appropriate or useful will depend on the selling situation:

- Sales brochures and literature
- Handbooks and product specifications
- Up-to-date price lists and credit details
- Samples
- Demonstration kits/films/videos/computer laptop spreadsheets
- Graphs, models and other supporting material
- Trade directories
- Order book
- Pens, calculator and stationery
- Credit card – although not a sales aid it is useful for settling fuel and entertainment bills, and possession of a company card confers 'seniority'.

Journey planning

The professional salesperson should have an organised plan for appointments and other calls on a daily basis. Planning should consider both current customers and prospects (people to whom the company does not sell, but wishes to in the future).

Because face-to-face sales time is at a premium and because so much of the salesperson's time is spent travelling, it is important that itineraries are well planned. One method is known as *differential call frequency*. In many industries it is common for more substantial customers to receive a higher frequency of personal calls other than clients. In the following illustration, the salesperson's overall *call cycle* is eight weeks and the overall territory can be divided into four

Key point
Because face-to-face sales time is at a premium and because so much of the salesperson's time is spent travelling, it is important that itineraries are well planned.

Table 8.1 Differential call frequency plan

Week no.	Customer type		
	A Area	B Area	C Area
1	1 + 3	1	$\frac{1}{2}$ of 1
2	2 + 4	2	$\frac{1}{2}$ of 2
3	3 + 1	3	$\frac{1}{2}$ of 3
4	4 + 2	4	$\frac{1}{2}$ of 4
5	1 + 3	1	other $\frac{1}{2}$ of 1
6	2 + 4	2	other $\frac{1}{2}$ of 2
7	3 + 1	3	other $\frac{1}{2}$ of 3
8	4 + 2	4	other $\frac{1}{2}$ of 4

approximately equal areas. The customers are then classified in terms of their relative importance, with Group A the most frequent purchasers and Group C the least frequent. The frequency of personal calling is related to the customer type:

- Group A (20 customers) – call every two weeks
- Group B (50 customers) – call every four weeks
- Group C (130 customers) – call every eight weeks.

On this basis, a *differential call frequency plan* can be drawn up. A typical plan for such a situation is shown in Table 8.1.

The differential call frequency plan shows, for example, that in Week 4 the salesperson will call on all Group A customers in Areas 4 and 2, and all Group B customers and half of Group C customers in Area 4. In Week 8, the salesperson calls again on all Group A customers in Areas 4 and 2, on Group B customers and the other half of Group C customers in Area 4. If this plan is followed the salesperson's objectives will be achieved, in that all Group A customers receive a call every 2 weeks, Group B customers every 4 weeks and Group C customers every 8 weeks, thus completing what is termed the *sales journey cycle*.

There are, however, a number of factors that complicate the operation of this system, for example: type of area (urban or rural); one area being more difficult to plan than another; ease of obtaining appointments (in certain industries, such as the licensed trade, there are certain times of the week or day when visits are not convenient to the customer); unequal distribution of customers; sales visits taking longer than expected, perhaps because of a complication in the negotiating process; and seasonal factors (e.g. the clothing trade is dictated to by seasonal demand, so buyers will purchase at certain times of the year in readiness for 'spring' or 'autumn' collections).

There are a number of suggestions that can help the salesperson in this respect:

1 Make firm appointments to avoid being kept waiting unnecessarily

2 Adhere as closely as possible to the allotted time for each visit

3 Budget time for contingencies

4 Budget time for prospecting new accounts

5 Use a customer record card or laptop computer for recording important 'background' information

6 Personal preparation prior to going into the interview (e.g. composure and pausing beforehand so as not to give the impression of 'rushing', which may give the buyer the impression that he or she is simply being 'fitted in' between other 'more important' meetings), including, needless to say, appropriate dress, general grooming and personal hygiene.

8.6.2 Approach

The manner in which the salesperson approaches a prospective customer (called a 'prospect') is a fundamental skill of professional selling. To be able to evaluate a situation quickly and judge the mood and type of personality of the prospect are valuable and necessary skills. Some pointers are:

● First impressions are important, and the salesperson should be prepared, alert and of good appearance (not meaning good looks!).

● The opening of the sales interview should be pleasant and businesslike. This is important if it is the first interview. In such a situation, opening remarks should be considered very carefully.

● The salesperson should discuss the business at hand as soon as possible to avoid wasting valuable selling and prospecting time.

● If the prospect sets a time limit, the salesperson should strictly adhere to it.

● If another appointment is made, the salesperson should enter the information in a diary and note any relevant conversational details on a record card.

● The salesperson should ask relevant questions and 'actively' listen to the answers.

● If any debts are to be discussed, it is advisable to do this at the beginning of the interview. The customer then feels that the debt is paid and any new negotiation can take place without the complication of previous dealings.

8.6.3 The presentation and/or demonstration

Key point
The salespersons should cast him/herself in the role of the buyer and establish the level of explanation that will be required.

The first stage was 'preparation', and this and subsequent stages depend on good foundations. The salespersons should have cast him/herself in the role of the buyer and established the level of explanation that will be required. Presentations are much more effective when the needs of potential customers are studied beforehand, and such information should be available from customer record cards.

It is said that during a sales presentation and/or demonstration, the role of the salesperson is to communicate specific product or service benefits of interest to the potential customer. Products or services have many features, and *'customers buy benefits, not features'*. A salesperson should examine the product range and list the major selling points of each product. The most important selling points are those that are unique to the product or service in question, and give some sort of advantage over similar products offered by competitors. These important selling points are referred to as the *unique proposition (USP)*.

The salesperson should have already identified the product benefits required by the customer during the preparation stage. People buy for a variety of different reasons and the sales professional must quickly assess the customer's buying motives, which may be economic, social or psychological. The most common ones revolve around performance, economy and price, durability, appearance, safety, comfort and adaptability, and Chapter 6 discussed these motives in detail.

Such a presentation can also help to overcome buying objections. If the dialogue is carried out on a 'to-and-fro' basis, the seller may find it worthwhile to encourage objections in the knowledge that they can be dealt with adequately.

Whenever possible, the salesperson should refer to the needs of the prospect and talk in a language that the prospect can readily understand. For example, when householders purchase a new central-heating boiler, they do not always want to know all about the technical details of the equipment. It is generally sufficient for the prospect to know how many litres of water the boiler will heat, how many baths or showers it will provide, that it will heat all radiators needed to warm the house, and for how long it will be guaranteed. However, if the boiler is being sold to the building trade, technical information is likely to be a major part of the presentation.

Many sales are lost because the salesperson over-presents too much technical detail. If the prospect gives the salesperson *buying signals*, an attempt should be made to close the sale (a *trial close*), which is dealt with later.

Key point
A salesperson should examine the product range and list the major selling points of each product.

8.6.4 Negotiation

Howard Raiffa (1982) claims that negotiation goes to the very heart of the selling process; in effect, it is the key element. This process usually involves two parties who wish to bring about an agreement that is favourable or acceptable to both sides. One party, usually the seller, makes a presentation and an offer in terms of price, credit, delivery, etc. The other party evaluates the points that the seller has made. Each party knows what it would like to achieve from negotiation and how far it is prepared to go in offering concessions. Hence, sales negotiation is a process of presentation, evaluation, counterproposal and concession. Each party has an 'optimal' result in mind, but concedes that the achievement of this goal is rarely possible and that it must be prepared to compromise. The 'gap' between the 'optimal' result and the 'minimum acceptable limit' gives each party 'room for manoeuvre'. This important

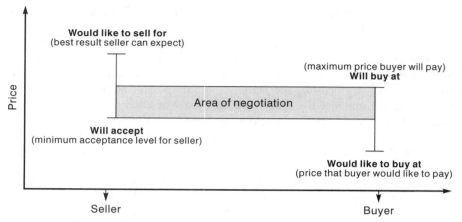

Figure 8.1 The 'room for manoeuvre' concept in negotiation.

concept in the sales negotiation process is illustrated in Figure 8.1. The example given concerns price, but the concept is equally valid for any area that is open to negotiation like credit terms, delivery or quality.

8.6.5 Closing

Definition
The fundamental objective of the selling process is to obtain an order to make a sale.

The fundamental objective of the selling process is to obtain an order to make a sale. It is therefore essential that a salesperson has detailed knowledge of appropriate closing techniques. Perhaps even more important is an appreciation of when and under what circumstances to use each technique; this comes with experience.

Some of the more common closing techniques are described below.

Basic close

When the salesperson sees buying signals from the prospect, he or she starts filling in the order form. If there is no objection, a successful sale is achieved. The techniques that follow are variations of this basic approach.

Alternative choice

This is really a *trial close* technique. When the salesperson has received buying signals from the prospect, he or she attempts to close by offering the prospect an alternative choice. For example, a prospect is showing serious interest in purchasing a new car and asks about delivery that is taken as a buying signal. The salesperson might then ask 'What would be your preferred colour?' and, if the prospect states a preference, a sale is made. This is one of the most common methods of 'trial close (i.e. a method of 'fishing' for a definite closing signal from the prospect).

'Puppy dog' technique

If you give a family a small puppy to look after for two weeks, they are likely to grow fond of it and will be reluctant to part with it at the end of the period. The same principle can be applied to any product that might be loaned out for a period. This technique is used by companies who offer their machines free or at a greatly reduced rental for a 'trial period'. It is hoped that the prospect will get used to having the machine and that at the end of the trial period there will be strong resistance to sending it back.

Summary question

This technique is used when the salesperson is experiencing sales resistance. The salesperson has discovered the main cause of resistance through a process of elimination. For example:

● 'Is it the price?' 'No!'

● 'Is it the colour?' 'No!'.

Each time the prospect says 'No', he or she is eliminating potential causes of resistance. This allows the salesperson to concentrate on the most important area of resistance.

Similar situation

This method is best illustrated by an example. Imagine a salesperson selling security devices 'door-to-door'. Upon meeting resistance, he could point to a similar situation: 'The Smith family in Winchester Avenue said exactly the same as you. They thought the product rather expensive and wanted more time to think about it. One week later they were burgled! They were also underinsured!'

The selling implication is obvious, and this technique can be powerful in influencing a prospect's decision, especially if the prospect can easily relate to the analogy.

Sharp angle

When a prospect requests information, the salesperson uses the reply to ask for a sale. For example:

Customer: 'Have you got it in green?'

Salesperson: 'Do you want it if we have it in that colour?'

Final objection

This is a mixture of 'summary question' and 'sharp angle' techniques. If the prospect is showing resistance, the salesperson uses summary questions to ascertain the most important objection and refutes that one.

Imagine a potential customer in a showroom considering purchasing a new built-in kitchen unit:

Salesperson: 'Is it the price?'

Customer: 'No, the price is fine; in fact it seems good value.'

Salesperson: 'Is it the credit terms, then?'

Customer: 'No, those seem very fair.'

Salesperson: 'You mentioned earlier that you were a little concerned about its size. Is this still troubling you?'

Customer: 'Well yes, it is really. You see at weekends my family all come to lunch and I need to be able to cook a meal to feed 10 people. I need to cook a really large joint or a turkey.'

Salesperson: 'So, what you are really concerned about is the oven capacity?'

Customer: 'Yes.'

The salesperson then demonstrates to the prospect's satisfaction that the oven has the capacity to cook a roast meal for 10 quite adequately by reference to the instructional manual and by envisioning food in the oven.

The techniques listed are not exhaustive. The real skill is in knowing which technique is appropriate in a given situation.

8.6.6 After-sales service

Key point
Increasingly, it is part of the salesperson's task to provide or to offer advice and information after the sale has been made.

Increasingly, it is part of the salesperson's task to provide or to offer advice and information after the sale has been made. Where appropriate, the salesperson should encourage the customer to take out a service contract and provide information about service centres. Good after-sales service is vital in securing post-purchase satisfaction and valuable repeat business, especially in the case of a major purchase. It is well known that 'cognitive dissonance' often follows, and this phenomenon was discussed in Chapter 7. It is in the salesperson's own interest to ensure that the customer is entirely satisfied after a major sale, and part of this process should ideally include after-sales service arrangements.

Vignette 8.3

Glanbia plc uses personal selling to sell 'Gain Feeds' to agricultural customers

Glanbia plc is an international food company based primarily in Ireland, UK and the USA. The company serves markets for dairy and meat products across the world. With an annual turnover of more than £1.5 billion and employing 8500 people, Glanbia ranks among the world's leading dairy businesses as well as holding significant regional meat interests.

Glanbia plc manufactures a comprehensive range of premium quality, high performance concentrates for the animal feed market made from select high quality ingredients. Glanbia brand these feeds as GAIN FEEDS. Rigorous enforcement of quality and the design of effective quality assurance systems form a key component of the Glanbia plc business philosophy.

The Gain Concentrate Range is specially formulated to fulfil the nutrient requirements of high-performing animals. The firm's sales representatives form a key part of the firm's success. Gain's sales team consists of highly professional people with extensive product knowledge. Many of them are graduates with degrees in biology, chemistry or some other form of scientific discipline. The sales team is also highly trained in all aspects of the business, including negotiation and sales skills, key account management, and customer care and customer relationship management. Personal selling is still the most important marketing communication tool in business-to-business marketing situations. Once an account is opened routine re-ordering can be carried out by telephone, although pro-active ordering has been recently introduced by Gain. This means that, if the customer wishes, the firm contacts the customer rather than the customer contacting the firm when re-ordering is due. This saves the customer time and expense. However, the initial opening of new accounts requires a very personal approach. Much of the success of the company has been achieved through the professional skills of its sales force.

8.7 Sales management

8.7.1 Setting the size of the sales force

Calculating the optimum sales force size is a basic task for sales management. There are a number of factors that need to be taken into account in reaching such a decision:

1 The company's financial resources

2 The number of customers to be reached

3 The average number of calls required per customer, per week, per month, etc.

4 The average number of calls that can be made by a salesperson in a given period

5 The distribution policy of the firm – for example, does the company operate a policy of exclusive, selective or mass distribution (Chapter 9 details these categories)?

Some companies use bespoke formulae for calculating the optimum size of a sales force, which take the above criteria into account.

8.7.2 Evaluating sales force performance

Looking at an individual salesperson's performance in terms of sales volume relative to his or her sales colleagues is too simplistic and can be misleading. Comparative sales performances are meaningful only if there are little or no variations from territory to territory.

There may well be differences in market potential and workload (e.g. Birmingham with its industrialised profile will clearly differ in market potential from Cornwall, which is largely rural. In terms of workload, travelling around Cornwall will involve greater distances between calls, but driving and parking will be less of a problem than in Birmingham). There may also be differences in promotional support, competition, the length of time the company has operated in a given area, and the degree of goodwill that the company has built up.

Measures of individual evaluation

Measures of individual evaluation can be qualitative or quantitative, for example:

1 Qualitative:

- degree of product knowledge
- quality of sales presentation and demonstration
- self-organisation (use of time, journey planning, etc.)
- intelligence
- patience
- tenacity
- enthusiasm, motivation and ambition
- grooming and general appearance.

2 Quantitative:

- sales volume
- number of orders secured
- number of new orders
- number of customers/orders lost
- number of sales calls made
- number of service calls made
- expenses incurred
- amount of market intelligence gathered.

Sales forecasts can also be used as a basis for evaluation. Once potential sales in relation to each area and then each salesperson's individual territory have been forecast, these are then translated into sales targets or sales quotas that each salesperson is budgeted to sell (some companies call it the 'sales budgetary' process). These area-by-area forecasts represent the potential contribution to the company's net profit. Actual contribution can then be compared to potential contribution once the forecasted period has been reached. A ratio of 1 : 1 would mean that the salesperson had exactly obtained all the forecasted potential business in a particular area, and would have exactly reached the agreed sales target or quota.

8.7.3 Remuneration of salespeople

Salespeople are paid by one of the following methods:

- salary only
  - salary plus commission or sales-related bonus
  - commission only
  - percentage of profits from a given territory.

There is much disagreement as to whether sales force compensation should be linked to what they actually sell. Day and Bennett (1964) carried out the first piece of extensive research in this area in the United States.

Straight salary offers the least incentive for salespersons to sell more, but it does offer stability and security of earnings. Sales management should expect any reasonable task to be performed. It is increasingly appropriate when salespersons have to consider customers' best interests in terms of aspects of customer care that must be performed in order to retain customers. This is increasingly important within 'lean manufacturing' situations when it is acknowledged that customer retention is, in most instances, more important than winning new customers. In some circumstances straight salary is linked to a group bonus, whereby all members of a team share a bonus relating to profitability during the previous period.

Salary plus commission (or sales-related bonus) is the most popular method of compensation. Some companies use *escalator* commission/bonus schemes, where the higher the sales, the higher the commission/bonus *pro rata*. The ratio between fixed basic salary and commission differs from company to company. Generally, the salary element provides a living basic wage, with the commission element acting as a sales incentive. In most cases this commission is linked to the sales target or quota system described earlier. Once a salesperson sells above an agreed target or quota, then some kind of escalator commission structure is sometimes applied. This escalator may work on the basis of ever-increasing commission percentages once certain levels of sales have been reached within a given period.

Key point
Salary plus commission (or sales-related bonus) is the most popular method of compensation.

The *commission only* method is usually used for self-employed manu-facturers' agents. Some organisations, like life assurance companies and home improvement organisations, often employ part-time salespeople on this basis. The method can be advantageous to the company, as the cost of each salesperson is directly related to their sales achievement. There is also a big incentive for salespersons to be successful, as their level of income is determined by their individual efforts. The main disadvantage is that such salespersons feel less a 'part' of the organisation, so after-sales service relationships with customers may suffer. Indeed, many such sales tend to be 'one-off' purchases.

Vignette 8.4

Arrow Industrial Supply Inc., industrial fastener distributor, uses a network of personal selling professionals to expand business

Arrow Industrial Supply Inc. is based in Ohio, USA, and is a major US industrial fastener distributor stocking over 75 000 individual items for the industrial plant maintenance market. The firm uses a range of marketing communications tools to sell its products to the plant maintenance market. Telephone marketing plays a big part in its communications strategy for existing customers. The firm prides itself on its personal touch, and does not use voice mail or automated attendants. Only real people answer the telephone and take orders.

Arrow Industrial Supply Inc. is always looking for sales people for new accounts, and offers an outstanding opportunity for sales professionals, whether on a full- or part-time basis. Arrow's sales people are independent sales professions working on a commission-only basis. Earnings range from $25 000 to $80 000 annually. Full product training is given, although most of the sales team already has considerable experience in the industrial fasteners market. In this business, a personal approach is vital. Catalogues and Internet marketing all have their place, and can be very useful in gaining the attention of potential customers or for existing customers to re-order over the Internet. New accounts are, however, generated by a personal sales call and the establishment of a customer–supplier relationship.

8.7.4 Recruitment and selection of salespeople

It is not possible to describe a 'typical' salesperson. The job itself, and the suitable person, will vary according to the product or service to be sold. The following job description is, therefore, only a general guideline.

1 *Responsibility.* The representative will be responsible directly to the sales manager.

2 *Objective.* To achieve the annual sales target across the product range in the area for which he/she is responsible, as economically as possible and within company policy.

3 *Planning.* To become familiar with company policy and plan how to achieve the defined objectives within the limits of that policy; to submit this plan to higher management.

4 *Implementation*

- To act as an effective link between customers and head office

- To organise own travel itinerary

- To develop a comprehensive skill in selling

- To maintain and submit accurate records

- To gather market intelligence and report this to Head Office

- To assess the potential of the area in terms of visits, outlets for company products, activity of competition

- To protect and promote the company image

- To protect the company's business by avoiding unnecessary expense

- To achieve harmony with fellow staff by setting a good example and maintaining loyalty towards superiors.

The following is a general checklist for evaluating prospective candidates for a selling position:

- age and marital status

- health

- interests

- education

- previous employment and experience

- location

- clean driving licence

- references

- appearance

- intelligence

- integrity

- motivation.

This is not an exhaustive list, and nor are the criteria in any order of importance. These criteria (and any others) can be incorporated into a rating matrix using an evaluation scale (e.g. excellent, very good, good, fair, poor). Coner and Dubinsky (1985) have done a lot of research in this area of sales evaluation.

Possible sources of recruitment are:

- inside staff (i.e. current employees)

- salespeople from outside the company (i.e. in many cases from the company's competitors)

- advertising in the press and other media

- specialist recruitment agencies.

The topic of personal selling has links with Chapters 2 and 3, and to a certain extent with Chapter 4. In this chapter a distinction has been made between selling and the more global view of marketing. Clearly, personal selling relates to the wider role of marketing communications that has been discussed in Chapter 7.

8.8 Summary

✓ Personal selling is a highly effective but expensive marketing communications tool. The cost of employing an additional member of the sales force is not just the remuneration of the salesperson, but also includes the 'add on' costs of vehicle depreciation, overhead allocation and support services like sales administration. In a sense, personal selling and other forms of non-personal communications, e.g. sales promotions, direct mail, exhibitions and trade fairs, complement each other.

Key point
Personal selling is a highly effective but expensive marketing communications tool.

✓ The obvious way to view the role of selling is that its function is to make a sale. However, the selling process is complicated and requires high levels of training.

✓ The term 'selling' encompasses a range of selling situations and activities. Some sales tasks are simply no more than 'order taking', whereas other situations involve many psychological complexities. Some salespeople specialise in selling in consumer markets, and others in selling within industrial or public sector markets. Whatever the industry and sales setting concerned, there is a common theme running through all situations that relates to professionalism and ethical practice.

✓ The modern salesperson has a more expanded role than was the situation 25 years ago. Selling is still the primary function of the task, but modern sales activity involves many other marketing tasks like attending exhibitions, gathering market intelligence, contributing to marketing plans and helping to formulate sales forecasts.

Questions

1 Planning is an essential part of the selling process. What should be included in the weekly calling plan, and what information should be recorded after each visit is made?

2 The primary task of a sales representative is to sell the company's product or service. What additional tasks could a sales representative be expected to undertake, and how might these affect the representative's selling role?

3 In order to determine how well or how badly each salesperson is performing, a sales manager needs an appraisal system. Why is this important, and what questions should such an appraisal system be able to answer?

4 How can the field sales force contribute to the process of achieving long-term relationships with customers through relationship marketing and customer care? Give specific examples.

References

Coner, J. M. and Dubinsky, A. J. (1985). *Managing the Successful Sales Force*, pp. 5–25. Lexington Books.

Day, R. L. and Bennett, P. D. (1964). Should salesmen's compensation be geared to profits? *Journal of Marketing Research*, **May**, 39–43.

Raiffa, H. (1982). *The Art of Science of Negotiation*, p. 10. Harvard University Press.

Rubin, J. Z. and Brown, B. R. (1975). *The Social Psychology of Bargaining and Negotiation*, p. 18. Academic Press.

Further reading

Armstrong, G. and Kotler, P. (2000). Integrated marketing communications: personal selling and sales promotion. *Marketing: An Introduction*, 5th edn, Chapter 13. Prentice Hall.

Blythe, J. (2001). Marketing communications and promotional tools. *Essentials of Marketing*, Chapter 9. Person Educational Ltd.

Cateora, P. R. and Ghauri, P. N. (2000). Personal selling and negotiations. *International Marketing: European Edition*, Chapter 17. McGraw Hill.

Davies, M. (1998). Marketing communications 2: public relations, personal selling and direct mail. *Understanding Marketing*, Chapter 9. Prentice Hall.

Jobber, D. and Lancaster, G. (2000). *Selling and Sales Management*. Pitman Publishing.

Keegan, W. J. and Green, M. S. (2000). Global marketing communications decisions 2: sales promotions, personal selling, special forms of marketing communications. *Global Marketing*, 2nd edn, Chapter 15. New Media, Prentice Hall.

Lancaster, G. A. and Reynolds, P. L. (1998). Managing selling. *Marketing*, Chapter 11. Macmillan Press.

Lancaster, G. A. and Reynolds, P. L. (1999). Personal selling. *Introduction to Marketing: A Step by Step Guide to All the Tools of Marketing*, Chapter 7. Kogan Page.

Mancrief, W. (1986). Selling activity and sales position taxonomies for industrial salesforces. *Journal of Marketing Research*, **Aug**, 261–70.

McMurry, R. N. (1961). The mystique of super salesmanship. *Harvard Business Review*, **Mar–Apr**, 114.

Plamer, A. (2000). Selling and sales management. *Principles of Marketing*, Chapter 18. Oxford University Press.

Channels of distribution

9

9.1 Introduction

This chapter investigates the routes marketing companies take when attempting to ensure that their goods and services reach the intended market or market segments.

The term 'distribution system' refers to that complex of agents, wholesalers and retailers through which manufacturers move products to their intended markets. Marketing channels are usually made up of independent firms who are in business to make a profit. These are known as marketing intermediaries or *middlemen*. Distribution outlets can include combinations of owned and independent outlets, or arrangements like franchising.

Definition
The term 'distribution system' refers to that complex of agents, wholesalers and retailers through which manufacturers move products to their intended markets.

9.2 Direct versus indirect systems

In designing a distribution system, a manufacturer must make a policy choice between selling directly to customers and employing salespeople, and using intermediaries – i.e. selling through agents, wholesalers and retailers. Initially, the decision is usually based on cost factors. Distribution costs are largely a function of:

- the number of potential customers in the market

- how concentrated or dispersed they are

- how much each will buy in a given period

- costs associated with the practical side of the distributive operation (e.g. transport, warehousing and stockholding, all of which are dealt with in detail in Chapter 10).

If the manufacturer has a large enough potential sales volume, there may be a strong case for selling direct and employing a sales force.

Industrial goods manufacturers tend to use direct selling and often deliver direct to the user/customer, although in some cases wholesalers or 'factors' are used. Consumer goods manufacturers tend to use a network of marketing intermediaries because of the dispersion and large numbers of potential customers. Again, there are exceptions (e.g. Avon Cosmetics, which sells direct to homes through agents). Most often manufacturers will sell to wholesalers, who in turn break bulk, add on a mark-up and sell to retailers. However, with the increased size and power of the large food multiples, manufacturers sell direct to them and they perform their own wholesaling function. Whether selling through retail chains, or wholesalers then retailers, the important point is that the manufacturer relies on these middlemen for ultimate marketing success, as it is these intermediaries who have the responsibility of taking the product to the ultimate consumer.

9.3 The nature of distribution

Distribution arrangements tend to be long term in nature. Because of this time horizon, channel decisions are usually classed as strategic, rather than tactical or operational ones. There are two reasons for treating channel decisions in this way:

Key point
Distribution arrangements tend to be long term in nature.

1 Channel decisions have a direct effect on the rest of the firm's marketing activities. For example, the selection of target markets is affected by, and in turn affects, channel design and choice. Similarly, decisions about individual marketing mix elements (e.g. pricing) must reflect a company's channel choice.

2 Once established, a company's channel system may be difficult to change, at least in the short term. Although distribution channels are not impervious to change and new channels emerge as old, established channels fade, few companies are able to change their channel structure with the same ease of frequency as they can change other marketing mix variables like price or advertising strategies. Because channel arrangements are likely to change slowly over time, manufacturers need continually to monitor the distributive environment and reassess their existing channel structure in an attempt to exploit and capitalise on any change. However, they should be aware of developments that are taking place, so as not to be caught off guard. Nowhere is this truer than in the case of the speed of development of the Internet as a direct retailing medium, which has caught many traditional distributors off balance.

9.4 Strategic elements of channel choice

An important consideration for marketing management in formulating channel policy and the number of marketing intermediaries used is the degree of market exposure sought by the company for its products. Three distribution strategies, resulting in varying degrees of market exposure, can be distinguished: intensive, exclusive and selective.

9.4.1 Intensive distribution

Products, when viewed by consumers in their totality, are seen as a *bundle of attributes* or satisfactions, including possession utilities and time and place utilities. Producers of convenience goods and certain raw materials aim to stock their products in as many outlets as possible (i.e. an intensive distribution strategy). The dominant factor in the marketing of such products is their place utility. Producers of convenience goods such as pens, confectionery and cigarettes try to enlist every possible retail outlet, ranging from multiples to independent corner shops, to create maximum brand exposure and maximum convenience to customers. With such products, every exposure to the customer is an opportunity to buy, and the image of the outlet used is of less significance in the customer's mind than the impression of the product.

9.4.2 Exclusive distribution

For some products, producers deliberately limit the number of intermediaries handling their products. They may wish to develop a high-quality brand image. Exclusive distribution to recognised official distributors can enhance the prestige of the product. Exclusive (or solus) distribution is a policy of granting dealers exclusive rights to distribute in a certain geographical area. It is often used in conjunction with a policy of exclusive dealing, where the manufacturer requires the dealer not to carry competing lines. Car manufacturers have such arrangements with their dealers. With the arrangement goes a stipulation by the manufacturer that the distributor is able to uphold appropriate repair, service and warranty handling facilities. By granting exclusive distribution the manufacturer gains more control over intermediaries regarding price, credit and promotional policies; greater loyalty, and more determined selling of the company's products.

9.4.3 Selective distribution

This policy lies somewhere between the extremes just described. The manufacturing firm may not have the resources adequately to service or influence the policies of all the intermediaries who are willing to carry a particular product. Instead of spreading its marketing effort over the whole range of possible outlets, it concentrates on the most promising.

Channel members should have certain facilities in order to store and market products effectively – for example, frozen food products require that intermediaries have adequate deep freeze display facilities. Specialised resources may be necessary; for example, certain ethical pharmaceutical products require that intermediaries are capable of offering advice as to the use and limitations of the product, so such products might be restricted to pharmacies. The product may have a carefully cultivated brand image that could be damaged by being stocked in limited line discount outlets where products are displayed in a functional way to reduce overheads and the final price. Selective distribution is used where the facilities, resources or image of the outlet can have a direct impact on customers' impressions of the product. An example here is 'upmarket' brands of perfume.

9.5 Changing channel systems

Cravens (1988) stated that channels do change and manufacturers often respond too slowly to such evolution. Individual changes may be small when viewed in isolation, but cumulative change can be significant. When planning long-term channel strategy, companies need to monitor such change and attempt to anticipate future macro-environmental developments. A good example of such change that is now upon us has just been cited in relation to Internet developments.

Change occurs at all levels in a channel system, but it has been very noticeable in UK retailing. Significant changes in retailing practice have occurred over the past three decades. This period has seen an increasing polarity in the distribution turnover of retail firms. At one end of the spectrum there are large-scale operators: multiples, discount chains and the co-operative movement. At the other end there are many small shops. Some of these are completely independent retailers who purchase from wholesalers and 'cash-and-carry' outlets, or who have joint purchasing agreements through 'retail buying associations'. Others are linked to wholesalers through the voluntary chain/group movement, sometimes called symbol shops (e.g. Spar), and are similar to franchises, explained later in this chapter. Numbers of shops have declined with an increased concentration of market share in the hands of a small number of large multiples that have grown at the expense of co-operatives, independents and smaller multiples.

Key point
When planning long-term channel strategy, companies need to monitor change and attempt to anticipate future macro-environmental developments.

Vignette 9.1

EMAZING.Com gives you a home repair tip of the day for free – and sells you lots of other things at the same time

EMAZING.com is an Internet service of AMAZING Inc. based in the USA. It offers a free subscription to an 'AMAZING – home repair tip of the day' service on the Internet. It is a very interesting site, and of great value to DIY enthusiasts all over the world. The site can be accessed on www.home-html@rtn.emazing.com, although many people come across the service as an advertising portal on another Internet site and access via a 'hot link'. On Wednesday 7 March 2001, for example, the 'tip of the day' was on the subject of 'troubleshooting'. Troubleshooting is the process of locating and repairing mechanical breakdowns. In the home, this might be the central heating system, the electricity system or the water supply system. The 'home tip' explains the process the DIY enthusiast should follow to eliminate all possible causes of the breakdown in a systematic manner, and then go on to identify the problem correctly.

The actual advice is only a few sentences long, but nonetheless often proves to be a useful tip to the homeowner. The rest of the Internet site is full of advertising and 'hot links' to other sites The object of these other sites is to sell you goods and services rather than simply offer you free advice. The free advice is really a 'honey trap' to get you interested and encourage you to visit the site and sign up for the daily, free service.

On the date given above the site was offering DIY books for Readers Digest, CD of the day, Gift of the day, DVD of the day and so on. The site also offered consumer finance at low interest rates and the chance to obtain a Visa Card, again at an especially introductory low rate of interest. Other products and services on offer were related to birthdays, holidays and security systems. EMAZING.com is an effective and novel channel of distribution system for a whole range of products and services people are likely to order over the Internet. It is an enjoyable site to visit, and gives the visitor something of value for nothing in the form of its 'household tip of the day'.

9.6 The wheel-of-retailing: growth of multiples, 'one-stop' and 'non-shop' shopping

Definition
The *wheel-of-retailing* concept refers to evolutionary change in retailing, and is similar to the product life cycle concept.

The *wheel-of-retailing* concept refers to evolutionary change in retailing, and is similar to the product life cycle concept that is dealt with in Chapter 12. The concept states that new retailing institutions enter the market as low status, low margin, low price operations, and then move upmarket towards higher status, higher margin and higher priced positions. New forms of retailing can be seen as going through various life cycle stages (i.e. introduction, growth, maturity and decline). The wheel-of-retailing appears to be turning with ever-increasing speed, with each new retail innovation taking less time to reach the maturity stage. For example, evidence suggests that it took approximately 50 years for the older-style department stores to reach the maturity (i.e. steady sales) stage; supermarkets took about 25 years, and hypermarkets only 10 years. The concept is even analogous to Charles Darwin's theory of evolution of plants and animals, which proposed that a changing environment leads to adaptation and hence evolution. Darwin also explained that there is no need for adaptation in a stable environment; there has to be change for the evolutionary process to occur. We will look at some of the environmental changes that have taken place which have instigated adaptation and evolution in retailing over the relatively short period just described.

9.6.1 The search for economies of scale

In search for greater profits, larger retail chains devised larger scale methods of operation and supermarkets have culminated in today's hypermarkets (stores with at least 50 000 square feet of selling space) and even larger 'megamarkets'. Each new retailing mode has led to greater economies of scale and better financial return.

9.6.2 The abolition of resale price maintenance (RPM)

Until the mid-1960s manufacturers' resale prices were protected by resale price maintenance (RPM), under which retailers had to sell at prices stipulated by the manufacturers; if they sold goods below the stipulated price, further supplies could be withheld.

RPM protected small independent retailers from price competition from larger multiples because these larger operators were legally unable to pass on their cost economies to customers. There were some very well-reported cases of multiples, notably Tesco, having supplies withheld for selling below a manufacturer's stipulated price (i.e. too cheaply), which was, of course, the best publicity that could have been attained.

Because RPM restricted price competition retailers relied heavily on non-price competition, and the level of service in many stores was arguably higher than consumers needed, since they would have preferred lower prices.

RPM was abolished by the Resale Prices Act (1964). This resulted in many small shops, and a number of wholesalers who traditionally supplied such outlets, going out of business. The market share that was 'freed up' fell into the hands of more efficient and powerful multiples, who used their purchasing economies to compete on price and pass savings on to customers. Thus, multiples expanded at the expense of independents and the wholesalers who supplied them, as well as the co-operative movement. The latter was ideally placed to take advantage of this environmental change (because of its size), but was too slow to react. This was largely because of its decentralised structure in terms of the movement consisting of a large number of individual retail societies whose democratically elected members (their customers) controlled them. Ironically, the co-operative movement (which was founded in Rochdale in 1844) was the first to innovate 'self-service' facilities during the Second World War. This was, however, done for social reasons of freeing up labour to help in the war effort, and at the end of the war the movement did not capitalise on this innovation and reverted to personal service.

9.6.3 Selective employment tax (SET)

This was a tax on 'non-productive workers' (i.e. a tax charged on selective occupations) that was introduced in 1966. Its effect was to increase shop workers' wage costs by 7 per cent, as it was the employer, not the employee, who paid the tax. SET made labour more expensive and, relatively speaking, capital investment cheaper. This encouraged many retailers (who were the largest employers of non-productive workers) to invest in capital systems (e.g. central checkout systems) that made them less reliant on labour. This gave a further push to the widespread introduction of self-service shopping. Such large investments meant that operators demanded larger and quicker turnover. Quicker turnover meant that consumer goods had a shorter shelf life, so they were fresher when purchased. Thus, indirectly, SET helped the multiples to expand at the expense of their smaller competitors.

9.6.4 Greater market power of multiples

As the power of the multiples increased they were able to cut out traditional wholesalers and purchase centrally, directly from manufacturers. Consumer goods manufacturers could ill afford not to be included in the multiples' product lines. Consequently, multiples were able to command very advantageous discounts from manufacturers. Independents still had to purchase through traditional wholesalers, and even though some formed wholesale groups through voluntary chains/groups, they still had difficulty in matching multiples' prices. Indeed, multiples in the 1970s were dubbed with the description 'pile it high; sell it cheap'.

The early to mid-1980s saw the introduction of 'own label' merchandise – ranges of brands commissioned by individual multiple chains bearing their own logotype (logo). In the 1970s, multiples introduced their own 'economy brands' without any logo, the idea being that such merchandise was a cheap alternative to manufacturer branded and packaged merchandise. However, consumers quickly realised that such goods, although cheaper, were usually of inferior quality.

The first operator to bring in 'own label' merchandise was Sainsbury's. Other multiple operators were quick to follow, with the result that power within food retailing channels has passed from manufacturers' brands to retailers' brands. Most food manufacturers now supply retail chains with 'own label' merchandise, with a few notable exceptions (e.g. Nestlé and Kellogg) who still do not supply 'own label' because they feel that this could diminish their power within the channel (which relies on strong brands). A feature of their advertising is along the lines of: 'you will only find XXXX in an XXXX jar/pack'. This makes it clear to customers that they do not manufacture for multiples (even though their brands are often displayed alongside multiples' 'own brands', often in similar packaging). Their advertising emphasises the 'uniqueness' (USP) of their product (i.e. product characteristics that cannot be replicated).

Despite these few manufacturers who do not supply 'own label' products, in the UK the power within retail channels has definitely switched from manufacturers to retailers – unlike many other countries, where power still rests with manufacturers of strongly branded products.

Some measure of the extent of change in retailing in the UK is the fact that co-operatives had more than 25 per cent share of the retail market in the early 1960s, with independent retailers commanding over 50 per cent. Now the co-operative share is down to less than 6 per cent, Tesco is more than 15 per cent and Sainsbury's is more than 12 per cent. The total share of independents' market share, including those who belong to voluntary groups, is now down to 20 per cent.

9.6.5 Scrambled merchandising

In an affluent society like the UK, consumption of food products is relatively income-inelastic. In other words, people do not buy more food when they have more money. Instead, they tend to 'trade up' and consume better quality foods. Therefore, in order to expand their businesses large multiples have diversified, stocking non-food products to further their turnover and profits. Many multiples now sell such items as electrical goods, garden supplies and clothing, and many no longer seem like 'food stores'. However, some of these multiples have decided to go back to their core business of food retailing, or clearly differentiate such business from their core activities (as in Sainsbury's Homebase), because of the confused *scrambled merchandising* images associated with non-food retailing.

9.6.6 'One-stop' shopping

Multiples have introduced hypermarkets and megastores to capitalise on the desire for the concept of 'one-stop' shopping. As well as shopping for most of a family's needs (from gardening materials and electrical goods to food) under one roof, there is an increasing tendency for customers to shop less frequently (perhaps fortnightly or even monthly instead of weekly). Payment is increasingly made by credit card or switch cards, where the customer's bank account is debited immediately the transaction has been completed, rather than with cash. These trends have been brought about, and will continue for the following reasons:

1 Growth in car ownership and the number of two-car families. This has brought increased mobility and the ability to travel to 'out-of-town' sites. Such stores have large catchment areas, sufficient to warrant the investment in land, building and facilities. Usually, major operators are also able to attract ancillary shops such as travel agents, newsagents and florists to open shops on the same site, so the complex becomes like a little 'town' in itself. An extension of this idea is the establishment of 'metro centres', which are usually located near large urban conurbations. Such complexes are designed for car travel as parking is easy, and these complexes are closed to the elements (e.g. covered walkways from car parks as well as the retail centre itself). The idea is not only to make shopping a more 'pleasant' experience, but also to encourage larger, bulk purchases.

2 A greater proportion of married women work, which means that family time is often at a premium, especially if there are children to look after. Time is no longer available for the luxury of 'browsing' in the shopping sense. The rise in average total family income has meant that a wife's income is often a major contributor to the household budget, especially now that the notion of 'equal pay for equal work' has legal status.

3 Greater ownership of freezers coupled with wider car ownership means that shoppers can transport and effectively store larger volumes of food, thereby benefiting economically from bulk purchasing. In addition, universal microwave cooker ownership has boosted sales of 'instant' meals, many of which are cooked from frozen.

4 A shift in the population from urban to suburban centres has occurred (unlike in poorer countries, where the shift is usually toward the cities). City congestion discourages car drivers, who prefer to shop in large out-of-town establishments where parking is adequate and usually free. However, this trend has recently been reversed with the 'gentrification' of some inner city areas to provide high capacity living accommodation mainly for younger people.

5 The 'division of labour' within marriage is no longer clearly defined. 'Modern' husbands, especially those in the B, C1 and C2 social categories, share roles previously regarded as being the province of their wives. They now help with shopping unselfconsciously, and share tasks like looking after children, which most husbands 30 years ago would not have considered.

Key point
Multiples have introduced hypermarkets and megastores to capitalise on the desire for the concept of 'one-stop' shopping.

'Family shopping' (with a far wider range of merchandise being offered) has now become the 'norm'.

Vignette 9.2

Staples Inc. put office supplies at the very centre of the retailing experience

Office supplies were something that concerned businesses, and were generally a pretty 'dry and dreary' sort of purchase. The shops selling office supplies were usually out of the way places, often located in the less visited areas of town and cities or on 'industrial' type estates. The products on offer were also fairly mundane and standard. Shopping for office supplies was a necessary evil conducted by those responsible for furnishing offices in corporations, or by the owners of smaller firms. The general public had not usually heard off the office supply company, and had no business or interest in shopping there.

Staples has changed all of this, and has brought office supplies into the centre of many peoples' shopping experience. Most people (at least in the countries where Staples have a presence) have heard of the company, and many people have visited a branch and actually purchased something, if only some replacement staples. Staples have located into the new retail parks, which are sprouting up on the edge of town centres both in the USA and Europe. Staples' retail operations in the UK are located next to the likes of Curry's, B&Q DIY Superstores, PC World and other major retail 'sheds' on free parking, close to town sites. People see the Staples store when shopping for other things, and often go in just to see what it's all about. Many of Staples' retail customers have nothing to do with business. Children like the store because they can stock up on things they need for school. Many people work from home today, and need supplies for their home 'office' or study areas.

Staples' product and service range offers a comprehensive office supply facility to customers. Everything a small business could possibly want is available under one roof. Large organisations also order from Staples. Increasingly, the educational market is using Staples. Many people are studying at home using distance learning methods and on-line program for degrees and professional qualifications such as law and accountancy. Many school and college children have a workstation in their bedroom and a personal computer. Staples sell PCs and all the additional products required by the PC user, from chairs and computer desks to paper and printer cartridges. It sells cash tills, mobile telephones, furniture and software, and offers business services such as printing, money management, legal and insurance, sales and marketing and office operations. Products can be purchased using the Staples catalogue over the telephone, or from their Web page.

In the Spring of 1985, Tom Stemberg was fired as president of First National Supermarkets in the USA. He had graduated from the prestigious Harvard University Business School with an MBA degree in 1973. His business interests were in the retailing field. He decided to set up on his own, and was looking for a retailing idea. He was convinced that the way office supplies were marketed, especially to the smaller business, needed improving. By offering very low prices he was certain he could get customers to come to the store and select and carry away their own supplies rather than have them delivered by a standard office supply company. He also thought that he could improve the product mix and the general design of things such as office furniture to appeal to the more style-conscious customer. He decided to locate the stores where people could see them, in large purpose-built 'sheds' in the main retail parks. Stemberg has been very successful in his choice of channel strategy, and the company continues to expand and prosper.

9.7 'Business format' franchising

To franchise means to grant freedom to do something (derived from the French verb *affranchir*, meaning 'to free'). Franchising is a system of marketing and distribution constituting a contractual relationship between a seller (franchiser) and the seller's distributive outlets (owned by franchisees). The common basic features of franchising are:

1 The ownership by an organisation (the franchiser) of a name, idea, secret process or specialised piece of equipment or goodwill

2 A licence granted by the franchiser to the franchisee that allows the franchisee to profitably exploit that name, idea or product

3 The licence agreement includes regulations concerning the operation of the business in which licensees exploit their rights

4 A payment by the licensee (e.g. an initial fee, royalty or share of profits) for the rights that are obtained.

Franchising is highly developed in the USA, and although it is popular in the UK it is a relatively recent phenomenon. This has led people to believe that it is an 'imported' idea. However, its roots can be traced back to the Middle Ages, when important 'personages' were granted the right to collect revenues in return for various services and considerations (e.g. to carry out trades to the exclusion of others in certain areas).

The 'tied' public house (where the publican only sells ale brewed by the brewery to which it is 'tied') is an example of franchising that has existed in Britain since the eighteenth century. This has been ameliorated since the early 1990s because monopolies legislation has compelled breweries to sell off many 'tied houses', as it was viewed as a restrictive practice. Franchising has come a long way since its early origins. It has been taken from the UK to the USA, where it evolved and developed, and has been re-exported back to the UK in a more sophisticated form.

The development of franchising in the USA dates back to the end of the American Civil War (1865), when the Singer Sewing Machine Company franchised exclusive sales territories to financially independent operators. In 1898, General Motors used independently owned businesses to increase its distribution outlets. Rexall followed with franchised drugstores, and the soft-drink manufacturers Coca-Cola and Pepsi-Cola licensed bottling.

The modern American concept of the *business format franchise* has gathered strength in Britain since the early 1960s. It contains all the

Definition
To franchise means to grant freedom to do something (derived from the French verb *affranchir*, meaning 'to free').

Key point
The modern American concept of the *business format franchise* has gathered strength in Britain since the early 1960s.

Key point
The 'formula' is very
carefully prepared so
as to minimise risk
when opening the
business.

components of a fully developed business system. The franchiser's brand name and business format are used for the exclusive purpose of marketing an agreed product or service from a 'blueprint', with the franchiser providing assistance in organisation, training, merchandising and management, in return for a 'consideration' from the franchisee. The 'formula' is very carefully prepared so as to minimise risk when opening the business. The basic principle that attracts new franchisees is that other people have followed the same scheme, and since they have been successful, new entrants should also be successful. The franchiser (normally a large business) supplies a franchisee with a business package or 'format', a trade name, and specific products or services for sale to the general public. In most cases, the franchisee pays royalties and, in turn, is granted exclusive access to a defined geographical area.

Vignette 9.3

Business format franchising has helped make Dyno-Rod one of the UK's most dynamic service organisations

Dyno-Rod is one of the pioneers of business format franchising within the UK, and one of the founder members of the highly respected British Franchise Association. This is the organisation that acts as an overseeing professional body for the franchise sector and sets high ethical business standards for its members. Dyno-Rod is rated as one of the most dynamic service organisations within the UK and one of the best franchise opportunities available. Dyno-Rod is a business that basically provides a professional service for the cleaning, inspection and refurbishment of pipework, particularly sewers and drains. It may not sound a very attractive business, but it provides good margins and a healthy bottom line.

There is always a need for services such as these from both the general public and industry. Much of the business is repeat business. The organisation offers a 24-hour emergency and contract maintenance basis service to residential, industrial and municipal markets. Dealing with blocked drains is really what the business is all about. The company offers a complete cleaning, maintenance and repair service for all drains and pipework. It offers a specialist surveying service for pipework using a slimline camera (CCTV) system, and also a drain-lining service that avoids the complete replacement of pipework by putting a 'sleeve' within the existing pipe.

The business is a mixture of drain services, which demands good managerial skills. Franchisees usually start with two liveried vans containing all the necessary equipment. This includes specialist tools and hoses, and a television system for drain inspection. At first the business can be run from home, but as it expands dedicated premises are required. Dyno-Rod franchisees operate in a specific geographic territory with a minimum residential population of 500 000 and a good mix of commercial and industrial premises. Dyno-Rod offers its franchisees a complete system of doing business. If the franchisee is taking over an existing operation, then a revenue stream will be on tap from the first day of operation from existing customers. The total package requires about £30 000 of investment, of which £8000 needs to be supplied by the franchisee. The remainder can be financed.

9.8 Growth in 'non-shop' shopping

During the past 30 years, as well as the many developments of new types of stores in retail marketing channels (e.g. supermarkets, hypermarkets, limited line discount stores) there has also been a marked increase in various forms of 'non-shop' selling. These are now discussed.

9.8.1 'Door-to-door' direct selling

This is a relatively expensive operation, but having no wholesaler and retailer margins means that the expense is counterbalanced. Firms that use this type of selling include Avon Cosmetics and Betterware. It means that manufacturers' agents have to build up their clientele among customers in the local community in the expectation that they will purchase from a catalogue on a regular basis.

9.8.2 Party plan

This method of direct selling is popular for products such as cosmetics, plastic ware, kitchenware, jewellery and linen products. A 'party' is organised in the home of a host or hostess, who invites friends and receives a 'consideration' in cash or goods based on the amount that these friends purchase. It is sometimes resented, as friends often feel there is a moral obligation to purchase.

Definition
A 'party' is organised in the home of a host or hostess, who invites friends and receives a 'consideration' in cash or goods based on the amount that these friends purchase.

9.8.3 Automatic vending

This form of retailing has grown dramatically since the 1960s, and is now used for beverages, snacks, confectionery, personal products, cigarettes and sometimes newspapers. Vending machines are placed in convenient locations (e.g. garage forecourts, railway and bus stations, colleges, libraries and factories). Automatic vending also supplies entertainment through jukeboxes and arcade games.

Vending machines can also be used to provide services, as seen by the widespread introduction of cash-dispenser machines provided by financial institutions. As well as dispensing cash, these machines answer balance enquiries, take requests for statements and chequebooks, and receive deposits.

Vignette 9.4

Coca-Cola uses vending machines for maximum distribution of the product

Coca-Cola™ is a world icon of the twentieth century and beyond. Its distinctive name, taste, shape of bottle, and design of label and can graphics make it easily recognisable by virtually everyone.

Coca-Cola is a truly 'world brand' and is in great demand, particularly from the young, all over the world. In developing countries with their emerging markets Coca-Cola is seen as a symbol of Western affluence and capitalist culture. The young aspire to purchase Western goods, whether in Russia or Taiwan, where Coca-Cola is almost viewed as a fashion accessory and as a 'designer drink'.

Coca-Cola Inc. is determined that this demand will be met by making the product widely available in all the areas where it might be expected that someone would want to purchase the product. This is achieved through a policy of intensive distribution using supermarkets, smaller stores, bakeries and sandwich shops, delicatessens, public houses, cafés, sport centres and cinemas, plus a plethora of other less conventional channels. Vending machines are at the centre of Coca-Cola's intensive distribution strategy.

Vending machines offering Coca-Cola and other drinks can be found in every 'nook and cranny' possible – on the various floors of hotels next to the ice machine, in university halls of residence and teaching areas, at schools, sports centres, garages, railways stations, airports, subways, art galleries, museums and a host of other similar locations. If you want a Coca-Cola, no matter what time of the day or night, the company has given you no excuse for not satisfying your desire. Vending machines fill the 'gap' left by the more conventional channels for this beverage. The vending machine itself is often designed in Cola-Cola livery, and acts as a further advertising source for the product. The company will continue to use innovatory channel strategies, and new developments in vending technology will further strengthen the firm's intensive coverage of the world market for this product.

9.8.4 Mail order catalogues

Definition
Businesses that use mail order selling are either catalogue or non-catalogue.

Businesses that use mail order selling are either catalogue or non-catalogue. The former relies heavily upon comprehensive catalogues to obtain sales, but sometimes uses local agents to deal with order collection and administration. Products can be purchased interest free, and extended credit terms are available for major purchases. There are also a number of specialist mail order houses dealing with a limited range of often 'unusual' or 'exclusive' lines that are difficult to find in shops.

Non-catalogue mail order usually relies on press and magazine advertising, and is used to sell a single product or limited range of products. 'Craft' products are often promoted in this way.

9.8.5 Other 'direct' marketing techniques

Definition
The use of direct mail is where a promotional letter and order form is sent through the post.

The use of direct mail is where a promotional letter and order form is sent through the post. Organisations using this method include book and record clubs. Television is also used, with orders being placed through a telephone call to a freephone number and paid for with a credit card. Sometimes impersonality is carried to the ultimate through an answering machine. Telephone ordering is often combined with newspaper advertising, especially in colour supplements, as described in Chapter 7 under the discussion of telemarketing and direct mail techniques.

9.8.6 Future developments

Television shopping via on-line computers is developing and will become a more popular medium along with the Internet. As opportunities for leisure activities increase (e.g. sports centres and specialist activity clubs), this kind of shopping will become popular because it will free up more time to pursue such activities. This very direct kind of shopping should also make goods cheaper, since orders can be placed directly with the manufacturers without the high costs of intermediaries and their associated overheads. Credit facilities will be immediately available through electronic debiting. As computer systems become more sophisticated and people become less 'afraid' of this new technology, it should become the growth area of retailing in the future.

Key point
As computer systems become more sophisticated and people become less 'afraid' of this new technology, it should become the growth area of retailing in the future.

9.9 Summary

✓ This chapter has dealt principally with channel arrangements for consumer products, and has not said too much about industrial or organisational channels. For these latter routes options are usually limited, as their preference is to deal direct. Chapter 10 provides a fuller discussion of the logistical implications of organisational channels, and the notion of the decision-making unit has already been covered in Chapter 6.

✓ Chapter 10 covers the second part of the 'place', or placement, element of the 'Four Ps', which is the subject of 'logistics'.

Questions

1 *Retailing*
How do you account for the fact that non-shop selling has, in recent years, been one of the fastest growing areas of distribution?

2 *Channels*
What should an organisation consider when it contemplates changing its channel of distribution?

3 *Distribution*
In what circumstances would a company wish to adopt (a) intensive distribution, (b) selective distribution, (c) exclusive distribution?

4 *Channel power*
How has 'power' within retail channels switched from brands to retail chains over the past 30 years?

References

Cravens, D. W. (1988). Gaining strategic marketing advantage. *Business Horizons*, **Sep/ Oct**, 44–5.

Further reading

Adcock, D. (2000). Channel management and value added relations. *Marketing Strategies for Competitive Advantage*, Chapter 12. John Wiley & Sons.

Armstrong, G. and Kotler, P. (2000). Distribution channels and logistics management. *Marketing: An Introduction*, 5th edn, Chapter 10. Prentice Hall.

Blythe, J. (2001). Distribution. *Essentials of Marketing*, Chapter 8. Person Educational Ltd.

Cateora, P. R. and Ghauri, P. N. (2000). The international distribution system. *International Marketing: European Edition*, Chapter 15. McGraw Hill.

Davies, M. (1998). Distribution. *Understanding Marketing*, Chapter 8. Prentice Hall.

Hollander, S. C. (1960). The wheel of retailing. *Journal of Marketing*, **Jul**, 37–42.

Keegan, W. J. and Green, M. S. (2000) Global marketing channels and physical distribution. *Global Marketing*, 2nd edn, Chapter 13. Prentice Hall.

Lancaster, G. A. and Reynolds, P. L. (1998). Channels of distribution. *Marketing*, Chapter 9. Macmillan Press.

Lancaster, G. A. and Reynolds, P. L. (1999). Channels of distribution. *Introduction to Marketing: A Step by Step Guide to All the Tools of Marketing*, Chapter 12. Kogan Page.

Plamer, A. (2000). Channel intermediaries. *Principles of Marketing*, Chapter 14. Oxford University Press.

Rosenbloom, B. (1991). *Marketing Channels: A Management View*, p. 212. The Dryden Press.

Physical distribution management 10

10.1 Introduction

Chapter 9 described the decisions that must be taken when a company organises a channel or network of intermediaries who take responsibility for the management of goods as they move from the producer to the consumer. Each channel member must be carefully selected, and the company must decide what type of relationship it seeks with each of its intermediate partners. Having established such a network, the organisation must next consider how these goods can be efficiently transferred, in the physical sense, from the place of manufacture to the place of consumption.

Physical distribution management (PDM) is concerned with *ensuring the product is in the right place at the right time.*

'Place' has always been thought of as being the least dynamic of the 'Four Ps'. Marketing practitioners and academics have tended to concentrate on the more conspicuous aspects of marketing. It is now recognised that PDM is a critical area of overall marketing management, and much of its expertise is 'borrowed' from military practice. During the Second World War and the Korean and Vietnam Wars, supplies officers had to perform extraordinary feats of PDM, in terms of food, clothing, ammunition, weapons and a whole range of support equipment having to be transported across the world. The military skill that marketing has adopted and applied to PDM is that of logistics. Marketing management realised that distribution could be organised in a scientific way and so the concept of business logistics developed, focusing attention on and increasing the importance of PDM.

As marketing analysis became increasingly sophisticated, managers became more aware of the costs of physical distribution. Whilst the military must win battles, the primary aim of business is to provide customer satisfaction in a manner that results in profit for the company. Business logistical techniques can be applied to PDM so that costs and customer satisfaction are optimised. There is little point in making large savings in the cost of distribution if, in the long run, sales are lost because of customer dissatisfaction. Similarly, it does not make economic sense to provide a level of service that is not really required by the customer and leads to erosion of profits. This cost/service balance is a basic dilemma that faces physical distribution managers.

Definition
Physical distribution management (PDM) is concerned with ensuring the product is in the right place at the right time.

191

A final reason for the growing importance of PDM as a marketing function is the increasingly demanding nature of the business environment. In the past, it was not uncommon for companies to hold large inventories of raw materials and components. Although industries and individual firms differ widely in their stockholding policies, nowadays stock levels are kept to a minimum wherever possible. Holding stock is wasting working capital, for it is not earning money for the company. A more financially analytical approach by management has combined to move the responsibility for carrying stock onto the supplier and away from the customer. Gilbert and Strebel (1989) pointed out that this has a 'domino' effect throughout the marketing channel, with each member putting pressure on the next to provide higher levels of service.

A logistical issue facing physical distribution managers today is the increasing application by customers of just-in-time management techniques or lean manufacturing. This topic was discussed in Chapter 4, but it is re-emphasised here. Hutchins (1988) stresses that companies who demand 'JIT' service from their suppliers carry only a few hours' stock of material and components, and rely totally on supplier service to keep their production running. This demanding distribution system is supported by company expediters whose task it is to 'chase' the progress of orders and deliveries, not only with immediate suppliers, but right along the chain of supply (called 'supply chain integration'). Lean manufacturing has been widely adopted throughout the automotive industry, where companies possess the necessary purchasing power to impose such delivery conditions on their suppliers. Their large purchasing power also necessitates stringent financial controls, and huge financial savings can be made in the reduction or even elimination of stockholding costs where this method of manufacturing is employed.

Definition

Physical distribution management (PDM) is concerned with the flow of goods from the receipt of an order until the goods are delivered to the customer.

To think of the logistical process merely in terms of transportation is much too narrow a view. Physical distribution management (PDM) is concerned with the flow of goods from the receipt of an order until the goods are delivered to the customer. In addition to transportation, PDM involves close liaison with production planning, purchasing, order processing, material control and warehousing. All these areas must be managed so that they interact efficiently with each other to provide the level of service that the customer demands and at a cost that the company can afford.

Vignette 10.1

Virtual logistics: top Web research firm Alexa Research says Web traffic is becoming less concentrated

Alexa Research is a leading Web intelligence and traffic measurement organisation based in the USA. It uses a number of mathematical and statistical measures to establish trends in the use of the Internet as a commercial distribution network. The most recent trend, established by monitoring Web traffic over the last 6 months of 2000, is that Web traffic in general is increasing quite dramatically and that the top Web sites are facing severe competition from other Web sites – i.e. the increased traffic is actually visiting a greater range of Web sites, and the top sites are seeing less congestion in traffic. However, despite the shift in concentration Alexa Research has established that the 50 leading web sites still account for 25 per cent of all Web traffic. It is very much a 'Pareto' type situation, where a relatively small proportion of sites accounts for a large proportion of site visits (see the work of economist Vilfredo Pareto, 1848–1923).

Research shows that in the period under review, the top 10 Web sites accounted for 11 per cent fewer page views at the end of the period than at the beginning. Among the 100 most popular Web sites, research found that the Web was 12.2 per cent less concentrated. Amongst the top 1000 sites, it was found that concentration was 9.4 per cent less. Despite the changes, one in every four pages viewed on the Web was at one of the top 50 sites, and half of all the pages on the Web were viewed at the top 1210 sites.

Generally, the research seems to show that the top Web sites still manage to pull in billions of page views each month, but that their relative share of overall Web traffic is falling. As people are becoming more used to the Web they seem to be coming more confident, and are branching out and exploring different sites. However, by far the largest amount of traffic is still visiting a very small proportion of the millions of sites on the Web. An additional indication of decreasing top Web site concentration, and an increase in general Web traffic in general, is that a larger number of sites are achieving large monthly 'hits' to their sites. Research shows that 17 sites managed more than one billion hits in January 2001, whereas in June 2000 only four sites achieved this number.

10.2 Definitions

This chapter considers the four principal components of PDM:

1 Order processing

2 Stock levels or inventory

3 Warehousing

4 Transportation.

PDM is concerned with ensuring that the individual efforts that go to make up the distributive function, are optimised so that a common objective is realised. This is called the '*systems approach*' to distribution management, and a major feature of PDM is that these functions are integrated.

Because PDM has a well-defined scientific basis, this chapter presents some of the analytical methods that management uses to assist in the development of an efficient logistics system. There are two central themes that should be taken into account:

1 The success of an efficient distribution system relies on integration of effort. An overall service objective can be achieved, even though it may appear that some individual components of the system are not performing at maximum efficiency.

Definition
PDM is concerned with ensuring that the individual efforts that go to make up the distributive function, are optimised so that a common objective is realised.

2 It is never possible to provide maximum service at a minimum cost. The higher the level of service required by the customer, the higher the cost. Having decided on the necessary level of service, a company must then consider ways of minimising costs, which should never be at the expense of, or result in, a reduction of the predetermined service level.

10.3 The distribution process

The distribution process begins when a supplier receives an order from a customer. The customer is not too concerned with the design of the supplier's distributive system, nor with any supply problems. In practical terms, the customer is only concerned with the efficiency of the supplier's distribution – that is, the likelihood of receiving goods at the time requested. *Lead-time* is the period of time that elapses between the placing of an order and receipt of the goods. This can vary according to the type of product and the type of market and industry being considered. Lead-time in the shipbuilding industry can be measured in fractions or multiples of years, whilst in the retail sector days and hours are common measures. Customers make production plans based on the lead-time agreed when the order is placed. Customers now expect that the quotation will be adhered to, and a late delivery is no longer acceptable in most purchasing situations.

10.3.1 Order processing

Order processing is the first of the four stages in the logistical process. The efficiency of order processing has a direct effect on lead times. Orders are received from the sales team through the sales department. Many companies establish regular supply routes that remain relatively stable over a period of time, providing that the supplier performs satisfactorily. Very often contracts are drawn up and repeat orders (forming part of the initial contract) are made at regular intervals during the contract period. Taken to its logical conclusion, this effectively does away with ordering and leads to what is called '*partnership sourcing*'. This is an agreement between the buyer and seller to supply a particular product or commodity as and when required without the necessity of negotiating a new contract every time an order is placed.

Key point
Order-processing systems should function quickly and accurately.

Order-processing systems should function quickly and accurately. Other departments in the company need to know as quickly as possible that an order has been placed, and the customer must have rapid confirmation of the order's receipt and the precise delivery time. Even before products are manufactured and sold, the level of office efficiency is a major contributor to a company's image. Incorrect 'paperwork' and slow reactions by the sales office are often an unrecognised source of ill will between buyers and sellers. When buyers review their suppliers, efficiency of order processing is an important factor in their evaluation.

A good computer system for order processing allows stock levels and delivery schedules to be automatically updated, and management can rapidly obtain an accurate view of the sales position. Accuracy is an important objective of order processing, as are procedures that are designed to shorten the order-processing cycle.

10.3.2 Inventory

Inventory, or stock management, is a critical area of PDM because stock levels have a direct effect on levels of service and customer satisfaction. The optimum stock level is a function of the type of market in which the company operates. Few companies can say that they never run out of stock, but if stock-outs happen regularly then market share will be lost to more efficient competitors. Techniques for determining optimum stock levels are illustrated later in this chapter. The key lies in ascertaining the re-order point. Carrying stock at levels below the re-order point might ultimately mean a stock-out, whereas too high stock levels are unnecessary and expensive to maintain. The stock/cost dilemma is clearly illustrated by the systems approach to PDM, which is dealt with later in this chapter.

Stocks represent *opportunity costs* that occur because of constant competition for the company's limited resources. If the company's marketing strategy requires that high stock levels be maintained, this should be justified by a profit contribution that will exceed the extra stock-carrying costs. Sometimes a company may be obliged to support high stock levels because the lead times prevalent in a given market are particularly short. In such a case, the company must seek to reduce costs in other areas of the PDM 'mix'.

Key point
Stocks represent *opportunity costs* that occur because of constant competition for the company's limited resources.

10.3.3 Warehousing

American marketing texts tend to pay more attention to warehousing than do British texts. This is mainly because of the relatively longer distances involved in distributing in the USA, where it can sometimes take days to reach customers by the most efficient road or rail routes. The logistics of warehousing can, therefore, be correspondingly more complicated in the USA than in the UK. However, the principles remain the same, and indeed the European Union should be viewed as a large 'home market'. Currently, many companies function adequately with their own on-site warehouses from which goods are despatched direct to customers. When a firm markets goods that are ordered regularly but in small quantities, it becomes more logical to locate warehouses strategically around the country. Transportation can be carried out in bulk from the place of manufacture to the respective warehouses, where stocks wait ready for further distribution to the customers. This system is used by large retail chains, except that the warehouses and transportation are owned and operated for them by logistics experts (e.g. BOC Distribution, Excel Logistics and Rowntree Distribution). Levels of service will of course increase when numbers of warehouse locations increase, but cost will increase accordingly. Again, an optimum strategy must be established that reflects the desired level of service.

To summarise, factors that must be considered in the warehouse equation are:

● Location of customers

● Size of orders

- Frequency of deliveries

- Lead times.

10.3.4 Transportation

Transportation usually represents the greatest distribution cost. It is usually easy to calculate, because it can be related directly to weight or numbers of units. Costs must be carefully controlled through the mode of transport selected amongst alternatives, and these must be constantly reviewed. During the past 50 years, road transport has become the dominant transportation mode in the UK. It has the advantage of speed coupled with door-to-door delivery.

The patterns of retailing that have developed, and the pressure caused by low stock holding and short lead times, have made road transport indispensable. When the volume of goods being transported reaches a certain level, some companies purchase their own vehicles, rather than use the services of haulage contractors. However, some large retail chains like Marks and Spencer, Tesco and Sainsbury's have now entrusted all their warehousing and transport to specialist logistics companies.

For some types of goods, transport by rail still has advantages. When lead time is a less critical element of marketing effort, or when lowering transport costs is a major objective, this mode of transport becomes viable. Similarly, when goods are hazardous or bulky in relation to value, and produced in large volumes, then rail transport is advantageous. Rail transport is also suitable for light goods that require speedy delivery (e.g. letter and parcel post).

Except where goods are highly perishable or valuable in relation to their weight, air transport is not usually an attractive transport alternative for distribution within the UK, where distances are relatively short in aviation terms. For long-distance overseas routes it is popular. Here it has the advantage of quick delivery compared to sea transport, and without the cost of the bulky and expensive packaging needed for sea transportation, and higher insurance costs.

Key point
Exporting poses particular transportation problems and challenges.

Exporting poses particular transportation problems and challenges. Chapter 15 discusses the need for the exporter's services to be such that the customer is scarcely aware that the goods purchased have been imported. Therefore, above all, export transportation must be reliable.

The development of roll-on roll-off (RORO) cargo ferries has greatly assisted UK exporters who distinguish between European and Near-European markets that can usually be served by road once the North Sea has been crossed. 'Deep sea markets', such as the Far East, Australasia and America, are still served by traditional ocean-going freighters, and the widespread introduction of containerisation in the 1970s made this medium more efficient.

The chosen transportation mode should adequately protect goods from damage in transit (a factor just mentioned as making air freight popular over longer routes, as less packaging is needed than for long sea voyages). Not only do damaged goods erode profits, but frequent claims increase insurance premiums and inconvenience customers, endangering future business.

Vignette 10.2

Kleeneze 'clean up' using a multi-level marketing physical distribution system

Kleeneze Ltd is a household products company based in the city of Bristol, UK. The firm has been trading for many years, since 1923 in fact, and is a well-known name within the UK. The company started off producing brushes and selling them door-to-door, using a conventional sales force to sell the products; the sales person also delivered the product to the customer. Today Kleeneze sells a wide range of products, although many of them are still related to the 'core business' of the firm – i.e. household-related merchandise.

It is not so much the product mix the company now offers that has changed radically over the years; as already pointed out, many products are still to do with cleaning and household maintenance. What has changed dramatically from the company's early years is the method of distribution the firm employs. Kleeneze has now changed over to a system of multi-level marketing (MLM), sometimes referred to as 'network marketing', as a distribution system.

The system harnesses the entrepreneurial power of individuals by allowing them to become registered Kleeneze agents by effectively running their own network marketing business under the banner of the Kleeneze corporate brand name. Kleeneze is a direct selling business, engaged in the network marketing of its products and business opportunity. The MLM system employed offers the opportunity for economic independence, personal growth and professional development. The programme offers an opportunity for all those who seek an outlet for their own commercial and entrepreneurial drive. Rewards can be substantial. Part-time agents, selling via catalogue door-to-door, can earn £200 per week. The big rewards come from developing a network of agents and managing them as a team. People start off as a 'direct agent' and can progress to full 'distributor'. The distributor gets downstream commission from all other agents recruited, on the basis of their sales. The distributor also gets further secondary downstream commission on the sales made by further agents recruited by the original agents, and so on. Some full-time agents can realise over £100 000 per year pre-tax.

Kleeneze is a founder member of the Direct Selling Association (DSA), and as such adheres to a strict code of business practice and ethics. The firm is a publicly quoted company on the London Stock Exchange, and has a reputation, built up over many years of successful trading, of being committed to innovation and quality. All their products are fully guaranteed. All of the firm's products are environmentally friendly and biodegradable, and the firm does not test any of its products on animals.

10.4 The systems or 'total' approach to PDM

One of the central themes of this text has been to highlight the need to integrate marketing activities so they combine into a single marketing effort. Because PDM has been neglected in the past, this function has been late in adopting an integrated approach towards it activities. Managers have now become more conscious of the potential of PDM, and recognise that logistical systems should be designed with the total function in mind. A fragmented or disjointed approach to PDM is a principal cause of failure to provide satisfactory service, and causes excessive costs.

Within any PDM structure there is potential for conflict. Individual managers striving to achieve their personal goals can frustrate overall PDM objectives. Sales and marketing management will favour high stock levels, special products and short production runs coupled with frequent deliveries. Against this, the transport manager attempts to reduce costs by selecting more economical but slower transportation methods, or by waiting until a load is full before making a delivery. Financial management will exercise pressure to reduce inventory wherever possible and discourage extended warehousing networks. Production managers will favour long production runs and standard products. It is possible for all these management areas to 'appear' efficient if they succeed in realising their individual objectives, but this might well be at the cost of the chosen marketing strategy not being implemented effectively.

Burbridge (1987) has provided guidelines to how levels of service to customers can be provided at optimal cost. Senior management must communicate overall distribution objectives to all company management, and ensure that they are understood. Ideally, the systems approach to PDM should encompass production and production planning, purchasing and sales forecasting. Included in the systems approach is the concept of total cost, because individual costs are less important than the total cost. The cost of holding high stocks may appear unreasonable, but if high stocks provide a service that leads to higher sales and profits, then the total cost of all the PDM activities will have been effective. Costs are a reflection of distribution strategy, and maximum service cannot be provided at minimum cost.

PDM as a cost centre is worth extensive analysis, as this function is now recognised as a valuable marketing tool in its own right. In homogeneous product markets, where differences in competitive prices may be negligible, service is often the major competitive weapon. Indeed, many buyers pay a premium for products that are consistently delivered on time. Similarly, the salesperson whose company provides a comprehensive spare-parts and service facility has a valuable negotiating tool when discussing prices.

Key point
Distribution is not an adjunct to marketing; it has a full place in the marketing mix and can be an essential component of marketing strategy.

Distribution is not, therefore, an adjunct to marketing; it has a full place in the marketing mix and can be an essential component of marketing strategy. In terms of marketing planning, a well-organised business logistics system can help to identify opportunities as well as supplying quantitative data that can be used to optimise the marketing mix as a whole.

Vignette 10.3

FedEx® Global Logistics provides business with a totally integrated, full-service global logistics facility

The FedEx® Corporation provides integrated transportation, information and logistics solutions through a group of companies that operate as separate strategic business units (SBUs), but also together as an integrated group. The emphasis here is on the word 'integrated', and the FedEx Corporation provides a good example of the need to take a holistic and total cost approach to the subject of logistics management. The FedEx Corporation is a $20 billion global enterprise consisting of the following SBUs:

- FedEx Express, the worlds largest express transportation company
- FedEx Ground, North America's second largest provider of ground small-package delivery
- FedEx Freight, a leading provider of regional freight services
- FedEx Custom Critical, the world's largest surface expedited carrier
- FedEx Trade Networks, a high-tech customs broker and trade facilitator
- FedEx Global Logistics, which offers integrated logistics, technology, and transportation solutions.

FedEx Global Logistics is particularly interesting in the context of this chapter. The subsidiary company specialises in integrated transportation management, integrated logistics and consulting services. The company specialises in targeting the aerospace, automotive, health care, high technology, industrial and consumer products industries. FedEx Global Logistics helps their customer become more efficient and cost effective by streamlining their supply chains. There are three main reasons that customers come to FedEx® Global Logistics:

1 *Cost-effective logistics solutions* with a strategic mix of transportation and logistics services designed to help customers reduce costs

2 *Increased product visibility* across the entire supply chain; information intensive services include crossdock, returns management and merge-in transit logistics

3 *Added convenience* of a third party resource to help manage transportation, audit freight bills, allocate charges appropriately, provide regular electronic invoicing and even operate facilities. The aim is help the customer reduce costs and increase profits.

10.5 Monitoring and control of PDM

The objective of PDM is to get the right goods to the right place at the right time for the least cost.

The objective seems reasonable, although it gives little guidance on specific measures of operational effectiveness. Management needs objectives or criteria that in turn allow meaningful evaluation of performance. This is the basis of monitoring and control.

Definition
The objective of PDM is to get the right goods to the right place at the right time for the least cost.

10.5.1 Basic output of physical distribution systems

The output from any system of physical distribution is the level of customer service. This is a key competitive benefit that companies can offer existing and potential customers to retain or attract business. From a policy point of view, the desired level of service should be at least equivalent to that of major competitors.

Table 10.1 An example of a simple delivery delay analysis

Delivery date	Number of orders	Percentage of total orders
As promised	186	37.2
Days late		
1	71	14.2
2	49	9.8
3	35	7.0
4	38	7.6
5	28	5.6
6	14	2.8
7	13	2.6
8	10	2.0
9	8	1.6
10–14	17	3.4
15–21	15	3.0
22–28	10	2.0
28+	6	1.2
	500	100.0

The level of service is often viewed as the time it takes to deliver an order to a customer, or the percentage of orders that can be met from stock. Other service elements include technical assistance, training and after-sales services. The two most important service elements to the majority of firms are:

1 Delivery – reliability and frequency

2 Stock availability – the ability to meet orders quickly.

To use a simple example, a company's service policy may be to deliver 40 per cent of all orders within seven days from receipt of order. This is an operationally useful and specific service objective that provides a strict criterion for evaluation. A simple delivery delay analysis (see Table 10.1) will inform management whether such objectives are being achieved, or whether corrective action is necessary to alter the actual service level in line with stated objectives. Such an analysis can be updated on receipt of a copy of the despatch note. Management can be provided with a summary, in the form of a management report, from which they can judge whether corrective action is necessary. There can, of course, be over-provision of service, as well as under-provision.

Key point
Provision of customer service is not free, and its cost can be calculated in terms of time and money.

10.5.2 Service elasticity

Provision of customer service is not free, and its cost can be calculated in terms of time and money. This applies particularly in industrial markets, where potential customers often consider service more important than price

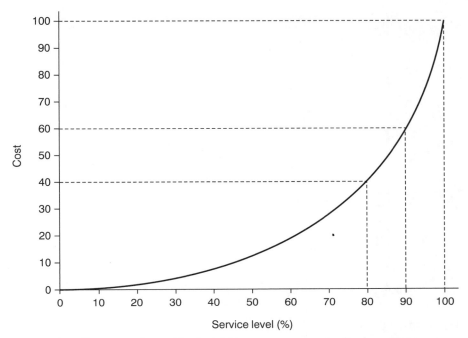

Figure 10.1 Illustration of possible diminishing returns to service level provision.

when deciding to source supplies from a particular company. Service levels are of course a competitive marketing tool for companies supplying the automotive industry, which applies lean manufacturing techniques.

The concept of diminishing returns, for marketing companies wishing to raise their service levels, is illustrated in the following example.

Suppose it costs a marketing firm £x to provide 75 per cent of all orders from stock, with 60 per cent of all orders delivered within seven days of receipt of purchase order.

To increase either of these targets by, say, 10 per cent may well increase the cost of service provision by 20 or 30 per cent. To be able to meet 85 per cent of orders out of stock, stockholding on all inventory items would have to increase. Similarly, to deliver 70 per cent of orders within the specified time may necessitate the purchase of extra transport, which might be under-utilised for a large part of the time. Alternatively, the company might use outside haulage contractors to cope with the extra deliveries, which would add to costs.

The illustration in Figure 10.1 further illustrates this point. In this example, 80 per cent of the total possible service can be provided for approximately 40 per cent of the cost of 100 per cent service provision. To increase general service levels by 10 per cent brings about a cost increase of approximately 18 per cent, while 100 per cent service provision means covering every possible eventuality, which is extremely expensive.

In reality, maximum consumer satisfaction and minimum distribution costs are mutually exclusive, and there has to be some kind of trade-off. The degree

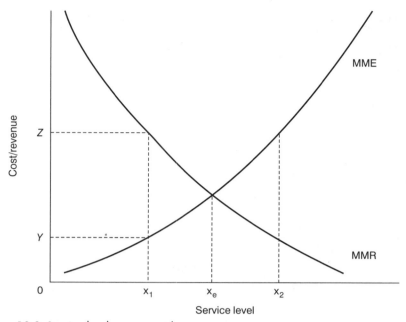

Figure 10.2 Service level versus cost/revenue.

of trade-off will often depend on the degree of service sensitivity or service elasticity in the market or market segments. Two industries may use the same product and may purchase that product from the same supplier, but their criteria for choosing a supplier may be very different. For example, both the sugar processing and oil exploration industries use large high-pressure 'on-line' valves, a sugar processing company to control the flow of its sugar beet pulp in the sugar-making process, and an oil exploration company to control the flow of drilling fluids and crude oil on the exploration platform. The oil industry is highly service-sensitive (or elastic) and when dealing with suppliers price is relatively unimportant, but service levels are critical. Because of the very high costs of operations, and the potential cost of breakdown, every effort is made to cover every contingency. On the other hand, the sugar processing industry is more price-sensitive. Sugar processing is seasonal, with much of the processing work being carried out within two months; so as long as these critical two months are not disrupted, service provision can take a relatively low priority for the remainder of the year.

In theory, service levels should be increased up to the point where the marginal marketing expense equals the marginal marketing response. This follows the economist's profit maximisation criterion of marginal cost being equal to marginal revenue. Figure 10.2 illustrates this point, and it can be seen that the marginal expense (MME) of level of service provision x_1 is Y and the marginal revenue (MMR) is Z. It would pay the firm to increase service levels, since the extra revenue generated by the increased services (MMR) is greater than the cost (MME). At service level x_2, however, the marginal expense (Z) is higher than the marginal revenue (X), so service provision is too high. Clearly, the theoretical point of service optimisation is where marginal marketing expense and marginal marketing response are equal, service level x_e.

Vignette 10.4

UPS Logistics Group teams up with The Ford Motor Company in the USA to facilitate vehicle delivery improvements

The Ford Motor Company teamed up with the logistics experts UPS Logistics Group, a subsidiary of the United Parcels Service, in February 2000. One year later, spectacular improvements in new vehicle delivery times were there for all to see. The strategic alliance has been hailed as a tremendous success by the Ford distribution network. Shorter delivery times are not only improving dealer and customer satisfaction, an important achievement for such a marketing- and customer-driven organisation, but it has also resulted in significant cost savings for Ford.

By working together the two firms have been able to reduce vehicle delivery time by 26 per cent, roughly equivalent to four days off the delivery schedule. The final goal is to reduce vehicle delivery time by 40 per cent, and the alliance between the two companies is well on track to achieve these goals. The delivery improvement initiative is already six months ahead of plan. The real winners are Ford's dealers and customers, who are now much more confident that new vehicles will be delivered on time. By reducing delivery times by four days, Ford has been able to re-engineer the distribution network and save over £1 billion in vehicle inventory and more than £4125 million in annual carrying costs.

Ford and UPS Logistics Group launched the alliance 12 months ago to re-engineer Ford's delivery system and to improve the reliability of Ford's delivery promises to the trade and the final customer. UPS Logistics Group set up a new subsidiary company, known as UPS Autogistics, as a separate strategic business unit (SBU) to deal with the work. Order fulfilment is fundamentally about customer satisfaction. The improvements have resulted in less damaged vehicles as well as faster delivery times. One of the initiative's achievements has been to integrate the supply chain and be able to track the journey of each vehicle along the transport route via a Web-enabled system. The new system provided by UPS Autogistics will give Ford up-to-date information on vehicle transit status at any time. This data can then be forwarded to dealers to keep them informed of progress. The new integrated logistics system has meant huge savings for Ford, good earnings for UPS Autogistics, and improved dealer and customer satisfaction. All in all, the alliance between the two companies has been a 'win win' situation.

10.5.3 Inventory management

Inventory (or stockholding) can be described as 'the accumulation of an assortment of items today for the purpose of providing protection against what may occur tomorrow'. An inventory is maintained to increase profitability through manufacturing and marketing support. Manufacturing support is provided through two types of inventory system:

Definition
Inventory (or stockholding) can be described as 'the accumulation of an assortment of items today for the purpose of providing protection against what may occur tomorrow'.

1 An inventory of the materials for production

2 An inventory of spare and repair parts for maintaining production equipment.

Similarly, marketing support is provided through:

1 Inventories of the finished product

2 Spare and repair parts that support the product.

If supply and demand could be perfectly co-ordinated, there would be no need for companies to hold stock. However, future demand is uncertain, as is reliability of supply. Hence inventories are accumulated to ensure availability of raw materials, spare parts and finished goods. Generally speaking, inventories are kept by companies because they:

- act as a 'hedge' against contingencies (e.g. unexpected demand, machinery breakdown)

- act as a 'hedge' against inflation, price or exchange rate fluctuations

- assist purchasing economies

- assist transportation economies

- assist production economies

- improve the level of customer service by providing greater stock availability.

Inventory planning is largely a matter of balancing various types of cost. The cost of holding stock and procurement has to be weighed against the cost of 'stock-out' in terms of production shutdowns and the loss of business and goodwill that would undoubtedly arise. These various costs conflict with each other.

Larger inventories mean more money is tied up in stock and more warehousing is needed. However, quantity discounts are usually available for large orders (e.g. of materials for production), and if fewer orders have to be placed, then purchasing administrative costs are reduced. Larger inventories also reduce the risks and costs of stock-outs.

When the conflicting costs just described are added together, they form a total cost that can be plotted as a 'U-shaped' curve. Part of management's task is to find a procedure of ordering resulting in an inventory level that minimises total costs. This 'minimum total cost procurement concept' is illustrated in Figure 10.3.

The economic order quantity (EOQ) is based on the assumption that total inventory costs are minimised at some definable purchase quantity. The EOQ method simply assumes that inventory costs are a function of the number of orders that are processed per unit of time, and the costs of maintaining an inventory over and above the cost of items included in the inventory (e.g. warehousing). The EOQ concept is simplistic in that it ignores transportation costs (which may significantly increase for smaller shipments) and the effects of quantity discounts. Because of these limitations, the EOQ concept

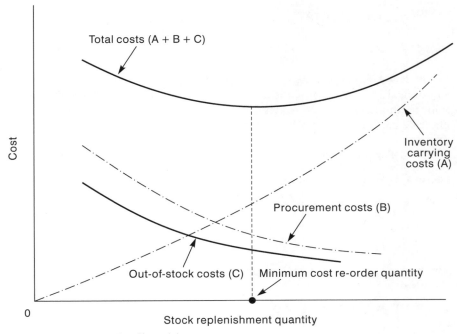

Figure 10.3 Cost trade-off model.

decreased in significance in the management of inventory, but the widespread adoption of business computing has allowed the use of more sophisticated versions of EOQ. An example of the traditional EOQ method is provided to give a general understanding of the principles. The economic order quantity can be calculated using the following formula:

$$EOQ = \sqrt{\frac{2AS}{I}}$$

where A = annual usage (units),
   S = ordering costs (£), and
   I = inventory carrying cost as a percentage of inventory value.

For example, if annual usage = 6000 units, ordering costs = £13, inventory carrying cost = 17% (= 0.17), and unit cost = £1.30:

$$EOQ = \sqrt{\frac{2 \times 6000 \times £1.30 \times £15}{0.17}}$$

$$= \sqrt{\frac{202,800}{0.17}}$$

$$= \sqrt{1,192,941.18}$$

$$= £1092.22 \text{ or } 840 \text{ units at } £1.30 \text{ per unit}$$

The EOQ concept and its variations basically seek to define the most economical lot size when considering the placement of an order. The order point method can be used to determine the ideal timing for placing an order. The calculation uses the following equation:

$$OP = DL_t + SS$$

where OP is the order point,

D is the demand,

L_t is the lead time, and

SS is the safety stock.

For example, if demand = 150 units per week, lead time = 6 weeks, and safety stock = 300 units:

$$OP = (150 \times 6) + 300$$

$$= 900 + 300$$

$$= 1200 \text{ units.}$$

Therefore, a replenishment order should be placed when inventory levels decrease to 1200 units. The actual size of the order placed when stock reaches this level can be calculated using the EOQ formula.

As with EOQ, the order point method incorporates certain assumptions. The order point assumes that lead times are fixed and can be accurately evaluated, which is rarely the case. However, despite the limitations of both the EOQ and order point models, the basic principles are valid, and form the basis of more realistic and useful computer-based inventory models.

10.6 Summary

✓ Discussion of PDM usually takes place from the viewpoint of the supplier. Understanding of physical distribution is, however, just as important to the purchaser. In addition to understanding the distribution tasks that face the supplier, the purchasing department must also appreciate logistical techniques for inventory control and the order cycle. There is consequently a close link between PDM and purchasing.

✓ Work study techniques and operations management can also be linked with PDM because management is concerned with efficiency and accuracy throughout the distributive function. Whilst a logistical system should not be inflexible, if routines can be established for certain functions they will assist the distribution process.

✓ As a function of the marketing mix, PDM is linked to all other marketing sub-functions and is an important element that plays a large part in achieving the goal of customer satisfaction.

Questions

1 Why has the marketing function of physical distribution management (PDM) grown significantly in importance with organisations over the past 30 years?

2 Explain, using quantitative and non-quantitative examples, the idea that diminishing returns can sometimes be faced by marketing firms when raising the level of service provided to certain customers or market segments.

3 Discuss the concept of service 'elasticity' and show how this concept can be applied by management when setting levels of service, and how these are priced in the following sectors: (a) the oil exploration sector; (b) a company supplying the automotive industry.

4 Outline and discuss the four main components of a 'systems approach' to PDM.

References

Burbridge, J. J. Jr (1987). The implementation of a distribution plan: a case study. *International Journal of Physical Distribution and Materials Management*, **17(1)**, 28–38.

Gilbert, X. and Strebel, P. (1989). From innovation to outpacing. *Business Quarterly*, **Summer**, 19–22.

Hutchins, D. (1988). *Just in Time*, pp. 27–47. Gower.

Further reading

Adcock, D. (2000). Channel management and value added relations. *Marketing Strategies for Competitive Advantage*, Chapter 12. John Wiley & Sons.

Armstrong, G. and Kotler, P. Distribution channels and logistics management. *Marketing: An Introduction*, 5th edn, Chapter 10. Prentice Hall.

Blythe, J. (2001). Distribution. *Essentials of Marketing*, Chapter 8. Person Educational Ltd.

Cateora, P. R. and Ghauri, P. N. (2000). The international distribution system. *International Marketing: European Edition*, Chapter 15. McGraw Hill.

Christopher, M. (1986). *The Strategy of Distribution Management*. Butterworth-Heinemann.

Davies, M. (1998). Distribution. *Understanding Marketing*, Chapter 8. Prentice Hall.

Keegan, W. J. and Green, M. S. (2000). Channels and physical distribution. *Global Marketing*, 2nd edn, Chapter 13. Prentice Hall.

Lancaster, G. A. and Reynolds, P. L. (1998). Logistics management. *Marketing*, Chapter 10. Macmillan Press.

Lancaster, G. A. and Reynolds, P. L. (1999). Logistics management. *Introduction to Marketing: A Step by Step Guide to All the Tools of Marketing*, Chapter 13. Kogan Page.

Plamer, A. (2000). Physical distribution and logistics. *Principles of Marketing*, Chapter 15. Oxford University Press.

Rosenbloom, B. (1991). *Marketing Channels: A Management View*. Dryden Press.

Stern, L. W. and El-Ansary, A. I. (1977). *Marketing Channels*. Prentice Hall.

Pricing 11

11.1 Introduction

Whatever strategic route a company chooses in its approach to pricing, the end price of its products is the ultimate determinant of the amount of money a company is able to make. Company objectives are guided and influenced by market conditions and price must be a function of such conditions, so the achievement of company objectives often necessitates compromise over the amount of profit that can be realised. The importance of price as a function of the marketing mix varies from market to market, but it is not always the most important factor in the buyer's decision-making process. For the seller, since price determines the amount of profit or loss, it is crucial that pricing is approached in a disciplined and orderly manner. Price provides a source of revenue, while the other elements of the marketing mix represent costs.

Marketing writers criticise approaches to pricing that are too cost-orientated. This criticism is justified in that costs do not necessarily reflect market conditions or company goals – at least in the longer term. Companies can design marketing strategies that put costs into the perspective of a long-range strategic approach. For example, the acquisition of a high market-share may drive down costs in the long term. An image-building strategy may invoke high costs initially, but it allows the company to charge higher prices in the long term. A purely cost-orientated approach to pricing is too narrow as a basis for pricing. Cost is, however, a logical starting point, and prices charged must ultimately exceed costs if a company is to remain in business. As Gerard Tellis explains (Tellis, 1986):

> A *strategy* is a broad plan of action by which an organisation intends to reach its goal. A *policy* is more of a routine managerial guide to be implemented when a given situation arises. Giving certain price discounts when a certain amount of product is ordered in an example of a *policy*.

Equipped with this awareness of costs, companies should consider price in terms of marketing objectives that are also designed to achieve financial goals. The key word in pricing is *realism*. Pricing objectives should be well defined, attainable and measurable. Having laid down objectives, the company can use a variety of pricing strategies to achieve them.

Key point
Pricing objectives should be well defined, attainable and measurable.

11.2 The nature of price

Price influences and affects all our lives. Whether we are consumers or involved directly in the industrial process, price affects our individual living standards and work, and, ultimately, the functioning of our national economy. As marketers we are more specifically interested in the role of price in the buyer–seller relationship. The buyer views price as a cost that is paid in return for a series of satisfactions. Whatever these satisfactions, the price itself is usually perceived as a negative factor. The seller sees price as a means of cost recovery and profit. Both buyer and seller need to understand how price works for pricing structures to be implemented and managed efficiently. Economics provides a starting point from which such an understanding can be gained.

From economic theory we learn about the closely related concepts of 'utility', 'value' and 'price'. Utility is that aspect of an item that makes it capable of satisfying a want or need. Value is the expression used to quantify utility, whilst price describes the number of monetary units the value represents.

A further assumption of economic theory is that of the downward sloping demand curve, or the assumption that customers will buy more of a product as the price falls, as shown in Figure 11.1.

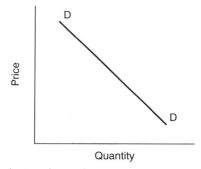

Figure 11.1 Downward sloping demand curve.

Conversely, the supply curve is the opposite way around, the assumption being that suppliers will be willing to supply greater amounts at a higher price. This is illustrated in Figure 11.2.

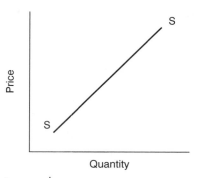

Figure 11.2 Upward sloping supply curve.

Where demand and supply intersect is the market price, and this is shown in Figure 11.3. It can be seen that at price 'P', quantity 'Q' will be the amount demanded.

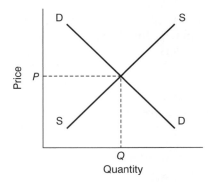

Figure 11.3 Demand and supply curves showing market price.

When companies attempt to plot a demand schedule, or demand curve, for a particular product, they must also consider the concept of elasticity of demand. Elasticity describes the sensitivity of consumers to changes in price. A product can be said to have elastic demand when price changes greatly affect the level of demand. Inelastic demand is relatively insensitive to price changes. These two notions are explained in Figure 11.4.

Key point
A product can be said to have elastic demand when price changes greatly affect the level of demand.

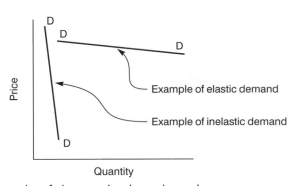

Figure 11.4 Examples of elastic and inelastic demand.

In reality, very few products have totally elastic or inelastic demand. Even when demand is elastic, there is usually some point on the demand curve where a further price reduction makes little or no difference to demand. Determining the exact position of this point is important in demand analysis, because clearly it makes little sense to reduce a price if this will not result in an increase in sales sufficient to offset the price reduction.

Companies must also establish a cost curve that relates costs to varying levels of output. The economic theory of the firm assumes that companies will always attempt to increase output to levels where profits are maximised. This is the point at which marginal costs are equal to marginal revenue, i.e. when the cost of one more unit of output is equal to the addition to total revenue that this last unit provides.

A final economic concept that is explored here is the notion of 'oligopoly', because many companies, especially in the fast-moving consumer goods (FMCG) field, operate in near-oligopolistic situations. In such circumstances, there are relatively few sellers who produce similar goods and produce below their maximum capacity. Price as an instrument of competition is less effective, so rather than engage in 'price wars', manufacturers place more emphasis on 'non-price competition'. This is epitomised by attempts to brand products and engage in above-the-line promotion. Generally, advertising tends to be defensive, as the market is saturated and demand is relatively inelastic because it reflects regular demand and not new or increased levels of demand. Examples include washing detergents, breakfast cereals, canned and packaged soups, soft drinks and car tyres, and aluminium producers and petrol companies.

Figure 11.5 illustrates the concept of oligopoly. It can be seen from demand curve 'D' that at price 'P', quantity 'Q' is the amount that would be demanded under normal demand considerations. If price is reduced to 'P1', then the expectation would be that Q – Q1 would be the additional amount demanded. However, under oligopoly the demand curve kinks to 'D1', which means that Q – Q2 is the additional amount demanded, so price competition is less effective in producing more sales.

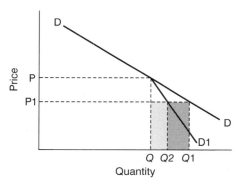

Figure 11.5 The concept of oligopoly.

If a company lowers its prices then it must expect competitors to lower their prices, and, given inelastic industry demand, the company's own demand curve is relatively more inelastic at lower prices. Oligopolistic situations not only apply to product groups and industries, but to local markets as well. A community might be served by, for example, many petrol stations or hairdressing establishments competing for local custom, and in such cases their behaviour equates to oligopoly.

Only the simplest assumptions that economic theory makes about the behaviour of the marketplace have been described here. Students of economics will appreciate that many variations in this behaviour can be described, and marketers will be aware that economics only describes markets to a limited extent. Economics largely ignores the effects of sociological and psychological influences on the consumer. However, when considering price, knowledge of economics is essential as a starting point for understanding the market. The fact that most marketing textbooks include a section on economics in relation to price illustrates this importance.

Thus, with economics as a foundation, marketers have an insight into pricing which can be related to specific pricing situations. As with any aspect of marketing, the task of pricing should be approached in a formal, structured manner. This helps to ensure professionalism, as well as affording the opportunity to 'look back' if revision or modifications are necessary.

Key point
As with any aspect of marketing, the task of pricing should be approached in a formal, structured manner.

Vignette 11.1

Dell Computers reduce price in an effort to stem the fall in the demand for PCs

Dell Computers, the Texas-based manufacture of personal computers, has totally underestimated the global slowdown in the demand for personal computers. This has resulted in the company cutting 1700 full-time jobs, or about 4 per cent of its workforce, and a significant fall in the firm's share price of about 5 per cent when the news of a profit warning was made in mid-February 2001. The forecasting side of Dell's predicament is discussed further in a case given in Chapter 14; here we will investigate the pricing implications.

As a strategic response to the worrying demand figures, especially in the USA consumer sector, Dell has cut its prices dramatically. The global PC market is already highly competitive, with Dell's competitors, such as Compaq and Gateway, fighting for a share of the same market segments. Industry analysts are worried that Dell's strategic response to the demand slowdown might precipitate a huge price war in a market where margins are already dangerously slim. Dell has been fortunate in enjoying a fall in its component prices; this fall has enabled the firm to pass on their reductions in the form of lower PC prices to the customer. The PC market is highly price sensitive, although there is a perceived relationship between quality and price. Dell needs to be careful not to damage the perceived value of its brand in the minds of consumers through the use of aggressive price reductions.

11.3 Pricing objectives

As with all aspects of marketing, the first stage in the pricing process should be to establish the objectives the company wishes to achieve. Price is a tool or instrument of the marketing mix that differs from the other mix elements in that it is a financial as well as a marketing tool. We should therefore be aware that some pricing objectives might arise from 'non-marketing' sources. For example, in public limited companies pressure may exist to pay a certain level

Definition
Price is a tool or instrument of the marketing mix that differs from the other mix elements in that it is a financial as well as a marketing tool.

of dividend to shareholders. Price may also be seen as a means of recouping recent investment. It is very important that pricing objectives originating from outside the marketing department are established in conjunction with marketing strategy. There is little point in planning the role of price in the marketing mix if finance decrees that price should be at a certain level, regardless of the marketing implications that such a price may have. Pricing objectives must therefore be set in co-operation with other departments so that conflict with corporate objectives does not arise. This involves consideration of price at the highest management level, giving an indication of the ultimate importance of price.

Most pricing objectives are set with the marketplace in mind because the market is a reality of business life, but these objectives should also reflect the financial objectives of the firm.

11.3.1 Return on investment

A fundamental pricing objective is to achieve a target return on investment from net sales. When costs have been established, the company decides on the percentage profit it wants to achieve. Whilst this percentage may remain constant, fluctuations in demand will affect the monetary value of the profits made. To achieve this objective successfully and consistently the company is likely to be a market leader, and so less vulnerable to changes in the market place than its competitors. Achievement of this objective is relatively easy to measure, but in reality it is not always practical to attain for an individual product. Most companies have a clear idea of the annual revenue that they need to realise, and can thus estimate the profit margins needed to achieve this. This overall profit margin is usually the result of several pricing strategies applied to a variety of products in response to changes in the market place. Care should be taken to avoid confusion between a 'target return' pricing objective and 'cost plan', which is a pricing technique.

11.3.2 Improvement in market share

Improvement or maintenance of market share is a common pricing objective that is market based. A firm might feel it is earning an appropriate and reasonable return on investment, but if the market is expanding, existing prices may not encourage a corresponding improvement in the market share. A price modification (i.e. a reduction) could increase sales in an expanding market to a level where the return on investment increases in monetary terms although percentage return may have fallen. The acquisition of market share for its own sake is a contentious issue. It appears, though, that high market share companies enjoy advantages over smaller competitors, and market share is regarded as the key to profitability. Certainly market share is an accepted indicator of a firm's general health, and a decline in share is an important danger signal.

Maintenance of market share is at least a key to survival, and price carries much of the burden of responsibility in a marketing mix designed to maintain or improve market share. In terms of measuring success, it is not too difficult to establish the size of the market and estimate respective market shares.

11.3.3 Maintaining price stability

A pricing policy with the objective of maintaining price stability and margins might appear to detract from marketing creativity and free choice. Whilst it is true that some products can be promoted and priced as prestige items, most firms have little or no influence over the general level of prices in a given market. They must organise their businesses so that costs are at a level that will permit them to fall in line with the prices charged by market leaders. Prices tend, therefore, to be 'market led', with little scope for radical deviation from the established price structures.

Provided a company's returns are considered adequate, there is considerable justification for maintaining the *status quo* by meeting competitive prices established by the market leaders. The market or price leaders themselves do not stand to gain very much by distancing their prices too much (either upwards or downwards) from their smaller competitors. Price adjustments are usually only made in response to changing market conditions.

Certain conditions may require an aggressive approach to pricing. During the introduction and growth stages of the product life cycle, price usually plays a less significant role. It is during maturity and growth (where most products are situated) that the major 'price wars' are usually fought. However, whilst changes in market share can be achieved by price cutting, as a general rule this is to be avoided as it works to the detriment of everyone.

The idea of a 'price leader' does not imply any kind of monopolistic situation, or that one company is exploiting the market because of its position of power. The position of leadership is not absolute; it can be threatened and will certainly be attacked by competitors if the power is abused. Finally, it should be noted that price leadership does not equate to absolute authority. Many price leaders are not the principal market shareholders, although they will be major participants. Price leadership does not render a firm impervious to competitors who engage in non-price competition. Companies can improve their market share by judicious use of the marketing mix, whilst at the same time pursuing a price stability objective. The party with the ultimate influence in price setting is usually the consumer or buyer. We should also be aware of the fact that the consumer has much less influence in some markets than in others. For example, the market for petrol is one where the consumer has no real choice of substitutes and consequently little influence on price.

Key point
Price leadership does not render a firm impervious to competitors who engage in non-price competition.

11.3.4 Controlling cash flow

In the next chapter we will discuss how pricing objectives vary according to the product's position in the product life cycle. Financial managers will be particularly anxious to recoup the often very high costs of development as early as possible in the product's life cycle. Controlling cash flow is therefore a common pricing objective. The financial manager may be willing to bear the development and marketing costs of launching a new product, but will also highlight a variety of other demands on the company's limited resources.

11.3.5 Growth in sales

The advantages of price stability objectives notwithstanding, at certain times and under certain conditions a legitimate pricing objective is simply to achieve a growth in sales. Providing the firm fully appreciates the competitive conditions under which it operates, price (in particular a low price) is probably the most effective competitive weapon at its disposal.

If rapid growth in sales is called for, price can be used as the major component of the marketing mix. Such a move should always be made with caution. Sudden price reductions may affect the effectiveness of other marketing mix elements. In addition, it is important to be aware that it is always easier to implement a growth-in-sales objective by price reductions than it is to regain previous higher pricing levels.

11.3.6 Profit maximisation

Most companies have an overall pricing objective of profit maximisation. This objective runs parallel with any other pricing objectives that a company may employ. Market conditions usually make it impossible to maximise profits on all products, in all markets, simultaneously. For this reason a number of companies employ pricing techniques that may promote sales but reduce profits on certain products in the short term, with the overall objective being to maximise profit on total sales of the company. The company's product mix should therefore be considered as a unit rather than a series of products whose profits should be maximised individually.

Key point
The term 'profit maximisation' is often unjustly associated with exploitation.

The term 'profit maximisation' is often unjustly associated with exploitation. A company needs to make profits to survive, and attempts to overcharge are usually counterbalanced by competitors as well as buyers themselves. The ethical issues that this gives rise to are discussed throughout Chapter 16.

Vignette 11.2

California is priced out of electricity

California's retail utility companies, which transmit the state's electricity to users along their various transmissions systems, have had difficulty in absorbing increased costs from electricity generators who sell electricity to them wholesale. The reason is that the retail utility firms are heavily regulated under state law as to the prices they can charge consumers, whereas the wholesale utility generators are largely unregulated and can basically charge what they want to the retail utility firms, up to maximum of $250 per megawatt hour. The regulators set this amount, but to many it seems an unrealistically high amount compared to what the retailers are allowed to charge. Because of this rather strange state of affairs, the retail utility companies' profits have turned into losses. Basically the market has broken down, and the usual laws of supply and demand, which are so efficient at clearing the market at an acceptable price under free market conditions, no longer work in this market.

The retail firms are in debt, and some of them cannot even service their debt commitments. The result has been electricity 'blackouts' throughout California, which have cost the 'golden' state's industries $millions. These losses include those made by the high technology industries, which are the very backbone of the state's economy. The authorities separated electricity generation from the retailing of electricity because they thought it would improve competition within the market. They thought that new firms would enter the electricity generation market and thus bring prices down. In fact the cost of building electricity-generating plant is so high and the political regulation so risky that few investors have ventured into the field. This has left the generators with virtually monopoly power. Their prices are capped at an unrealistically high $250 per megawatt hour, and because they are trying to maximise their profit opportunity the generators fix their prices at the maximum permitted level. In the short run authorities can subsidise the electricity bills of consumers, but eventually the debt incurred by the state in doing this will have to be paid by future taxpayers. The only long-term solution would seem to be market reform by the authorities.

11.4 Essential steps in price determination

To ensure profitability, prices must ultimately exceed costs. It seems logical, therefore, to consider cost as the first stage in price planning. In fact, the problem should be approached from the opposite direction. In line with marketing orientation in general, pricing strategy should begin with the consumer and work 'backwards' to the company. Costs cannot be ignored, but pricing must be consumer- or customer-orientated, the customer being the person who finally decides whether or not the product is purchased. The steps described below should be followed.

Key point
In line with marketing orientation in general, pricing strategy should begin with the consumer and work 'backwards' to the company.

11.4.1 Identify the potential consumer or market

This step may appear to be too obvious to be worth mentioning, but its purpose is to focus the planner's mind on the market from the outset. It also prevents price from being viewed as separate from the other marketing mix elements.

11.4.2 Demand estimation

The likely volume of sales will directly affect the manufacturer's costs and thus the price necessary for profit maximisation. Demand analysis is a highly skilled process, and is dealt with in further detail in Chapter 14. Ideally, demand analysis should provide the company with a schedule of predicted demand levels at differing prices. This establishes the position and slope of the demand curve. The price a company is able to charge for a certain product will vary from market to market, and also within markets and between different market segments. This variation calls for comprehensive market research before the decision is taken to enter a particular market. Both qualitative and quantitative primary research techniques can be used. The company can also learn much about price from secondary analysis. Chapter 13 discusses these techniques in more detail.

Demand analysis should provide the following basic information, from which it should be possible to construct a demand schedule showing levels of demand at varying price levels:

1 General marketing information – demographic and psychographic data that help planners to understand consumer needs and preferences.

2 Income – in general, the demand for a product rises in line with increases in disposable income. The effect of prosperity varies according to the nature of the product, and the company should try to establish the income-sensitivity of demand for their products.

3 Substitute products – knowledge of the availability of substitutes will help the company form an opinion of the price elasticity of demand.

The results of demand analysis must be used with an element of caution; statistical methods are based on hypotheses that can only estimate real life behaviour. Those responsible for setting prices should also be aware that potential customers might say that they would pay a certain price for a product, but in reality their behaviour might be totally different. A further cautionary consideration is that of the expected price. Expected price is the value that consumers, consciously or subconsciously, place on a given product.

Regardless of their inherent or built-in value (from the producer's point of view), certain products fall into a group where the consumer 'expects' them to be at a certain price level. The manufacturer may price products too high or too low relative to the expected price. Irrespective of production and marketing costs, consumers would not, for example, expect to pay a very low price for a luxury item; a low price would detract from the quality image of such a product. The concept of an expected price, high or low, can also be extended to wholesalers and distributors.

11.4.3 Anticipating competitors' prices and potential competitor reaction

The complexity and nature of a competitor's pricing structure is usually difficult to ascertain. Of course consumers (i.e. other manufacturers and final consumers) can easily compare selling prices, but this does not give any real insight into a competitive manufacturing pricing structure, as it relates to the various members of the marketing channel. Buyers often compound this difficulty by inventing 'special prices' and 'non-existent discounts', not really offered by competitors, but stated as being real during the negotiation process in order to help when bargaining for a lower price.

When products are easily initiated and markets are relatively easy to enter, the price of existing or potential competitive products assumes major importance.

Even when products have substantial distinctiveness, it is not usually too long before other companies will enter the market.

Competition stems from three major sources:

1 'Head-on' competition from directly similar products

2 Competition from substitute products

3 Competition from products that are not directly related, but compete for the same disposable income. For instance, watch manufacturers are often in competition with fountain pen manufacturers because their products are often bought as gifts. Hand knitting is a leisure activity in the main, so yarn producers face competition from other 'handcraft' hobbies to seek the potential customer's free time. This is an aspect of competition often overlooked when setting prices.

11.4.4 Market share analysis

If the company is seeking a large market share, the price for the product will need to be competitive. Management should ensure that production capacity is sufficient to meet the demand that this anticipated market share might create. If production capacity is limited, there is little point in setting low prices that might attract orders that cannot be fulfilled.

The steps discussed so far in price determination have been concerned with the marketplace rather than the internal workings of the firm. Market considerations should be the major determinant of price, so it would not make sense to develop a product whose price did not fall approximately in line with competitive prices. The level of potential demand at given price levels is, therefore, an important consideration.

11.4.5 Cost analysis

The company should by now have established, from a basic assessment of costs, whether or not a potential market is attractive and practical. If the market seems promising, a more detailed cost analysis should be the next step. The likely level of demand should by now have been estimated for varying levels of output.

For example, if demand analysis has predicted that a price level of £1.80 per unit will generate a demand level of 100 000 units per annum, the company needs to know the effect that this level of production will have on costs. (In this example, the price of £1.80 per unit would be a figure derived from an overall market demand schedule, whilst 100 000 units could represent the share of the total market the company wishes to obtain). In order to ascertain the viability of such a price and level of output, a break-even point must be calculated from an analysis of the relationship between costs and output.

Fixed costs are those that the company must pay regardless of the level of output (e.g. depreciation and maintenance costs of machinery, and the costs of a minimum labour force). Variable costs are a function of the level of output (e.g. energy and raw material costs, and perhaps those of additional labour as production levels rise). Total costs are the sum of the fixed and variable costs. The break-even point occurs when the number of units sold at a given price generates revenue to exactly equal total costs.

In Figure 11.6, demand analysis indicates that a price of £1.80 per unit would be attractive to the market, and the desired market share would require a production level of 100 000 units per annum. Fixed costs for production of the product are £100 000. Variable costs rise as production increases; at a production level of 100 000 units, total costs are £150 000. The company

Definition
The break-even point occurs when the number of units sold at a given price generates revenue to exactly equal total costs.

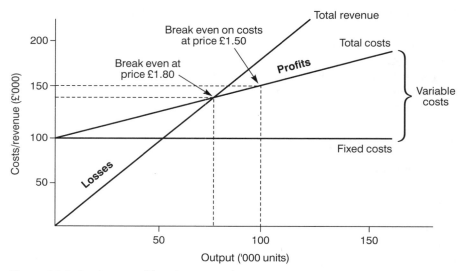

Figure 11.6 Application of break-even analysis.

knows, therefore, that it must charge at least £1.50 per unit in order to break even at this volume. However, this is a break-even figure based solely on cost. The break-even point can be modified by changing the price – at a higher price, fewer units are required to break even.

In this example, the company has already estimated that £1.80 is a desirable price in market terms. If this price is used with information from Figure 11.6, the following equation can be used to calculate the number of units required to break even at this price.

If fixed costs   = £100 000,

variable costs = £0.50 per unit and

selling price   = £1.80:

Number of units required to break even at a given selling price = n

Total costs will be equal total revenue when $100\,000 + 0.5n = 1.8n$

Therefore, $n = 77\,000$ (approx.), and total costs = £138 500 (approx.).

The company had planned to produce and sell 100 000 units. When the price is set at £1.80 per unit, break-even will be approximately 77 000 units. This price provides for profitable production at all points above 77 000 units.

This is a demand-orientated approach to pricing. The manufacturer determines the likely market price, and then looks back at the cost structure to establish the feasibility of such a price.

11.4.6 Profit calculation

When pricing objectives were discussed, it was said that they differed according to the nature of the market. The cost and demand analysis just described does not reduce flexibility in setting price objectives. Rather, it provides management with information it requires to make further decisions. Taking the example in Figure 11.6 again, the company could use £1.80 at 100 000 units as its basis for setting a price if the objective was other than to break even. Once equipped with cost and demand data, various price levels that might be appropriate to a chosen marketing strategy can be considered. Several break-even points can then be plotted along the line of total cost. As long as the output level is to the right of any given break-even point, the company will generate profits. Thus the break-even point is a function of price, which is in turn a function of the chosen marketing strategy.

Key point
Thus the break-even point is a function of price, which is in turn a function of the chosen marketing strategy.

It is appropriate to re-emphasise that the determination of price and profit is a practical and not an academic exercise. Marketing practitioners should recognise that profit is the only means of survival for a company, and price is the major tool through which profits can be realised.

Once a price has been chosen, management should review costs regularly in case savings can be made without affecting the product's quality. In addition, provided that production capacity, delivery and strategy permit, the sales force should strive to increase the sale of units and so increase profits (seen in Figure 11.6 as moving output along the line of total costs away from the break-even point).

Vignette 11.3

British supermarket chains keep food prices sky high despite the fall in British farm prices

February 2001 was not a particularly good month for British livestock farmers. Having had to put up with the BSE (mad cow disease) problem for years and seeing their exports banned or restricted to many world markets, especially Europe, then having to contend with very wet weather and in some cases severe flooding, they thought nothing else could go wrong. They were wrong. February saw a massive outbreak of foot and mouth disease within the UK, resulting in hundreds of thousands of animals being destroyed. The problems in British agriculture over the years, the loss of export markets, relatively cheap imports from all over the world, increased slaughtering and other costs and the loss of consumer confidence in British meat, particularly beef, has taken its toll on the health and pockets of the British farmer.

The most important outcome has been a dramatic fall in British farmers' incomes, in some cases to unsustainable levels. Thousands of farmers are selling up and realising what they can financially, and getting out of the industry altogether. Others are moving to France or Spain, where land is cheaper and there are less financial burdens on the farmer. The price farmers receive for their produce, especially meat, is in some cases so low in the UK that it costs farmers more to get an animal slaughtered than they realise on the open market for the meat. In other words, many farmers are operating at a loss at the present market price. However, what the British public find hard to understand is how the British farmers receive so little for beef, lamb, pork and poultry when the cost of British meat is still so high in the British supermarkets. In fact, as of March 2001, the supermarkets are forecasting a further 15 per cent rise in the retail price of British meat because of shortages caused by the restricted movement of livestock as a result of the foot and mouth disease outbreak.

The general public are suspicious, and many are accusing the British supermarket chains of profiteering and an abuse of monopoly power in fixing retail sale prices of British meat firmly in their own favour. At the end of February the British Prime Minister entered the fray himself, with a scathing speech denouncing the conduct of the British retail multiple chains. He said that the large retail organisations have a 'stranglehold' on the farming industry, who are in a sense being blackmailed by the supermarkets to keep prices down otherwise the supermarkets will buy from overseas. Many claim that the continual pressure on British farmers by the supermarkets has increased health risks to the British consumer as farmers relax their standards of animal husbandry, including animal welfare. Many claim this has been done in order to produce British meat at the lowest possible price, even if this does mean 'cutting a few corners'.

Basically, the large UK multiple chains are so big and powerful that between them they can virtually dictate pricing policy to the British consumer. Farmers are paid pence per pound or kilo in the wholesale market, and yet consumers are charged pounds per pound or kilo in the shops. The supermarkets claim that preparation and transport charges are the same no matter what is paid for produce at source. But British consumers feel they are being 'taken for a ride', and it would seem that the British Labour Government also feels the supermarkets are taking advantage of the situation and abusing their considerable market power. Calls have been made for the competition regulators to investigate the pricing policies of British retail chains and recommend divestment if monopoly power is thought to exist within the retail market. British supermarkets need to consider their position before they lose the goodwill of the British customer and bring down the wrath of the UK Government on their pricing strategies.

11.5 Price selection techniques

Key point
The chosen price will depend on the overall marketing strategy to be employed.

The procedure for price determination should have prepared the company with as much information as possible to use when selecting a specific price. The chosen price will depend on the overall marketing strategy to be employed. Examples are given here of demand- and market-orientated treatments of price determination. Some pricing techniques pay less attention to demand and concentrate on cost, whilst others put more emphasis on the other elements of the marketing mix as well as on aspects of consumer behaviour that affect the way that price is perceived.

11.5.1 Break-even analysis related to market demand

The principal value of this technique is that, insofar as demand estimation is accurate, management is dealing with reality. We must begin with the premise that at too high a price there will be no demand, whilst at too low a price the company will make losses. The company must therefore choose a price that is acceptable both to itself and to the market place. For simplicity only one price is considered in Figure 11.6, and there is thus only one function for total revenue (i.e. total revenue = demand × unit price). If demand is estimated at various price levels, it is possible to produce a series of total revenue lines. The various total revenue lines can be plotted to form a demand curve for the product in question. Usually, a company will choose a price and a corresponding level of demand that will maximise profit. In practice, this may not be possible because of limitations on the firm's production capacity, or because of a need to utilise production capacity as fully as possible.

Whilst demand-orientated pricing is preferable to cost-based pricing, we should be aware of certain practical limitations when it is related to break-even analysis.

First, it assumes that costs are static, whereas costs can vary considerably in a practical setting. Revenue too is over-simplified, because market conditions can change rapidly. Even if they return to the condition on which the analysis was based, the actual revenue will not be as predicted. If these considerations are taken into account, break-even analysis related to demand is an extremely effective price selection technique, particularly when costs and demand levels are relatively stable, if only in the short term. Accurate demand estimation is difficult, and more insight is provided later in Chapter 14.

11.5.2 Cost-based price selection techniques

These have the advantage of being easier to administer than demand-based techniques. It is simple for a firm to arrive at an accurate estimation of the cost of producing a unit of production. Cost-plus pricing takes the cost of production and adds to this an amount that will provide the profit the company requires.

Definition
Cost-plus pricing takes the cost of production and adds to this an amount that will provide the profit the company requires.

Mark-up pricing is a cost-plus technique that is widely used in the retail sector. The retailer takes the cost price of the product it is offering for sale and adds to this a percentage mark-up that is sufficient to cover overhead costs and provides a pre-determined percentage profit. Usually mark-up is calculated as a percentage of cost price using the following formula:

100% + required % mark-up × cost = selling price

Retailers favour mark-up pricing, because it is convenient and straightforward. Demand analysis might also have been carried out by the manufacturer, who may then suggest a retail price area to the retailer. This is not to say that retailers ignore demand. Usually, the faster the turnover, the lower the percentage mark-up. Retailers are also in the almost unique position of being able to experiment with sales effectiveness at varying price levels and receive quick feedback. Although mark-up pricing tends to prevail in retailing, it is also common in manufacturing, principally because it is easier to estimate cost than demand. If a long-term view of price is taken, there is no need to make continuous demand-related pricing adjustments. In some industries, where a particular mark-up is considered 'standard', the market is correspondingly more stable, and this benefits both producers and customers alike.

Target pricing is another cost-based approach, which considers output as well as costs in determining price. The company decides on a given rate of return or 'target price', and then calculates the level of output necessary to achieve this. Break-even analysis is used to determine the level of output where profits will begin. The linear rise in variable costs as output increases will determine the company's total costs. The company then chooses a price that will produce a revenue line which achieves the target profit.

Definition
Target pricing is a cost-based approach, which considers output as well as costs in determining price.

Target pricing is used by many skill-based companies and also business-to-business companies whose price philosophy is one of a 'fair return on investment'. In most marketing situations, the technique has limitations. In particular, demand elasticity is ignored. Thus although a given level of output may be prescribed which only requires a relatively low price, there is no guarantee that this volume will be bought by the market. Conversely, if the company wishes to reduce output and still reach the target profit, a higher price must be charged and this may not be acceptable to the market.

11.5.3 Psychological pricing techniques

It is the marketplace and not the company that exerts the greatest influence when prices are being determined. Although an individual company cannot significantly alter the basic market structure, it has some influence if marketing implications are considered. Marketing management is faced with a general level of demand for a given product or product type. Inside this demand level are opportunities for strategies to be developed which focus specifically on consumers. The importance that consumers attach to prestige value allows for psychological pricing techniques to be developed. Many consumers believe that price is an indication of quality; they use this perceived quality to enhance the image of their lifestyle.

The purchase of a 'prestige' product therefore becomes an expression of 'self-concept'. Designer clothes are a good example of prestige products; their perceived value is greater than their cost. Consumers see value in exclusivity and the ability to display it, and are prepared to pay high prices for such fashionable items.

The influences on the consumer that make prestige pricing possible are numerous, and were discussed in Chapter 6. In order to satisfy the consumer's psychological needs, other elements of the marketing mix (such as promotion and distribution) must support the image reflected by the price. For example, Cartier jewellery and Gucci accessories are only advertised in prestige media and not in the popular press; nor would we expect to find them in our local supermarket.

Demand for prestige goods produces an unusual curve, as shown in Figure 11.7. Although demand increases to some extent as prices are reduced, below

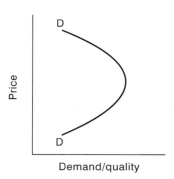

Figure 11.7 Prestige price demand curve.

a certain price further reductions actually decrease the level of demand. This is because the product loses its prestigious image if its price becomes too low.

Other psychological price factors concern consumer perceptions of the price itself. For some products, there are price bands within which price reductions have little effect on demand. However, if price is reduced so that it falls into the next psychological price bracket, then demand will increase. This results in a step-like demand curve, and is the basis of odd/even pricing (called price lining). Somehow, £4.99 appears a lot less expensive than £5.00. Similarly, for higher-priced products, an even figure reduction appears to encourage demand. The figure of £68 'appears' disproportionately less than its true difference from £70. Odd/even pricing is widely practiced in retailing, although its scientific basis is unclear and the technique owes as much to tradition as it does to consumer analysis.

11.5.4 Going-rate pricing

Some companies price their products according to the going rate. Clearly they must ensure that their cost structures and profit requirements are compatible with this, but it is also a popular method when companies that are 'price leaders' feature in the market. Thus, if the main pricing objective is to meet competitive prices, going-rate pricing is appropriate. Generally, when companies collectively apply this technique in a market, prices are stabilised and price wars are avoided.

Vignette 11.4

Small UK construction firms often price at a loss in times of recession in order to show a full order book

Evidence from the available literature on small- and medium-sized enterprises (SMEs) shows that smaller firms are not very sophisticated in their setting of price (Reynolds and Day, 1993, 1994). Nowhere is this more evident that in the UK small firm construction sector. There are a plethora of very small building and construction firms within the UK, and in times of recession many are fighting for their lives to simply meet their payroll obligations at the end of the week. During the last serious UK recession in the first half of the 1990s, many small building and construction firms ceased trading and a large number of these were declared bankrupt. This brought misery to many people; not only to those construction workers that found themselves out of a job, but also to the owner of the business and his or her family. Many entrepreneurs lost their homes as a result of their small business failure.

Many small building and construction firms were existing on bank finance. During this recessionary period, many of the main high street banks kept a close watch on the firms to whom they had made loans. The banks often withdrew their support at the first signal of trouble, and this was one of the main reasons for many businesses failing. Often they were trading successfully but had cash-flow problems, sometimes because of late payment by customers.

If firms had tried to use marketing tools other than price, they may well have been able to attract work at a price that would have at least allowed them to make a profit. Many small firms were very busy but were making no money. Their payroll and other expenses were often financed by bank loans, and the interest payments on these loans turned a potentially profitable job into a loss situation. The lesson here is that firms can rely too heavily on price competition alone. In times of trading difficulties, too much emphasis on price turns the service provided by such firms into a basic 'commodity'.

11.6 Pricing strategy

Whatever technique is used to arrive at a selling price, marketing management must devise an overall pricing strategy that is compatible with strategies attached to other elements of the marketing mix. It is not always possible to set a price and apply this rigidly to all customers in all market situations. A pricing strategy therefore denotes how a company will price its products in particular periods or particular market conditions. Demand-orientated pricing sets a base price which the company must endeavour to achieve, but it also assumes that price will be modified in line with changes in demand. Manufacturers must also consider that customers are not the same. Some will purchase in far greater quantities than others, or be situated in areas that are more costly to reach.

Definition
Demand-orientated pricing sets a base price which the company must endeavour to achieve, but it also assumes that price will be modified in line with changes in demand.

If a target return-on-investment price is set, this may only be appropriate during the maturity stage of the product life cycle, which is explained in Chapter 12. During introduction or growth, it is usually necessary to employ a pricing strategy that will enable the target return to be achieved over the long term. Again, this is explained more fully in Chapter 12.

A company's ability and willingness to formulate pricing strategies is a reflection of its willingness to adapt and modify price according to the needs of its customers and the market conditions that prevail.

11.6.1 Discounting

The discount structure a company employs is a major element of pricing strategy and an indicator of the firm's flexibility. If customers buy products in large quantities, they may reasonably expect to be charged a lower price than that set and applied to smaller purchases. The seller may also offer discounts voluntarily in order to encourage large orders, which facilitate economies of scale and assist effective production planning. Such quantity-related discounts can refer to individual orders or be based on an estimated off-take that is planned over a given period. In certain markets, price discounting is very important. George Day and Adrian Ryans (1988) say that, if used with imagination and creativity, this can provide a firm with a strong competitive advantage.

Manufacturers can also offer discounts to encourage sales of a new product, or to accelerate demand for a product whose stocks are high owing to an overall reduction in demand that might be exceptional or the result of seasonal or cyclical demand variations. In the production context, it is desirable that a constant rate of output is maintained. If market conditions are not conducive to this, a price modification by means of discounting might encourage sales sufficiently to counteract variations in the level of demand.

A discounting strategy might also be applied to payment terms. It is common in industrial marketing to offer a percentage discount to firms who settle their monthly account promptly. Finance should arrive at a 'sliding scale' for discounts in relation to speed of payment that is a reflection of interest rates. The firm may then not have to wait for 30, 60 or even 90 days for settlement of many of its accounts. Discounting is a reality of marketing pricing strategy, but it is not necessarily a standard procedure.

Within guidelines set down by management in relation to pricing, the task of negotiating specific prices usually falls to sales. There are situations where the buying power of customers gives the salesperson little alternative but to offer some discount, but this should only be given as a 'last resort' in the price negotiation process. Temporary discounts in particular should be applied with caution; these might come to be regarded as the normal price, and, although it is easy to reduce prices, it is more difficult to increase them later. When discounts are promotion-related, they should have strict time limits defined from the outset. In some circumstances discounting is regarded (by buyers) as a sign that the company wishes to dispose of surplus capacity, and buyers may then use this discounted price as the base level for further downwards negotiation.

11.6.2 Zone or geographic pricing strategies

In order to export, a company should take competition and local conditions into account before a price level can be decided. Sometimes, even within the country of manufacture, customers in certain areas can be charged a price that reflects additional delivery costs. Customers, however, tend to view their location in relation to the supplier's manufacturing base as being the supplier's problem. As a result, most UK and European companies tend to be unsympathetic to arguments that the cost of transportation merits a price premium. There is almost always a competitor who is willing to supply even the furthest location at a price that is the same as locally delivered prices.

In the USA, distances are so great that producers often apply zone or geographic pricing strategies – their customer-bases being spread over an area several times larger in geographical terms than the market afforded by the total European Union. The subject of pricing for export markets is dealt with in more detail in Chapter 15.

11.6.3 Market skimming and market penetration

Chapter 12 considers marketing strategy at various stages of the product life cycle (PLC). Of particular interest here are the strategies available to companies launching new products, and the pricing approach of innovative, rather than imitative, new products is considered. In the introductory stage of the PLC, marketing management has two basic strategic pricing alternatives; marketing skimming and market penetration.

Market skimming

Market skimming implies that a company will charge the highest price that the market will bear, given the relative merits of the product in question. A skimming strategy is directed at only a small proportion of the total potential market. This is likely to be made up of innovators and early adopters, who are receptive to new ideas and whose income and lifestyle makes them less sensitive to price (Figure 11.8). Diffusion theory, which is dealt with in the next chapter, suggests that these customer groups influence subsequent buyer categories, and acceptance of an innovative product 'filters' down to a larger number of consumers. In order to reach this wider group of customers, the company must plan to reduce prices progressively while at the same time 'skimming' the most advantageous prices from each successive customer group. The signal for each planned price reduction is a slowing down in sales. The price reductions are successively introduced until the product has ultimately been offered to the bulk of the overall target market. A variation of this market skimming approach is to launch a highly sophisticated version of a new product, and then reduce the price successively by producing cheaper, simpler, alternative or modified products at each successive stage of the strategy. For a skimming strategy to be successful, the product must be distinctive enough to exclude competitors who may be encouraged to enter the market by the high prices that a company is able to charge in the earlier stages. Other elements of the marketing mix should support the skimming strategy by promoting a high quality, distinctive image. The company must also be prepared and able to forgo high volume production in the initial stages of the product's life, bearing in mind that overall the volume of sales and the price charged must be high enough to achieve profitability.

Figure 11.8 illustrates that the first to adopt a new product (as first-time adopters and not replacement buyers) might be the upper middle social class A – which might well be the case in high fashion. However, for a new type of computer software, innovator categories (explained in Chapter 12) might be a

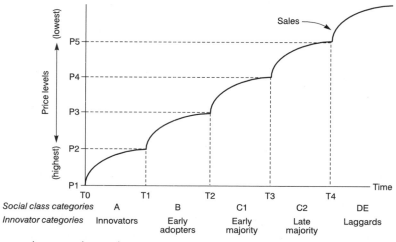

Figure 11.8 Skimming the market.

better indicator of a propensity to adopt. It could be that in this case 'innovators' might well be 'technical' people who may largely belong to the C2 category social class. It should also be noted that the first price charged (P1) is the highest, and, as demand begins to slow at T1, the price is lowered to P2 and so on. Price P5 is the final skim.

Market penetration pricing

When a company has a high production capacity that must be utilised as quickly as possible, a penetration pricing strategy is appropriate to the marketing of a new product. A penetration strategy relies on economies of scale to allow production to be pursued at a price low enough to attract the greatest number of buyers to the market as early as possible. This in turn should preclude potential competitors by erecting price barriers, in the form of large capital set-up costs, to market entry. The longer-term goal is to acquire a high market share and to hold on to this during the later stages of the product's life through further economies of scale, which might allow further price reductions to be made to fight off competition if necessary. Figure 11.9 illustrates penetration pricing, and it can be seen that market share is quickly gained through the adoption of a low initial price.

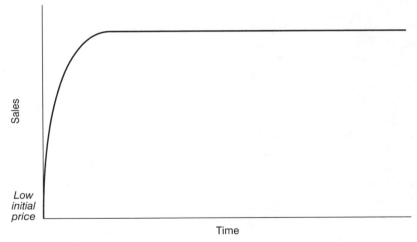

Figure 11.9 Penetration pricing.

11.6.4 Discriminatory pricing

Where markets are easily segmented, companies are often able to charge different prices to each respective segment, even though the product on offer is basically the same. This is referred to as a price discrimination strategy. Sometimes only very minor modifications to a product can allow a discriminatory price to be charged. In other cases discrimination may be based on non-product factors, such as the time of year, customer type or location.

Key point
Sometimes only very minor modifications to a product can allow a discriminatory price to be charged.

The term 'discrimination' does not infer exploitation, as customers can exercise choice. The manufacturer's rationale for discrimination is based on filling capacity by serving new markets. Discrimination on a customer basis can pose problems, as Michael Morris (1987) points out: 'Flexible, discriminatory pricing may generate considerable ill will amongst customers'. Volume discounting is a form of discrimination not always accepted by smaller customers. If the purchase level that qualifies for discount is 1000 units, a customer who only needs to purchase 900 units may feel aggrieved at being excluded from the discount structure.

A popular form of customer discrimination is the variety of discounts offered to children, students and older persons for what are essentially the same services as are offered to the public at large. Apart from any altruistic aims that a company may have, it anticipates that these groups may be encouraged to participate in activities that they could not normally afford, thus increasing the company's total market.

Key point
Discriminatory prices based on time are popular with manufacturers and services industries experiencing seasonal demand.

Discriminatory prices based on time are popular with manufacturers and services industries experiencing seasonal demand. The travel industry regularly offers cheaper prices during the low season. The objective is to attract customers who might not have considered a particular holiday if it had not been for the fact that it was offered at an attractive price. Similarly, transport operators often offer lower rates during off-peak hours, or to stand-by passengers. If the journeys are scheduled in any case, any extra sales (at however low a price) will make a contribution to covering fixed costs.

Often only minor modifications to a product can attract a new market segment to which a company can apply a discriminatory price that is disproportionate to the added value. Swatch^{TM} watches are an example of such a case. The basic production cost for any watch is the mechanism. Swatch^{TM} watches have attractive faces and straps, and are marketed skilfully to enable a premium to be charged for what is essentially a standard production item.

When applying a price discrimination strategy, the market segments chosen should be easily identifiable and separable so that they can be managed and addressed in a manner that distinguishes them from each other. This will reduce feelings of ill will that would otherwise arise from those who are in higher-priced segments of the market.

11.7 Summary

✓ At the beginning of this chapter the usefulness of economic theory to the marketer was qualified in relation to pricing, but a sound knowledge of basic economics is desirable for marketing practice in general. It is especially relevant to the study of demand and cost behaviour.

✓ Price embodies more than a monetary unit that is exchanged for a product or service. It is therefore also desirable to develop knowledge of consumer behaviour, which helps to explain why purchases are made, and buyer behaviour has already been covered in Chapter 6. Although price is important, non-price competition is also effective in achieving sales. Price wars can be damaging, as James Miller (1989) points out in relation to the beer market.

✓ Segmentation strategy, as covered in Chapter 5, is also linked with pricing. If a company's marketing mix strategy for a specific market segment is considered, the role of pricing in the context of its relationship with its other marketing mix partners should become apparent.

✓ Later chapters on market research, including demand analysis as well as forecasting, deal further with the implications of pricing, and also with ethical considerations.

Questions

1 Whilst cost considerations form an essential element of the price determination process, a company's costs have little or no relevance to its customers. Discuss in relation to your organisation's customers.

2 Whenever possible, a company should avoid competing on the basis of price and should instead compete on the basis of superior value. Discuss the role of price in the price/quality relationship. Apply this to your own firm's pricing.

3 What factors should be taken into consideration when pricing *new* products or services.

4 How important are non-pricing factors in the marketing of your organisation's products or services? List the factors in order of importance.

5 Under what circumstances can 'positively high pricing' or 'prestige' pricing be used with effect? Is it used in your firm's pricing strategy? If so, how?

References

Day, G. S. and Ryans, A. B. (1988). Using price discounts for a competitive advantage. *Industrial Marketing Management*, **Feb**, 1–14.

Miller, J. (1989). Anheuser-Busch, slugging it out, plans beer price cuts. *Wall Street Journal*, **26 Oct**, 31.

Morris, M. H. (1987). Separate prices as a marketing tool. *Industrial Marketing Management*, **May**, 79–86.

Reynolds, P. L. and Day, J. (1993). Crisis pricing in times of recession – an investigation into the UK timber and joinery industry. In: *Emerging Issues in Marketing*, Proceedings of the 1993 MEG Annual Conference, 7–9 July, Vol. 2, p. 857. Loughborough University Business School.

Reynolds, P. L. and Day, J. (1994). Pricing for survival – crisis pricing in small firms as a survival strategy. In: *Research at the Marketing/Entrepreneurial Interface* (G. E. Hills and S. T. Mohan-Neill, eds), pp. 300–313. The University of Illinois at Chicago.

Tellis, G. J. (1986). Beyond the many faces of price: an integration of pricing strategies. *Journal of Marketing*, **Oct**, 146–160.

Further reading

Armstrong, G. and Kotler, P. (2000). Pricing products: pricing considerations and strategies. *Marketing: An Introduction*, 5th edn, Chapter 9. Prentice Hall.

Blythe, J. (2001). Pricing strategies. *Essentials of Marketing*, Chapter 7. Person Educational Ltd.

Davies, M. (1998). Pricing. *Understanding Marketing*, Chapter 7. Prentice Hall.

Day, J. and Reynolds, P. L. (1995). The response of entrepreneurial and non-entrepreneurial firms to crisis points on their growth path: an application to the pricing strategies of UK timber and joinery firms. Paper presented to the Small Business Development Conference, April 1995, University of Leeds.

Keegan, W. J. and Green, M. S. (2000). Pricing decisions. *Global Marketing*, 2nd edn, Chapter 12. Prentice Hall.

Lancaster, G. A. and Reynolds, P. L. (1998). Price. *Marketing*, Chapter 8. Macmillan Press Ltd.

Lancaster, G. A. and Reynolds, P. L. (1999). Price. *Introduction to Marketing: A Step by Step Guide to All the Tools of Marketing*, Chapter 11. Kogan Page.

Plamer, W. (2000). *Principles of Marketing*, Chapters 12 and 14. Oxford University Press.

Reynolds, P. L. and Day, J. (1995). The marketing of public sector professional building services in a compulsory competitive tendering environment. Abstract in *Making Marketing Work*, Proceedings of the MEG Annual Conference, Bradford University, 5–7 July.

Product policy 12

12.1 Introduction

The success of a marketing plan relies on how the 'Four Ps' are used in ways that support and complement each other. Different products and markets call for a different mix, but in all cases mix elements need to be applied to a marketing situation whatever the emphasis given to any one of them. The 'product' is especially important. A product strategy presupposes the existence of something to 'take to the market'. The product is the centre or focus of the marketing mix, because it is the product that is ultimately delivered to the consumer. The actual product or service ('product' and 'service' are interchangeable words in the context of this discussion) is that which gives satisfaction to the consumer, fulfilling the overall aim of marketing.

Product policy or strategy is concerned with how the product is presented to the consumer, how it will be perceived, and how long it will last.

Definition
Product policy or strategy is concerned with how the product is presented to the consumer, how it will be perceived, and how long it will last.

12.2 Defining the product

Although consumers or customers (again, interchangeable terms) pay money for something specific and identifiable, they are in fact paying for something that incorporates promotion, availability and perceived value. This has been termed a 'bundle of satisfactions', which can be tangible and intangible (see Figure 12.1). Unless marketers understand and utilise this broad view of the product, any product strategy is likely to be disjointed, poorly targeted and potentially unsuccessful. The task of the marketer is to organise the marketing mix in such a way as to present consumers with an assortment of 'satisfactions' identified as being appropriate to their needs. The marketing mix creates the 'product' in this wider sense, and all its efforts are devoted to delivering something that most exactly matches a defined consumer want or need.

'Product' has been defined at its broadest level. Sometimes known as the 'extended product', this definition considers the product as the total sum of marketing effort. Many who are unfamiliar with marketing restrict their view of a product to one of a physical object, but it is necessary to include 'service' in any definition of the product.

233

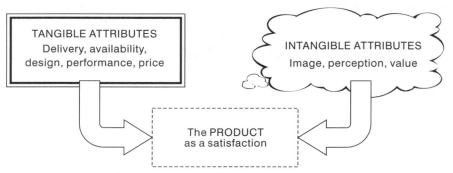

Figure 12.1 Product dimensions – the wider viewpoint.

A holiday is a product in the leisure market, and an insurance policy is a product in the securities and investment market. To the consumer, the product is a satisfaction. Whilst a washing machine is a physical object, the real product features (customer satisfaction) are labour saving and time saving. A frozen ready-prepared meal is composed of physical ingredients; but the satisfaction is convenience. To an industrial buyer, the main feature of a product may be speed of delivery or technical support.

The product can therefore be a physical object, a service or a benefit that can be perceived or real. For the marketer, the product is a want-satisfying item; to the consumer, it is a satisfaction. Having clarified the concept of a product, we now describe products in terms of classification systems.

Vignette 12.1

Bob the Builder builds profits in America

Bob the Builder. the children's character owned by Hit Entertainment, has become a big hit on the other side of the Atlantic and has dramatically improved the profits of the company. UK characters do not always travel well. Characters that are popular to a UK children's audience are not always so well received in other countries, even in those countries that speak English as a first language and have a similar culture. However, dear old Bob has gone down well in the States, and the company intends to make the Bob character a worldwide brand.

Hit Entertainment is a licensing and merchandising company, and holds a 70-year copyright on Bob. The character appeals more to pre-school age children, who are less changeable in their liking and loyalty towards toys and characters such as Bob. The company thinks Bob has a long-term future, and that the Bob brand will support a growing portfolio of Bob products such as dolls, videos, books, clothes and even rugs. Sales of Bob's products continue to grow in the US, and if this growth continues then there are further possibilities to expand the Bob network to other markets such as Canada, Australia, New Zealand and Japan. Bob was developed primarily for the UK market, and appeals to the tastes of pre-school UK children. The company is very fortunate that American children have also taken Bob to their hearts.

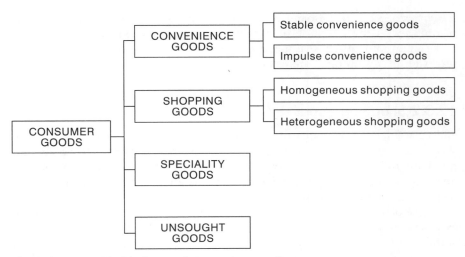

Figure 12.2 Formal classification for consumer goods.

12.3 Product classification (consumer goods)

We are aware that a product has intangible as well as tangible attributes. With this broad perspective in mind, it is now appropriate to consider products in identifiable groups. This is done through a classification that assists market planning. We also ascribe to each group a customer view of products, and thereby ascertain why and how they are purchased.

The first distinction made is between consumer goods and industrial goods. Industrial goods are those bought by manufacturers who then use them to make a product that is in turn sold to make other products. Consumer goods are finished products that are sold to the ultimate user, and these are sub-categorised as shown in Figure 12.2.

12.3.1 Convenience goods

Normally, these are relatively inexpensive items whose purchase requires little effort on the part of the consumer. The weekly shopping requirement mainly comprises convenience goods. The decision process is clouded by the existence of brands that require the consumer to make comparisons and choices. One of the principal tasks of competitive advertising here is to attempt to predetermine the purchase decision for convenience goods, so that the consumer buys (or subconsciously notes) a certain brand rather than first thinking of the generic product and then making a brand-choice decision.

Convenience goods can be further divided into staple and impulse items. Staple convenience goods are those consumed almost every day (e.g. milk, bread and potatoes). Product differentiation for staple items tends to be negligible. If a sudden need arises for a product that might have been overlooked during a major shopping trip, then even less thought is put into the purchase decision. Small grocery stores owe much of their trade to the

Definition
Staple convenience goods are those consumed almost every day (e.g. milk, bread and potatoes).

purchase of such overlooked items. As the name implies, there is no pre-planning with the purchase of impulse convenience goods. The decision to make an impulse purchase is made 'on the spot'. Supermarket displays and the provision of 'dump bins' are often designed to promote impulse sales.

12.3.2 Shopping goods

This classification includes major durable or semi-durable items. Because shopping goods are generally more expensive than convenience goods and purchase is less frequent, their purchase is characterised by pre-planning, information search and price comparisons. The infrequency of such purchases usually means that the consumer is not aware of product availability prior to purchase planning. The purchase of a furniture item, for example, will involve extensive consideration of the relative merits of the products on offer. In addition to product features, the consumer will consider price, place of purchase, purchase (credit) terms, delivery arrangements, after-sales service and guarantees.

The quality of sales staff in stores is a significant factor to success in the marketing of shopping goods. Promotional strategies aim to simplify the decision process for consumers by ensuring that they have a high level of brand awareness before purchase planning begins.

Shopping goods can be further classified into homogeneous or hetero-geneous items. White goods, furniture, DIY equipment and lawnmowers are homogeneous in nature because, although they are important to the consumer, they are not really exclusive. They are goods that are virtual necessities, and in market terms are not very differentiated from each other in terms of price, prestige or image. Heterogeneous shopping goods are stylised and non-standard. Here, price is of less importance to the consumer than image. Behavioural factors play an important role in the purchase decision process.

12.3.3 Speciality goods

Definition
The purchase of speciality goods is characterised by extensive search and a reluctance to accept substitutes once the purchase choice has been made.

The purchase of speciality goods is characterised by extensive search and a reluctance to accept substitutes once the purchase choice has been made. The market for such goods is small, but prices and profits are relatively high. Consumers of speciality goods pay for prestige as well as the product itself. Companies marketing these goods must be skilful at creating and preserving the correct image. If marketing is successful, the customer's search period can be reduced or even eliminated. For instance, some consumers will decide on a particular model of car or a designer label for clothes or jewellery long before the purchase is considered.

12.3.4 Unsought goods

Promoting and selling 'unsought' goods makes up an area of marketing that is susceptible to criticism. By definition, the customer has not considered the purchase of these goods before being made aware of them, and could often do without them. Unsought goods also often satisfy a genuine need that the consumer had not actively considered, for example a life insurance policy, or the need for a funeral to be arranged.

The consumer is often at a disadvantage when confronted with unsought goods, because there probably has been no opportunity for evaluation and comparison. The consumer may view with suspicion any 'special offer', which is often the hallmark of less scrupulous companies. Unsought goods should be marketed in a sensitive manner. Methods of marketing are usually direct mail, telephone canvassing, door-to-door calling and the practice of 'sugging' (or 'selling under the guise of market research', which is described in Chapter 13).

The marketing implication of the system of classification that has been described is that it accurately reflects buying behaviour for large groups of consumers. Naturally, a company is likely to segment its market within a given product class, but the classification system allows for a basic understanding of buyer behaviour as a function of the product. A segmentation strategy that is consumer-orientated, as described in Chapter 5, can then be formulated using this classification basis.

12.4 Product classification (industrial goods)

A classification of industrial goods gives an insight into the uses to which goods are put and reasons for their purchase, which provides a better understanding of the market.

Only some goods classed as 'industrial' are directly essential to manufacture. Machinery and raw materials are prime necessities. However, the company could not function without a whole range of other items that, whilst not being integral to the manufacturing process, are still essential to the overall running of the company. For example, a company needs office furniture and equipment, stationery and cleaning materials, which are ancillary to the manufacturing process.

Goods and services required by industry are formally classified as shown in Figure 12.3.

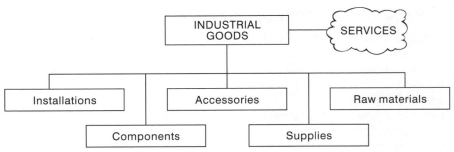

Figure 12.3 Classification of industrial goods.

12.4.1 Installations

These are expensive and critical purchases, and are typically major items of plant and machinery required for the production of a manufacturer's products. If a company makes a mistake in its choice of office equipment or building maintenance services this can be costly, but it is unlikely to be a serious threat to the company's future. However, if a range of machinery is purchased that is subsequently found to be unsuitable, this could affect the entire production base. The purchase of installations should therefore be the result of a very extensive search process. Although price is important in such a decision, it is seldom the single deciding factor. Much emphasis is placed on the quality of sales support and advice, and subsequent technical support and after-sales service.

12.4.2 Accessories

Like installations these are regarded as capital items, but they are usually less expensive and are depreciated over fewer years. Their purchase is important for the company, but not as critical as installation purchases. Accessories include ancillary plant and machinery, office equipment and office furniture. In the case of a haulage company, forklift trucks, warehousing equipment and smaller vehicles would be classified as accessories.

12.4.3 Raw materials

The purchase of raw materials often accounts for much of the time and work of a typical purchasing department. There is a direct relationship between raw material quality and the quality of the company's own finished product, so quality, consistency of supply, service and price are important. Price is also important because these goods are purchased continuously and have a direct and continuous effect on costs, and the more a class of material belongs to the commodity end of the market, the more important price will be.

Even in commodity markets, there are often distinctions in quality of service that can affect the speed of processing or the number of machinery breakdowns. Certainly, raw material suppliers can do much in terms of differentiation to emphasise the fact that they provide a good service.

12.4.4 Component parts and materials

Supply criteria are similar to those for raw materials, and include replacement and maintenance items for manufacturing machinery. In this sense they are different to 'accessories'. This category is a very important part of the purchasing process, particularly in assembly plants, where purchases range from computer chips to casings, fascia panels and even components as large as car bodies. This category also includes those products that facilitate, or are essential in, the manufacturing process, but which do not form part of the finished product – e.g. oils, chemicals, adhesives and packaging materials.

12.4.5 Supplies

These can be likened to the 'convenience goods' of industrial supply, and include such items as office stationery, cleaning materials and goods required for general maintenance and repairs. The purchasing process is often routine and undertaken by less senior employees. Most supplies are relatively homogeneous in nature, and price is likely to be a major factor in the purchasing decision.

12.4.6 Industrial services

The use of outside suppliers of industrial services, especially in the public sector, has risen over recent years. Many organisations now find it is less expensive to employ outside agencies (with the expertise they can offer) to carry out certain tasks than to employ their own personnel. Cleaning, catering, maintenance and transport are such industrial services. So long as the suppliers can meet the standards required by the organisation, it makes economic sense to use outside providers whilst the company concentrates on its own areas of expertise in producing and marketing their products. *Ad hoc* services like management consultancy also fall within this category.

The industrial product classification system that has been described can be linked to organisational buying behaviour. Organisational purchasing has a more rigid routine compared to consumer purchasing. The industrial buyer is dealing with someone else's money, and the amounts spent are large in comparison to individual consumer purchases. This means that the consequences of error are greater. Industrial decision-making is thus generally more considered than for consumer purchases. Industrial buyers are, however, only human, and base decisions on a variety of criteria in addition to those of price, quality and delivery.

Key point
Organisational purchasing has a more rigid routine compared to consumer purchasing.

12.5 New product development

New product development forms part of product strategy as well as being an element of overall marketing strategy. New products should be a prime concern of all levels within an organisation, from top management to the shop floor.

New products are key to a company's continued survival, but their development is a risk-laden undertaking. Large sums of money can be lost, but product failure can also damage a company's image and allow other companies to gain competitive advantage. Naturally, the objective of new product strategy is to launch a successful product, but it is essential that any such strategy be designed to reduce risk throughout individual stages of development.

In consumer markets, new products appear regularly. Confectionery firms, for instance, launch new products, many of which disappear shortly after the initial product promotion. Consumers are often unaware of the work and investment that goes into product development. The development of a new

Key point
New products are key to a company's continued survival, but their development is a risk-laden undertaking.

car, for example, is a multi-million pound investment, although success or failure is of little consequence to the consumer. For many companies, new products represent 'make or break' decisions.

As marketers, it is useful to consider the definitions of various types of new products:

1 *Innovative products* are by definition 'new' to the market. They provide completely different alternatives to the existing products in existing markets. Successful new drugs are 'innovative', as were laser beams and micro-processors and, in their day, the internal combustion engine and the television.

2 *Replacement products* are new to consumers, but 'replace' existing products rather than providing a total innovation. Photographic equipment has been 'replaced' constantly since cameras were invented. The compact disc player and microwave oven are replacement products ('replacing' other methods of sound reproduction and cooking). The technology and some of the component parts of such products are innovative in the marketing sense of new product definitions, but the products themselves are replacements.

3 *Imitative products* is the category into which most new products fall. Once a firm has successfully launched an innovative or replacement product, other firms usually follow. These are sometimes described as 'me too' products. Not all companies have the necessary resources to develop new product ideas, but if a firm has resources, it is often preferable to be a market leader rather than a follower. Some companies do, however, have a deliberate 'me too' approach, preferring to let another company complete costly market development before launching their imitative product. Often a powerful imitator can quickly gain market share from an innovative initiator.

4 *Relaunched products* form the final category, and it must be considered that in more abstract terms the nature of a product is always to be found in the consumer's perception. If a product is successfully relaunched using a different marketing strategy (perhaps by changing the emphasis of product benefits), then it can be called a new product even if its physical characteristics have not substantially altered.

Key point
The product is central
to all marketing
strategy.

The product is central to all marketing strategy. It is easy to overlook the fact that without a product, no other marketing activity would be possible. Not only does the sale of the product (or service) provide revenue, it is also the medium through which a company fulfils the marketing concept. Given the importance of new products and the risks involved in their development, it is essential that any development programme should be carried out in a pre-determined and scientific manner through a new product development programme.

The notion for individual phases in new product development was developed by the American consultants Booz-Allen & Hamilton, and is explained in Figure 12.4.

This study was done in 1968, and it found that it took 58 new product or service ideas to generate one successful product. The study was repeated in 1981, but it was then found that it only took only seven new ideas to come up

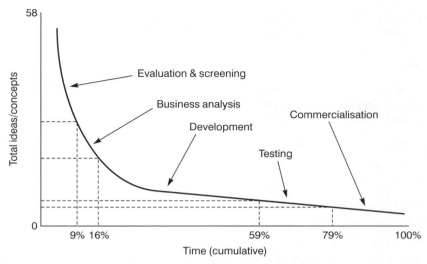

Figure 12.4 Decay curve of new product ideas (from research by Booz-Allen & Hamilton 1968 and 1981).

with one successful product. However, it is the 1968 study that is the most popularly cited one, and it is our belief that it generally takes more than seven new concepts to produce a successful product.

Refinement has taken place since this experiment in relation to the stages of new product development, and the process described in Figure 12.5 represents what is currently viewed as being each of the stages in this process.

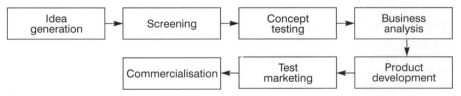

Figure 12.5 Stages in the new product development process.

Idea generation

Of prime importance here is the attitude of management and the atmosphere in which new ideas are encouraged and created. Ideas can spring from many sources, including workers in research and development or production, who are in a good position to see ways of modifying and improving the product. The sales team is ideally placed for reporting on competitive products and providing customer feedback. Senior management, in addition to being responsible for creating an idea-orientated mentality, should hold regular meetings and brainstorming sessions concentrating on the issue of new product development. They can set up venture teams and planning commit-tees to include a mixture of personnel from management to the shop floor.

Market information can provide ideas based either on what other companies are doing or on changes that are taking place in the marketplace.

Screening

The aim of screening is to reduce the pool of ideas to a manageable number by identifying the most potentially viable ideas. Answers must be provided to a number of questions:

- Is there a real consumer need?

- Does the company have the resources and technical competence to market and manufacture the new product?

- Is the potential market large enough to generate profits that correspond to the company's needs?

If the answer to any of these questions is negative, then no further work should be undertaken. Many new products fail because these basic questions have not been asked.

To develop an effective screening technique, the firm should isolate those factors that research has shown to be desirable in the market place. Factors desirable to the firm should also be included, because the firm should attempt to develop products that make best use of production and marketing strengths. An internal appraisal of the company's strengths and weaknesses, together with input from marketing research, should establish what these criteria must be. Statistical weighting techniques can be used to make the selections. The products that best satisfy these criteria should be selected for further development.

Concept testing

During this phase a small number of key decision-makers from within the company, and also potential buyers, are presented with the product idea in a simple format, perhaps accompanied by drawings and a written description. This is in order to ascertain their feelings about the product's likely success in the marketplace. Concept testing uses small resources, and it allows an organisation to test out initial reactions prior to any commitment to more costly research, design and development.

Business analysis

Definition
Business analysis is concerned with the more detailed financial, rather than practical, viability concerns of the concept testing phase.

Business analysis is concerned with the more detailed financial, rather than practical, viability concerns of the previous phase. The company should estimate demand, costs and profitability. Cost analysis needs to take into account marketing costs, as well as the physical costs of raw materials and production.

Product development

Considerable time and energy will have already been expended, as well as some financial outlay, especially if research surveys have been commissioned;

however, compared with the costs of physical product development, the energy and expense so far devoted to the product is likely to be small. By means of thorough pre-analysis, the company has attempted to minimise risk and isolate and validate a new product idea by this phase. During the product development stage, the company develops a prototype product in order to confirm this validity in physical terms. Once a prototype has been developed satisfactorily, the company must again turn to the market place to obtain feedback on the product's suitability in terms of performance and customer attitude. The prototype should correspond as closely as possible to the envisaged production model so as to obtain accurate customer reactions. At this stage, the product can be modified or 'fine tuned'.

It is possible to abandon the idea at this stage if market reaction is perceived to be negative. It is important that the company be ruthless at rejecting products at any stage of development. The fact that a flaw is found in the feasibility of the product at this late stage should not influence the decision to abandon the idea, even though it may appear to be wasteful, as subsequent failure will be far more costly.

If the product development stage is successful, the firm should then have the confidence to go ahead with a product launch. This decision is critical, and requires considerable business competence and courage. If the product is rejected at this stage, a valuable opportunity might be lost. On the other hand, the decision to go ahead commits the company to the relatively large costs of production and the marketing costs associated with a new product launch.

Test marketing

This is the final check on whether or not the new product is being marketed properly. It is an error to consider a test market as a final 'screen' for a new product. In fact, when a company enters a test market the decision to launch the product has already been taken. The purpose of a test market is to test the appropriateness of the proposed marketing strategy and associated tactics, to refine them if necessary, and to predict the effect of such strategy in terms of potential market penetration.

For consumer markets, test marketing is made simpler by the existence of Independent Television areas. These divide the UK into well-defined areas that can be used as test market areas. They are particularly appropriate when television advertising is a component of marketing strategy. No matter how the test market area is chosen, it is important that the chosen area should be as closely representative of the final total market as possible. If this is not the case, the whole objective of 'testing' is lost. Sometimes companies will run two test markets at the same time in different geographical locations. This offers opportunities for experimentation. Variations of the marketing mix can be tested simultaneously to try to find the best balance possible within an optimum budget.

Market research agencies now provide sophisticated services to companies when they test market. In FMCG markets, it is important to establish the rate of 'penetration' for a given brand. The increasing use of modelling techniques, aided by computer technology, has greatly improved the accuracy of predictive analysis. Statistical analyses can also reduce the need for large scale testing.

Definition
The purpose of a test market is to test the appropriateness of the proposed marketing strategy and associated tactics, to refine them if necessary, and to predict the effect of such strategy in terms of potential market penetration.

Test markets are sometimes 'sabotaged' by competitors, who can create artificial conditions of increased marketing activity in the test area for a short period with the intention of causing disruption and creating market conditions that are not representative. For this reason test markets should be as unobtrusive as possible, and many companies confine such test marketing activities to a small geographical location – smaller than a television area.

A number of 'test towns' now exist in the UK, which are said to represent as closely as possible a microcosm of the UK as a whole. Examples of such towns are Darlington, Croydon, Bristol and Southampton.

In industrial markets, where the number of customers may be small, testing can be achieved by initially marketing to a few co-operating customers who provide feedback before a full-scale launch takes place. There are more correctly termed 'product placement tests'. This testing technique is also used for consumer items like washing machines.

Commercialisation

Various ideas have been filtered out by now, so a viable proposition has been selected. The production, financial and commercial criteria have been examined, and a suitable product, acceptable to the marketplace, has been prepared. Test marketing has permitted the company to make any final adjustments to the chosen marketing strategy. The product can now be 'commercialised' on a full-scale basis.

New products have a high failure rate, and this can only be lessened through a scientific analysis of the market along the lines described. Figure 12.6 illustrates the relationship between cost and the various stages of product development. Development costs increase as commercialisation comes closer. The importance of screening is re-emphasised; it is essential to reject unsuitable product ideas as early as possible to minimise development costs.

Key point
Development costs increase as commercialisation comes closer.

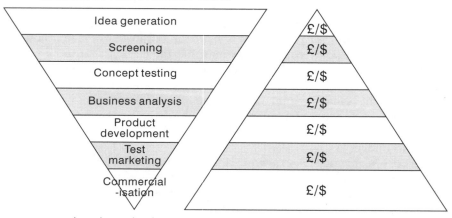

Figure 12.6 The relationship between cost and product development.

Vignette 12.2

Rolls-Royce big 'down under' in the superjumbo stakes

The UK aeroplane engine manufacturer Rolls-Royce has once again 'flown the flag' for the home country and managed to win a major order 'down under' against fearsome competition from the major American aerospace firms. The $10.7 billion Airbus project to develop the 555-seat A380, the biggest civil aircraft in the world, is the most impressive project ever undertaken by the European aerospace industry. Rolls-Royce is now firmly at the centre of things, and is in fact the leading aircraft engine supplier so far within the whole programme. Rolls-Royce's victory was won from under the nose of the rival 'Engine Alliance', which is a strategic alliance of the might of US aerospace manufacturers Pratt and Whitney and General Electric.

Rolls-Royce is to supply the Australian airline Qantas with engines to power the 12 A380s that the airline has on order. Qantas is not the only airline to consider Rolls-Royce engines the best there is. In addition to winning the Qantas order, the Rolls-Royce Trent 900 engine has also been ordered by Virgin Atlantic, Singapore Airlines and the International Lease Finance Corporation. Rolls-Royce's major strategic advantage is product quality and reliability, including excellent ongoing servicing and after-sales programmes. The firm spends an enormous amount of time and effort on product development. The quality of its aerospace products is acknowledged as being possibly the best in the world.

12.6 The product life cycle

The idea of the product life cycle (PLC) is central to product and marketing strategy. It is based on the premise that a new product enters a 'life cycle' once it is launched on the market. The product has a 'birth' and a 'death', described as 'introduction' and 'decline' respectively, and the intervening period is characterised by 'growth' and 'maturity'. By mapping a product's course through the market like this, it is possible to design marketing strategies appropriate to the relevant stage in the product's life. In addition to the stages outlined, an additional stage is that of 'saturation', which is a levelling off in sales once maturity is reached and prior to decline.

There is much enthusiasm for the PLC concept, but it must be used with caution. Not every product fits conveniently into the theoretical curve it proposes. It is also true that where a product's demise seems inevitable, there is often a great deal that creative management can do to extend the course of the curve.

Key point
There is much enthusiasm for the PLC concept, but it must be used with caution.

Figure 12.7 shows the course for the hypothetical life cycle of a product. The marketing environment is dynamic, so even basically similar products are likely to react differently during their life span. The PLC is influenced by:

- the intrinsic nature of the product itself

- changes in the macro environment

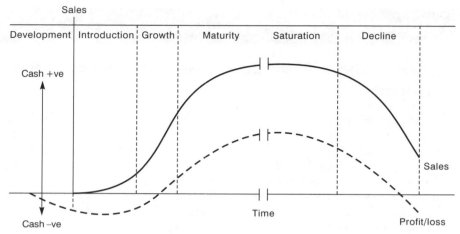

Figure 12.7 Product life cycle (PLC).

- changes in consumer preferences, which are affected by the macro- and micro-environment

- competitive actions.

The 'market influence' on the shape of the curve can also influence the time span of the life cycle, which can range from weeks to decades.

A daily newspaper is often cited as a product with a very short life cycle, because it is of little use the day after publication. However, this is a poor example, because in considering a newspaper the real product is the newspaper as a 'name' rather than an individual edition. However, newspaper titles, whilst not short PLC examples (distribution strategy, for example, varies little over time), do provide good examples of introduction and decline and, in particular, life cycle extension. Changes in format, use of colour and changed editorial content are designed to revive flagging interest in a newspaper suffering from falling circulation figures.

In strategic terms, the tasks of marketing management are to:

1 Estimate the likely shape of the total curve

2 Design an appropriate strategy for each stage

3 Identify the product's movement from one stage to another.

Key point
The value of the concept is that once the stage has been identified, markets are seen to display certain characteristics that suggest specific strategic reactions.

The value of the concept is that once the stage has been identified, markets are seen to display certain characteristics that suggest specific strategic reactions. The life cycle stages highlighted in Figure 12.7 will now be examined, along with their associated strategies.

12.6.1 Development

During this phase, of course, no sales are made, and as time proceeds so development costs accrue. This can be seen on the lower negative cash flow curve.

12.6.2 Introduction

This is the period relating to the new product launch, and its duration depends on the product's rate of market penetration. The period ends when awareness of the product is high enough to attract wider user groups and therefore sales increase at a steeper rate.

Typical conditions associated with the introduction stage are:

- A high product failure rate

- Relatively few competitors

- Limited distribution (often exclusive or selective)

- Frequent product modifications

- Company losses, because development costs have not yet been recouped, promotional expenditure is relatively high in relation to sales, and economies of scale are not yet possible.

The goal at this stage is to create awareness. This usually involves a disproportionate level of marketing expenditure relative to sales revenue. This must be regarded as an investment in the product's future. Promotion is the marketing mix element used to create this product awareness. The sales function is also important in communicating the product's benefits to users.

The introductory pricing strategy will depend on the type of product in terms of its degree of distinctiveness. The company may wish to achieve high sales levels in a short space of time, or slowly to establish a profitable niche in the marketplace. Price is also affected by competitive activity, as this determines how long any product distinctiveness is likely to last.

The company has two strategic options:

1 A skimming pricing strategy involves the application of a high price to a small target group of consumers (typically innovators and early adopters, as discussed in Chapter 11). Whilst the product remains distinctive, growth can be encouraged by a planned series of progressive price reductions.

2 A penetration pricing strategy to attract the largest possible number of new buyers early in the product's life. This involves pricing the product at a low level, and is appropriate where demand is elastic and there is a high level of competitive activity.

Definition
A skimming pricing strategy involves the application of a high price to a small target group of consumers.

In both cases, the role of pricing is to establish the product in such a way as to permit further strategy to be implemented in the subsequent stages. A skimming approach should 'set the scene' for product distinctiveness to be retained as long as possible. Whilst profits are not necessarily forthcoming during introduction, the introductory pricing strategy should prepare for profitability in the future.

Distribution decisions are determined by expected penetration or skimming, and it is important that the product is available to the intended market. Out-of-stock situations provide competitors with opportunities to take market share that can be costly to win back.

12.6.3 Growth

During growth the product is still vulnerable to failure (although most failures occur early during this stage). Competitive products, launched by more powerful companies, can enter the market at this stage and pose a sufficient threat to cause some companies to withdraw.

The characteristics of growth are:

● More competitors and less product distinctiveness

● More profitable returns

● Steeply rising sales

● Company or product acquisition by larger competitors.

Promotional expenditure still features strongly, because this is the best time to acquire market share. It should, however, be at a level that does not drain profits, although it is not unusual for high levels of expenditure to continue throughout growth in order to achieve profitable market dominance during the maturity stage. The emphasis of the promotional effort changes from creating product awareness to specific brand or trade name promotion.

Distribution retains its importance during growth. In FMCG markets in particular, success often depends on finding shelf space in retail outlets, although these now tend to be dominated by a small number of operators (as discussed in Chapter 9). Once a 'hierarchy' of brand leaders has been established, powerful buyers in retail multiples may attempt to rationalise their list of suppliers. Distribution is a key factor in such decisions, because retailers will wish to keep their stock levels to realistic levels. In other markets distribution is equally important because, during growth, suppliers are in competition with each other to establish dealership and distributive outlet agreements.

A company should attempt to optimise the product's price during growth, especially if a skimming policy is in operation, and towards the end of this period profits are usually at their highest. The end of growth is often characterised by reduced prices at the end of skimming (even though profits may be still high as a result of higher volumes). As the growth period moves towards maturity, market shares tend to stabilise and a hierarchy of brand or market leaders will probably have emerged.

12.6.4 Maturity

At any one time, the majority of products are normally in the maturity stage of the product life cycle. Much marketing activity is devoted to this stage.

The major characteristics of the maturity stage are:

● Sales continuing to grow, but at a much decreased rate

● Attempts to differentiate and re-differentiate products

● Prices falling in battles to retain market share, and profits falling correspondingly

- Increasing brand and inventory rationalisation amongst retailers and distributors

- Marginal manufacturers retiring from the market when faced with severe competition and reduced margins.

A key task of marketing strategy during maturity is to retain market share. The promotional role should be to reinforce brand loyalty.

It should be emphasised that exponential market growth has ceased by this stage. Any growth is achieved at the expense of competitors. There is therefore a need for sustained promotional activity, even if only to retain existing customers. Deciding the level of promotional expenditure can be a problem in view of contracting profit margins.

In line with the aims of promotion, distribution strategy should be designed to retain outlets. A retail outlet or distributorship that is lost during maturity is unlikely to be easily regained at a later stage. To this end, the major thrust of promotional effort may move from the consumer to the distributor.

Key point
A key task of marketing strategy during maturity is to retain market share.

12.6.5 Saturation

This stage is considered in many textbooks as being part of the maturity phase, but it does have characteristics that make it slightly different. It is where the peak of 'maturity' has been passed, and is just before the final decline. Saturation is the period when 'price wars' are common and lower-priced producers have entered the marketplace, as they have been able to replicate the manufacturing technology, often in low labour cost countries. Price wars should be avoided, although the problem is that the market is so saturated that this is the inevitable result. The result is an overall reduction in revenue for all participants, although it is good news for consumers. The aim of price-cutting should be to increase purchases sufficiently to offset any revenue loss, but the reality is that it is often a signal for more established players to exit from the marketplace before decline.

12.6.6 Decline

The shape of the PLC curve is theoretical and should not be regarded as inevitable, but persistently falling sales signify the decline stage of the product. Market intelligence should be able to identify and predict this phenomenon. Consumer preferences may have changed, or innovative products may have displaced existing products.

Characteristics of decline are:

- Sales falling continually for the total period

- A further intensification of price-cutting

- Producers deciding to abandon the market.

As stated earlier, the decision to abandon a market poses problems for the firm and is often made too late. However, some companies believe that it is worthwhile extending the product's life well into decline, whilst the number of competitors is falling, in the belief that in a declined market there will be few competitors but still a residual demand. In such circumstances it is often the case that price reductions can be halted, or prices can even be increased, as there are few or no competitors to make a challenge.

Whilst continuing in the marketplace, during this phase management's attention is likely to move from active marketing to cost control. Cost control and cost reduction is always an important element of management activity, but during decline this may be the only method of maintaining profitability.

Vignette 12.3

It's the real thing but forget the fizz

The Coca-Cola Company has always had the strategy of making Coke available anywhere it can possibly be sold, and getting as many people to drink it as often as possible. The firm employs an intensive distribution strategy to this end, placing the product in all kinds of retail outlets and using vending machines to close any gaps in the product's distribution. The company has been completely focused in selling Coke world-wide, and its advertising is some of the most recognised in the world. For example, the large red Coke bottle is one of the best-known icons in Times Square, New York.

But things seem to be changing within the heart of the Coca-Cola Company. Has the firm lost its strategic direction? The company has decided on a joint venture with Nestlé to sell tea and coffee, a joint venture with Proctor and Gamble to sell juices and snacks, and an agreement with Walt Disney to sell Disney-branded children's drinks. In fact, many of these products will not have the Coca-Cola brand on them at all.

The world trend seems to be away from 'fizzy' carbonated drinks full of sugar or sugar substitutes and towards a wider range of beverages that are non-carbonated and more health-orientated. The company sees the world drink market in terms of four segments. The traditional Coke drink falls into one of these segments, carbonated drinks. The other segments are health and nutrition, rejuvenation, and replenishment. These segments require a completely different beverage portfolio to the traditional Coke drink. The joint venture strategy makes sense. It will allow the firm to give the marketing of the drinks in these other segments to the partners of the joint venture, and allow the Coca-Cola Company to concentrate on what it does best, marketing the traditional Coke.

12.7 The PLC as a management tool

There are a number of detractors to the notion of the PLC, and like any theory it can pose a problem if it is taken too literally (for example, a product might be prematurely discarded if there is a downturn in sales in the belief that it has started to decline, but what management might be witnessing is a temporary downturn at the end of the introduction stage). The key to successful use of the concept is the ability to identify accurately the transition from one stage to another, which requires the company to use marketing research and intelligence. Management will then have the framework for using the PLC as a long-term strategic planning tool. In particular, use of the PLC provides two valuable benefits:

1 A predictable course of product development for which appropriate strategies can be planned and budgeted

2 The scope to plan beyond the life of the existing product.

In some cases there might be an overlap in the lives of two products. The launch of the second product should ideally be funded from the profits of the first product's growth period. The timing of new product launches should be synchronised with the life cycles of existing products, enabling the company to perpetuate its presence in the market.

The PLC provides a 'framework' for planning, but management should be master of the theory. In difficult trading conditions, it may be judicious to bring the product's life to a premature end in order to afford the company a better allocation of resources. Alternatively, the product need not necessarily fall into decline at all; its life can be extended by finding new end uses, or by finding new markets.

Key point
The PLC provides a 'framework' for planning, but management should be master of the theory.

Normally, an extension of the life cycle does not involve too many product modifications. If the basic product is altered radically, it can be argued that this is a new product, albeit not an innovative one.

In understanding the PLC concept, it is important to distinguish between the specific and the generic product. Following the launch of a truly innovative product (e.g. the video recorder), many imitative products will emerge. Some of these will follow the typical PLC pattern, and others will not. This will depend on the skill of company management, and strategic decisions as to their future course in the marketplace. As a generic product the video recorder is likely to follow a typical life cycle course, with a stretched maturity point representing replacement buyers, until an innovative alternative is launched.

The identification of the transition period from one stage to another is a difficult task. Where innovative products are concerned there will be no empirical data on previous products, so the product represents a unique situation. If the concept is adhered to too rigidly, management planners may 'think' themselves into successive stages and thus into decline, which may not be the case. Critics contend that the PLC becomes a self-fulfilling prophecy, and that management is liable to miss opportunities because of too dogmatic an approach to the theory. Marketing is a creative process, and the PLC concept is meant to provide a guide to strategy.

12.8 The product adoption process

The product adoption process has already been introduced in Chapter 6 insofar as it relates to buyer behaviour. The PLC concept has considered the product in relation to the marketplace. From the product adoption process, described in Figure 12.8, we can learn something about users or consumers who are the targets of marketing strategy. The relationship is simple, yet positive enough to enable us to draw conclusions about the characteristics of

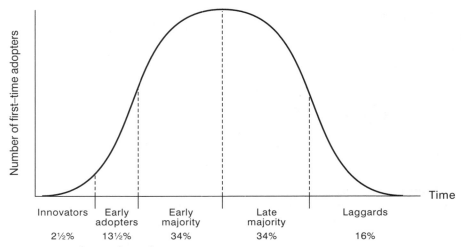

Figure 12.8 The product adoption process.

the consumers in each adopter category. The theory is applicable to both industrial and consumer markets. It is important to remember that consumers will not necessarily fall into the same category for all products. An early adopter of a photographic innovation could be a laggard in the garden-tool market.

The rate at which the product moves through these adopter categories is termed the 'diffusion of innovations', i.e. the extent to which each adopter category successively influences another towards adoption. This theory is widely acknowledged in marketing. Chapter 6 has already dealt with the diffusion process in terms of a detailed discussion of the various adopter categories, but it has been discussed here in the context of the product.

12.9 Product (and market) management

Definition
Product management is the function responsible for the 'fortunes' of the product, and covers tactical and strategic marketing issues as the product follows its course along the life-cycle curve.

Product management is the function responsible for the 'fortunes' of the product, and covers tactical and strategic marketing issues as the product follows its course along the life-cycle curve. The managing director is of course responsible for managing the whole company, and managing the marketing of products is delegated to the marketing director or manager. The marketing manager then delegates responsibility further throughout the marketing function. Just as many companies employ an advertising manager, a marketing research manager or a sales manager, there is often justification for employing somebody whose role is specifically concerned with products or brands. In FMCG companies, the term 'brand management' is usually substituted for product management.

How marketing is organised depends on the type of company, the nature of its products, and the markets in which it operates. A simple marketing structure is outlined in Figure 12.9.

Figure 12.9 A functional marketing organisation.

As the number of products to be marketed increases problems might develop, as responsibility for individual products may become blurred. Some products may become neglected, and marketing mix elements might be misallocated.

A product-management structure offers a solution to this problem in that a manager is made directly responsible for each product's success and for the allocation of marketing resources. It is the product manager who decides the level and type of support required from the marketing functions. Figure 12.10 shows the product manager's position in relation to other functional marketing specialists.

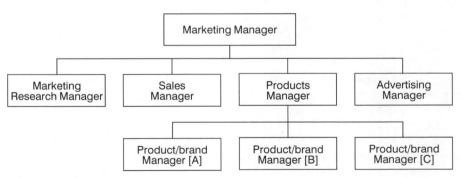

Figure 12.10 A product/brand management structure.

A products manager will oversee the overall management of the company's products or brands, and is responsible to the marketing manager. In a large company, a group product manager might take control of a range of similar products (e.g. frozen foods, agrichemicals or cosmetics). Product (or brand) managers serve under that person with responsibility for individual brands. In this way, control and management of the product is focused. The product manager is responsible for all aspects of the product's welfare, through liaison with other functional managers within the marketing function.

A product management system is appropriate when companies have a large number of products, or where products differ widely in nature. A criticism of this system is that product managers are not functional experts, and must rely on liaison with the other functional managers to execute their ideas. This can lead to conflicts of interest between these parties, and also to conflict between

Key point
A product management system is appropriate when companies have a large number of products, or where products differ widely in nature.

individual product managers. It is important, therefore, that individual roles are clearly delineated.

The term 'market manager' is occasionally used in a similar philosophical context to that of product management. Here, the company markets similar products, but to diverse customer groups. An example is computer applications to banks, educational establishments, public sector, retailing and so on. Here, user needs differ widely, so the overall head is a 'markets manager', with an individual 'market manager' in charge of each of these individual market groupings.

Vignette 12.4

Product quality counts in the minds of consumers: a lesson for Mitsubishi Motors

Mitsubishi Motors used to have a good reputation for quality and value for money. That is until last year, when the company chairman resigned after it became known that the company had been covering up the degree of serious customer complaints for 30 years. A number of senior staff within the firm were also prosecuted as a result of this cover-up. In 2000, the company recalled about one million cars due to poor product quality. Analysts thought that the worst was behind the company, and that important product quality lessons had finally been learnt. However, in February of 2001 the firm said it was going to recall another 1.4 million cars at least, due to serious mechanical faults.

The German/US car maker DaimlerChrysler purchased 34 per cent of the company in 2000, and has faced many problems since the deal was completed. DaimlerChrysler has put money aside to restructure Mitsubishi in a 'no stone left unturned' reorganisation, which will probably involve serious job losses and plant closures as well as a restructuring of Mitsubishi's distribution network. Experts estimate Mitsubishi's losses for 2001 to be in the region of 47 billion Yen, an estimate that has already seriously affected the organisation's share price, which fell 8 per cent on the news. DaimlerChrysler intends to put its own staff in senior positions within Mitsubishi, including the position of chief executive. Many think the class of cultures between the Japanese and the German–American management teams will cause additional problems.

12.10 Product line and product mix

Definition
The product mix is the total assortment of products that a company markets.

The product mix is the total assortment of products that a company markets. So this assortment can be more easily managed, products can be grouped into product lines or groups of products that are similar in terms of their functions, or because they are sold to similar groups of customers.

A food manufacturer might market a range of beverages as well as other products like convenience foods. Beverages can be arranged as a product line. It may even be appropriate to arrange different beverages into their own individual product lines. Thus, the coffee product line might include different varieties of instant coffee, coffee beans, ground coffee and coffee sachets. The length of a product line will then denote the number of individual products in the line; the width of the product mix denotes how many lines go to make up the mix.

This system allows management to look objectively at its product mix and decide whether or not certain lines should be lengthened, shortened or even deleted. As well as allowing the development of line strategies, this organised method of looking at the products of a company shows where profits are being made. These profits can then be directly related to marketing expenditure.

12.11 Summary

✓ A study of the product is inevitably bound up with other areas of marketing, in particular with consumer and organisational buying behaviour. This topic was covered in Chapter 6, which highlighted how new products are accepted by purchasers and how information relating to these new products is disseminated throughout the marketing system. This chapter has now related this knowledge to its applicability to the notion of the product life cycle concept.

✓ Another area that is linked with the product is that of market segmentation and product positioning, and this was the focus of Chapter 5.

✓ The whole area of portfolio analysis is one of strategy, and this is tied in very closely to product. A full discussion of this aspect takes place in Chapter 17.

Questions

1 *New products*
   (a) Why is it necessary for a company to develop new products?
   (b) How can a company stimulate the generation of new product ideas?

2 *Product classification*
   Why is it helpful to have a system that classifies products and services into a number of different categories?

3 *Product life cycle*
   Is the PLC concept more useful for looking at sales of products for an individual company or sales of products for an industry as a whole?

4 *Product management*
   Do you feel that the product/brand management system only has applicability for fast-moving consumer goods, or is there some applicability for industrial products?

Further reading

Armstrong, G. and Kotler, P. (2000). *Marketing: An Introduction*, 5th edn, Chapters 7 and 8. Prentice Hall.

Blythe, J. (2001). Products, branding and packages. *Essentials of Marketing*, Chapter 6. Person Educational Ltd.

Davies, M. (1998). Managing the product in the marketing mix. *Understanding Marketing*, Chapter 6. Prentice Hall.

Keegan, W. J. and Green, M. S. (2000). Product and branding decisions. *Global Marketing*, 2nd edn, Chapter 11. Prentice Hall.

Lancaster, G. A. and Reynolds, P. L. (1998). Products and services. *Marketing*, Chapter 7. Macmillan Press.

Lancaster, G. A. and Reynolds, P. L. (1999). Product and portfolio analysis. *Introduction to Marketing: A Step by Step Guide to All the Tools of Marketing*, Chapter 10. Kogan Page.

Levitt, T. (1983). *Differentiation of Anything: the Marketing Imagination*, pp. 72–93. Collier Macmillan.

Morse, S. (1994). *Successful Product Management*. Kogan Page.

Plamer, A. (2000). *Principles of Marketing*, Chapters 9 and 10. Oxford University Press.

Rogers, E. (1962). *Diffusion of Innovations*, p. 162. The Free Press.

Urban, G. L. and Hauser, J. R. (1993). *Design and Marketing of New Products*. Prentice-Hall.

Marketing research 13

13.1 Introduction

The American Marketing Association (AMA, 1961) defines marketing research as: 'the systematic gathering, recording and analysing of data relating to the marketing of goods and services'. Kotler (1994) defines it as: 'systematic problem analysis, model building and fact finding for the purpose of improved decision-making and control in the marketing of goods and services'. Doyle (1994) states that marketing management consists of five tasks, one of which is marketing research and explains: 'Management has to collect information on the current and potential needs of customers in the markets chosen, how they buy and what competitors are offering'.

Research attempts to find reliable and unbiased answers to questions. Marketing research provides information in a systematic way about the market for goods or services and probes people's ideas and intentions on many issues. As explained in Chapter 3, in a complex consumer society there is little direct contact between the producer and consumer. Marketing research can, by the collection, analysis and interpretation of facts, find out what it is that people want and ascertain why they want it.

Definition
Research attempts to find reliable and unbiased answers to questions.

Effective marketing decisions are as good as the information on which they are based. Decision-making underlies the management process at every level, and the terms 'managing' and 'decision-making' are synonymous. Marketing management is of course the process of making decisions in relation to marketing problems. Marketing research is utilised by marketing management when planning the marketing strategy of an enterprise. The application of the techniques and methodology of marketing research is as applicable in the not-for-profit sector as in profit-making organisations. A disciplined and systematic approach to research methodology in the area of investigation is needed, and a series of steps should be taken in developing, planning and executing research with a view to solving specific problems.

13.2 Main areas of marketing research

The underlying concept is an appreciation of the fact that to manage a business well, is to manage its future. Marketing research has a contribution to make in decisions involving any area of an organisation's marketing mix. Management needs information about its markets and competitors, and changes and developments in the external environment, to aid marketing decisions, whether these are operational, tactical or strategic.

13.2.1 Product research

This is generally concerned with all aspects of design, development and testing of new products, as well as the improvement and modification of existing products. Activities include:

- comparative testing against competitive products
- test marketing
- concept testing
- idea generation and screening
- product elimination/simplification
- brand positioning.

This last point is particularly important as heavy competitive pressures of the new millennium make it important that brand-positioning strategies be effectively developed, and this research has been particularly advanced by de Chernatony and Daniels (1994).

13.2.2 Communications research

Fast-moving consumer goods companies in particular spend a lot of money on marketing communications. The communications mix (including personal selling, direct mail, exhibitions, sponsorship and advertising) can be more effectively planned as a result of research information. Communications research activities include:

- pre- and post-testing of advertising
- media planning research
- readership surveys
- testing alternative selling techniques
- exhibition and sponsorship evaluation.

13.2.3 Pricing research

Techniques like the 'buy–response model' can be used to:

- assist in establishing a more market-orientated pricing strategy
- see what kind of prices consumers associate with different product variations (e.g. packaging)
- establish market segments in relation to price.

13.2.4 Corporate planning

Research activities that can assist corporate planners include:

- evaluation of companies for acquisition
- assessment of an organisation's strengths and weaknesses
- portfolio analysis
- corporate image studies.

13.2.5 Distribution research

Techniques such as the 'retail audit' can monitor the effectiveness of different types of distribution channels and detect regional variations.

This list is not exhaustive, but it illustrates the range of areas in which marketing research can aid decision-making. Other areas include industrial market research and international market research.

Vignette 13.1

Wholesale Electro Ltd uses simple customer surveys to boost business by 25 per cent in one year

Wholesale Electro Ltd (WEL) is a small family-owned electrical wholesaler (called a 'factor' in the UK). It is based in West Yorkshire, England, and has four branches in the region and an annual turnover of approximately £3 million ($4.5 million). It is a private limited company. Customers include independent (jobbing) electricians, small electrical contractors (usually two to five employees), and the maintenance departments of medium and sometimes quite large firms in the area.

The company's project range includes tools and testing equipment, safety wear, and general electrical equipment and fittings such as light fittings etc. Such a range constitutes most of that which an electrician or maintenance engineers would need on a regular basis. Particularly expensive equipment or out of the ordinary products can be ordered from the firm's own catalogue or from a range of manufacturers' brochures, which the firm supplies. Orders can be placed in person by calling at the trade counter, or by telephone or mail. A technical telephone advisory service is also available.

The company had been trading for six years (at case date), and in that time had grown from a total turnover of £250 000 in the first year to its present level. Management thought that it must have been doing the 'right thing' – after all, the company was successful – but they were not entirely sure. Hence they decided to commission a customer service appreciation survey, which was partly funded under a Department of Trade and Industry Small Firm Marketing Initiative.

The survey involved the use of a postal questionnaire, which was administered to all of their existing 1250 customers. The purpose of the survey was to allow the firm to establish the degree of satisfaction or dissatisfaction with various important elements of the business. The postal questionnaire itself, the covering letter, the return envelope and the outgoing envelope were all chosen and designed to be of the highest quality and standard. The questionnaire letters and envelope had the firm's name and logo incorporated, and all documents were professionally produced and printed. Particular attention was paid to the wording of the covering letter, principally to maximise the response rate of the survey, but also to deliberately convey the impression of concern and care for customer's needs. The intention was to demonstrate to the customer that WEL was a highly customer-oriented, market-driven firm that regarded customer care and customer satisfaction with the utmost importance. After two weeks a further letter, along with all the original material, was sent to non-respondents. After a further two weeks the survey was closed.

In the first two weeks the company received 265 completed questionnaires, and the second wave of responses produced another 94, making a total of 359 replies. Questionnaires had been pre-coded to provide the base for the analysis of classification variables – e.g. size of firm, type of firm, sales with WSE, etc. By relating their analysis of the questionnaires to specific companies, management was able to prepare highly operational action plans for the short, medium or long term. These plans were customer specific, formed the basis for targeted future marketing improvements, and acted as criteria for future evaluation.

The total cost of the survey was around £2500, 75 per cent of which was paid for by a government grant. As a result of carrying out the survey, WEL was able to address a number of key marketing weaknesses in a customer-specific manner. The company was able to improve dramatically the overall level of service to their existing customer base, and overall was able to increase sales by approximately 27 per cent from existing customers within 12 months (see Reynolds and Day, 1994, 1995).

13.3 Evaluating information

Key point
Information is vital to successful marketing in terms of its generation, processing and circulation.

Marketing information can be expensive to obtain (for example, a national *ad hoc* survey commissioned from a large agency). Information is vital to successful marketing in terms of its generation, processing and circulation. Extraneous information is often a problem with marketing research, and this is both expensive and a waste of time. Therefore the information function needs to be managed and controlled like any other area of the company's operations, and information should be:

- reliable
- relevant to users' needs
- adequate for the type of decisions being made
- timely
- cost-effective to obtain.

13.4 The marketing information system

Marketing research is a component part of a wider marketing information system (MkIS), which collects, processes and co-ordinates information from a

Figure 13.1 Marketing information system (MkIS).

wide range of sources. The MkIS is a computer-based decision-support system, and it has a number of inputs and one output (Figure 13.1).

The MkIS has inputs from marketing research, market intelligence and the internal accounting system. Its output is primarily for strategic marketing planning, but, as the marketing plan is implemented during the planned-for period, what is planned does not always match what happens in reality. These deviations from the plan are then fed back into the MkIS, so this is a double-headed arrow. Inputs from the internal accounting system relate to factors like sales analyses by time, by product group, by region, by customer type, etc. Market intelligence relates to information that has been obtained principally from the field sales force, who in the course of their work obtain information about customers, competitors, distributors, etc., and then feed this information into the MkIS. The MkIS in turn is part of the organisation-wide management information system (MIS).

Definition
Market intelligence relates to information that has been obtained principally from the field sales force, who in the course of their work obtain information about customers, competitors, distributors, etc., and then feed this information into the MkIS.

13.5 Marketing research as a problem-solving process

The solution of a marketing problem requires a systematic approach. This permits better application of available resources to the key elements of the problem, with a minimum loss of time. Every marketing problem has three vital dimensions:

1 *Time*. This determines the urgency of the situation. It is significant, because some research approaches that might otherwise be suitable may be impossible within the time before a decision must be reached.

2 *Profit*. This determines the relative importance of the particular problem given the financial situation of the company. It is helpful in assigning priorities to different problems competing for attention.

3 *Facilities*. The facilities dimension is concerned with the availability of personnel and other facilities required for a successful solution of the problem.

A problem-solving approach to marketing research planning involves six steps:

1 *Definition* of the marketing problem in specific terms

2 *Refinement* of the marketing problem, and its subdivision into various individual marketing research problems

3 *Development of a plan* for securing the facts or information needed

4 *Execution of the plan* by collecting facts or information

5 *Analysis and interpretation* of the facts in terms of the problem

6 *Summary* of the results in a report.

The objective of this problem-solving process is identify and isolate any problem elements. For example, in a complex marketing problem such as an unexplained sales decline, this can be subdivided into competitive, market and company elements. Hypotheses are developed and explored in the search for problem elements. Sometimes research is necessary, even in this diagnostic stage, to help define the problem. Marketing research is much more effective, and makes its maximum contribution when it is integrated into the problem-solving process at the marketing problem level than when the research function is simply assigned portions of the problem for exploration without the entire background to the problem.

Vignette 13.2

Leamington's Department Store uses marketing research to develop customer retention strategies

Leamington's (name disguised) is one of a few family-owned department stores in the UK, and is located in the centre of a traditional northern industrial town. The firm started as a small shop located in the city outskirts some 90 years ago, selling textile products such as curtains and towels often bought in bulk as 'seconds' and heavily 'stunted' (extensive use of sales promotions, in store, in order to sell the products). Today there is still only a single store, but this extends over three floors of a fully owned building in the middle of the city, comprising some 75 000 square feet of retail selling space and 500 000 square feet of shared parking facility. The firm offers a range of products, mainly textile based, and management has recently introduced a number of concessions to the store (other companies operating within the store).

The store's problem was to retain their existing customers. The threat to their existing market share came from another two similar stores in the region, plus the development of an out-of-town shopping centre. It was decided to make use of marketing research techniques to attempt to generate information that would help management devise a customer retention strategy. The company used a consultant to carry out the marketing research and produce a report.

Depth interviews were carried out with each of the family members (also the main shareholders) and the store manager. A group discussion was carried out with a range of staff. Both the group discussions and depth interviews were taped and transcribed. Questionnaires were used, on a sample survey basis, to interview customers personally in the store. A small food and beverage incentive was given to respondents. Information about the survey and participation incentive was posted at the store entrances. Five hundred questionnaires were completed and were analysed by age, gender, frequency of use of the store, degree of store loyalty and, in particular, the residential area of the customer by postcode.

The results indicated a number of areas that needed to be addressed. Two years after the survey the store had suffered some loss of sales due to the opening of the out-of-town shopping centre, but so had most stores in the area. A follow-up survey did indicate that customer satisfaction had improved because of the implementation of many of the recommendations resulting from the survey. The general feeling from management was that the survey had helped them in retaining a large number of customers who might have gone elsewhere.

13.6 Methods of marketing research

Information sources may be primary or secondary. Primary data is that which is collected as first-hand information for a specific project, normally generated from external sources through sample surveys or experiments. This work can be described as fieldwork or '*ad hoc*' research.

The starting point should be desk research using secondary data. This information is historical and, if it has been researched on a continuous basis, can indicate trends and tendencies. Analysis can highlight areas in need of further research. The company's own records are the raw material of a sales analysis. The main approaches are product, area or territorial, customer and time analyses. External publications are the next source to investigate. There are three principal sources: government/official publications, trade association publications and specialist publications (see Appendix 1 for lists of the main sources available in the UK).

When the data for a marketing problem cannot be found in secondary sources the company must then generate primary information, usually through a survey involving four major steps:

1 Setting objectives for the survey

2 Developing the survey method and sample design

3 Collection of data

4 Interpretation of data.

The first is important in cost terms, for without a clear statement of objectives a lot of interesting but irrelevant information might be obtained. There are several methods of obtaining information, and these are described below.

13.6.1 Personal interviews

These may be structured or unstructured, direct or indirect. Direct interviews are used to obtain descriptive information – getting at the facts. Unstructured direct interviews are used for exploratory work to make sure that the final questionnaire will be well structured and relevant to the problem. In structured interviews a set of predetermined questions is asked; in unstructured interviews the questions are put as the interviewer sees best.

When an unstructured indirect interview is used to establish motives it is known as a depth interview. Indirect interviews have developed into a specialised area called motivation research. Direct questions are often of little value for diagnostic purposes. Most motivation research techniques employ the principle of 'projection' – e.g. the 'third person' technique, word association tests, sentence completion tests, and thematic apperception tests (TAT), in which 'themes' are described by the perceptual/interpretative use of pictures, usually cartoons. The main problem with motivation research relates to sample selection and size considerations.

Advantages of personal interviews include:

- good sample control

- more reliable answers

- longer questionnaires are possible

- greater flexibility

- observation is possible.

Disadvantages include:

- high cost

- possible bias owing to personal contact

- difficulty in obtaining co-operation from respondents.

13.6.2 Telephone interviews

These are useful when information is sought quickly, and it is a relatively inexpensive method. So long as not too much information is sought, co-operation can be obtained relatively easily, especially during evenings. Sample bias is a problem, as telephone lists only include those respondents whose numbers are actually included in telephone directories and this excludes those who are ex-directory. In addition, the sample can be biased as it only includes co-operating respondents. A recent problem is that an increased use of the telephone to canvass for sales approaches has made respondents wary. There might also be difficulties if personal data are required.

13.6.3 Postal questionnaires

These can be sent to as many respondents as required, and the method offers cheapness, wide distribution and speed. If respondent anonymity is possible it will lead to frank answers, and interviewer bias is eliminated. However, there

Definition

In structured interviews a set of predetermined questions is asked; in unstructured interviews the questions are put as the interviewer sees best.

is usually a high non-response rate. The questionnaire cannot be too long, and risks of ambiguity are increased if more than dichotomous questions are asked. It might also be difficult to classify respondents.

13.6.4 Panel surveys

In the field of consumer goods there are retail audits, like those provided by A. C. Neilsen Co. and Retail Audits Ltd, which provide surveys on a continuous basis. There are also consumer panels, usually on a continuous basis, like those provided by the Attwood Consumer Panel (mainly for food products) or Audits of Great Britain (mainly for consumer durables). Consumer panels may be conducted through a diary, questionnaire or home-audit basis.

13.6.5 Marketing experiments

An experiment is a method of gathering primary data in which the researcher is able to establish causation of effect amongst the variables being experimentally tested. Experiments can be carried out in artificial 'laboratory' type settings, or as field experiments. 'Test marketing' is a good example, where researchers choose a 'representative' geographical area, or at least one where they can statistically adjust data to make them representative of a wider market area such as the UK as a whole. The test market then becomes a 'model' of the total market. Pat Seelig states that test markets are expensive, but being a field experiment they have the advantage of realism or 'external validity' over laboratory experiments (Seelig, 1989). Howard Schlussberg advocates 'simulated test markets' as a way of reducing costs (Schlossberg, 1989). These are not full test markets, and involve surveying a small sample of consumers and showing them pictures or samples of product and ascertaining their preference as if they were really shopping.

Other techniques include 'extended user tests', 'blind' and 'simple placement' tests. In addition, there are the techniques used in the pre- and post-testing of advertising themes and copy, like split-run copy testing. 'Group discussions' or 'focus groups' (as opposed to interview questioning) can get away from the notion of 'rational' thinking.

Definition
An experiment is a method of gathering primary data in which the researcher is able to establish causation of effect amongst the variables being experimentally tested.

13.6.6 Sampling

Although this is not a method of marketing research, it is appropriate to consider sampling under this heading as it underlies the validity of research. The sample design is a plan that sets out who is to be sampled, how many respondents are to be surveyed, and how they are to be selected. Sampling procedures may be on a probability (or random) basis or on a non-probability basis, usually a quota sample. In a probability sample, every member of the population has a known probability of being included and their selection is random. These probabilities are taken into account when making estimates from the sample. The following sample methods involve probability:

Definition
The sample design is a plan that sets out who is to be sampled, how many respondents are to be surveyed, and how they are to be selected.

- simple random sample

- systematic sample (e.g. every nth name on a list)

- cluster sample (blocks selected randomly)

- area sample (blocks are geographic)

- stratified sample (sampling within strata, e.g. different family sizes)

- multi-stage sample (random sampling within random clusters).

For a true random sample to be taken from a complete national sampling frame costs could be prohibitive, so the usual method is to take a quota sample. The characteristics required of respondents are determined in advance (usually to represent the demographics of the population as a whole). Interviewers are then required to obtain specific quotas of people to make up the sample they interview, but using their own resources to do this rather than through any other statistical method.

Key point
We need to be aware of the difficulties in obtaining information from a sample of respondents.

We need to be aware of the difficulties in obtaining information from a sample of respondents. The sample itself may be a source of error if it is not representative. It may start off being representative, but cease to be so as a result of non-response and possible substitution of other respondents. There may also be errors in responses obtained. Inaccurate information may result from an inability or unwillingness of respondents to help. Unwillingness is a complex area that may be due to a perceived loss of prestige, a resentment of invasion of privacy or a personal reaction to the interviewer.

Vignette 13.3

Lack of adequate sampling frames makes research difficult in Saudi Arabia

JMR Information Services Ltd is a small marketing research agency based in Wakefield, West Yorkshire, in the UK. The company has particular expertise in building materials; its founder is actually a qualified chartered building surveyor. The company was commissioned by a manufacturer of 'marble effect' building cladding materials to investigate the potential of the product in Saudi Arabia.

The country has an extensive ongoing building programme, and this material was thought to be particularly suitable to the climate and other conditions there. Conventional bricks and mortar construction is not really suitable in the Arab states because of the heat and the dryness of the air. This dries out the mortar before it can set and harden properly, and has caused problems for many builders because of the substantial defects resulting over time. The manufacturer wanted views on the suitability of the building materials from domestic householders and businesses interested in commercial buildings.

One of the partners from JMR went to Saudi Arabia on an exploratory study with the aim of designing a research plan to carry out more conclusive research. A number of problems were encountered. Sampling procedures, particularly the use of probability or 'random' sampling techniques, were considered to be a problem. The kind of problems in formulating a random sample included:

- no officially recognised census of the population

- no accurate maps of cities to allow clustering for sampling

- out-of-date and incomplete telephone directories

- no other lists that would serve as a sampling frame.

Other problems included interviewing. Door-to-door personal interviewing is illegal in the country. Females were reluctant to discuss spending patterns, as males mainly took these decisions. Males would not speak to female interviewers. Definitions of classification questions, such as the meaning of the word 'family', also posed difficulties. Translations of depth interviews and questionnaires, particularly open-ended questions, were also very time consuming and expensive. This list is not exhaustive, but does illustrate some of the additional problems that marketing researchers face when working overseas.

13.7 The research brief

This is the process through which management conveys the nature of marketing problems or information needs to market researchers working in the company or in a research agency. Research briefs should be expressed in writing, but more typically are given verbally.

Translating a marketing problem into a comprehensive research study can be difficult, and much depends on the ability of marketing personnel and researchers to communicate effectively with each other. The following are some typical problems that prevent a thorough brief being achieved:

1 Some marketing problems are difficult to define

2 The marketing person knows little about research or its limitations

3 Researchers often have a low status in the company, so a full and frank discussion of the problem is not possible for security reasons

4 The researcher is often seen as a 'fire fighter', brought in on an *ad hoc* basis, with no continuous understanding of the product/market

5 Marketing people can find it difficult ascertaining how accurate the data have to be (this affects costs and sample sizes), and often lack the statistical skills necessary to understand the relationship between accuracy, sample sizes and costs.

The task of the brief is effectively to bring the two parties together. A good brief (usually achieved after detailed discussion) should ensure that irrelevant information is not requested, and it should:

- state the population(s) to be surveyed/sampled (e.g. consumers not buyers, car owners not car drivers)

- state the appropriate variables to be measured

- by and large, not pre-empt the design of the research; many marketing personnel think they know how to do research, but in practice few can do it properly.

Key point
The task of the brief is effectively to bring the two parties (the marketing personnel and the researchers) together.

Once the researcher has a brief, it is then possible to prepare a research 'proposal'.

13.8 Exploratory research

Key point
The company should 'explore' the situation before investing in the production of more conclusive research.

Whatever the purpose of a research exercise (e.g. exploratory or descriptive), it is costly in terms of time and money. The company should 'explore' the situation before investing in the production of more conclusive research. In exploring the market, all available sources of facts and ideas should be consulted in order that a picture of the market can be built up *before* conclusive research is commenced. Sound exploratory research gives a clearer idea of the situation, and highlights possible areas of investigation.

Before designing a cost-effective survey it is necessary to be informed about the market, the population and the topics of interest in a particular area, because most full surveys are sample surveys rather than census surveys. Exploratory data are needed about population parameters (e.g. sex, age, socio-economic and geographical characteristics of the population) in order to design an appropriate sampling scheme. The sample may have to be broken down into quotas based on such characteristics.

Exploratory research is essential because the research methodology used in a sample survey is usually a questionnaire. Before a meaningful questionnaire can be designed (one with relevant questions that people can understand, arranged in a sensible order) it will be necessary to have an idea of consumer behaviour and attitudes towards various products, including competitors' products and substitutes. Such information will include brands available in the market and consumer attitudes towards them, the relative popularity of brands and the context in which the products/brands are used.

Exploratory research thus indicates which areas need to be investigated, in what depth, and the type of information required (e.g. qualitative or quantitative) as well as the amount of data to be collected. It allows the researcher to arrive at a set of assumptions on which to base the research. The more thought put into this stage, the less opportunity there will be for subsequent mistakes.

13.9 Stages in the research process

1 *Problem definition*. This leads to a preliminary statement of research objectives – usually to provide information, i.e. this stage is an identification of information needs:

● *What* information is needed?

Motivations – values, beliefs, feelings, opinions
Evaluations – attitudes, intentions
Knowledge – facts, behaviour, actions
Demographic – socio-economic, etc. (on/from people, stores, companies, brands, products).

- *Why* is information required?
  For exploration, description, prediction or evaluation.

- *Where* does information come from?
  Secondary data sources, both internal and external to a company
  Primary data sources (i.e. from fieldwork).

2 *Review of secondary data sources*:

- Company records, reports, previous research

- Trade associations, government agencies, research organisations

- Advertising/marketing research agencies

- Books, periodicals, theses, statistics, conference proceedings, etc.

- See Appendix 1 for lists of the main sources of secondary data in the UK.

3 *Select approach for collection of new/primary information*:

- Experimentation

- Observation

- Surveys – mail, telephone, personal

- Motivational research techniques – depth interviews, group interviews, projective techniques.

4 *Research design*:

- Methods

- Sampling issues

- Design.

5 *Data collection*.

6 *Analysis and interpretation*.

7 *Evaluation* of results and recommendations to management.

13.10 Methods of collecting data

13.10.1 Experimentation

Experimentation is used to test/assess the effect of some element(s) in the marketing mix (e.g. product, package, price change, advertising, promotion, type of outlet). There are two main types:

1 *Field experiments*, which are controlled experiments where a change in an experimental variable(s) is related to a resulting level of sales, advertisement recall/recognition, or attitudes (e.g. coupon trials, split-run advertisements and test-markets). Possible problems are:

- 'contamination' of control units

- influence of uncontrolled variables

- short-run response (evaluation of the results must consider carry-over effects and present sales being at expense of future sales).

2 *Laboratory experiments*, which involve using individual consumers or consumer groups/juries/panels. The researcher has a high degree of control, and can introduce and exclude stimuli to create laboratory analogues of real-life situations to measure attitudes towards products, prices, packages, advertising or promotion, as well as preferences and intentions to buy.

The problem is that the situations are artificial, and it must be asked to what extent the information collected will reflect actual future reaction/behaviour in the market place.

13.10.2 Observation

This method is used to describe rather than to explain. Observations are selective and can be of people or physical phenomena, observed by people or by mechanical devices.

1 *People observing people*. This includes watching people in shops, children with toys etc. Only overt behaviour is measured. There is no interviewer or response bias, but because motivations, preferences, intentions or attitudes cannot be observed, problems can arise in the interpretation of observations.

2 *Mechanical devices observing people*:

- eye camera – changes in pupil size measure interest (e.g. in response to advertisements)

- tachistoscope – a projection device to present visual stimuli for a short time (e.g. to measure brand-name awareness)

- psycho-galvanometer – a device that measures galvanic skin response (e.g. to measure response when exposed to different types of advertisement)

- tape-recordings: (e.g. of salespeople with customers)

- photographic and movie cameras, video recorders.

3 *Physical phenomena observed by people*:

- analysis of documents (e.g. content analysis of advertisements)

- observation of physical characteristics

- inventories: store/retail audits, information on brand/stock levels

- 'pantry' audits of products/brands on hand (many consumer audits/panels are comprehensive and also include diaries on product consumption, media exposure, purchasing habits and even opinions).

4 *Physical phenomena observed by mechanical devices*:

- traffic counters
- television (and radio) audiometers.

13.10.3 Surveys (using questionnaires)

Surveys can be conducted by mail, telephone or personal interview; questionnaires can be self-administered or used in an interview situation. The choice is determined by:

- cost
- timing
- type of information needed
- amount of information needed
- ease of questioning
- accuracy required.

When choosing a method, consider cost and value of alternative methods, and also:

- using pilot surveys
- sample size(s)
- method of analysing results.

Types of survey – some questions to consider

Postal surveys:

- Who is the respondent? Industrial buyer, middle/lower class consumer, doctor, etc.?
- Nature of the survey: will motivation to respond be high?
- Questions: how simple must they be?
- Length of the questionnaire: what is the limit?
- Response bias (there should be none from interviewers, only from the sample)
- To what extent do respondents differ from non-respondents?
- Sample selection: size may be related to expected response rate
- Is a 'list' (of potential respondents compiled by/bought from an external source) being used? If so, how accurate is it?
- Should respondents be provided with prepaid reply envelopes?

- Response rate: this will affect cost/value of the survey; if response is relatively slow, it may be appropriate to send reminders to follow up non-respondents

- Importance of cover letter, request for co-operation and/or instructions

- Cost: this should be relatively low per response.

Telephone surveys:

Considerations as above, plus:

- Who is the respondent? Are telephone subscribers who are not ex-directory representative of the required population?

- Telephone contact is impersonal; how important is credibility of the interviewer?

- Questions should be short and simple

- The interviewer can only talk to one person at a time (usually); is it the right one?

- The respondent cannot consult other people, company records, etc.

- This method is relatively cheap and fast.

Personal interviews:

Similar considerations, plus:

- Who is the respondent?

- Where is the respondent – in the home, office, street, a cinema queue?

- Factors affecting motivation to participate in an interview (see Figure 13.2), which gives an 'outline' of the problems of personal interviews

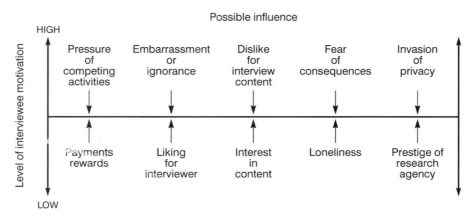

Figure 13.2 Factors affecting interviewee participation.

- Response bias in reaching the sample – non-contact, interviewer error, refusal to be interviewed

- Bias in responses – incorrect and/or untruthful answers, omissions, and interviewer's perception of the interviewee

- Who is the interviewer: salesperson, housewife, freelance researcher? What qualifications and training do they need?

- The cost of this method is usually high.

Questionnaires:

- Types of questions

  - Open-ended, structured (yes/no, multiple-choice, rankings, paired comparisons, checklist, 'which of these . . .?'

- Wording of questions

  - Avoid ambiguity; the question must have the same meaning for all respondents

  - Respondents' ability to answer will relate to their level of education and language; questions must be self-exploratory and fully understood

  - Respondents' willingness to answer – they may be reluctant, for example, to answer questions on personal matters such as income

  - Avoid influencing the answer (e.g. 'Do you brush your teeth every day?')

- Sequencing of questions (and alternatives within questions)

  - Initial questions should provide motivation (and encourage further co-operation)

  - Questions should follow a logical order, from general to the specific

  - Rotate questions/sub-questions to eliminate bias

  - Place personal questions at the end, or 'bury' them in the middle.

- Scaling techniques for attitude measurement – these usually determine content and direction of attitudes rather than intensity. More commonly used techniques are:

  - Paired comparisons

  - Likert summated ratings (agreement on a five-point scale)

  - Thurstone's equal appearing intervals (paired comparisons)

  - Osgood's semantic differential: a bipolar scale used to measure opinions about ideas, products, brands, stores, companies, etc.

  - Guttman's scalogram

  - Stephenson's sort technique

- Other considerations:
  - Length of questionnaire
  - Use of cue cards (e.g. rotating lists of alternative responses)
  - Aids to recall (e.g. pictures of advertisements)
  - Presentation (especially if the questionnaire is to be self-administered)
  - Methods of coding and analysis of data will affect design and structure of questions.

13.10.4 Motivational research techniques

Definition

Motivational research techniques aim to discover the underlying motives, desires and emotions of consumers that influence their behaviour.

Motivational research techniques aim to discover the underlying motives, desires and emotions of consumers that influence their behaviour. These techniques often penetrate below the level of the conscious mind, and uncover motives that consumers themselves conceal or of which they are not aware.

There are two approaches to motivational research: *the psycho-sociological approach*, this relies on group behaviour of consumers and the impact of culture and environment on their opinions and reactions; and *the psychoanalytic approach*, which relies on information drawn from individual respondents in depth interviews and projective tests. Freudian interpretations dominate such analysis.

Techniques used include:

- *Depth interviewing*, which employs interviewing and observational methods. The interviewer chooses topics for discussion and, through non-structured, indirect questioning, leads the respondent to free expression of motives, attitudes, opinions, experiences and habits in relation to advertisements, products, brands, services, etc.

- *Group interviewing*, where the interviewer is responsible for moderating and stimulating group discussion, to encourage freedom of expression and interaction between individuals.

- *Projective techniques*, which may help to reveal what the respondent might cover up in direct questioning. Examples of such techniques include:

  - Verbal projection – for example, asking 'Why do you think people do . . .?', i.e. asking about someone else with the expectation that answers will actually apply to respondents themselves

  - Word association tests

  - Sentence completion exercises (e.g. 'People buy on credit when . . .', 'Prices are high because . . .')

  - Response to pictures (thematic apperception tests, or TAT – respondents give a description of a pictured situation based on their own experience and attitudes)

  - Interpretation of ink blots (Rorschach tests).

Vignette 13.4

Slackman's Ltd, of London, develops a variation on the conventional qualitative group discussion

Slackman's Ltd is a successful marketing research company based in London in the UK. It carries out all types of marketing research but specialises in qualitative research, particularly depth interviews and group discussions. The management of the company had been dissatisfied for some time with some of the interviews resulting from their group discussion work, particularly when conducting work into new product development and related areas such as advertising. In their view, some of the interview material was somewhat superficial and lacked the depth and clarity needed for their clients.

The conventional 'rules' covering the organising and conduct of conventional consumer-based group discussions state that participants should not know one another, as this tends to influence the responses of others in the group. Also, participants should not be 'professional group discussion members', i.e. ideally they should not have participated in a group discussion before. Abiding by these 'rules', obviously people attending a consumer group discussion for the first time took a little time to get used to the proceedings and 'settle in'. Often consumer group discussions were conducted along the lines of 'party plan' type bases. Someone allowed his or her house to be used for the discussion, receiving a fee for doing so. The research company provided food and beverages, and the respondents were invited to take part in the interview. Again respondents received a small incentive, usually in the form of a holiday or grocery voucher. When respondents arrived, they would have a drink and a 'bite to eat' and get to know the others taking part. The moderator then explained the reason for the interview to the group and the interview took place, lasting some two hours. Proceedings were often taped, both visually and on audiotapes, for further analysis.

Respondents knew virtually nothing about the marketing process or the type of information the moderator wanted. Respondents found the moderators' probing into the psychological aspects of products and brand image particularly difficult to grasp, and techniques such a 'word association' and 'role playing' exercises both difficult and at times embarrassing.

Slackman's decided to experiment with reconvened trained group discussions. They called this new group concept a 'sensitivity panel'. Group members were originally selected for their potential in being able to be productive in a group discussion setting. They were then given six months' training in marketing and in conducting group discussion work. By the end of the training period the group knew one another very well indeed, and had a good grasp of the principles of qualitative research and group discussions. They knew about the marketing process in detail, and understood the kind of information and detail the researcher was after in a successful group discussion. The firm claimed that the sensitivity panel provided clients with data that were more robust and at a much deeper psychological level. This was particularly important for new product development studies and work on product and brand image. Because the respondents were trained, it saved time at the interview because they already knew each other and could get straight down to work. The interviews were therefore more efficient and more productive.

On the down side, the interviews were also more expensive. Respondents had to be paid to be trained and, because they were trained, expected a reasonable fee to take part in any further reconvened discussions. The sensitivity panel has not overtaken the conventional group discussion, but does offer an interesting alternative for situations where very detailed and deep psychologically-based responses are required from group members.

13.11 Problems in research exercises

The practical problems encountered in the planning and execution of a sample survey vary with the type of material and the nature of the information required. Investigations can be broken down into four phases: planning, execution, analysis and the report.

13.11.1 Planning

The following aspects require consideration in the planning stage.

1 *Specification of the purposes of the survey.* It is important to be clear as to what the problem is in the first place, and then determine which aspects of it are appropriate to a solution using survey techniques. A basic question must be asked: Is a sample survey the best way of solving the problem? If the advice of a statistical expert is to be sought, then this should be done at the earliest possible stage.

2 *Definition of the population.* The categories or types of respondents to be included in a survey, its scope, etc., are largely determined in broad outline by the purposes of the survey. However, marginal categories require special consideration because:

- Excluding them can simplify the survey (cheapen its cost) without materially affecting the outcome

- The inclusion of certain marginal categories can be valuable where relationships are discovered between sub-groups of the population and variables being measured

- In many situations multi-phase sampling would answer doubts on this matter.

3 *Determination of the details of information to be collected.* List the information required to solve the original problem. This list may be expanded by contacting people in the company who might find the results of the survey useful. The list should be as extensive as possible at this stage so no omissions are made. A selection then has to be made within the practical limitations of the survey (expense, time, etc.).

4 *Practicability of obtaining the required information.* Each item of information selected should be considered in terms of how practical it is to obtain, given the level of accuracy required. For example, it should be asked:

- Do the respondents have the knowledge required to answer the questions?

- Will it involve them in a lot of effort?

- If the information is to be obtained by observation, can it be observed or measured accurately?

Considerations like this may lead to further modifications.

5 *Methods of collecting the information.*

6 *Methods of dealing with non-response.* Unless non-response is confined to a relatively small proportion of the whole sample, the results cannot claim any general validity. This problem becomes particularly acute in postal surveys and in random samples from human populations, where response can be very low. In such cases, follow-up letters/calls can increase the response. However, the results of the sample can be weighted for non-response by identifying the characteristics of the initial non-respondents who reply on follow-up.

7 *The sampling frame.* The whole structure of the survey is to a considerable extent determined by the sampling frame. Until details of the frame have been obtained, no comprehensive planning of the survey can be undertaken. Care must be taken to ensure that the frame is accurate, complete, not subject to duplication, and up-to-date.

Key point
Care must be taken to ensure that the sampling frame is accurate, complete, not subject to duplication, and up-to-date.

8 *Pilot surveys.* The practicability of any survey is best checked by a pilot survey(s). They are designed to check:

a. The questionnaire

- Use a broad quota sample (mainly lower socio-economic groups)

- Good investigators should be used with instructions to follow up diversions, to check the meanings of words, check respondents' train of thoughts and, as far as possible, record all that is said

- The last pre-test should use the final approved questionnaire.

b. The sample

- Check the ease of getting the smallest sub-group wanted

- Check the number of interviews possible in the time allowed

- Check that the selection process and the call-back/substitution procedure are feasible.

c. The survey contact

- Check additional fields of enquiry shown up by (a), and also the appearance and 'feel' of the pilot results. Sometimes results obtained in the field will reorient the basic approach to the survey.

13.11.2 Execution of a survey

After the planning stage, the execution of a survey involves:

- Administrative organisation to cover the supervision of the field operations, the investigations, follow-ups, check calls, etc. and the central task of collation, tabulation and computation

- Selection, training and supervision of field investigators

- Briefing conference

- Control and accuracy of the fieldwork

- Editing of schedules
- Coding of answers to open-ended questions
- Data analysis.

13.11.3 Analysis of the results

Numerical accuracy during the analysis should be verified by repetition, by cross-checks or by using different methods of computation to arrive at the same result. If the sampling procedure is defective in some way, the result can sometimes be adjusted to compensate for the defect. For example, if the sample contains incorrect proportions of certain classes of the population, this is sometimes overcome by weighting the results of the sample.

13.11.4 The report

The following features should be included in a survey report.

1 A general description of the survey:

- statement of purpose of the survey
- description of material covered
- nature of information collected
- method of collecting of the data
- sampling method
- accuracy
- period of time of the survey
- cost
- who is responsible for the survey
- references.

2 Design of the survey. Here, the sampling design of the survey should be specified.

3 Methods of selecting sampling units.

4 Personnel and equipment used.

5 Findings of the survey.

13.12 Questionnaire design

The results of a survey are no better than the accuracy of the information it obtains, so the design of a questionnaire is an important feature of survey work. The ultimate objective of a questionnaire is to design questions that have

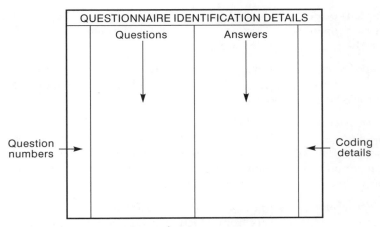

Figure 13.3 A specimen questionnaire layout.

the same meaning, a single meaning, and the intended meaning to everyone.

13.12.1 Physical layout

The general layout of a questionnaire is shown in Figure 13.3.

- Each question should be numbered
- Use capital letters for the main sections
- Instructions to be given to the investigator concerning the conduct of the interview (alternative routes in the questionnaire) should be in bold face, capital letters and underlined
- Arrange answer codes, boxes, etc. as near to the right hand side as possible
- Lines drawn at suitable intervals can bring clarity to the design of the questionnaire
- Arrows can be used to indicate the routes through 'skip' questions.

13.12.2 Types of questions

There is no general rule that can be used to decide which type of question is most suitable to elicit particular types of information. The following are the types of questions most commonly used:

1 *Open-ended questions.* An open-ended question provides the clue as to what answer might be expected from the respondent. For example, a question which begins 'What do you think of . . .?' will bring forth comments over a full range of opinion. With a large sample, the mass of diverse data collected cannot be statistically analysed since verbatim answers (and they must be so

recorded) can only be hand-summarised and then not always satisfactorily. However, open-ended questions are useful in the pilot stage of a survey to show the range of likely answers.

2 *Unaided recall questions.* The basic rule here is *not* to mention the nature of the answer material, and to avoid asking leading questions like: 'How did you travel to the station to catch this train?'

3 *Dichotomous questions.* A dichotomous question offers two answer choices, basically 'yes' and 'no'. A third possible answer ('don't know') is implicit in this type of question. It has been found that as long as the researcher does not mention this alternative, then people who understand the question will simply choose one of these two alternatives.

4 *Multiple-choice ('cafeteria') questions.* The informant is given a graduated range of possible answers from which to choose a preferred response. The possibilities should be listed in rank order from one extreme to the other. It may be necessary to reverse the order on half of the questionnaires in order to prevent listing bias. In general, an even number of items is preferred, because where an odd number of potential answers are offered there sometimes a tendency for respondents to select the middle (or neutral) choice.

5 *Thermometer questions.* This is an evolution of multi-choice questions that seeks to minimise the disadvantage of a discrete classification. Informants are asked to rate their feelings on a numerical scale, e.g. 0–10 or 0–100. It is presumed that errors in this type of question cancel each other out.

6 *Checklists.* A checklist is the standard way of prompting a respondent's memory without the interviewer biasing him or her in relation to any item on the list. Care must still be taken to avoid bias, as too many items can lead to 'fatigue' on the part of the respondent and a preference for the earlier items. This bias can be avoided by rotating the items during the survey. A further problem is that brand leaders may be selected more frequently because of the weight of advertising rather than the criterion that is being investigated.

13.12.3 General rules for question design

- Use simple words that are familiar to everyone, e.g. shop, not outlet; shopkeeper, not retailer.

- Questions should be as short as possible

- Don't ask double-barrelled questions – e.g. 'Have you a radio and television set?'

- Don't ask leading questions – e.g. 'Do you buy instant coffee because it is the quickest way to make coffee?'

- Don't mention brand names – e.g. 'Do you consider 'Hitachi' to be the best audio equipment?'

- Don't ask questions that might offend – e.g. 'When did you last wash your hair?', 'Do you work or are you a housewife?'

- Avoid using catch phrases or colloquialisms.

- Avoid words that are not precise in their meanings – e.g. 'Does this product last a reasonable length of time?', 'Are there sufficient comedy shows on TV?'

- Direct questions will not always give the expected response. Perhaps not all-possible answers have been foreseen. A question such as 'Are you married?' does not cover the possibilities of divorce, separation, etc.

- Questions concerning prestige goods may not be answered truthfully. Careful rewording can avoid this. For example, 'Have you a television capable of receiving teletext transmissions?' might be better asked by: 'How many hours per week do you watch television?' followed by: 'Do you watch teletext transmissions, i.e. Ceefax or Oracle?'

- Only questions that the respondent can answer from knowledge or experience should be asked. It would be pointless, for example, to ask a housewife if she prefers cooking by gas if she has never experienced cooking by other means.

- Questions should not depend on the respondent's memory.

- Questions should only allow one thought to be created in the respondent's mind; where multiple thoughts are created, confusion can result and an inappropriate answer may be given, or one that does not accurately represent the respondent's opinion (where the respondent has to choose between possible answers). This particularly applies to questions commencing 'Why . . .?'

- Avoid questions or words with an emotional bias – e.g. use Conservative/ Labour; not Tory/Socialist.

13.12.4 Positioning of questions

The first question asked should be easy to answer and gain the interest of the informant. If possible, it should require a factual answer. Generally, the questionnaire should begin with easier questions and proceed to the more difficult ones, but the questions of the greatest importance should be about one-third of the way through the questionnaire.

Information about the respondent (age, address, full name, occupation, etc.) should appear at the end of the questionnaire unless it is necessary to obtain it at the beginning of the interview (as in quota sampling).

The transition from question to question should be smooth and logical. Any 'jumps in thought' should be introduced before the next question is asked.

13.12.5 Miscellaneous information

A questionnaire should have a title to identify it. Standard information can include the respondent's name, home address, sex, age (usually asked for in groups, e.g. 20–25, 26–30, . . .), income group, occupation, interviewing district identification, the place and date of interview, and the interviewer's name.

13.12.6 Recording answers

If possible, ensure that the investigator or respondent uses one of the following methods to record the respondent's answers:

- writing a number
- putting a cross (×) or a tick (3) in a box
- underlining correct answers
- crossing out incorrect answers
- writing in a predetermined symbol
- ringing a number or letter.

When open-ended questions are used, enough space should be allowed for answers to be recorded verbatim.

13.12.7 Questionnaire length

A questionnaire should be as short as possible in relation to the data to be secured. For a standard questionnaire investigation among householders in their own homes, a typical limit is what can be reasonably printed on both sides of an A4 sheet. For interviewing people in the street, one side of an A4 sheet is a reasonable limit. If the schedule is lengthy, interview appointments should be made, and in such cases interviews of up to one hour are reasonable.

13.12.8 Questionnaire evaluation

The following is a list of basic questions that should be asked about any questionnaire:

1 Is each question clearly worded?

2 Does it break any of the rules of question design?

3 Is each question concerned with one single factor?

4 Are the questions ones that will elicit the answers necessary to solve the research problem?

5 Is each question unambiguous, and will both the investigator and the informant have the same understanding of the question?

6 Are all the possible answers allowed for?

7 Are recording arrangements foolproof?

8 Will the answers to each question be in a form in which they can be cross-tabulated against other data on the same or other questionnaires?

9 Will the answers be in a form that will allow at least some to be checked against established data?

13.12.9 An example questionnaire

A complete evaluation of the questionnaire is of paramount importance. Such an evaluation should be carried out before the final survey work is undertaken. A poorly structured and designed questionnaire can ruin a survey exercise and can result in loss of time and money. Pilot testing and evaluation of questionnaires are a necessity for good market research and not an option. The question facing the researcher is not whether or not to evaluate the questionnaire, but how to evaluate. The precise method used will depend on the nature of the research exercise and the population being surveyed.

13.13 Summary

✓ Marketing research is the starting point of the business process in a marketing-orientated organisation. This chapter is linked with Chapter 2, which explained marketing orientation. Thereafter marketing research provides inputs into each of the 'Four Ps', essentially covered by Chapters 7–12.

✓ In practice, marketing research also provides valuable input for areas such as segmentation, targeting and positioning (Chapter 5), and planning and control (Chapter 17).

✓ Whilst marketing research is an important function in its own right, it is only part of a wider marketing information system. Information can be collected internally and market intelligence can be gathered from employees like sales staff. Information collected from formal marketing research can be enhanced by computer modelling etc. Hence marketing research provides a valuable source of input data to the overall marketing information system.

Activities

1 Use examples to illustrate how marketing research can aid marketing decision-making.

2 Exploratory research has a specific role to play in the overall marketing research process. Examine this role, and outline the research techniques that might be utilised at the exploratory stage.

3 Under what circumstances would qualitative research techniques be more appropriate than quantitative research techniques? Give specific examples.

4 List the advantages and disadvantages of using a telephone survey compared with a postal survey. Under what circumstances might a telephone survey be particularly appropriate?

5 Compare and contrast probability sampling with non-probability sampling. Under what conditions might a market researcher have no other choice but to use a non-probability sampling procedure?

References

American Marketing Association (1961). *Report of the Definitions Committee of the American Marketing Association*. AMA.

Doyle, P. (1994). *Marketing Management and Strategy*, p. 39, p. 124. Prentice-Hall International.

de Chernatony, L. and Daniels, K. (1994). The importance of market research in brand positioning. *Proceedings of the Marketing Education Group (MEG) Annual Conference*, The University of Ulster, pp. 158–167.

Kotler, P. (1994). *Marketing Management, Analysis, Planning, Control and Implementation*, p. 257. Prentice-Hall International.

Reynolds, P. L. and Day, J. (1994). The use of customer service appreciation surveys by small and medium sized firms to leverage more business from existing customers. In: *Marketing: Unity in Diversity: Proceedings Of The 1994 MEG Annual Conference*, The University of Ulster, p. 779.

Reynolds, P. L. and Day, J. (1995). A low cost and low risk scheme for small entrepreneurial firms to enable them to increase both sales and profitability from their existing customer base. In: *Research At The Marketing/Entrepreneurial Interface: Proceedings of the MEG Annual Conference, Bradford University* (G. E. Hills, G. Omura, F. Danial and G. A. Knight, eds), pp. 551–6.

Schlossberg, H. (1989). Simulated vs traditional test marketing. *Marketing News*, **23 Oct**, 1–2, 11.

Seelig, P. (1989). All over the map. *Sales and Marketing Management*, **Mar**, 58–64.

Further reading

Armstrong, G. and Kotler, P. (2000). Marketing research and information systems. *Marketing: An Introduction*, 5th edn, Chapter 4. Prentice Hall.

Blythe, J. (2001). Market research. *Essentials of Marketing*, Chapter 5. Person Educational Ltd.

Chisnall, P. M. (1992). *Marketing Research*, 4th edn. McGraw Hill.

Crimp, M. (1992). *The Marketing Research Process*. Prentice Hall.

Davies, M. (1998). Marketing research. *Understanding Marketing*, Chapter 3. Prentice Hall.

Keegan, W. J. and Green, M. S. (2000). Global information systems and market research. *Global Marketing*, 2nd edn, Chapter 6. Prentice Hall.

Lancaster, G. A. and Reynolds, P. L. (1998). Marketing research. *Marketing*, Chapter 6. Macmillan Press Ltd.

Lancaster, G. A. and Reynolds, P. L. (1999). Marketing information systems. *Introduction to Marketing: A Step by Step Guide to All the Tools of Marketing*, Chapter 4. Kogan Page.

Plamer, A. (2000). Marketing research. *Principles of Marketing*, Chapter 6. Oxford University Press.

Sales forecasting

14

14.1 Introduction

The act of preparing for the future implies forecasting, consciously or subconsciously, tomorrow's condition. In our personal lives, such predictions are usually made on an informal, subjective basis. If they turn out to be wrong, we can usually adjust our personal circumstances. However, we rarely enjoy the same degree of flexibility in our working lives. There, decisions are usually of a more formal nature and greater consequence.

The very nature of managerial decision-making involves forecasting future conditions. Forecasts may be required for an important 'one-off' decision – for example, the company may be considering expanding by acquisition, diversifying into a totally new market or modernising its production processes. Such decisions tend to be long term and strategic, rather than operational. In such situations, because of the importance of the decisions being made it is important that forecasting receives careful consideration, meaning an investment of time and money in the forecasting process.

Managerial decisions are not always strategic and much of a busy manager's time is taken up with day-to-day operational issues, which, although not of the same magnitude as strategic decisions, are nonetheless important to the manager because of the proportion of time they occupy. Management requires forecasting information to assist in making operational decisions, although the required time horizon for such forecasts is shorter than for strategic decisions. For example, for the marketing manager to set monthly sales targets, operational expense or advertising budgets, he or she may require regular short-term forecasts for each product, broken down according to product type, size, colour, salesperson's territory, channel of distribution, and even by individual customer.

Whatever type of decision is being made, forecasting is required. Forecasting is a key to success, but poor forecasting can lead to high inventories and associated stockholding costs which must be paid for out of working capital, or

> **Key point**
> The very nature of managerial decision-making involves forecasting future conditions.

285

to under-production and unrealised market potential. Stanton *et al.* (1991) contend: 'The cornerstone of successful marketing planning is forecasting the demand for a product'.

The recognition of the importance of forecasting was first illustrated by the results of a major research exercise carried out in the United States by Ledbetter and Cox in 1977. They found that forecasting techniques were used by 88 per cent of the 500 largest industrial companies in the USA. It was also established that no other class of planning technique was used as much as forecasting.

Although forecasting is important in most functional areas of a firm, the forecasting of sales is particularly important. The sales forecast is the bedrock on which company plans are built, and for this to be sound the forecast must be built on a firm scientific foundation.

The central issue facing businesses is not whether to forecast, but how to forecast. The forecaster can choose 'subjective' or 'objective' methods, or a mixture of both.

Key point
The sales forecast is the bedrock on which company plans are built, and for this to be sound the forecast must be built on a firm scientific foundation.

14.2 Forecasting terminology

The terminology used in the literature to describe forecasts can be confusing. Many writers make a distinction between prediction and forecasting, using 'forecast' to refer to objective, quantitative techniques, and 'predict' to denote subjective estimates. This distinction is pedantic, and the debate is a matter of semantics. 'Forecast' is of Saxon origin, meaning 'to throw ahead', implying that there is something in hand. In the context of this discussion, it would be historical data that can be extrapolated into the future. 'Predict' is of Latin origin, literally meaning 'to say beforehand', and no empirical basis is indicated. Dictionary definitions are unhelpful, a forecast being defined as 'a prophecy or prediction' and prediction, in turn, as 'something predicted, a forecast'. Consequently, the use of the terms *subjective and objective* forecast is recommended, and these terms are used throughout.

The availability of appropriate data is of central importance to the development of a forecasting system. Depending on the degree of accuracy required, most forecasting techniques require a considerable amount of data to be collected and analysed in terms of usefulness and validity before being used in the forecasting process.

Selection of the most suitable forecasting method from the choice of techniques available depends on the availability of existing data and/or the company's ability to acquire relevant data. For example, a technique requiring a long historical time series would be of little use if data were only available for the past year. If the accuracy or validity of data were questionable, it would not be worthwhile or cost-effective to spend time and effort using a sophisticated technique known for its precision. In forecasting, the principle of '*garbage in/ garbage out*' applies; a forecast will only be as good as the data used in its compilation.

Definition
'Forecast' is of Saxon origin, meaning 'to throw ahead', implying that there is something in hand.

Vignette 14.1

Sales forecasting is difficult, especially for the future – Fujitsu gets profit forecasts wrong by 78 per cent

Some say that forecasting is an art, others, especially those who favour the use of more objective quantitative forecasting methods, claim that forecasting is more of a science. Whatever position you take on the arts/science debate, what is clear is that forecasting future market conditions, and hence profitability conditions, is very difficult. So difficult, in fact, that some of the world's most respected and sophisticated companies get their profit forecasts embarrassingly wrong.

Nowhere is this inherent difficulty so well illustrated as in the case of the high technology company Fujitsu. On 2 March 2001, the company cut its forecast consolidated net profit forecast for the year by a staggering 78 per cent. The company says that many business environmental factors impacted on sales and hence forecast profits. Nearly 40 per cent of Fujitsu's sales are made overseas. The USA is a particularly important market for the firm. The economic slowdown in the USA has hit high technology products, and especially product components, hard. Computers, disk drives, microchips for computers and other electronic devices have all suffered from a dramatic downturn in demand.

Fujitsu is amongst Japan's most respected companies. The organisation is proud of its management staff, many of whom are selected from the elite of Japan's top universities and business schools. It has a highly trained and educated team producing sales and profit forecasts for its markets all over the world. Some of the top forecasting brains in Japan's international business community are involved in the production of its forecasts. This illustrates very well how difficult it is to produce robust commercial forecasting information even only one year into the future.

14.3 Data collection

Once the company has decided how much time, energy and money is to be spent on data collection, it must determine where it will obtain the data. The most promising sources depend on the individual situation.

There are two main categories of existing data:

1 Internal data generated within the company itself, e.g. previous company plans, sales statistics and other internal records. For certain situations this may be sufficient.

2 Secondary data from external sources, e.g. government and trade statistics, and published marketing research surveys.

Both are important, and in many forecasting situations it is necessary to utilise them both.

A third category of data is that generated specifically for the forecasting task through some form of marketing research, such as a sample survey, a test-marketing experiment or an observational study. This is usually the most expensive source of data, and before commencing a full study should be made of existing data sources, both internal and external.

14.3.1 Internal data sources

In the immediate and short-term forecasting that is used for operational decision-making and control purposes, much of the necessary data can be gathered from internal sources. There may be questions that can only be answered by a detailed investigation of the firm's own data, so it is essential that internal data are collected, recorded and stored as part of a firm's routine administrative procedures. Desk research into internal company records is a useful and economic source of data, and should be a starting point for data collection in any forecasting exercise. An advantage is that the departmental manager concerned can give an indication of the accuracy of data and the relevance to the forecasting situation. A disadvantage is that although the company's internal system may contain useful information, it may be difficult for the forecaster to obtain it in an appropriate form as it has been compiled for different purposes.

Key point
Success in obtaining past data from within the firm will depend to a great extent on knowing the firm and its staff.

Success in obtaining past data from within the firm will depend to a great extent on knowing the firm and its staff. Much information can be obtained by consulting heads of departments and other staff. Obtaining access to information may sometimes be a problem, so it is important that such exercises have the authority of top management to obtain maximum co-operation.

The first stage is to take a systems analysis approach and trace the documentary procedures of the firm. The forecaster should look carefully at what records are kept, and how data are obtained, altered, processed and circulated throughout the firm. Every document should be recorded, possibly using some form of flow chart. The type of document, as well as the function it serves, should be noted, along with its origin and destination.

Administrative and documentary procedures vary, but most company systems start with a customer enquiry and end with the customer's invoice. With detailed analysis, it is possible to identify the main steps in the procedure within each department. The idea is to build up a picture of the overall system from individual employees to the total departmental system and, ultimately, the company. 'Unofficial' records are sometimes kept for contingency purposes. Such sources may be useful to the forecaster, and may only be discovered by probing.

14.3.2 Data from the sales department

The sales/marketing department is the main point of commercial interaction between the company and its customers. Consequently, it is the chief source of information including:

1 *Sales volume by product and by product group.* This information can be combined to give total sales volume, but it also allows each product or product group in the overall product mix to be evaluated in terms of its contribution to total volume.

2 *Sales volume by area.* This may be divided according to salesperson territories, standard media areas as used by the Joint Industry for Television Advertising Research (JICTAR), or other geographical areas (e.g. countries).

3 *Sales volumes by market segment.* The basis for segmentation may be regional or, especially in industrial markets, by type of industry. Such information will give an indication of which segments are likely to remain static, which are declining, and which show growth possibilities. Where the firm deals with a few large customers, segmentation may be by customer, and any change in demand from any of these may be significant in terms of forecasting sales.

4 *Sales volume by type of channel of distribution.* Where a company has a multi-channel distribution policy, it is possible to calculate the effectiveness and profitability of each type of channel. It also allows for trends in the pattern of distribution to be identified and taken into account in forecasting future channel requirements. Channel information by geographical area may indicate a difference in the profitability between various types of channel in different parts of the country, allowing for geographical differentials. Information gathered by type of retail outlet, agents, wholesalers and distributors can contribute to a more realistic forecast. Such information allows marketing to identify and develop promising channel opportunities, resulting in more effective channel management.

5 *Sales volume over time.* In terms of actual sales and units sold, this allows seasonal variations to be identified and inflation and price adjustments to be taken into consideration.

6 *Pricing information.* Historical information relating to price adjustments by product types allows forecasters to establish the effects of price increases or decreases on demand. The forecaster is then able to judge the likely effects of future price changes.

7 *Communication mix information.* The effects of previous advertising campaigns, sponsorship, direct mail or exhibitions can be assessed. Various levels of expenditure in marketing communications can be evaluated. This information will act as a guide to the likely effectiveness of future communication mix expenditures.

8 *Sales promotional data.* The effectiveness of past promotional campaigns, such as reduced-price packs, coupons, self-liquidating offers and competitions, can be assessed. Trade incentives aimed at distributive intermediaries can also be assessed in terms of their individual influence on sales.

9 *Sales representatives' records and reports.* As described in Chapter 8, sales representatives should keep files on 'live' customers. Often such records hold considerable detail, ranging from information on customer interests to personal information, as well as information about the customer's firm, its product range, diversification plans and likely future purchases. Even what the customer last said to the salesperson may be recorded. In addition, sales representatives make reports to the sales office on such matters as orders

lost to competitors, customers holding future purchasing decisions in abeyance, and information on quotations that never materialised as orders. This information is potentially useful to the forecaster.

10 *Enquiries received and quotations sent.* Customers submit enquiries asking for details of price, delivery, etc., and records should be kept of verbal enquiries. Customers make enquiries to a number of companies. Enquiries lead to a detailed quotation being submitted to the customer. This information can be useful to the forecaster, especially if patterns can be established in the percentage of enquiries that mature into orders and the time between a quotation being submitted and an order being received. The number of requests for quotations can provide a guide to economic activity in the marketplace and, as firms are likely to request quotations from a number of sources, the number of quotations successfully converted into orders gives an indication of the firm's market share.

14.3.3 Data from other departments

Accounts department

The management accountant will be able to provide accurate cost data. Other useful information can be gained from previous management reports. Management information requirements differ between firms, but such reports may contain very accurate information on such matters as:

- number of new customers in a given period

- number of withdrawals

- number of items sold by product in volume and monetary terms

- total sales by salesperson, area, division, etc.

Management accounting reports give information on staff matters such as absenteeism. Such information can be useful when attempting to accurately forecast production capacity. Past budgets with variance analysis will show budgeted figures against actual figures.

The accounts department will also keep statistics on current operations such as orders received, orders dispatched and orders on hand. Such information is kept for internal management information needs, and to fulfil legal requirement when presenting accounts. This information may duplicate information held elsewhere, but may be most accessible in the accounts department. Since such information has been collected independently, it can be used as a 'check' on information gathered from other sources.

Purchasing department

Copies of purchase orders, material lists, requisitions, material status schedule reports and information on suppliers (e.g. reliability of delivery, lead times, prices) can be useful. Purchasing will also be able to provide stock control data relating to re-order levels, buffer and safety stock levels, economic order quantities and stock-turn by inventory item. The forecaster may need to take

Key point
Past budgets with variance analysis will show budgeted figures against actual figures.

such information into account. Stock availability and short lead times are part of the general level of service offered by the firm to customers. Depending on the service sensitivity of the market, service levels can have a significant influence on demand. Present and future service levels will have a bearing on both sales and materials management, as an increase in the level of service would mean more stock and a greater variety of materials being held.

Dispatch department

The dispatch department will have its own information system detailing goods dispatched and transportation methods as well as advice notes and other delivery documents. Such information may be useful for forecasting in its own right, or act as a check on information gathered elsewhere.

Production department

The production department should be able to supply documentation relating to production control, e.g. copies of works orders, material lists and design information. Information will be available on orders placed with the company's own workshops, requisitions for materials to stores, orders subcontracted to other suppliers, manufacturing times, machine utilisation times and order completion dates.

14.3.4 Departmental plans

Not only should historical and current internal information be available to the forecaster, but this should also include short-, medium- and long-term plans relating to individual departments.

Activity and changes in company policy or methods of operation already planned could have a considerable bearing on a forecast. For instance, plans to expand the sales department or to increase promotional activity will affect a sales forecast. Investment in capital equipment such as new machine tools or a new material handling system may significantly affect both materials requirements and future sales.

Key point
Activity and changes in company policy or methods of operation already planned could have a considerable bearing on a forecast.

The sources mentioned are not an exhaustive list of the sources or types of internal information available to the forecaster. Other departments (e.g. human resource management, research and development, work study etc.) might also hold useful information. The choice of sources will depend on the type of forecast required.

Vignette 14.2

Dell Computers lowers sales forecasts

On Thursday 15 February 2001, Dell Computers announced a first round of job losses. This was to be the first reduction in personnel in the history of the company, spanning over 16 years of successful trading. The company had got its sales forecasts badly wrong and totally underestimated the worldwide fall in demand for personal computers and related products. Dell is a high-tech firm, and employs some of the best business brains the world's business schools can generate. The management makes full use of a range of sales forecasting techniques, including both qualitative and quantitative methods, running forecasting software on powerful computers. However, even Dell's level of sophistication and expertise could not prevent them from mis-forecasting the global slowdown for their products, particularly in the USA consumer sector, where the largest slowdown has occurred.

The global PC market is still uncertain, and the company admits it does not have a clear picture of what market conditions will be like beyond the short term, about four months. Even the professional independent analysts got it wrong, and so did other leading computer manufacturers such as Compaq and Gateway. This scenario illustrates the difficulty of producing reliable sales forecasts even up to 12 months ahead of current time, where market conditions are volatile. The slowdown in PC demand growth has been blamed partly on the world economic uncertainty and the concern about general economic slowdown in the USA particularly. Businesses and individuals are feeling less secure, and are deferring the purchase of a new or replacement PC.

14.4 Forecasting methods

14.4.1 Subjective methods

Definition
Subjective methods of forecasting are generally qualitative techniques in that they rely largely on judgement rather than numerical calculations.

Subjective methods of forecasting are generally qualitative techniques in that they rely largely on judgement rather than numerical calculations. They are sometimes called 'intuitive' or, unkindly perhaps, 'naïve' techniques, being applied through a mixture of experience and judgement. Subjective techniques include the executive opinion and sales force composite methods, and customer-use projections.

The executive opinion (or jury) and sales force composite methods

This method involves the sales or marketing manager making an informed subjective forecast. This is sometimes done initially in conjunction with the field sales force (in which case is it the 'sales force composite' method), and then by consulting other executives in production, finance and elsewhere. The group forms a 'jury', which delivers a 'verdict' on the forecast. The final forecast is thus based on the collective experience of the sales force, and has the backing and input of experienced executives in the company. Proponents of this technique claim that the informed opinions of such people provide as valid a prediction as any other method. Such panels are often used in the final stages of the development of a forecast. Where subjective forecasts have been obtained from various sources, there is usually a need to assess and evaluate each one before consolidating them into a final forecast.

Advantages:

● The forecast is compiled by people who have experience of the industry.

● The final forecast is based on the collective experience of a group, rather than on the opinion of a single executive.

- Because the final forecast is based on consensus of opinion, variations in individual subjective estimates are 'smoothed out'.

- Because of the status of individuals contributing to the forecast, the figures are perceived to have a high level of source credibility by people who make use of the forecasting information.

Disadvantages:

- If salespersons know that the resulting sales quotas or targets are linked to bonus payments or commission rates, they may deliberately produce pessimistic forecasts in order to be in a better earning position.

- As forecasting is only a subsidiary activity of the salesperson, the forecast may often be based on guesswork rather than on careful reasoning. Salespeople are often too concerned with everyday events to devote sufficient time to produce realistic forecasts. They have a much wider role than, say, 15 years ago (as discussed in Chapter 8), and are already expected to attend exhibitions, contribute to marketing plans, provide market intelligence and carry out numerous other related activities. Add to this time spent travelling and waiting to see clients, and there is little time available for forecasting activity. This would particularly apply if a large number of product forecasts were required on a regular basis.

Customer-use projections

This method uses survey techniques to ascertain purchase intentions of customers and/or users. Such surveys range from the sales representative merely talking to existing and potential customers and reporting back to head office, to more formal market research surveys. In consumer markets, where the population is often large, a sample survey is usually undertaken. Such a survey can be at two levels; the customer's intention to buy, or the distributive intermediary's intention to stock and promote the product(s). In industrial markets, where the number of customers may be relatively few, sampling may not be necessary. This method is seldom used on its own, but more often in conjunction with other forecasting methods. Test marketing is also used to produce forecasts, and is similar to surveys. A small representative area is used, and the results form the basis of a forecast. Seelig proposes using simulated test marketing – i.e. a test market in a laboratory (Seelig, 1999).

Key point
In consumer markets, where the population is often large, a sample survey is usually undertaken.

Advantages:

- The information on which the forecast is based comes from prospective purchasers, and the rationale is that only they really know what and how they are likely to purchase in the future.

- The technique utilises proven marketing research methodology such as sample surveys, projective techniques and questionnaires to elicit information.

- The task of producing sales forecasts can be subcontracted to professional research agencies, which is useful if executive or salespeople's time is at a premium.

Disadvantages:

- Sample surveys, particularly if they involve face-to-face contact with customers and potential customers, can be very time-consuming and expensive. This cost must be compared with those of alternative methods of producing a forecast using a cost–benefit approach. If forecasts are required on a regular basis, then such a method is likely to be expensive, particularly if forecasts are required in a disaggregated form (e.g. product line by product line over time).

- There may be a difference between what respondents say they are going to purchase and their actual purchases.

- There is a limit to how often the same people (e.g. purchasing managers) can be approached and expected to participate in such a fact-finding study.

Where subjective forecasting techniques are used, the jury of executive opinion and sales force composite methods have greater application than customer-use projections. This is true in industrial markets, as the success of these techniques depends on a close relationship between the supplier and customers.

14.4.2 Bayesian decision theory

The methods of subjective forecasting described do not form an exhaustive list. Some other methods are variations on the techniques described. The main exception is Bayesian decision theory, which is a mixture of qualitative and quantitative techniques. The method is named after the Reverend Thomas Bayes (1702–1761), a statistician. Despite the fact that it was developed in the eighteenth century, it has only recently been widely adopted.

The method incorporates the firm's guesses at data inputs for the statistical calculation of sales forecasts. It uses network diagrams showing the probable outcome of each decision alternative considered. These are shown together with expected values and associated probabilities, initially derived on a subjective basis.

Definition
Bayesian statisticians differ from 'purist' statisticians in the respect that 'purists' view the concept of probability as the relative frequency with which an event might occur.

One of the problems of using probabilities in statistical models is in ascertaining initial probabilities to commence the forecasting process. Bayesian statisticians differ from 'purist' statisticians in the respect that 'purists' view the concept of probability as the relative frequency with which an event might occur. The Bayesian view is that probability is a measure of our belief, and that we can always express our degree of belief in terms of probability. Although the initial probabilities are derived subjectively (i.e. the figures are based on judgmental opinion rather than on objective calculation), proponents of Bayesian theory believe that such probabilities are perfectly valid and hence perfectly acceptable as initial starting points in an extensive quantitative forecasting process. It is the subjective nature of arriving at the initial probabilities that makes the Bayesian approach useful in solving business problems for which initial probabilities are often unknown and are difficult or impossible to calculate using objective methods.

To use the Bayesian approach, the decision-maker must be able to assign a probability to each specific event. The sum of the probabilities of all events considered must be unity (one). These probabilities represent the magnitude of the decision-maker's belief that a particular event will take place.

In business situations, such decisions should be delegated to personnel who have the knowledge and experience to assign valid initial subjective probabilities to the occurrences of various business events. These initial probabilities are based on previous experience of information (such as published secondary data) acquired prior to the decision-making process. For this reason, the initial subjective probabilities are referred to as 'prior probabilities'.

When making business decisions, the financial implications of actions must be taken into account. For example, when a manager is considering investing a firm's surplus cash, he or she must consider the probability of making a profit (or loss) under different economic scenarios, and also assess the probability of such scenarios or events occurring. Applying Bayesian decision theory involves selecting an option and having a reasonable idea of the economic consequences of choosing a particular course of action. Once the relevant future events have been identified, the decision-maker assigns prior subjective probabilities to them. The expected pay-off for each act is then computed, and the act with the most attractive pay-off is chosen. If pay-offs represent income or profit, the decision-maker usually chooses the act with the highest expected pay-off.

Key point
When making business decisions, the financial implications of actions must be taken into account.

To illustrate the theory just described, a practical example is now discussed.

Shepley Textiles produce high quality Axminster carpets. Such carpets are made from 80 per cent wool and 20 per cent nylon (for strength). In the UK, the product retails for approximately £22 per square metre. Axminster carpets are very popular among higher income households in Australia, where only small quantities are produced. The product is perceived by Australian higher social groups as being a luxury purchase. For Shepley Textiles to gain economies in freight charges export consignments need to be relatively large, and it is planned that the first consignment will be worth £3 000 000. Because of its high-status image in Australia, the carpet can command a premium price (about £36 per square metre sterling equivalent). However, such a product is a deferrable purchase, and demand is only likely to remain high if the Australian economy remains strong. Management foresee a possible decline of the Australian economy as the main risk factor in this venture. The first 12 months are particularly important, as this is the time during which the first consignment is expected to be sold, given the present economic climate. Economists have predicted an economic downturn over this period if monetary conditions tighten in response to rising domestic inflation and poor trade figures.

The decision facing Shepley Textiles' management is whether to risk going ahead with the Australian centre now, when present demand for their product is likely to be high, or to postpone the decision, waiting for the economic outlook in Australia to become more stable. If the decision is postponed, fashion tastes may change away from this type of product in the interim.

The management of Shepley Textiles assesses that the Australian economy is likely to go in one of three directions over the next 12 months:

Table 14.1 Subjective prior probabilities of alternative future economic scenarios

Event	Probability
(a) Economic conditions remain the same	0.4
(b) Slight deterioration in the economy	0.3
(c) Significant deterioration in the economy	0.3
Sum of probabilities	1.0

a. It will stay the same

b. Slight deterioration

c. There will be a significant deterioration.

Management assigns subjective initial probabilities to each of the possible economic scenarios (Table 14.1). Note that the sum of the probabilities of the three possibilities considered is unity (1.0).

The direction of the Australian economy is an event (E) that is outside the control of the company. Management decides on three possible courses of action (A):

1 Export now while conditions are relatively good

2 Delay six months, by which time the direction of the Australian Government's economic strategy is likely to become clearer

3 Delay one year to observe the longer-term economic trends.

Management then forecasts expected profit for each course of action under different economic conditions (Table 14.2).

The prior probabilities are now incorporated into a decision tree (Figure 14.1). This is made up of 'nodes' and 'branches', with the decision point represented by a square and chance events by circles.

The expected value (EV) is now calculated for each forecast and then totalled for each alternative course of action (A). This is done using pay-off tables where the expected profit for each event is multiplied by its assigned probability and the resulting products summed (see Table 14.3).

Table 14.2 Expected pay-offs for different decisions under different economic conditions

Events (E)	Actions (A)		
(a) Economic conditions remain the same	1 600 000	1 200 000	1 000 000
(b) Slight deterioration in economy	900 000	740 000	400 000
(c) Significant deterioration in economy	−648 000	100 000	160 000

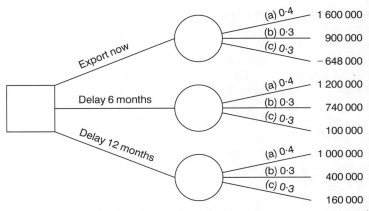

Figure 14.1 Decision tree for Shepley Textiles Ltd: (a) economy remains same; (b) slight deterioration; (c) significant deterioration.

By examining the total values for each of three possible actions, management sees that A2 (i.e. delay action for 6 months) gives the maximum expected pay-off (£732 000). Since the action is selected under conditions of uncertainty, the EV is referred to as the 'EV under uncertainty' and the action chosen as the 'optimal action'.

Table 14.3 Expected value (EV)

Event	Probability	Expected profit (£)		Expected value
A1 – export now:				
(a)	0.4	1 600 000		620 000
(b)	0.3	900 000		270 000
(c)	0.3	–648 000		–194 400
			Total EV	695 600
A1 – delay 6 months:				
(a)	0.4	1 200 000		480 000
(b)	0.3	740 000		220 000
(c)	0.3	100 000		30 000
			Total EV	732 000
A1 – delay 12 months:				
(a)	0.4	1 000 000		400 000
(b)	0.3	400 000		120 000
(c)	0.3	160 000		48 000
			Total EV	568 000

In this example, the probabilities assigned to events were prior probabilities. They were subjective, largely based on the decision-makers' beliefs in the probability that certain events will occur. Such an analysis, carried out using prior probabilities, is called a prior analysis.

After prior analysis, the decision-maker has two choices: to go ahead with the optimal action indicated by the prior analysis, or to collect additional primary data, re-evaluate the probabilities in the light of further information and carry out new calculations. Additional information may be obtained by carrying out a market research survey or some other form of primary data collection procedure (as described in Chapter 13). If additional information is gathered and another analysis carried out, the term for these new calculations is 'posterior analysis'. Clearly, it is going to cost the decision-maker time and money to collect further information. A decision must be made as to whether the better-informed decision will be worth the extra cost or not.

Vignette 14.3

Long-range economic forecasts dampen the spirit of Palermo

On Saturday 17 February 2001, ministers and bankers from the Group of seven industrialised countries (G7) met for a summit in Palermo's Plazzo dei Normanni to discuss the implications of the latest spate of economic forecasts. They were seeking co-operation and harmony to avoid world-wide economic recession in the face of the continuing USA slowdown in demand. Macro-economic forecasts for the US economy predict that the slowdown in demand is continuing, although Alan Greenspan, the Chairman of the US Federal Reserve Bank, is putting a brave face on it, and claims the USA will not experience a severe economic recession. However, even the great Greenspan's forecasts can be wrong.

Whatever the Federal Reserve bank in the USA says, the main theme of the discussion at Palermo was the size of the US slowdown and its likely effect on the world economy. Forecast figures released just before the meeting showed a fourth fall in US industrial production and confirmation that the US economy is experiencing virtually no growth at all. A further worrying trend is the rise in US producer prices, making any interest cut from the Federal Reserve a risky strategy because of its possible impact on fuelling inflation.

On a more positive note, economic long-range forecasts show that Japan is likely to experience continued positive economic growth. However, even this forecast has been reduced from previous forecasted figures because of the reduction of Japanese imports from Japan to the US due to the slowdown. Japan's growth will not compensate for the slowdown in the USA, and is not powerful enough to function as an economic engine for the rest of the world. However, positive growth in Japan over the long term, even if it is relatively modest, is still good news in an uncertain world. Forecasts for Europe also indicate hope for the future, with news that the Italian economy is growing by nearly 3 per cent – the highest growth rate since 1996. The Palermo scenario indicates the importance of forecasting at the macro level. Many of the macro-economic forecasts for industrial sector demand are in fact an aggregate of forecasts made from individual forms within a particular sector.

14.4.3 Objective methods

Objective methods of forecasting are quantitative in nature. Historical data are analysed to identify a pattern or relationship between variables, and this pattern is then extended or extrapolated into the future to make a forecast. Objective methods fall into two groups: 'time series' and 'causal' models.

Time series models

Time series analysis uses the historical series of only one variable to develop a model for predicting future values. The forecasting situation is treated rather like a 'black box', with no attempt being made to discover other factors that might affect its behaviour.

Because time series models treat the variable to be forecast as a function of time only, they are most useful when other conditions are expected to remain relatively constant, which is most likely true of the short term rather than the long term. Hence such methods are particularly suited to short-term, operational, routine forecasting – usually up to six months or one year ahead of current time.

Time series methods are not very useful when there is no discernible pattern of demand. Their whole purpose is to identify patterns in historical data, model these, and extrapolate them into the future. Such methods are unlikely to be successful in forecasting future demand when the historical time series is very erratic. In addition, because it is assumed that future demand is a function of time only, causal factors cannot be taken into consideration. For example, such models would not be able to incorporate the impact of changes in management policy.

Causal models

Causal models exploit the relationship between the time series of the variable being examined and one or more other time series. If other variables are found to correlate with the variable of interest, a causal model can be constructed incorporating coefficients that give the relative strengths of the various causal factors. For example, the sales of a product may be related to the price of the product, advertising expenditure and the price of competitors' products. If the forecaster can estimate the relationship between sales and the independent variables, then the forecast values of the independent variables can be used to predict future values of the dependent variable (in this case, sales).

Such techniques are illustrated by two of the simpler models, *moving averages* and *exponential smoothing*, which are discussed here. Other, more sophisticated, time series models include decomposition models and auto-regressive moving averages (Box–Jenkins) techniques, which are the subject of more advanced study.

Definition
Causal models exploit the relationship between the time series of the variable being examined and one or more other time series.

Moving averages (time series)

Simple moving average:
The simple moving or 'rolling' average is a useful and uncomplicated method of forecasting the average expected value of a time series. The process uses the

average individual forecasts (F) and demand values (X) over the past *n* time periods.

A suffix notation is used, which may seem complicated but is quite simple: the present is referred to as time *t*, and one period into the future as *t* + 1, one period into the past by *t* − 1, two periods by *t* ± 2, and so on. This is best appreciated with reference to a time diagram (Figure 14.2)

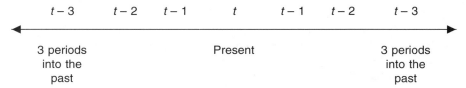

Figure 14.2 Time scale diagram.

The simple moving average process is defined by the equation:

$$F_{t+1} = F_t + \frac{1}{n}(X_t - X_{t-n})$$

where: F_{t+1} = forecast for one period ahead
F_t = the forecast made last time period for the present period
n = the number of time periods considered in the calculation
X_t = actual demand at the present time
X_{t-1} = actual demand for period *t* − *n*.

Weighted average:
The simple moving average has the disadvantage that all data in the average are given equal weighting, i.e. $1/n$.

More recent data may be more important than older data, particularly if the underlying pattern of the data has been changing, and should therefore be given a greater weight. To overcome this problem and increase the sensitivity of the moving average, it is possible to use 'weighted averages', with the sum of the weights equal to unity, in order to produce a true average. In decimal form, a weighted moving average can be expressed as:

$$F_{t+1} = 0.4X_t + 0.3X_{t-1} + 0.2X_{t-2} + 0.1X_{t-3}$$
(Notation as defined for the simple moving average).

Problems common to all moving average procedures are that a forecast cannot be made until *n* time periods have passed, because it is necessary to have values available for the previous *n* − 1, etc. periods. The sensitivity or speed of response of moving average procedures is inversely proportional to the number of periods *n* included in the average. To change the sensitivity it is necessary to change the value of *n*, which creates problems of continuity and much additional work.

The methods of simple and weighted moving averages discussed so far are only suitable for reasonably constant (stationary) data – they are unable to deal with a significant trend. An example of a 'stationary time series' is shown

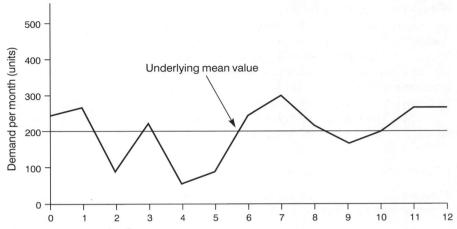

Figure 14.3 Example of a stationary time series.

in Figure 14.3. It can be seen from the graph that over a period of nine months the time series fluctuates randomly about a mean value of 200 units that is not increasing or decreasing significantly over time.

In the times series shown in Figure 14.4, the underlying mean value of the series is not stationary. If a line of best fit is drawn through all of the points, it can be seen that while the actual values are fluctuating randomly, the underlying mean value is following a rising linear trend.

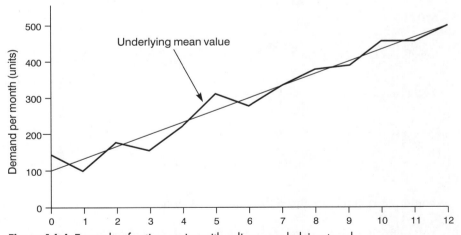

Figure 14.4 Example of a time series with a linear underlying trend.

Double (linear) moving average:
A method of moving averages designed for a reasonably stationary time series cannot accommodate a series with a linear trend. In such situations the forecasts tend to lag behind the actual time series, resulting in systematic

errors. To counter such error factors, the method of 'double' (or 'linear') moving averages has been developed. This method calculates a second (or double) moving average that is a moving average of the first one. The principle is that a single moving average (MA_t^1) will lag behind the actual trend series X_t, and the second moving average (MA_t^2) will lag behind MA_t^1 by approximately the same amount. The difference between the two moving averages is added to the single moving average MA_t^1, to give the level (a_t). The difference between MA_t^1 and MA_t^2 can then be added to the level (a_t) to produce a one- or m-period-ahead forecast.

The 'double moving average procedure' is summarised as follows:

1　The use of a simple moving average at time t (denoted as MA_t'').

2　An adjustment, which is the difference between the simple and the double averages at time t ($MA_t'' - MA_t'$).

3　An adjustment for trend from period t to period $t + 1$ (or to period $t + 1$ (or period $t + m$, if the forecast is for m period ahead).

The updating equations for the double moving average are as follows:

Single moving average:

$$MA_t'' = \frac{X_t + X_{t-1} + X_{t-2} + \ldots + X_t - N + 1}{N}$$

Double moving average:

$$MA_t' = \frac{MA_t'' + MA_{t-1}'' + MA_{t-2}'' + \ldots + MA_t'' - N + 1}{N}$$

Level component, $a_t = MA_t'' + (MA_t'' - MA_t') = 2MA_t'' - MA_t'$

Trend component, $b_t = \dfrac{2}{N-1}(MA_t'' - MA_t')$

Forecast, $F_t + m = a_t + b_t m$.

The general principle of the double moving average is shown in Figure 14.5.

(Notation as defined for the simple moving average).

Although the double moving average has the advantage of being able to handle data with a trend, it has the disadvantage of requiring extra data. N data points are required to update each MA_t'' and MA_t', i.e. $2n$, or twice the number required for the simple moving average, must be stored. The necessity for substantial data storage makes the double moving average less attractive in practice than other techniques that provide similar results from less data. This is particularly so if short-term forecasts are required on a routine basis (e.g. weekly) for a large number of items.

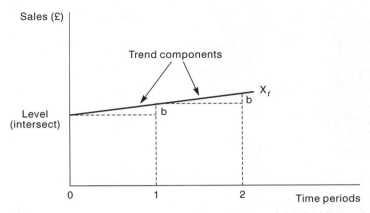

Figure 14.5 Diagrammatical representation of the principle of the double moving average.

Exponential smoothing (time series)

The use of exponentially-weighted moving averages was first developed from a number of unpublished reports by C. Holt, of the Carnegie Institute of Technology. This overcomes some of the shortcomings and limitations of the moving average method.

Simple exponential smoothing:
When using simple exponential smoothing, weights used in the averaging process decrease exponentially over time, allowing greater weight to be given to more recent values. This is achieved by means of a smoothing coefficient, the value of which can be chosen to give the required weight to each piece of historical data used in the calculation of the forecast. To illustrate the principle, let the weighting function used to smooth the random fluctuations from the time series be denoted by α (alpha). A series can be constructed:

$$\alpha + (1 - \alpha) + \alpha (1 - \alpha)^2 + \alpha(1 - \alpha)^3 + \alpha(1 - \alpha)^4 \ldots + \alpha(1 - \alpha)^n$$

For $0 \leq \alpha \leq 1$, as n gets larger the sum of the series will approximate to 1. For example, if $\alpha = 0.4$ and $n = 15$, the series will sum as follows:

0.4 + 0.24 + 0.144 + 0.0864 + 0.0518 + 0.0311 + 0.0187 +

0.0112 + 0.0067 + 0.004 + 0.0024 + 0.0015 + 0.0009 + 0.0005 +

0.003 = 0.995

Rounded up, this is 1.0.

To illustrate how the technique is used in forecasting, we use the notation discussed earlier for simple moving averages (i.e. the one-step-ahead forecast produced in current time is denoted by $F_{t + 1}$ and the actual current demand value by X_t). Using the weighting coefficient series, we produce the following equation:

> **Definition**
> When using simple exponential smoothing, weights used in the averaging process decrease exponentially over time, allowing greater weight to be given to more recent values.

$$F_{t+1} = \alpha X_t + \alpha(1-\alpha)X_{t-1} + \alpha(1-\alpha)^2 X_{t-2} + \alpha(1-\alpha)^3 X_{t-3}$$
$$+ \ldots + \alpha(1-\alpha)^n X_{t-n}$$

Transcribing this equation to an expression for F_t (by subtracting 1 from all the subscripts) we obtain:

$$F_t = \alpha X_{t-1} + \alpha(1-\alpha)X_{t-2} + \alpha(1-\alpha)^2 X_{t-3} + \ldots \alpha(1-\alpha)^{n-1} X_{t-n}$$

The equation for F_{t+1} can be written as follows:

$$F_{t-1} = \alpha X_t + (1-\alpha)[\alpha X_{t-1} + \alpha(1-\alpha)X_{t-2} + \alpha(1-\alpha)^2 X_{t-3}$$
$$+ \ldots + \alpha(1-\alpha)^{n-1} X_{t-n}]$$

The expression in the square brackets is exactly the same as that derived for F_t. Substituting F_t, we obtain the basic equation defining a simple exponentially-weighted moving average from which all other models or exponential smoothing are derived:

$$F_{t+1} = \alpha X_t + (1-\alpha)F_t$$

(More correctly, the process is a geometrically weighted moving average, the exponentially weighted moving average being its analogue in continuous (series) form).

The technique of simple exponential smoothing is historically very important, as it was the first 'adaptive forecasting' method to be proposed. It is adaptive in the sense that the current forecasting errors are used to update the model: A more compact form of equation can be achieved by noting that $X_t F_t$ represents the value of the current forecasting error e_t', and that the equation for simple exponential smoothing could be written as:

$$F_{t+1} = F_t + \alpha(X_t - F_t)$$
$$F_{t+1} = F_t + \alpha(e_t)$$

Thus, the previous forecast is updated by a proportion (α) of the current error (e_t).

An example is given, in Table 14.4, where the one-period-ahead forecast (weeks, months or years) for a hypothetical product is calculated using this last equation. Different values of smoothing coefficient have been used in the calculation ($\alpha = 0.1$, 0.5 and 0.9). In the first period, no earlier forecast is available to use as an F_t value. The normal convention of using the observed value X_t for F_t in the first calculation has been followed.

Double exponential smoothing:

> **Key point**
> Simple exponential smoothing is only appropriate for a relatively stationary time series.

Simple exponential smoothing is only appropriate for a relatively stationary time series. In particular, the method will perform badly if the series contains a long-term trend. Like the simple moving average, if simple exponential smoothing is applied inappropriately to a time series with a trend, the forecast will continually lag behind the actual value of series X_t.

Table 14.4 Example of one-period-ahead forecasting using the equation $F_{t+1} = F_t + \alpha(e_t)$

Time period	Observed demand (X_t)	Exponentially smoothed forecast values (units) (F_t)		
		$\alpha = 0.1$	$\alpha = 0.5$	$\alpha = 0.9$
1	2000	-	—	—
2	1350	2000	2000	2000
3	1950	1935	1675	1415
4	1975	1937	1813	1897
5	3100	1941	1894	1967
6	1750	2057	2497	2987
7	1550	2026	2124	1874
8	1300	1978	1837	1582
9	2200	1910	1569	1328
10	2775	1939	1885	2113
11	2350	2023	2330	2709
12	—	2056	2340	2386

The method of double exponential smoothing is technically known as 'Brown's one parameter linear exponential smoothing'. This method introduces additional equations to those of the simple exponential smoothing to estimate a trend. The method uses the same principle as the double or linear moving average; that is, that if simple exponential smoothing is applied to a time series with a significant trend, it will lag behind. If single exponential smoothing is applied again to the first smoothed series, the second smoothed series (S^2_t) will lag behind the first (S^1_t) by approximately the same amount as the first smoothed series (S^2_t) lagged behind the original time series (X_t). This is illustrated in Figure 14.6.

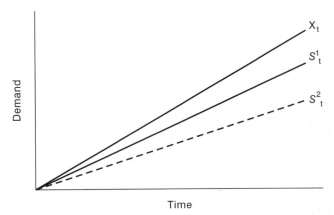

Figure 14.6 The lagged response of a simple exponential smoothing model applied to a series with a linear additive trend.

Brown's method accepts that after initial transients have died down, S^1_t will lag behind X_t by amount A. A second single exponentially weighted average (S^2_t) will lag behind the first (S^1_t) by the same amount, A. At time t, the difference between S^1_t and S^2_t is added to the S^2_t to give the level component a_t. A proportion of the difference between S^1_t and S^2_t is then used to provide a trend component, b_t, which is multiplied by the number of periods ahead to be forecast, m, and the product added to the level a_t to produce a forecast for m steps ahead (see Reynolds and Greatorex, 1988).

Brown's model of double exponential smoothing is made up of two components: a level component or intercept (α), and a trend component (β). These components are combined to provide a forecast, as illustrated in Figure 14.7.

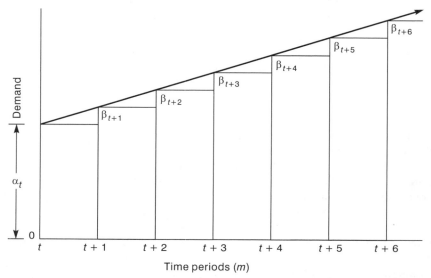

Figure 14.7 The level (α_t) and trend (β[ts]+[ts]m) components of Brown's double exponential smoothing.

The updating equations for Brown's model are:

Single smoothing:	S^1_t	$= \alpha X_t + (1 - \alpha)S^1_{t-1}$
Double smoothing:	S^2_t	$= \alpha S^1_t + (1 - \alpha)S^2_{t-1}$
Level component:	α_t	$= S^1_t + (S^1_t - S^2_t) = 2S^1_t - S^2_t$
Trend component:	β_t	$= \dfrac{\alpha}{1 - \alpha}(S^1_t - S^2_t)$
Forecast:	F_{t+m}	$= \alpha_t + \beta_t m$, where m is a multiplier of the trend component, i.e. the periods ahead to be forecast.

Winter's trend and seasonal model:

The exponential smoothing models discussed so far cannot deal with seasonal data. When seasonality does exist, these methods may perform poorly because the seasonality will produce a systematic error pattern. Such a data series requires the use of a seasonal method to eliminate the systematic pattern in the errors. 'Winter's trend and seasonal model' is based on three smoothing equations – one for stationary series, one for trends and one for seasonality. The updating equations for this model are as follows:

Overall smoothing: $\quad S_t \quad = \alpha \dfrac{X_t}{I_{t-L}} + (1 - \alpha)\, I_{t-L}$

Trend: $\quad Z_t \quad = Y(S_t - S_{t-1}) + (1 - Y)(Z_{t-1})$

Seasonality: $\quad I_t \quad = \beta \dfrac{X_t}{S_t} + (1 - \beta)I_{t-L}$

Forecast: $\quad F_{t+m} = (S_t + mZ_t)I_{(t-L+m)}$

Where: L   is the length of seasonality (e.g. the number of months or quarters in a year)

$\quad Z_t$ is the trend component

$\quad I_t$ is the seasonal adjustment factor

$\quad F_{t+m}$ is the forecast for m periods ahead

X, Y and β are the smoothing coefficients for overall smoothing, trend and seasonal components respectively.

Vignette 14.4

Using exponential smoothing and a tracking signal to monitor the commercial health of small firms

Researchers at the University of Huddersfield in Yorkshire, UK, and Macquarie University in Sydney, Australia, have been experimenting with using short-term forecasting methods in a rather unusual way. Many small firms fail in the important first five years from start up. Something goes wrong, but the management often fails to spot the problem before it is too late. What is needed is some form of early warning system to alert the managers of small firms that things are starting to go wrong. The researchers' idea was to feed various commercial parameters, such as sales, orders, profitability etc., into a semi-automatic short-term forecasting system. The system is run on a standard PC computer and utilises exponential smoothing forecasting techniques. A range of models is available for different input data patterns, including simple exponential smoothing, Holt's method (which can handle a linear trend) and Winter's model (which can also deal with seasonality or cyclicality). The time series data are tracked by a signal itself computed from the forecasting errors. Tracking signal 'trip' limits are set within the system. When errors from forecasts are large enough to 'trip' the system, an error message is generated, which warns management that the situation needs investigating.

Such a system is widely used in process control situations and for stock control systems. However, it is the first time that such a system has been used to try and monitor the commercial health of small firms by monitoring a range of parameters. Early results look promising, and the system might be of use to bank managers and other small firm advisors who need to monitor a large number of small firms simultaneously (Reynolds and Day, 1994, 2000; Reynolds *et al.*, 2001).

14.5 Summary

✓ Forecasting is the starting point for business planning, so if the forecast is incorrect then all strategic and tactical plans will be affected. It follows that the most important link is with marketing planning and control, which is the theme of Chapter 17. Forecasting does, of course, impinge on other areas like marketing research, the subject of Chapter 13, and this is an important forecasting tool when the product is new to the market.

Questions

1 What are the advantages and disadvantages of the various qualitative forecasting methods available to a market researcher wishing to forecast sales up to one year ahead of current time?

2 'Good forecasting becomes a key factor in company success. Poor forecasting can lead to overly large inventories, costly price mark-downs, or lost sales due to being out of stock' (Philip Kotler). Critically evaluate this statement, using examples to illustrate the points being made.

3 What is the difference between sales forecasting up to one year ahead of current time and the annual sales budget? Show how each contributes to the marketing planning and control process.

4 What advantages do exponential smoothing forecasting techniques have, if any, over the method of moving averages techniques?

5 List the types of decision-making that involve either subjective or objective forecasts of future events or states.

References

Ledbetter, W. N. and Cox, J. F. (1977). Operations research in production management, and investigation of past and present utilisation. *Production & Inventory Management*, **18**, 84–92.

Reynolds, P. L. and Day, J. (1994). The commercial health monitoring of small entrepreneurial firms using process control techniques (abstract). In: *Frontiers of Entrepreneurship* (W. D. Bygrave *et al.*, eds), pp. 210–11. Babson College Centre for Entrepreneurial Studies.

Reynolds, P. L. and Day, J. (2000), Helping the SME to survive? Moving towards a robust control technique to monitor and control key marketing parameters within small firms. *Entrepreneurial SMEs – Engines for Growth in The Millennium*, International Council for Small Businesses World Conference 2000, Brisbane, 7–10 June. ICSB.

Reynolds, P. L. and Greatorex, M. (1998). Monitoring short-term sales forecasts. *Proceedings of the Marketing Education Group (MEG) Annual Conference, Huddersfield University*, July, pp. 578–86.

Reynolds, P. L., Day, J. and Lancaster, G. A. (2001). Moving towards a control technique to help small firms monitor and control key marketing parameters: a survival aid. *Management Decision*, **2**, pp. 113–120.

Seelig, P. (1989). All over the map. *Sales and Marketing Management*, **Mar**, 58–64.

Stanton, W. J., Etzel, M. J. and Walker, B. J. (1991). *Fundamentals of Marketing*, 9th edn, p. 571. McGraw Hill.

Further reading

Blythe, J. (2001). *Essentials of Marketing*, Chapters 4 and 5. Person Educational Ltd.

Bolt, G. J. (1981). *Market and Sales Forecasting: A Total Approach*. Kogan Page.

Lancaster, G. A. and Lomas, R. A. (1985). *Forecasting for Sales and Materials Management*. Macmillan Press.

Lancaster, G. A. and Reynolds, P. L. (1998). Marketing information systems and forecasting. *Marketing*, Chapter 5. Macmillan Press.

Lancaster, G. A. and Reynolds, P. L. (1999). Sales forecasting. *Introduction to Marketing: A Step by Step Guide to All the Tools of Marketing*, Chapter 5. Kogan Page.

Makridakis, S. and Wheelwright, S. C. (1978). *Forecasting Methods for Management*. Wiley.

Plamer, A. (2000). *Principles of Marketing*, Chapters 6 and 18. Oxford University Press.

International marketing

15

15.1 Introduction

Trading between nations can be traced back many centuries. People have always traded goods that were surplus to their requirements. Early traders recognised that certain goods and commodities, regarded as commonplace in their own countries, were highly sought after by other nations.

At the turn of the nineteenth century, trading was 'one-sided' in the historical context, but the framework that was laid down fostered the idea of contemporary international trade. During the twentieth century, as empires eroded, trade between nations evolved on a fairer and more meaningful 'buyer' and 'seller' basis. Some nations possess natural resources in excess of their needs which have a value placed on them by other nations, and this forms the basis of trading.

Since the advent of industrialisation, the concept of 'trading' has become more complicated. National expectations have risen such that people are no longer content with the basic essentials of life. Manufacturers have responded by producing goods designed to fulfil these higher expectations. In order for economies to grow and develop, they must earn money that comes from outside their own countries. Governments have a vested interest in promoting international trade and attempting to ensure that their balance of trade is not adverse.

The marketing concept has developed and been accepted as a way of business management that is valid internationally. The pursuit of customer satisfaction, which is very demanding in home markets, requires additional skills when operating in the international sphere. A new marketing mix is often developed to suit foreign markets, and caters for differences in language and culture. International marketing involves precise documentation, and it is often frustrating when dealing with problems not normally encountered in home-based marketing. It can, however, be very rewarding. As the late John F. Kennedy said: 'world trade leads to world peace'.

Key point
As the late John F. Kennedy said: 'world trade leads to world peace'.

310

15.2 Defining subdivisions of international activity

A degree of confusion exists between the terms 'multinational marketing', 'international marketing' and 'exporting'.

Multinational marketing refers to a relatively small number of companies whose business interests, manufacturing plants and offices are spread throughout the world. Although the overall strategic headquarters and control may be based in an original 'parent' country, multinational companies operate alongside their national counterparts so that they are not immediately distinguishable from them. Multinational companies are not principally exporters; they actually produce and market goods within the countries that they have chosen to develop.

The difference between exporting and international marketing is less clear-cut. A company that engages in simple exporting considers it to be a peripheral activity. Most firms have some export involvement, and the term 'exporting' is commonly applied to firms whose export activity represent less than 20 per cent of total turnover. This implies that their international activities are sporadic and lacking in commitment to the degree of modification they should be prepared to make to their products and marketing mix strategy in order to sell successfully in overseas markets.

A company's overseas activities can be described as international marketing once overseas sales account for more than 20 per cent of turnover, at which point it is reasonable to assume that a company has made a firm strategic commitment to overseas involvement. The term implies that:

1 A strategic decision has been taken to enter foreign markets

2 The necessary organisational changes have been carried out

3 Product and marketing mix adaptations for these markets have been made

4 The company has made 'mental' and 'attitudinal' adjustments appropriate to an international marketing strategy.

In essence, international marketing is concerned with any conscious marketing activity that crosses national frontiers. Multinational corporations and exporters (as just defined) represent extremes on the international marketing scale. Between these two extremes are firms who market overseas and who are involved in some way in distributing their products from home manufacturing bases.

Definition
In essence, international marketing is concerned with any conscious marketing activity that crosses national frontiers.

Many companies have developed their overseas activities by means of licensing agreements or joint ventures. Such forms of distribution are discussed later, and the concepts of marketing are as pertinent to them as to home manufacturer/overseas customer arrangements. International marketing is not separate from national marketing; the underlying marketing concept is still valid.

It is considered separately here because of the frequent, and often essential, requirements for modifications to the marketing approach. The product may need to be physically modified, and international marketing might require the firm to change its internal organisation. Even when products are left physically unchanged, to be successful overseas it may be necessary to employ completely different marketing mix strategies from those in operation in the domestic market.

The 'rules' for international marketing are no different from those applied to basic home-based marketing. Management must set objectives that the international strategy should achieve. This strategy must be implemented through the marketing mix being organised in a way that is appropriate to the market being considered. It is likely that an individual marketing mix strategy will need to be developed for each market. Marketing research, advertising and promotion, packaging or sales management all possess the same rationale in both market types; what differs is the way in which these functions are performed.

Key point
International marketing can be demanding, and companies considering international markets should be aware that additional and different demands are made in fulfilling what is already a difficult task.

The design and implementation of an advertising campaign or a marketing research survey is often more difficult in international markets. Language and culture are the principal areas of difficulty. Physical communication can sometimes pose additional problems for international marketers. Face-to-face contact is the best way of conducting negotiations, but even in a firm that has a large-scale international commitment, day-to-day international communication can be limited compared to domestic activities.

Whatever market is considered, the underlying marketing concept does not change. International marketing can be demanding, and companies considering international markets should be aware that additional and different demands are made in fulfilling what is already a difficult task.

15.3 Why enter overseas markets?

Some firms originate with the intention of seeking overseas involvement. The products or services they offer may be so specialised that the domestic market alone will not provide sufficient sales. This is commonplace in industrial markets where, for example, specialist machinery manufacturers make relatively few sales because the rate of repeat purchase is low. Although the value of each sale may be high, the interval between re-buys dictates that as wide a market as possible must be sought. Other firms may start out on the basis of having identified a buoyant foreign market.

The majority of companies, however, begin their overseas involvement from the basis of a well-established home market. The decision to 'go international' can be due to a variety of reasons, including the following:

1 Saturation of the home market. Many companies in mature markets find that the scope for growth is limited. Competitive action may be threatening their market share. Overseas opportunities must be sought to maintain the viability of existing production capacity. This action might also extend the life cycle of a product.

2 To facilitate growth. The actions of competitors might mean there is pressure on a company to increase production capacity and sales volume. Growth markets might present a situation in which a company that does not

grow with market trends becomes relatively smaller in relation to competition and is less able to compete in terms of lower costs and innovation. Access to overseas markets facilitates growth by providing new outlets for increased production.

3 To achieve lower unit costs. The core business may remain in the domestic market, whilst new markets abroad afford the opportunity to increase production and lower overall unit costs. Such cost advantages allow a company to keep pace with market expansion and may even permit the company to expand its domestic market share, provided that the returns on overseas activity are sufficient to make a contribution to fixed costs and cover the variable costs of increased production.

4 Depressed demand in the home market. Some companies regard overseas markets as marginal cost areas. At times of depressed demand in the home market, exporting can maintain production capacity and make a contribution to fixed costs. The ability to pursue such a 'hit-and-run' strategy depends on the type of market in which the company is involved. For price-sensitive commodity markets, this is a viable strategy. However, international marketing is usually dependent on long-term involvement. Companies that turn to export markets in times of need and return to the home market when it is convenient are usually unsuccessful.

An indirect advantage of international marketing is that the company gains a new perspective on its activities. Involvement in foreign markets gives the firm a yardstick by which to measure its efforts at home, and reduces the likelihood of complacency. It also follows that risk is spread more widely with each new market that is successfully entered.

Key point
An indirect advantage of international marketing is that the company gains a new perspective on its activities.

Vignette 15.1

The Philippines is Wal-Mart's next target as part of its ongoing Pacific Rim emerging market retail strategy

The USA retail giant Wal-Mart has made its mark in Europe with the taking over of Asda. It now has its sights fixed on the potential lucrative markets of the Asian-Pacific emerging economies. At present the company has the Philippines on its strategic mind. A retail liberalisation law passed in the country in 2000 lifted a 46-year-old restriction on foreign companies entering the retail market. Up until now, few companies have taken advantage of the relaxation in the regulations. Wal-Mart may be minded to create a chain of retail stores in the country, as well as setting up a regional headquarters. Infrastructure in the country is reasonably well developed – a crucial factor for a business such as Wal-Mart, where distribution and logistics in general is so important.

The firm may develop its own distribution and logistics capability, or it might, at least in the initial market entry stages, form a strategic alliance with an indigenous company who has strength and expertise in the logistics area. The Aboitiz Group is in negotiations with Wal-Mart to provide advice and assistance in logistical matters. Aboitiz has interests and considerable expertise in shipping, air transport, and cargo handling. As the economy develops, per capita GDP increases.

The population has more disposable income and, like any other population, wants to spend some of it shopping. Wal-Mart's no-nonsense approach to retailing and their competitive pricing policies should go down well with the local people, who understandably like to get value for money and appreciate a bargain when they see one.

15.4 How does international marketing begin?

Implicit in the earlier definition of international marketing activity was the idea that simple exporting is a pursuit that accounts for only a small part of a company's overall affairs. The implication is that exporting does not involve the company in any major modifications to its home-based marketing. The term 'international marketing' is used to describe the activities of firms that have made a positive decision to enter overseas markets and are prepared to implement whatever is required to achieve success in such markets.

Many firms begin exporting in a passive way. Whilst being exclusively involved with the home market, they may receive unsolicited enquiries for their products from abroad. These could be as a result of a press or magazine article, or simply through 'word-of-mouth'. Such extra business is likely to be welcomed, as long as it can be undertaken without making any alterations to the existing marketing structure. Requests for modifications to the product or payment terms are unlikely to be considered, because these would detract from the company's main marketing effort. Such action may also involve financial commitment that the company feels could be better employed elsewhere.

When a company's capacity is not being fully utilised, export orders will probably be welcomed. As long as marketing strategy is home-based, these orders will tend to take second place when the home situation begins to improve. Such sporadic commitment can continue for a long time, and is a viable policy as long as customers are prepared to conduct business in this manner. However, it is likely that the overseas customer will look for some kind of security of the supply route. In the long term, it is in the interests of both buyers and sellers to establish such a working relationship.

This sporadic type of exporting can provide the basis for further export involvement. At some point in a company's life, a decision has to be made on whether to develop exporting or not. Clearly, a strong relationship exists between the level of exports and how far a company is prepared to change in response to this. As the level of exports grow, a company is more likely to adopt an 'international marketing' philosophy. As export growth increases, the company will become less passive and more actively involved in exporting, thus taking on an international marketing orientation. The company can initiate this growing commitment gradually by making small changes, but at some stage a conscious decision should be made to devote more marketing effort to exports.

The gradual evolution towards export commitment may be punctuated by the following actions:

1 Allocation or engagement of employees with specific responsibility for internal aspects of exporting such as export documentation, shipping and basic customer liaison

2 Minor modifications to payment terms and conditions

3 Involvement in export marketing research

4 Engagement of overseas agent(s) and/or distributor(s)

5 Engagement of export sales personnel

6 The decision to carry out product modification to suit individual overseas markets

7 Involvement in overseas promotion, including participation in international trade fairs and exhibitions.

Although a gradual evolution of export activity is common, some companies make a single decision to become involved in international marketing without prior involvement. This may represent a major element of an expansion strategy that might be achieved by selling directly to overseas markets or entering into some form of joint venture.

15.5 The international decision – a strategic commitment

An undertaking to become involved in international marketing is strategic in nature. As with all aspects of strategic decision-making, information is needed and careful preparation is essential. The decision will involve financial outlay and organisational change.

The company's first step should be to examine the strategic alternatives. It may be that some other option is easier to implement and carries less risk. If an international strategy is the chosen route, profitability and accessibility to the market should be thoroughly considered and the markets with the greatest profit potential should be identified. Some markets might appear to be highly profitable, but have features that might increase risk. Such influences may be physical, cultural, government- and/or market-related. Some markets might be so well served by domestic suppliers or existing exporters that the level of competition might be a barrier to entry.

The key to making the correct decision is adequate research. Desk research should identify potential markets that should then become the subject of extensive field research. Marketing research and subsequent market selection represent one side of the company's strategic preparation process.

As well as looking 'outward' to the marketplace, the company should prepare and organise its internal structure to meet the challenges that international marketing will present. Production and transport should be organised to meet additional demands, and new commercial procedures might be needed. If the new export business can be accommodated within existing office procedures this will be more cost effective, but inevitably some new

Key point
Marketing research and subsequent market selection represent one side of the company's strategic preparation process.

systems must be devised. It is a common error to try to 'fit exporting in' with existing office systems, treating exporting as a subsidiary activity. To be successful, overseas business must be considered as an entity in its own right and not just an adjunct to domestic marketing arrangements. Such commitment involves adjustments in attitudes, as well as physical adjustments.

15.6 The international mentality

Key point
Just as an understanding and acceptance of the marketing concept should permeate a firm, those involved in export activity should extend the concept overseas with a committed approach to their markets.

An 'international mentality' is an intangible attribute, and it is unlikely that a firm will succeed in international markets without it. Just as an understanding and acceptance of the marketing concept should permeate a firm, those involved in export activity should extend the concept overseas with a committed approach to their markets.

Too often, overseas markets are afforded second-class treatment whilst the domestic market receives priority. When export markets are less profitable than those at home, such an attitude might be understandable but it cannot be condoned. Once the 'international decision' has been taken, overseas customers should expect the best service the firm can offer. It is only by providing service at least as good as local suppliers that the international marketer can hope to succeed.

The mentality required means a genuine interest in overseas customers and their countries, plus a willingness to adapt, and a high degree of patience and tolerance. This is an indispensable characteristic in higher management and international sales personnel, and it is the task of managers to encourage and develop this amongst their staff through training and explanation.

Vignette 15.2

India is branching out in the international defence market

India is becoming an increasingly important country in the international defence industry market. The country's importance has grown not only as a consumer for military products and services, but also as a producer. India's achievements in this important and very lucrative international market have been achieved largely through the use of strategic alliances in the form of joint ventures with other countries. Indian defence organisations have also made use of licensing agreements that have enabled India to produce high technology defence products locally. In February 2001, for example, India signed a $650 million deal to produce Russia's latest tank, the T-90, and will also purchase 100 of the tanks as part of the deal. This is good news for Russia, which desperately needs to earn money from overseas and generate foreign exchange.

This deal come hot on the tail of another successful deal with Russia which enables the Indian authorities, in partnership with the Indian aircraft maker National Aeronautic, to produce the Sukhoi 30 MK1 Fighter jet – Russia's most advanced fighter jet – locally. India's greater involvement in international defence agreements is partly due to fear of similar activities by

Pakistan and a cooling of relations between the two countries. Pakistan has recently acquired 300 of the slightly older T-80 tanks from the Ukraine. India also had a need to upgrade its rather ageing armoury anyway, again because of fears of developments in Pakistan, which India regards as a rogue state. Another over-riding reason is India's strategic long-term decision to become a major player in the international defence market over the next 20 years. India continues to accumulate expertise and technology in a wide range of high technology industries, including the defence industry, and is now well on its way to becoming a major force within the global defence industry in the future.

This case illustrates that international marketing can successfully take place between developing countries. India is still regarded as part of the 'third world', whereas Russia is regarded as a member of the 'second world' despite its former 'superpower' status.

15.7 Organisation for international marketing

15.7.1 Internal organisation

Once a company begins to operate internationally, organisational provision should be made. Export documentation is often complicated and requires specialist expertise, particularly when it relates to developing nations, and staff must be specially trained or recruited to carry out this work. Some firms manage their own freight forwarding, which also demands specific skills. As export activity increases, it might be necessary to establish a complete export administration department.

Communication between the company, its customers and intermediaries might seem to be a basic observation, but the speed of response to electronic mail, fax, postal and telephone messages is a measure of the firm's efficiency. When communication is efficient, it denotes a business-like attitude; rapid response to requests for samples or technical information demonstrates that the company is interested in its customers. The fact that a customer is on the other side of the world often has the effect of decreasing the urgency of any request. The company should implement systems and procedures to ensure that communication, in the sense of customer liaison, is rapid and efficient.

15.7.2 External organisation – the method of supply

How the company organises its sales force (i.e. the people directly concerned with customers and intermediaries), and how agents and distributors are selected and managed, is an important practical consideration. Some firms approach their overseas markets directly, whilst others employ commercial agents and distributors to act in conjunction with and on behalf of the supplier.

Overseas agents are usually nationals of the country concerned. They can be individuals or companies. Their role, supported by the supplier, is to identify customers and provide 'on-the-spot' representation for the supplier. They are paid on a commission basis. Distributors operate by purchasing from the manufacturer and then re-selling after a mark-up has been added for their services. The market for industrial goods lends itself more to agency agreements than that for consumer goods, where distributorships are more common.

The agent/principal relationship is vital to the success of any overseas operation. Whilst agents are not direct employees, they should be afforded the attention and co-operation that company employees might expect. The agent should be able to demonstrate to customers that a positive relationship has been established with the principal in the form of a true 'partnership'.

Apart from financial reward, agents can be motivated by regular contact and sales support, prompt replies to their queries and requests, invitations to the principal's premises, and regular updates on company developments. The agent should respond by providing constant feedback and information about the marketplace. Agents should develop long-term objectives that will benefit both themselves and their principals in the form of a true partnership, which normally implies territorial exclusivity in relation to the product or service being represented.

Key point
The initial criteria for agent selection are similar to those applied to the appointment of any new employee.

The initial criteria for agent selection are similar to those applied to the appointment of any new employee. Most agents have more than one principal, and their existing activity should complement, but not compete with, what is proposed.

The agent search process is often carried out through commercial contacts, but can also include advertising or the employment of consultants to prepare a shortlist of potential agents. Government agencies such as the British Overseas Trade Board (BOTB), Chambers of Commerce and British Consulates in relevant countries can also be a useful source of contact.

The appointment of distributors is a similar process. The firm requires an overseas distributor who has relevant experience and contacts, and whose existing activities are in harmony with the proposed product range. The chief differences are related to the fact that, unlike an agent, the distributor actually purchases the goods from the supplier. They usually contract to maintain agreed minimum stock levels. Although distributors reduce risk and financial outlay for the suppliers, losing 'title' to the goods reduces the control the suppliers have over their marketing of their products.

Direct investment is a further organisational option, and is dealt with later in this chapter.

15.8 International marketing strategy

The decision to become involved in overseas markets is 'strategic'. The decision should be informed, and can only be implemented after adequate preparation. The implementation of international marketing strategy is particularly affected by the influences and constraints of the international marketing environment. Political, economic, socio-cultural and technological ('PEST') factors may differ, and home and overseas markets can exhibit wide environmental differences.

International strategy formulation should thus take the following course:

1 Investment analysis – can resources be better employed by adopting a strategic alternative, say in the home market?

2 Market selection – which markets appear most likely to fulfil the company's overall strategic objectives?

3 Broad-based functional decisions – how will the marketing mix be employed in order to implement the strategy?

The chosen strategy should possess specific objectives to permit subsequent measurement of results. These objectives must be realistic and within the capabilities of the firm, and take account of the environmental factors of the market. They should also be consistent and not conflict with each other. Typical objectives include a specific return on investment (ROI), a specific market share percentage and a specific time scale.

Only through a strategic approach can the company objectively assess its situation and plan a modified international marketing strategy. Related to the decision about how much of a company's turnover should be allocated to overseas markets is how much the company is prepared, or can afford, to spend to attain this goal. The amount or 'level' of investment is a key strategic issue that is governed by the method of entry into the market and the way in which the international marketing mix is employed.

The issues of environment have been dealt with in Chapter 3, and the nature of strategy and control is the concern of Chapter 17. Features that distinguish international strategy from that of the home market are:

- Environmental issues are more wide-ranging and complex

- There is a higher level of risk

- The level of investment is usually higher, involving not only the commitment of financial resources, but also additional organisational burdens.

Once overall strategy has been formulated, the company must develop a 'mix strategy' to achieve the strategic objectives set. The marketing mix is, therefore, the 'tool' of strategy. The essential elements are the same whether the market is international or domestic. Any home-based mix strategy is likely to require modification for international marketing.

The components of the international marketing mix are discussed below.

Key point
Any home-based mix strategy is likely to require modification for international marketing.

15.8.1 Product

In order to achieve economies of scale, companies attempt to streamline their organisational systems and standardise production. This can only be achieved when it is acceptable to the customer. The company must be willing to make changes. Basic, physical changes to the product are not normally a major source of problems to a company that has serious international intentions. More problematic are intangible factors such as image and product positioning.

Packaging is a major element of the product that can be affected by both legal and cultural aspects of the international market. For example, package sizes produced for the home market may not correspond to those in another country. In some countries certain colours have religious significance, and it would be offensive to associate such colours with material goods. Climate can also be an important factor when considering package type. For instance, in warmer, more humid climates, chocolate bar manufacturers put an extra layer of wrapping around the silver foil to prevent the product from melting. In industrial markets, some countries may be unable to handle goods packed in their existing form because of lack of appropriate materials handling equipment.

Labelling is a product-related area where local mandate or convention can dictate modifications. The information required on pharmaceutical products differs throughout the world, and sometimes specific package sizes are required by law. In some countries the level of literacy may require that important information be related graphically. Language presents an obvious need for label modification. Firms with a wide international involvement tend to repeat the information required in a variety of languages relevant to their major markets in a positive move to accommodate these markets, as well as reducing the number of label modifications. A brand name that sounds innocuous in the home market may have a different significance in another language. Even a logo can possess a connotation that might be negative.

Dealing in many markets allows the company to pursue a variety of product policies. At any one time it is likely that a single product's life cycle position will vary in different markets and countries. This implies that the marketing mix and product decisions should be adapted accordingly.

A feature of the past 25 years has been a consistent effort by internationally orientated firms to standardise their products. Although life-cycle positions may call for differing strategies, a goal has been to provide an internationally accepted product image. Whilst individual markets might require an individual mix strategy, product decisions can be simple; Coca Cola® and Levi jeans are famous examples.

Key point
A brand name that sounds innocuous in the home market may have a different significance in another language.

15.8.2 Promotion

Promotional tools and strategies for international markets are similar to those available domestically, but they are not equally appropriate to both situations. The greatest opportunities for simplifying the communications task exist when:

- all media are available
- there are no governmental restrictions on the type of advertising allowed
- advertising and promotion can be developed centrally
- the product is not affected by cultural variables.

A combination of all these circumstances is not common, and is least likely in developed markets like those of Western Europe. Despite similar economic circumstances, these markets have significant cultural variables whose influence only diminishes when marketing industrial commodities. The Americans have been criticised for their failure to recognise this, as they often regard Europe as a single, homogeneous market.

In addition to the obvious problem of language, most advertising must be otherwise modified to suit its target market. Cultural attitudes to family life, behaviour, good manners and sexual equality vary widely between nations. Legal restrictions may also forbid comparative advertising or restrict broadcasting time. This compounds the issue of copy translation and message. Unless it is carefully conceived and checked out by nationals of a country, the message and advertising copy might be totally misdirected.

Whilst the media available can vary between countries, the major criterion for media selection is universal. The appropriate medium is that which reaches the highest number of prospects within the target market at the most cost-effective rate, taking into consideration the specific task that the advertising is designed to achieve.

Sales promotional strategies also need to be 'tailored' to the market. Although standard techniques can be employed, where the product is readily distinguishable as 'imported' the promotional emphasis is normally centred on some form of joint effort organised by an agency of the exporting country (e.g. a Trade Association or a Chamber of Commerce). Large retailers in the target country might be persuaded to host in-store promotions that feature a variety of products from a particular country.

In industrial markets, trade fairs or exhibitions are valuable promotional tools. Companies can participate individually or through some co-operative venture. Participation in such events is often made more attractive by government aid or sponsorship. The benefits derived from attendance at exhibitions are sometimes difficult to measure. Exhibitions provide the company with an international meeting point for seeing a large number of customers in a short space of time. Naturally the company should set clear objectives, but often 'orders taken' provide the only clear yardstick of success. Other measures can include the number of enquiries. If the product is technical, it may be some time before enquiries are converted into orders.

15.8.3 Distribution

International distribution involves wide-ranging decisions. As well as physical distribution and logistics, the company must consider whether to use agents and/or distributors or to sell directly to the overseas customer.

Key point
International distribution involves wide-ranging decisions.

In general, transportation decisions are clear and can be refined as the company gains experience. Clearly, perishable products should be despatched by the fastest means. An expensive mode like air freight would not, on the other hand, be appropriate for bulky, low-value products.

The idea of 'total distribution' or the systems approach, as discussed in Chapter 10, is particularly applicable to international marketing. In commodity markets, or where there is local competition, service is frequently the major competitive tool. A company that consistently delivers on time will build up a level of loyalty that may never be achieved by promotional means. The organisation of the distribution mix is a function of the product and market type and, where international markets are concerned, distribution is a high-profile element of the overall marketing mix.

15.8.4 Price

The price element of the marketing mix in international markets is complicated by transportation costs and currency fluctuations. However, basic pricing strategies still apply. Unless the company is merely seeking to 'offload' excess capacity, research carried out before the market entry decision is made should establish that it is possible to make some level of profit given the cost structure of the company. Important questions include how much is the company able to change, and how much price is a function of the product and of the market situation?

Depending on the product/market relationship, the company can adopt one of three basic pricing strategies that have already been considered in Chapter 11:

1 Market penetration pricing

2 Market skimming

3 Market- (competitor-) based pricing.

When market conditions permit, opportunities for 'skimming' should be taken; innovative products lend themselves to this approach. A market penetration strategy should be considered carefully before being applied to export markets. The relatively volatile nature of overseas markets and the associated risks can bring about a change in the market situation before the company has had the opportunity to recoup its investment through a low-penetration price policy. Possible market changes include currency fluctuations, government action and aggressive competitive reaction from within the target country. Whilst opportunities for product and price differentiation in overseas markets are apparent, it is a feature of the twenty-first century that, in general (and especially in consumer markets), product standardisation is increasing. This means that a company often has little option than to charge a price established by competitors. In such situations it is essential that cost structures have been thoroughly examined and that the expected return on investment is considered to be acceptable before market entry. Where the company is obliged to operate within a predetermined price framework, it should attempt to differentiate its products by other means.

Procter & Gamble is an example of a company that is successful internationally and obtains high market share through an emphasis on promotion rather than price. International markets can offer special opportunities for obtaining high prices due to the prestige or novelty associated with the country of origin. Burberry clothes have a 'Britishness' sought after throughout the world. The French have a reputation for high quality cosmetics. International sales of some brands of whisky are probably due as much to their Scottish origin as to their taste.

As well as how much to charge, the question of how prices are to be applied must be considered. It has been stated that exporters should modify their approach to customers so as to minimise possible complications. Importers are not concerned with the problems of foreign suppliers, and simply require goods and services under conditions that are as similar as possible to those existing through normal purchasing channels. Modifications in price application might be necessary for successful international marketing, and this is the

Key point
International markets can offer special opportunities for obtaining high prices due to the prestige or novelty associated with the country of origin.

responsibility of the supplier. The main issues regarding international pricing concern the price quotation, where the main terms used in export/import transactions are:

- 'Ex-works' is where the importer is solely responsible for transport and insurance from the supplier's premises.

- 'FOB' (free on board) is where the supplier is responsible for the costs of transport and insurance until the goods are loaded immediately prior to export. Once loaded onto a ship or aircraft, the customer assumes responsibility for further costs.

- 'CIF' (cost, insurance and freight) is where the supplier's quotation includes all costs of delivery to a port convenient to the customer. A typical quotation may read 'CIF local port', but often the port of destination is specified.

- 'C & F' (cost and freight) is where insurance is not included in the price. This might be because the government of the importer insists on using the country's own insurance facilities. Sometimes the government of the importing country might specify the shipping line that the exporter must use.

- 'Delivered client's warehouse' (sometimes termed 'rendu' or 'free delivered') is a typical quotation used in trading within Europe, where lorries can deliver 'door-to-door'. The supplier is responsible for all costs, including customs clearance, but excluding any local duties or taxes.

- More specialist quotations, such as 'FAS' (free-alongside) and 'FOW' (free-on-wagon).

> **Definition**
> 'FOB' (free on board) is where the supplier is responsible for the costs of transport and insurance until the goods are loaded immediately prior to export.

Payment terms and conditions vary from country to country. Thirty-, sixty- and ninety-day credit terms are common within Europe. Discounts for prompt payment also vary.

'Letters of credit' are a normal trading condition in more distant markets. They provide protection for both parties, because funds are not transferred until conditions are met. Once they are fulfilled, the supplier is guaranteed payment by the bank. In some countries, especially those with balance-of-payments problems, payment can be deferred by as much as two years. Financial institutions exist that are able to factor payments to suppliers for a percentage of the cost involved. Means of payment must therefore be carefully considered before sales are negotiated.

Currency is an important consideration, and 'hard' currencies like the US dollar and the pound sterling are 'universal' currencies. However, they are not always the most convenient means of exchange for most international trade. From a marketing perspective, it can be preferable to make quotations in the customer's local currency as long as it is readily convertible and stable in international terms. This shows a commitment to the overseas customer. Where local competition is strong, quotations made in local currency can remove one of the distinctions that competition might use to argue against international sourcing. Financially, trading in foreign currencies carries an element of risk that can be offset by buying the currency 'forward'.

15.8.5 International sales management

Given the complexity and variety of international sales management, systems should be devised that are effective in each market being served. Export sales staff are often recruited from outside the firm, but it is not uncommon for home-based sales personnel to be given overseas responsibilities. The latter option might be feasible where a clear interest and commitment to international activity is evident. It is a mistake to transfer successful domestically based sales staff to overseas markets, as their effectiveness is often reduced. An 'international mentality' is a prerequisite, and this should ideally be supported by linguistic ability – or at least a willingness to learn the local language – as this can foster goodwill.

Many organisational options are available. An international sales team can be home-based and made up of nationals of the exporting country. Each salesperson will be responsible for one or more territories, with workloads being divided between home-based liaison and follow-up and actually visiting the markets. The amount of time spent abroad will depend on the market and product. Apart from the practical side of visiting customers to conduct business, such visits reinforce the commitment of the company to its overseas customers. It is essential when making visits that the salesperson has sufficient authority to take important business decisions 'on the spot'. This increases the salesperson's credibility, and raises the tone of the meeting from what might otherwise appear to be a courtesy visit. The need to make such decisions whilst abroad requires a level of managerial ability not always needed for domestic sales staff. International sales personnel should therefore be able to work with minimal supervision, which requires self-discipline and determination.

Key point
Maintaining an expatriate sales force is expensive and complex.

Expatriate sales personnel (nationals of the exporting country) can be domiciled in the target country. Although the business rationale for such a system is sound, management problems can occur. Maintaining an expatriate sales force is expensive and complex. The company might feel that control over its salespeople is reduced, and salespersons may feel personally isolated from the home country. Morale amongst staff living abroad for long periods can be difficult to maintain.

When a high level of sales is achieved in a particular country, it might be appropriate to engage a national sales manager and sales personnel. They have the advantage of familiarity with the language, customs and culture, which expatriate sales staff might never achieve. On the other hand, customers might consider a sales force of locals as 'once-removed' from the company and less directly involved in the marketing process. The company may also find that control measures are more difficult to apply.

15.9 International intelligence and information

The expense of entry into international markets places a burden on a company's MkIS (marketing information system), which must provide accurate information for strategic decision-making. The MkIS should function as it would for domestic purposes, but the breadth of information required is greater and information can be more difficult to obtain. Some companies employ specialist international agencies.

Field research is sometimes frustrated by language problems, in which case it may be necessary to engage local research agencies. In developing nations, organised data collection might not exist, levels of literacy can be low, and media available for promotion limited.

At the secondary stage, the research process should relate to:

- International trade directories and magazines

- Government statistics and reports

- Embassies and consulates

- Published surveys

- 'On-line' data services accessed directly or through specialist agencies

- International banks and other financial institutions.

As well as supplying information for marketing preparation, the intelligence system has a vital role to play in monitoring the international environment once business has begun. In the 'home' country, much information available through the media is taken for granted. The intelligence system should ensure a regular flow of information from the countries being monitored. It is part of the role of agents, distributors, sales personnel and other locally based employees to contribute information.

15.10 Cultural variables

As 'culture' is intangible and unwritten, it is assimilated rather than learned. Cultural variables can pose problems when devising marketing strategy. Advertisers need to be aware of differences in such aspects as humour, morality and the role and status of women. Colours have religious significance, or can signify good or bad luck. As mentioned already, care must be taken in package design and labelling. Sales personnel must observe rules of etiquette that are part of the socio-cultural context of an international market. International marketers should obtain assistance and advice from nationals before applying their own cultural and business values to marketing activities.

Key point
Colours have religious significance, or can signify good or bad luck.

Culture is an ethnic rather than geographic factor. A country may contain groups of people with radically different cultures; the Germans and the French recognise distinct cultural differences between the north and the south of their respective countries that are not immediately apparent.

15.11 Government and political activity

International marketers must consider the influence of governments on their activities. In recent years, some emerging economies in Africa have been politically unstable. Countries that have emerged following the break-up of the

Soviet Union have displayed volatility. Governments can also frustrate the efforts of international marketing in developed economies. A country might need to redress a balance-of-trade problem, and to do so might impose duties on imported goods that can effectively bar attempts to export to that country. Another reason for such action in developing countries is to protect local industries from foreign competition. Governments might subsidise certain industries to maintain employment, thereby changing the basis of competition.

The European Union has encouraged free trade between member nations, and this culminated in the 'harmonisation' accord at the end of 1992, which covers matters like customs procedures and differing legal requirements for labelling and product safety.

Vignette 15.3

Pacific Rim emerging markets offer European firms great opportunities but also great threats

Asia and the Pacific Rim area of the world promises enormous commercial opportunities to western firms as the emerging economies in the region continue to develop, despite the slight economic 'hiccup' in the late 1990s. Taiwan, Hong Kong (now part of China), Singapore and South Korea are once again showing signs of impressive economic growth, and are in fact designated 'newly industrialised countries' because of their spectacular growth and development compared to other emerging and developing economies in the region. Borneo, the Philippines, Thailand, Indonesia, Vietnam, Cambodia, Malaysia and other countries in the region are also showing encouraging signs of growth.

These markets offer great opportunities to many European firms, but they also represent a longer-term threat to their markets. The emerging Pacific Rim economies represent a potentially lucrative market for European goods; they also offer the possibility of manufacturing facilities with considerably lower labour and other costs. Many European firms are 'outsourcing' manufacturing to such low labour-cost countries, and many are making a direct investment in the region, setting up a subsidiary company or becoming involved with strategic alliances such as joint ventures with local companies in the region.

Hence involvement in the region could be profitable for European firms, but, as the region develops economically, it also poses a threat to Europe. Many of the goods and services produced in the region by indigenous firms will be targeted at European markets. Often these products and services will be at a lower cost and often technologically superior, having been produced using the latest processes and equipment. Already Europe has seen large sections of its industry under heavy pressure from cheaper foreign imports from the Pacific Rim area. Children's toys, sports shoes, cameras, hi-fi and many other product areas, including motor cars, are among those industries affected by the aggressive export drive of these countries. European firms will have to take the economic threats posed by the continual development of the region into account in their long-term strategic marketing plans. They managed to 'factor in' the profit potential of the region in their strategic plans a decade ago; now they must factor in the commercial threats posed by the same development.

15.12 Direct international investment

'Investment' has been used to describe resource allocation (financial or human) used to enter an overseas market. 'Direct investment' also implies a semi-permanent diversion of funds and expertise so the company is no longer transporting finished goods from the home base to export markets, but is manufacturing outside the home country or engaging in co-operation with foreign manufacturers.

15.12.1 Direct investment

This is normally considered when the firm's level of international involvement has reached a point where it is no longer practical or convenient to continue the physical transfer of goods from one country to another. Sometimes direct investment provides a method of entry into overseas markets that bypasses the export evolution process. By purchasing a foreign company, or by entering into a licensing or industrial co-operation agreement, a company gains immediate market access and revenue from abroad without necessarily having had prior international involvement.

15.12.2 Licensing

This involves one company allowing another to use a trademark or patent, or a manufacturing process, design or recipe, for which the user company makes a payment. It is a relatively easy method of entry into foreign markets, and it provides immediate revenue.

Licensing is much favoured by Japanese companies, although some have been criticised for using this as a 'back door' method of entry where, once the product has become established, they can take over the licensee and with it a ready-made marketing system for the original product.

15.12.3 International co-operative ventures

These involve the sharing of technology or manufacture between two companies from different countries. As well as sharing knowledge and expertise to mutual advantage, both companies benefit from sharing costs.

15.12.4 Joint venture

These operations involve two companies joining together to manufacture and market their products as one. They differ from co-operative ventures in that the companies are effectively merging, rather than sharing, their expertise. Often a new company is formed in which neither party has an over-riding shareholding. The maintenance of a 50 : 50 holding interest helps to ensure that conflict between the two parties is minimised, although in some countries there is an insistence that the 'local' partner has a controlling interest (i.e. 51 per cent or more).

In markets where there is not scope for licensing or joint manufacture, it might be possible to establish local sales and distribution centres overseas. Although costs are usually high compared with those of maintaining such centres at home, this system has the advantage of allowing the company to retain control over its activities. It is often a precursor to establishing the company's own manufacturing facilities overseas, which represents the sophisticated degree of international investment. Risk is associated with any large investment, but by installing its own capacity in a foreign country, control is retained and the opportunity exists to build up goodwill with both the community and the government.

15.13 Multinational and global marketing

Companies such as Ford, IBM, McDonalds, Shell and Mitsubishi can be described as multinational companies. Although they have their 'roots' in a single country, whose office may still hold overall strategic power, they are multinational in nature because their activities are world-wide, and in particular because they have established themselves in countries on an equal footing with indigenous companies. They operate as national companies in everything but name.

If such companies decide to divert their resources from one country to another, the consequences for local communities in which their operations decrease or cease can be severe. Their size and power can also tend towards monopoly, and it is the responsibility of governments and trading blocks to ensure that this power is not abused.

If the trend towards world-wide standardisation of products (whether it be cars, hamburgers or clothes) continues, and cultural groups grow increasingly alike in their tastes as societies become more 'cosmopolitan', the importance of multinationals is likely to increase. The rise of multinationals means that in product terms certain goods have 'global' appeal. These goods are successfully marketed in all countries with little or no attention to product or image modification. This is the phenomenon of global marketing.

In most countries one is able to see local people wearing Levi jeans, driving Ford or Toyota cars, drinking Coca Cola and listening to Sony personal stereos. Companies that achieve such standardisation simplify their marketing task and create effective competitive barriers. This is a trend that seems likely to increase with growth in multinational activity.

Warren Keegan (1969) put forward a theory that is now central to strategic thinking when considering international marketing. He considered the mix elements of product and promotion, and identified five possible strategies (see Figure 15.1). Explanations follow in relation to each of these strategies.

1 *Straight extension*: the product or service and the type of communication message is the same for overseas and home markets (e.g. Coca Cola).

2 *Communications adaptation*: the promotional theme is modified and the product or service remains unchanged (e.g. bicycles are promoted as basic means of transportation in developing countries, whereas in developed countries they are promoted as a means of recreation).

Key point
The rise of multinationals means that in product terms certain goods have 'global' appeal.

Products

	No change	Adapted	New product
No change	Straight extension	Product adaptation	
Adapt	Communication adaptation	Dual adaptation	Product invention

(Left axis label: Marketing communications)

Figure 15.1 Keegan's five strategies for international marketing.

3 *Product adaptation*: the product or service is different for home and overseas markets, whereas the promotion is the same for both (e.g. petrol has a different 'formula' for colder climates than for warmer climates).

4 *Dual adaptation*: the communication message and the product or service are altered for each market (e.g. clothing products, where designs and structure are different for each market, and promotion can emphasise functionality or fashion).

5 *Product invention*: the above strategies are appropriate where product needs and market conditions are similar to the home market, but in developing countries this may not be true. New product development might be required to meet customer needs at an affordable price (e.g. a hand-cranked washing machine is an example of 'backwards invention' to suit the needs of countries where there is an uncertain power supply and washing is done by hand).

Vignette 15.4

Japan uses non-tariff barriers to keep out competition in its telecom markets

Japan has a reputation for tacit protectionism in many of its markets. For years international organisations have been trying to persuade Japan to open its markets to foreign competition, as many countries of the world have been good enough to do for Japan. The minutes of the 'G7 Economic Summit', hosted annually in different parts of the world and attended by the world's finance ministers and other important financial and economic figures, have always criticised Japan for holding up the world economy through its protectionist practices and polices. Japan has signed under the GATT agreement, and is part of the World Trade Organisation (WTO) agreements that followed GATT. However, many say that Japan does not follow either the letter or the spirit of the agreements. The international telecom market is a case in point here.

Basically, the interconnection charge made by NTT, one of Japan's biggest telecom companies, is thought to be too high. This high charge stops Japanese consumers using the services of foreign network providers, because the interconnection rates make the price of the service much higher than the ordinary domestic rate charged to its customers by NTT. Japan has agreed to reduce the interconnection charge made to USA competitors by 20 per cent, but many in Europe say this is inadequate and needs to be more substantial. The European Commission is threatening to take Japan to the WTO if it does not come up with an acceptable solution. The EU does not consider that Japan is playing 'fair' and believes that it is not honouring its commitments made under the WTO agreements to liberalise telecom services throughout the world.

15.14 Help to UK exporters

For small and medium-sized enterprises (SMEs) and large companies who are new to international markets, the UK government offers a wide range of services to assist and promote marketing efforts.

15.14.1 Statistics and market information

The British Overseas Trade Board (BOTB) is able to supply a wide variety of information on specific markets throughout the world on request. The Export Intelligence service provides regular information on specific markets for a subscription. Such information can be augmented by direct application to British consular offices throughout the world through commercial officers who have detailed local knowledge of particular industries. These services include the preparation of shortlists of potential agents and distributors.

The BOTB sometimes provides direct financial assistance for market research projects aimed at export markets. Financial support from the BOTB is available to exporting companies.

15.14.2 Trade fairs and exhibitions

Companies wishing to participate in overseas trade fairs and exhibitions can do this through their Trade Association or local Chamber of Commerce. The BOTB also organises and subsidises trade delegations to selected overseas markets.

15.14.3 Market entry guarantee scheme

This is effectively a loan of up to 50 per cent of the costs involved in entering a new export market. If the venture is unsuccessful, the loss is shared by the exporter and the BOTB. The scheme is aimed at small to medium-sized firms.

15.14.4 Export Credits Guarantee Department (ECGD)

This is a government-organised insurance scheme that extends normal insurance cover to include non-commercial risks such as war, expropriation and balance-of-payment crises in countries to which goods have been sent.

15.15 Summary

✓ This chapter has described the operation of companies engaged in exporting at various levels of activity. The subject encompasses all topics within marketing. To be an international marketer, there should be no distinctions between countries; the only differences should be in terms of how the marketing mix is employed for different markets/countries.

✓ The decision to enter overseas markets is an important strategic consideration that cannot be effected without considerable preparation and willingness to adapt. International marketing is not a quick remedy for companies who find themselves in difficulty on the domestic front. An international strategy should be preceded by close examination of the available alternatives in the home market. Increasing sales volume through overseas markets may only be possible by means of extensive product and marketing mix modifications, the cost of which may negate the expected advantages. Similarly, an investment in a product life-cycle extension strategy aimed at overseas markets might be better utilised in the development of new products for the home market.

Questions

1 *Definitions*
Explain how overseas marketing differs from overseas trading.

2 *International involvement*
How can firms begin to increase their involvement in international markets? Discuss the relative merits of the methods you describe.

3 *Information sources*
Outline the statistical and other international market research information that is provided by the government in order to assist potential exporters. What limitations or problems are apparent when preparing to use such sources?

4 *Financial implications*
Why does the acceptance of a foreign order usually impose a proportionately heavier financial burden on the supplier than for a similar home market order? What steps can be taken to reduce this effect?

Reference

Keegan, W. J. (1969). Multinational product planning: strategic alternatives. *Journal of Marketing*, **33**, 58–62.

Further reading

Armstrong, G. and Kotler, P. (2000). The global marketplace. *Marketing: An Introduction*, 5th edn, Chapter 15. Prentice Hall.

Blythe, J. (2001). International marketing. *Essentials of Marketing*, Chapter 11. Person Educational Ltd.

Cateora, P. R. and Ghauri, P. N. (2000). Emerging markets and market behaviour. *International Marketing: European Edition*, Chapter 9. McGraw Hill.

Davies, M. (1998). International marketing. *Understanding Marketing*, Chapter 11. Prentice Hall.

Keegan, W. J. and Green, M. S. (2000). Introduction to global marketing. *Global Marketing*, 2nd edn, Chapter 1. Prentice Hall.

Lancaster, G. A. and Reynolds, P. L. (1998). International marketing. *Marketing*, Chapter 14. Macmillan Press.

Lancaster, G. A. and Reynolds, P. L. (!999). Macro issues in marketing. *Introduction to Marketing: A Step by Step Guide to All the Tools of Marketing*, Chapter 14. Kogan Page.

Plamer, A. (2000). *Principles of Marketing*, Chapters 14 and 23. Oxford University Press.

Societal marketing

16

16.1 Introduction

Marketing practice is the subject of criticism and debate that essentially revolves around two themes:

1 Aspects of business malpractice are frequently associated with, or grouped under the umbrella of marketing. This is due to a misconception of marketing's true meaning. Added to this is the fact that marketing orientation, which puts customers at the centre of business activity, grew out of sales orientation. Sales orientation puts production at the centre, and its philosophy is of course one of selling this production by any means, as was discussed in Chapters 1 and 2. This is associated with 'sharp practice'.

2 Social commentators question the ethics of marketing and its place in our social system. In a world of finite resources, they query whether we might be devoting too much to the gratification of materialistic wants to the detriment of the social good. It is suggested that marketing creates artificial wants, and that the resources channelled into competitive advertising, branding and packaging are a waste of money and might be better employed elsewhere.

It is, however, acknowledged that marketing is not merely a business practice, but a social influence that can be used to improve the quality of life in its widest sense. This influence should not be patronising; rather it should be exercised in co-operation with the individuals and groups who are consumers of marketing's offerings.

Linked to the idea of marketing as a beneficial social force is the extension of functional marketing into non-commercial activities. The pursuit of customer satisfaction is a valid aim, irrespective of the profit motive. Marketing as a discipline is appropriate to the not-for-profit sector, because its practice obliges managers to think and act efficiently with end-user needs in mind. Marketing is a style and philosophy of management that is not restricted to business. It also has social consequences. Implicit in true marketing-orientation is recognition that business responsibility extends beyond a company's immediate customers.

Definition
Marketing is a style and philosophy of management that is not restricted to business.

This chapter examines the validity of criticism aimed against the marketing system, but comes to no firm conclusions. Individuals must develop their own opinions and consider marketing from these perspectives. The issue of 'consumerism' is meant to assist this process. The chapter also extends the marketing concept into issues of social marketing and marketing for non-profit-making organisations.

Vignette 16.1

J. Sainsbury plc employs 'green' and socially responsible marketing in its battle for an increased market share of the UK grocery market

The population of the UK is reasonably static at about 57 million people. The average birth rate is falling, although population numbers are sustained through immigration and people living longer. The UK is a first world country and part of the EU. It is a participant of the EU's Common Agricultural Policy (CAP). There is no shortage of food in Europe; in fact, farmers are often paid not to produce certain crops in order to control supply and prices. Diseases such as BSE and foot and mouth sometimes result in temporary shortages of meat products.

The demand for food in the UK is again reasonably static in terms of quantity. If anything, many health conscious people are trying to eat less to avoid obesity. The demand for food is also reasonably income-inelastic. Unless you are really poor, when you double your income you do not double your consumption of food. Many people 'trade up' and buy more interesting or better quality foods, or may spend more money eating out. For a supermarket chain to increase its market share of the grocery business it has to capture market share from other stores. Part of Sainsbury's strategy is to employ environmentally friendly, ethical and socially responsible marketing policies. The company feels that this is what its customers want, and research indicates that customers care and are generally responsive to this policy. As a result of this policy many of Sainsbury's grocery products cost a little more, but this seems to be a cost that its customers are prepared to pay.

Sainsbury's complete strategy is too extensive to cover here, but two areas are highly indicative of the company's approach. The first area concerns the use of pesticides. Many people are worried about pesticides and the affect they are having on the natural environment. Sainsbury's is working with its suppliers and growers to bring the benefits of the latest scientific developments and changes in farming practices to its customers. The use of pesticides has reduced dramatically over the last 10 years, and Sainsbury's is ensuring that the produce it sells has been produced using the latest available techniques. Reducing pesticides and encouraging farmers to protect wildlife and the general environment is one of the strategies Sainsbury's is using as part of its 'green marketing' policy.

A second area that serves as a good example of Sainsbury's overall approach concerns the company's use of socially responsible sourcing. Sainsbury's customers want excellent quality and value for money, but not at the expense of other people. Sainsbury's is playing a leading role in many initiatives to protect the right of workers operating in developing countries. Sainsbury's operates a 'Fairtrade' policy, which increases awareness of disadvantaged and marginalised producers in emerging economies and developing nations. The 'Fairtrade' mark is an independent consumer label that guarantees a fair deal for marginalised farmers in developing nations.

Sainsbury's also works with its suppliers of own-brand goods, and has a code of practice covering issues such as health and safety, the protection of children, equal opportunities and socially responsible sourcing procedures. Basically, the code ensures that its suppliers adhere to internationally recognised standards in terms of employment conditions. Sainsbury's is also a leading light in the Ethical Trading Initiative (ETI), which is an association set up to monitor and negotiate standards for third-world suppliers.

16.2 Common criticisms of marketing

16.2.1 Customer dissatisfaction

The marketing system operates in an environment that rarely functions exactly as theory predicts. This does not negate the value of theory, but it should be remembered that the world of reality is not perfect and at best theory can only predict what is likely to happen. The marketing concept is often criticised when customer satisfaction is not achieved, but the concept at least provides a clear objective against which performance can be measured and necessary remedial action taken. The fact that companies acknowledge the marketing concept and pursue a customer-orientation does not excuse shortfalls in efficiency, but for many 'marketing' has become a generic term for 'business activity'. Amongst those active in business are firms who pursue a short-term 'sales-orientated' approach. Thus, as well as genuinely marketing-orientated companies who are sometimes less than efficient, consumers must contend with companies whose short-term goal is profit and for whom customer satisfaction is sublimated. Criticisms levelled against such companies include:

Key point
The marketing system operates in an environment that rarely functions exactly as theory predicts.

- poor product quality

- misleading packaging and labelling

- unreliable delivery

- poor after-sales service

- uninformative or offensive advertising.

Consumers have a right to be protected from such practices. This protection is particularly necessary when the product is complicated (e.g. insurance and credit). Governments and consumer bodies have taken steps to enforce protective measures. It must be noted that consumer sovereignty is a powerful safeguard against malpractice and, whilst it is not always the case, it is likely that companies who consistently fail to provide customer satisfaction will ultimately exhaust their supply of customers and go out of business. Customer pressure and legislation has decreased opportunities for companies to exploit consumers, and increased marketing orientation by companies acts in their favour.

The main debate about marketing is not concerned with customer satisfaction. Criticisms are voiced by philosophers and social, economic and political commentators, who question the ethos of the marketing system, looking at issues like the manipulation of society, efficient resource utilisation and the social effect of marketing on lifestyles and value systems. Brownlie and Saren (1992) have even argued that marketing has now outlived its usefulness.

Vignette 16.2

Protecting the small banana growers against the big three USA producers

The European Union (EU) developed new regulations relating to the import of bananas into the EU in 1993. The aim was to protect banana producers in the former European colonies who were smaller and less efficient than the large US banana growers – especially the biggest three US companies, Chiquita Brands International, Dole Foods and Fresh Del Monte. The smaller growers, many of whom were based in the Caribbean countries, relied on the sale of their produce to the EU in order to make their living.

Without the EU markets many families in these countries would face unemployment and severe financial hardship. The big American producers, on the other hand, had a diversified portfolio of products and did not depend on the EU banana market for their survival. The EU introduced restrictions on imports from a societal point of view. However, the EU banana market was a lucrative market, and although the American producers may not have depended on it for their continued existence, they had all worked hard to build their market shares in this market and did not want to lose them.

The American companies had known that restrictions of their produce into the EU had been in the planning stage for some time, and that they needed a long-term strategy to try and minimise the threat to their businesses. Basically, the American firms were faced with two strategic conceptual extremes; either they had to find a way to work within the system of EU regulations relating to the banana market, or they had to find a way of fighting the system. Different firms chose different long-term strategies, with different long-term consequences.

Chiquita Brands International (CBI) decided to fight the regulations. The company enlisted the help of the USA government in an attempt to have the restrictions lifted; they also have the World Trade Organisation (WTO) on their side. The WTO says that the EU restrictions are unlawful. CBI spent millions of dollars building its brand within the EU. The company invested heavily in the 1980s to dominate the EU market, where margins were almost twice those achievable in the USA. The company invested in a new refrigerated transport fleet for the European trade, and purchased extensive South American banana plantations. In order to finance its investment, the company went into debt. Since the EU restrictions on imports the firm has had difficulty servicing its debts and, despite the WTO ruling in the company's favour, is finding itself close to bankruptcy.

CBI's main competitors, Dole Foods and Fresh Del Monte, chose a different long-term strategic route. They realised that the EU restrictions would curb their sales of South American bananas into the EU, and started to invest in Caribbean and African plantations – countries that enjoyed preferential treatment from the EU. The companies also purchased European interests in Sweden and Spain. Both of these firms have in fact increased their market share in Europe, largely at CBI's expense.

16.2.2 Monopolies and limitation of consumer choice

The notion that marketing creates monopoly and limits consumer choice is a popular criticism. The idea that some companies will become powerful enough to dictate what, how and where consumers buy is an issue. In reality, it is rare and temporarily the case that consumers have only one source of supply. The existence of anti-trust laws in the USA and the Monopolies and Mergers Commission in the United Kingdom is evidence of official concern over the possibility of monopolies.

For the most part, such laws and commissions have been established to curtail monopoly by acquisition. A state of monopoly that is reached by continued increase in market share is, to a great extent, a reflection of consumer choice. In a capitalist system, marketing allows companies who are successful to tend towards monopoly. Marketing's critics suggest that 'pure competition' affords consumers more varied choice. This argument has a sound theoretical basis, but one of the conditions for a state of pure competition is that all buyers and sellers have perfect knowledge – the buyers being 'economic' and 'rational' consumers. Studies of consumer behaviour show that this is rarely the case. Moreover, companies that tend towards monopoly are subject to competition from firms who attempt to differentiate and improve their products and services so as to gain market share through customer satisfaction. This is a powerful safeguard against the risks of consumer exploitation.

This 'tempering' of power was aptly illustrated during the 1970s and 1980s:

1 At one point it seemed that a few large bakeries (in a powerful oligopoly) had begun to 'restrict' UK consumer choice to processed sliced bread. This product was initially adopted because it reflected consumer preference. The few companies involved in manufacture felt powerful enough to ignore market segments that preferred other varieties of bread, and made their manufacturing task easier by limiting consumer choice. After some time, these large bakeries encountered powerful consumer resistance. Today supermarkets have 'in-store' bakeries, and specialist independent bakers have experienced a revival.

2 Major breweries reduced their number of product lines and produced what was convenient and profitable, namely 'keg' beer. Breweries now provide beer whose selling points are traditional recipes and regional specialisation. These examples illustrate the power of consumer choice and sanction against companies who have neglected the marketing concept.

3 In the late 1970s in the UK, major banks dominated the consumer market. They have been obliged to revise their product offerings because of legislation and new initiatives taken by smaller banks, building societies and the Post Office.

In summary, it can be argued that companies will gain power only as long as they fulfil the essential criteria of the marketing concept.

16.2.3 Inefficient utilisation of resources

Another criticism of marketing is that the marketing system is wasteful. Could not the enormous sums spent on advertising be better used in product development or simply reducing costs to the consumer? Is it not wasteful for companies to transport basically similar goods all over the country, when these companies could concentrate on their immediate locality at a reduced cost? In other words, it is proposed that scarce resources should be deployed on producing goods rather than marketing them.

There is certainly a case to answer where advertising is purely competitive. In some countries, advertising that relies solely on direct comparison with competitive products is not permitted.

In the UK, the Advertising Standards Authority (ASA) 'watchdog' body requires advertisements to be 'legal, decent, honest and truthful'. The existence of such a body is evidence that some companies abuse the power that media expenditure allows them.

Key point
Creative and informative advertising plays a valid role in assisting consumer choice.

Ideally, advertising should be an informative form of promotion. Creative and informative advertising plays a valid role in assisting consumer choice. Although it seems wasteful to devote large sums to the promotion of essentially similar products, several products would not exist were it not for the fact that consumers themselves demand product differentiation. Any interference in this process would limit consumer choice rather than promote consumer welfare. Moreover, the situation is self-regulating in that companies cannot devote infinite amounts to advertising. Advertising expenditure is an extra cost that is ultimately governed by the price the consumer is willing to pay.

Distribution costs are also criticised. Goods must be transported from manufacturer to user, but critics believe that marketing extends this transportation needlessly because many goods are generically similar. In fact, these goods are usually highly differentiated with respect to style, price and design.

As discussed in Chapter 9, during the past 30 years the retail structure in the UK has altered significantly, and consumers are now served mainly by national chains. This phenomenon is noticeable in 'do-it-yourself' supplies. Companies set up on the periphery of towns in so-called 'sheds', which are effectively factory-type constructions. The result is that small hardware stores are rare today. Such distribution patterns are certainly efficient, and the success of the 'superstores' would indicate that consumers are being satisfied. In the long term, consumers must decide whether convenience outweighs the potential disadvantage of choice restriction. Whilst a complicated distributive structure may appear wasteful in the 'macro' sense, the right of the consumer to 'vote through the purse' is also an important criterion.

Distributive intermediaries are also criticised, and many retailers boast lower prices because they have 'cut out the middleman'. In many cases such claims are justified, but marketing intermediaries do perform valuable specialist functions that serve both consumers and manufacturers.

Marketing's critics must continually refer their arguments back to the issue of consumer choice. There is no evidence to suggest that, in centrally planned economies, the distributive systems used to supply goods and services bring about greater consumer satisfaction. As has been witnessed through the break-up of the old Soviet Union, the converse might well be the case. The concept of 'marketing' enables consumers themselves to apply sanctions against inefficiency and waste.

Key point
The concept of 'marketing' enables consumers themselves to apply sanctions against inefficiency and waste.

16.2.4 Social effects of marketing on lifestyles and values

The idea that marketing promotes materialism and creates artificial needs and values is perhaps one of the most difficult concepts to debate. Marketing has been accused of creating a 'dependence effect' by creating and satisfying wants that are not 'original' within the consumer. There is no doubt that a great deal of marketing activity caters to materialism. It is considerably less certain, however, that this is wrong in itself and, if so, where blame should lie. A defender of marketing would maintain that the marketing system merely reflects society's values. But who should determine our values and material ambitions? It is true that as consumers we surround ourselves with possessions that we do not 'need' to sustain life. Psychologists argue that many material goods satisfy hidden inner needs, and anthropologists point out that even amongst primitive societies value is placed on many functionally useless possessions.

Another factor in the 'materialism' debate concerns our quality of life or standard of living. Many consumer goods can be deemed materialistic, but most also provide a more comfortable way of life, reduce labour and release time to pursue other interests. At an individual level, many firms market goods and services whose value to society is questionable. At the macro level marketing has done much to improve the quality of life generally, even though the perceived value is likely to differ between different sectors of society.

Vignette 16.3

Save our *Schierlings-wasserfenchel*: European airbus consortium should be more socially and environmentally responsible, say Hamburg's protesters

The European Airbus project, to build the 555-seater A380, the largest civil jet aircraft in the world, is one of the biggest business projects world-wide right now. Many companies are trying to get contracts to supply components. Rolls-Royce, General Electric, and Pratt and Whitney are but three international aerospace companies interested in supplying engines for the new 'superjumbo'.

The commercial activity involved in building the new aeroplane has been spread around Europe. This for mainly for political reasons. In theory most of the final assembly and finishing could be carried out in France, probably at the Toulouse site. However, the European Aeronautic Defence and Space Company (EADS), which is made up of a merger of European aerospace firms, says that work has to be sent out to different countries, roughly according to each country's stake in the new superjumbo aircraft. Hamburg in Germany will be the home of operations involved in painting and furnishing the new aircraft. This is hoped to create over 4000 jobs directly and probably twice this number of jobs indirectly, many in local firms in or around Hamburg. There is unemployment in and around the city, so people are looking forward to this increased inward investment by Airbus and hope that it will improve the general prosperity of the area and also attract other large projects in the future.

However, there is a problem for Airbus. In order for the new aeroplanes to be flown from Toulouse (where the assembly is carried out) to Hamburg for painting and furnishing, Airbus will have to expand its operations and build a new runway. Airbus plans to develop its runway capacity at Hamburg's Muhlenberger Loch site, an area of natural beauty and one of the last examples of freshwater tidal ecosystems in Europe. It is one of the most sensitive environmental sites in Europe, offering summer sanctuary to migrating birds, including a number of rare species. It also happens to be the home of a rare plant, the *Schierlings-Wasserfenchel* or, in English, the hemlock water dropwort. Airbus's plans for the area will mean that about one-fifth of the site will be concreted over to extend the existing runway.

Although the people of Hamburg want the commercial activities and the jobs that the new superjumbo aircraft will bring to the area, the city is up in arms about the choice of the site of the development and is taking Airbus to court. The area is protected by three international environmental protection agreements; The European Union Flora, Fauna and Habitat Directive, the EU Bird Protection Directive, and the Ramsar Convention on Wetlands. Under these agreements, Germany designated the area of Muhlenberger Loch an area of international importance. Many people from Hamburg and the surrounding area enjoy the site, and many others from Germany and overseas visit it as part of their holidays. There are numerous bird-watching clubs, botany clubs and other organisations that regularly make use of the site.

However, for Airbus these agreements are worth sacrificing, even in the face of public protest. The company sees no alternative to Hamburg, and no alternative to the development of the Muhlenberger Loch site. The protesters say that the company should be more socially and environmentally sensitive to the needs of the people living in the area and beyond. Many environmentalists cannot see how firmly agreed environmental protection regulations can be rescinded because of the political needs to generate jobs for the area and for the Airbus consortium to be seen to be 'spreading' the commercial activity involved with the project around the EU. Protesters are hoping the courts will make Airbus reconsider, but the firm is in a dilemma, as it sees the use of this site as paramount to the success of the Airbus operation.

16.3 Consumerism

Arguments have been outlined for and against the marketing system in a socio-economic context and at a 'macro' level. The modern-day consumer movement, which had its roots in the 1970s, is mainly involved in specific issues. However, consumerism has macro dimensions, and is responsible for much of the social awareness displayed by many business organisations today. Such companies do not view consumerism as a threat, but as a movement that can be responded to positively, so as to serve their customers and society more effectively. There are, however, companies who have neglected the marketing concept and their social responsibilities, and their customers have a right to consumer protection and advice.

The organised 'consumer movement' had its origins in the USA. At first, its actions were sporadic in response to specific events in the early part of this century. The consumerist phenomenon really began to be noticed in the late 1950s. Social commentators such as Vance Packard and Rachael Carson began to alert the American public to the idea that the business community was more concerned with its own welfare than that of its customers. Vance Packard's book *The Hidden Persuaders* challenged the advertising industry, and Rachael Carson's *Silent Spring* attacked the business community for its neglect of, and disregard for, the environment. The idea that individuals could combat the power of huge corporations had been unimaginable until Ralph Nader published his indictment of the automobile industry, *Unsafe at any Speed*, which was particularly aimed at General Motors. This, and other campaigns, signified the foundation of organised consumerism.

In the United Kingdom the movement gained momentum more slowly, and its roots can be traced back to the magazine *Which*, published by the Consumers' Association and established in the 1960s. The magazine selects, tests and classifies products and services according to their relative performance. Such information was initially received with great interest, as the idea was totally new to British consumers. Perhaps more important than the specific information that *Which* provided was the conceptual breakthrough of the idea that consumers need not accept the offerings of manufacturers without question, and had a right to express their opinions about what was offered for sale. It was no coincidence that companies began to adopt the marketing concept as a business-orientated philosophy at the same time as consumers began to realise the potential of their influence.

Consumerism can be defined as 'a social movement seeking to augment the rights and power of buyers in relation to sellers'. Consumerism, therefore, accepts that both parties have rights.

Definition
Consumerism can be defined as 'a social movement seeking to augment the rights and power of buyers in relation to sellers'.

Buyers have the right:

1 Not to buy products offered to them

2 To expect the product to be safe

3 To expect that the product is essentially the same as the seller has stated.

Sellers have the right:

1 To introduce any product in any style or size, provided it is not injurious to health and safety, and provided potentially hazardous products are supplied together with appropriate warnings

2 To price products at any level, provided that there is no discrimination amongst similar classes of buyers

3 To say what they like in the promotion of their products, provided that any message is not dishonest or misleading in content or execution

4 To spend any amount of money they wish in order to promote their products, and to introduce any buying incentive schemes, providing that are not deemed to be unfair competition.

The idea of 'consumer sovereignty' or 'consumer veto' is central to arguments used to defend marketing. This power should never be underestimated, and is the consumer's chief weapon against business malpractice. A serious problem is the fact that if companies deliberately set out to deceive customers, the consumer is distinctly disadvantaged. Consumerists, therefore, rightly emphasise that the obligation is on business organisations to provide satisfactory goods in the first place. Why should customers only be able to veto goods and services after having been initially disappointed? The consumer movement augments the basic 'buyers' rights' just described by specifically stating what should be expected of the seller.

In 1962, President John F. Kennedy, in keeping with the mood of that era in the USA, made a classic declaration on consumer rights that still forms the basis of modern day consumerism. He proposed:

1 *The right to safety.* The consumer should be able to expect that there are no 'hidden dangers' incorporated into the product. Companies must seek safe alternatives to additives and components that are known to be harmful. In particular, the pharmaceutical industry can make consumers vulnerable if adequate testing is not carried out. The drugs Thalidomide and Opren have provided test cases in this respect. The suitability of polyurethane foam in upholstery, which can be a fire hazard, was a poignant *cause cél'ebre* of consumerism. Unfortunately it is true that, in many cases, legislation is necessary before positive steps are taken to reduce risks. Some manufacturers argue that consumers are unwilling to pay the higher prices that product improvements would require. Consumerists can at least alert buyers to potential risks before they make a choice between economy and safety.

2 *The right to be informed.* Whilst consumerists can increase consumer knowledge for many product categories, they might argue that the 'typical' consumer does not have the time, skills or specialist knowledge with which to make choices or understand product information if it is couched in technical jargon. Consumers have the right to expect sellers to provide the maximum relevant information about their products in an understandable manner. Consumers can only make reasoned purchase decisions after having received comprehensible information. Misleading product information can be conveyed in guarantees, product labelling, advertising and 'small print'. The travel industry is often criticised in this respect.

3 *The right to choose.* Closely linked with the need for protection of the customer against misleading information is the right of protection against confusing information. In order to make a reasoned objective choice, consumers should be able to distinguish 'real' competition in manufacturers' promotions. Products should be presented in such a way that is relatively simple for consumers to relate quality and quantity to cost before making purchases.

4 *The right to be heard.* Consumers have the right to express dissatisfaction not only to suppliers but also to other parties, so attention can be focused on poor service and product performance. This right implies the existence of a

Key point
Consumers have the right to expect sellers to provide the maximum relevant information about their products in an understandable manner.

mechanism for redress should a product prove unsatisfactory. The need for a mechanism that is organised and watched over by an external body is important, as manufacturers and consumers have become more distanced from each other. In the case of faulty goods, consumers sometimes find it confusing and difficult to discover to whom a complaint should be addressed. In the UK, the Consumers' Association and 'watchdog' TV programmes fulfil this role. However, for the vast majority of goods and services on sale today, there is never any need for recourse to such measures.

In addition to Kennedy's rights, two more rights can be added that reflect modern day circumstances:

1 *The right to privacy.* With the information revolution has come an increase in direct marketing through database management. Much of the promotional material that is distributed in this way is beneficial to consumers, and it is possible to make more directly targeted approaches to potential customers that are more likely to fit recipients' social class and consumption profiles. However, some people take the view that use of their details in databases is an invasion of privacy, and view such approaches as invasive 'junk mail'. They now have the right to be able to remove their details from such mailing lists through the Data Protection Act.

2 *The right to a clean and healthy environment.* Ecological awareness is a significant issue nowadays. Organisations like Greenpeace and Friends of the Earth have shed their 'cranky' image and achieved 'respectability' that they did not possess 20 years ago. Indeed, it is through many of the issues with which they have been associated that environmental legislation has followed and environmental polluters have been prosecuted. Recently, the government has introduced a voluntary 'Environmental Initiative' in which companies are subject to inspection and 'certification' that their manufacturing processes do not pollute the environment.

The consumerist movement has come a long way in obtaining a 'fair deal' for consumers. Companies are now more consumer aware. In the early 1960s, many companies actually believed that customers' needs and wants were being adequately satisfied. Consumerism has been an educational process, as well as a policing mechanism. Whether consumers are better served today because companies have made voluntary changes or because they have been coerced is not important; the fact is that individual consumers do receive a far better treatment from manufacturers and service providers.

Key point
Consumerism has been an educational process, as well as a policing mechanism.

Companies should develop their own customer orientation and concern for consumer welfare. Unfortunately, in order to protect consumers from companies who have not accepted this challenge, it has been necessary for governments to take action. Whilst UK governments and the legal system have always taken an interest in fair trading, the 1970s in particular witnessed the government's increasing concern for consumer affairs – spurred on by the consumer movement. Table 16.1 provides a list of statutes, allowing some insight into the nature of this development.

In the UK, there is no single 'consumer law' or specific code for consumer protection. In broad terms, the two most pertinent statutes relating to the

Table 16.1 Some examples of statutory instruments for consumer protection

Aerosol Dispensers (EEC Requirements) Regulations (1977)
Babies Dummies (Safety) Regulations (1978)
Business Advertisements (Disclosure) Order (1977)
Consumer Credit (Credit Reference Agency) Regulations (1977)
Consumer Credit Act (1974)
Consumer Protection Act (1987)
Consumer Safety Act (1978)
Cooking Utensils (Safety) Regulations (1972)
Cosmetic Products Regulations (1978)
Electric Blankets (Safety) Regulations (1971)
Fair Trading Act (1973)
Hire Purchase Act (1973)
Mail Order Transactions (Information) Order (1976)
Nightdresses (Safety) Regulations (1967)
Price Marking (Bargain Offers) Order (1979)
Pyramid Selling Schemes Regulations (1973)
Resale Prices Acts (1964 and 1976)
Supply of Goods (Implied Terms) Acts (1973, 1982)
Toys (Safety) Regulations (1974)
Unsolicited Goods and Services Acts (1971 and 1975)

consumer are the Sale of Goods Act (1979), one in a series of Sale of Goods Acts since 1893, and the Trade Descriptions Act (1972). In addition to these and other legal measures, the government established the Office of Fair Trading and appointed a Minister for Consumer Affairs. The Office of Fair Trading was established in 1973 and, together with the Consumer Protection Advisory Committee, was designed to monitor the activities of the business world, and investigate and publish information in consumers' interests. In liaison with industry, the Office encouraged self-regulatory activities and helped to establish Trade Associations.

All local authorities have Trading Standards Departments that oversee the proper execution of the Weights and Measures and Food and Drugs Acts as well as acting in an advisory capacity to consumers in cases of dispute, a task that was supported and developed by Consumer Advice Centres from 1972 until 1980, when these were abolished on the premise that consumerism was beginning to protect consumers too much, to the commercial detriment of manufacturers.

Key point
In truth, consumerism helped business to identify its own shortcomings as well as the real needs of its customers.

When the impact of the consumer movement was first felt, many companies felt threatened by the apparent restrictions that the movement sought to impose. In truth, consumerism helped business to identify its own shortcomings as well as the real needs of its customers. Many companies benefited by adopting a positive stance and, instead of attempting to hide product defects, made safety, honesty and service product 'features', including initiatives in areas of labelling, pricing and credit agreements. Such features enabled companies to appeal to the psychological as well as physical needs of buyers.

Consumerism is now a permanent feature of society, as there is always a need for vigilance against opportunist sellers. Consumerism is now involved with broader socio-economic issues as well as the basic aspects of consumer protection. Many of today's consumers feel positive about environmentalism. They are also concerned with pricing issues at a macro, in addition to micro, level. Consumer bodies now discuss these issues with governments. To this extent, consumerism has graduated from involvement in specific issues that affect small sections of the population to an interest and involvement in those issues that affect society as a whole.

Marketing has undergone a similar evolution. A new slant on the marketing concept must be adopted if firms are to prosper in a way that is acceptable to society. The essence of the marketing concept is still customer satisfaction; this must be achieved through a social as well as a customer orientation.

Definition
The essence of the marketing concept is still customer satisfaction; this must be achieved through a social as well as a customer orientation.

16.4 Social marketing

Marketing, as defined by the marketing concept, is a management system with customer satisfaction as the object of all marketing effort. Any extension to this definition simply adds to marketing's remit, but the basic tenet of customer orientation remains unchanged. The concept of social marketing holds that business activity should satisfy and be acceptable to society as well as to targeted customer groups; it refers to the study of markets and marketing activity within a total social system.

Definition
Marketing, as defined by the marketing concept, is a management system with customer satisfaction as the object of all marketing effort.

The requirement that marketing be socially acceptable is not new; it has existed as long as organised trading has been practised. The recognition of the role of social marketing has, however, gained momentum and crystallised in the past 25 years. Two factors have accelerated this development:

1 Sociologists' and economists' identification of the phenomenon of the post-industrial society. During the twentieth century, the major thrust of business activity centred on the provision of basic commodities. Compared to the nineteenth century, disposable income was severely limited. Even during the 1950s and 1960s, the aftermath of the Second World War restricted the availability and the means to obtain goods and services that could be described as luxury items. Although poverty has not been eliminated in developed nations, during the past two decades living standards have improved to such an extent that the basic needs and wants of a large proportion of their populations have been fulfilled. This has led to more people being able to choose how to spend an augmented disposable income, and increased leisure time in what has been described as the 'affluent society'. Marketing management has been efficient in catering for the affluent society, and in fulfilling society's so called 'meta-needs'. The affluence of the post-industrial society has brought with it social costs that are linked to profound changes in society's value systems. Perhaps it is not the task of marketing to dictate what is good or otherwise for society, but it is certainly the remit of 'social marketing' to question whether products and

services on offer have a detrimental effect on society. This social awareness should also be used in an attempt to ascertain whether consumers are really receiving satisfaction, and whether the products on offer provide long-term benefits to the quality of life, or whether they are merely for short-term gratification. Critics of marketing hold marketing partially responsible for 'cultural pollution'. Social marketing does not imply acceptance of 'guilt', but its existence implies that such views should be respected and considered seriously.

2 The second spur to the development of social marketing concerns scarcity of the earth's basic resources relative to the abundance of manufactured goods, as well as the way in these goods are produced. Marketing's success in providing for our material needs and wants has also contributed to their existence. The environmentalist is concerned with issues like pollution, waste, congestion and ecological imbalance. Social marketing recognises that it is not enough to provide customer satisfaction if, in doing so, society as a whole is adversely affected. The social marketer's task is to find new products or new production methods that do not pollute, damage or deplete scarce resources.

Definition
The environmentalist is concerned with issues like pollution, waste, congestion and ecological imbalance.

Two important and complex questions face today's marketing practitioners:

1 The debate can be simplified by considering the obviously harmful results that can be directly attributed to marketing action. The causes of industrial pollution are usually easy to identify, and quite often an alternative process can be devised which reduces or eliminates the problem. Such remedies can, however, be costly, and the question that is posed is, are consumers prepared to pay for a safer environment or should this cost be borne by the producer? The issue of lead in petrol provides an example of social marketing in action. The help of the government (which has kept the price of unleaded petrol lower than that of leaded petrol), combined with an open-minded attitude by consumers, has enabled a compromise to be reached that provides a needed product at a reduced social cost. Oil companies have been prepared to invest in research into unleaded petrol, in return for which consumers have been asked to accept modifications in their product usage.

2 The second question deals with a philosophical issue that cannot be easily answered. How much, for example, should governments or religious bodies influence our lives? Certainly consumers (in the form of society as a whole) are largely responsible for their own social and moral welfare. What steps do individual consumers take in order to minimise pollution or reduce wasteful consumption of energy? Usually some external organised body co-ordinates such actions. Consumerists call for social responsibility in business, but say little about the need for consumers also to accept a share of the responsibility.

Marketing is a social force that not only transmits a standard of living, but also reflects and influences cultural values and norms. Marketing can use its influence and expertise to work for the 'social good' in areas where it is popularly accepted that there is scope for improvement – for example:

- automobiles (pollution, congestion and safety)

- foodstuffs (additives, preservatives and pesticides)

- packaging (non-biodegradable materials)

- manufacturing (pollution, noise and safety).

Social marketing addresses these problems by seeking ways to provide customer satisfaction at a reduced 'social cost'. Consumerism and government legislation have to some extent coerced companies into a more socially responsible approach to their activities. Many companies have made voluntary moves towards social orientation. Manufacturers are putting more thought into packaging design by providing their goods in less wasteful packages that can be disposed of more easily. Aerosol manufacturers have discontinued use of a propellant that damaged the earth's ozone layer. While acknowledging that product costs and performance will always be key to success, producers have been urged to take on responsibility and liability for the products they sell.

Marketing's critics argue that such examples of a social orientation are attempts to gain popular appeal. We cannot always be sure of the motivation behind moves towards social marketing, but this is not really the issue. Whatever the motives behind such a shift in a company's business orientation, it is good that such movements are occurring. Whether these initiatives originate from within the company or are prompted by external pressure is irrelevant to consumer satisfaction. In the long term, however, it is preferable that social initiatives in marketing are made by the companies involved. Progress in social orientation is likely to be more beneficial and enduring if business is the voluntary initiator of social change, rather than change being imposed by external agents like government legislation.

Although social orientation benefits the consumer, marketing practitioners face considerable problems in implementing socially orientated strategies. In particular, many socially desirable modifications to products and marketing strategy involve extra costs for which the consumer is not prepared to pay. Automobile production is an example of an industry that is able to provide added safety features (such as anti-lock braking systems) where price is less sensitive, but they cannot easily incorporate such modifications into the sensitive lower price ranges.

The onus is on marketing to find ways of improving products at minimum extra cost, but consumers should be prepared to make some financial contribution towards their own welfare.

Our concern is not with matters that are 'functional' in the marketing sense. Marketing's social responsibilities imply a transition from a pure 'management' orientation. However, this added dimension does not suggest that profit is unimportant. Profit is the essential element of a company's survival, and companies cannot implement social programmes without financial security.

Key point
While acknowledging that product costs and performance will always be key to success, producers have been urged to take on responsibility and liability for the products they sell.

Vignette 16.4

Listening to your customers: the Co-operative Bank plc differentiates itself from other UK banks by using a strong ethical marketing policy

The Co-operative Bank plc is a UK bank, and its products are only available in the UK (including the Channel Islands and the Isle of Man) to residents of the UK. The bank operates one of the strongest ethical marketing polices in the world. The Co-operative Bank plc is a relatively small bank, with two million customers and a 5 per cent UK market share. It does not try to take the larger UK banks on 'head on', but rather operates a niche strategy. No other bank has as strong an ethical marketing policy as the 'Co-op'. The bank recognises that there is a relatively large niche segment of people who have sympathy with what the bank is trying to achieve. Even the bank's Visa cards are completely biodegradable.

The bank believes very strongly in listening to what its customers are saying and implementing what they want. Their philosophy is that it is the customers' money, so why not ask the customers how they think the money should be used and invested? The bank regularly appraises and reappraises customers' views, and develops their ethical stance accordingly. By using customer surveys, the bank has implemented the following ethical marketing strategies:

- *Human rights* – the bank will not invest or provide financial services for any regime or organisation that oppresses the human spirit or takes away the rights of the individual. It will have no dealing with the manufacturers of equipment that could be used in the violation of human rights.

- *Armaments* – the bank will not invest or provide any financial services for any business involved in the manufacture or sale of armaments to any country that has an oppressive regime.

- *Trade and social involvement* – the bank seeks to support and encourage the activities of organisations engaged in free trade. It takes a pro-active stance in ethical sourcing from developing countries. The bank ensures that its financial services are not exploited for the purposes of money laundering related to the trafficking of drugs. The bank will not get involved in currency speculation, which may damage the economies of sovereign states. It will not be involved in providing financial services to any company involved in tobacco products.

- *Environmental impact* – the bank seeks to encourage its customers to take a positive position on the environmental impact of their business activities, and will invest in those companies that show they avoid damage to the environment. The bank will not support organisations that contribute to problems such as climate change or acid rain, or the unsustainable harvest of natural resources such as timber.

- *Animal welfare* – the bank will not support organisations involved in animal testing, or engaged in exploitative factory farming methods, blood sports or fur farming.

The above list of examples is not exhaustive, but merely indicative of the bank's ethical stance on marketing and related issues.

16.5 Marketing in not-for-profit organisations

There has been a focus on the distinction between 'managerial' or 'systems' marketing and the wider remit of a 'societal' or a socially-orientated approach to marketing. Non-profit-making organisations provide an example of a reverse of the marketing transition that should be made by progressive companies. For the most part, non-profit organisations already perform roles designed to cater for social, rather than commercial, needs. To this extent their social orientation is already established, and what is required is the adoption of managerial marketing techniques to accomplish their tasks.

It may seem strange that services like the Health Service, public libraries or the police force should consider that marketing has anything to offer them. On further investigation, many parallels can be drawn between the functions of the profit and non-profit sectors.

Non-profit organisations have 'products' (usually services) and 'consumers' (users), and they function through organisational structures of purchasing, production and personnel. A parallel for 'selling' is not so readily apparent. For example, in a public hospital the 'customers' have little opportunity to exercise choice and, because of scarce resources, one hospital is not really acting in competition with another. Marketing implies customer satisfaction, and in this respect those who are directly involved with consumers in non-profit organisations have roles similar to those of sales personnel. This is not to suggest that doctors or nurses perform a 'sales function' in the accepted sense. They are, however, the last link between the organisation and the user, and in this sense represent the organisation and influence consumer attitudes towards its service/product. In addition to the physical similarities of profit and non-profit organisations they both have marketing problems, although this fact is not generally avowed. To a certain extent the government has attempted to address this in respect of health care with the introduction of general practitioner fundholder status and hospital trusts, with the object of making them more accountable in financial and marketing terms.

Key point
Marketing implies customer satisfaction, and in this respect those who are directly involved with consumers in non-profit organisations have roles similar to those of sales personnel.

The business sector is often criticised for poor marketing. Ultimately, unless companies resolve their marketing problems, consumers have the sanction of placing their custom elsewhere. The public sector receives criticism that is often frustrated and aggravated by the fact that in most cases the sanction of choice does not exist. Non-profit organisations, whose customer-orientation is poor, are still able to function, but when criticism develops into resentment the task is increasingly difficult.

If we recognise that not-for-profit organisations have marketing structures and marketing problems, we can then use marketing functions as tools for more effective action. The most important element of marketing for non-profit organisations is communication. Commercial enterprises find customers and communicate with them in order to make sales. In the non-commercial sector, it is easy to lose touch with customers. The idea that non-profit organisations can take their users for granted can be likened to sales orientation.

In non-profit situations, marketing orientation involves defining what the organisation is attempting to supply or achieve – which is similar to defining the market in the commercial sector. A public library does more than provide

Key point
In non-profit situations, marketing orientation involves defining what the organisation is attempting to supply or achieve – which is similar to defining the market in the commercial sector.

books; it also serves as a meeting place, a support to local schools and a source of information for a wide range of commercial activities. When seen through a marketing orientation, libraries are involved in providing leisure and information.

Non-profit organisations should fulfil their functions through the marketing mix. Apart from price, the mix elements are no different to those for commercial product or service marketing. The emphasis in the marketing mix varies according to the task. A local police force may place emphasis on public relations in order to foster a favourable image of the police within their community to facilitate the functional tasks of policing. The police visit schools so children can get to know them better and understand their place in the community. Police forces hold open days and run public relations campaigns, and view their task as a far wider one than catching criminals.

16.6 Quality and marketing

Quality should be integrated at all levels in a company, and for this to have meaning, marketing must be integrated throughout the company. This means that designers must fully understand customer requirements, which must be translated to the production process, with the final link being to produce the product when the customer wants it and at the right price. Engineering, without a true understanding of customer needs, can result in customer dissatisfaction. Equally, a marketing team, cut off from its technological base, is impotent and cannot hope accurately to interpret the capabilities of the company in relation to customer requirements. There must be a balance between these disparate functions, and removal of the exclusivity of the 'marketing' label, because marketing is what everybody does. This gives rise to the notion of the 'part-time marketer' (PTM), where everybody in the organisation is responsible for satisfying customer needs. Similarly, the concept of total quality management (TQM) holds that every member of the organisation is responsible for the image and service that the company puts forward. These two aspects are inseparable in helping to provide customer satisfaction.

Key point
There must be a balance between these disparate functions, and removal of the exclusivity of the 'marketing' label, because marketing is what everybody does.

Total quality management is a powerful tool if it is introduced to each audience in the right way. This is due to the differences in 'mind set' between marketing and manufacturing. By careful selection of methods of introduction it is possible for all to embrace the process, so that it can interface between marketing and manufacturing and between other functions effectively. In order to break down departmental barriers so that staff from different departments can work together to tackle problem solving (known as 'continuous improvement processes'), many companies have set up quality improvement teams so that synergy exists and interfaces between marketing, production, quality, purchasing and human resource management. The role of marketing in quality improvement teams is to be assured that the organisation is doing the right things in terms of building customer-valued quality products.

Taeger (1992) reported that the 3M Document Systems Group has formed a corrective action team to introduce improvements involving members of sales, marketing and other departments to look at the distribution of camera cards. By a process of communicating with each other, and reaching a consensus opinion about the important areas of business and how well the group was performing in these areas, the team has substantially improved the operation of the business.

Best practice benchmarking (BPB) as defined by the DTI (1993) involves the formation of a project team comprising people from multifunctional areas such as marketing production, quality and purchasing. The team's task is to obtain information on products or companies that have a higher level of performance or activity, and to identify areas in their own organisation that need improving. The team needs to be given the facility for research on product development and quality. Because of the benefits of shared knowledge in this multifunctional team, companies that implement BPB should find that this drives members of the team to meet new standards or even exceed them.

16.7 Summary

16.7.1 The macro dimension

✓ Research by Sheth (1992) has shown that four macro-economic forces are shaping global marketing strategies:

1 Regional integration

2 Technology advances, e.g. the adoption of information technology in business (Stalk *et al.*, 1992)

3 Emergence of an ideology-free world and the role of the market economy policy

4 Borderless economies due to global sourcing and competition (Schill and McArthur, 1992).

✓ To seek dominant market share, organisations may want to expand their marketing and manufacturing efforts to other geographical areas, and attain economies of scale through increased systemisation and interconnection between the process operations. Flexibility becomes a greater component of manufacturing systems, allowing relatively small batches to be produced on a mass production bases.

✓ Unisys Corporation's flexible manufacturing system enables it to assemble up to 2500 printed circuit boards per week in 64 different configurations, having 1327 components. The system enables time to market to be reduced significantly, because the components can be assembled in any sequence and even in lot sizes of one. Market segmentation is, of course, an important issue here. Willigan (1992) has reported that even high-powered marketing companies such as Nike have continued 'slicing up' their product ranges to add diversity. Kasturirangan *et al.* (1993) state that mature industrial markets have resorted to trade-offs, tailoring the mix for particular homogeneous needs and so leading to better use of resources.

✓ There is recognition that there must be a change from a production/cost-dominated strategy towards one of servicing the diverse needs of global customers through marketing. This process of interdependence formation has led to the development of relationship marketing, which involves building long-term relationships with customers through the practice of 'retention economics'. As the strategic geographical perspective of companies has changed from domestic to international marketing, the marketing paradigm has transformed from a transactional focus to a relationship focus. Customer-focused quality is also important because it involves a move towards customer-targeted activity. As we move towards a global economy, customers demand even better quality and place increasing importance on reliability, durability, ease of use and service.

16.7.2 From competitive strategy to strategic marketing

✓ Schill and McArthur (1992) contend that a new thinking emanated in the 1980s, known as the 'competitive strategy' era. An integrated/functional role within the overall task of formulating and implementing corporate competitive strategy led marketing theorists to take on a new dimension known as 'strategic marketing'. This attempted to integrate manufacturing, finance, human resources and other functions with marketing to support a cohesive competitive strategy focusing on such matters as cost leadership and product differentiation. The notion was established that company-wide solutions were necessary in providing solutions to customers' problems.

✓ Manufacturing supports overall business objectives through the design and utilisation of suitable manufacturing resources and capabilities. Alignment of manufacturing and marketing strategies will contribute significantly to the overall success of the organisation. Marketing-led strategies are usually based on the principles of growth throughout the product range. The relationship between marketing objectives and manufacturing strategies appears to be a critical factor affecting the success of the organisation, but the nature of this relationship is not well defined. Piercy (1991) refers to the 'strategic internal market' that should have the goal of developing a marketing programme aimed at the internal marketplace within a company that parallels and matches the marketing programme aimed at the external marketplace of customers and competitors. This model comes from a simple observation that the implementation of external marketing strategies implies changes of various kinds within organisations – in the allocation of resources, in the culture of 'how we do things here', and even in the organisational structures needed to deliver marketing strategies effectively in customer segments.

Key point
The role of marketing should be seen as one of co-ordination across the company's functional units.

✓ The role of marketing should be seen as one of co-ordination across the company's functional units. This is critical, because each department is likely to have different views of customers. Sheth (1992) summarises it when he says:

'It will become increasingly important for the left hand to know what the right hand is doing, especially in the market boundary of front line personnel in procurement, manufacturing, selling and service market offerings.'

The social, ethical and economic issues of marketing look at managerial systems from a 'bird's-eye' viewpoint. If we are to broaden our marketing scope further we must turn to other disciplines to gain an objective view of marketing's place in society. The role of profit in marketing assumes a capitalist economic system. A study of politics and economics allows the student to consider other systems. The ethical and moral questions raised by marketing can also be considered with reference to sociology, which helps us to understand how and why the population reacts to marketing activity.

✓ It is contended that quality as well as marketing must permeate the entire manufacturing operation, and this has given rise to the notion of TQM and the PTM. As marketing becomes central to all business activity, so its role changes from being a function of management to that of a company-wide philosophy with total quality as its driving force.

Questions

1 *Use of marketing by non-profit organisations*
Marketing is increasingly being used by non-profit organisations such as colleges, libraries and political parties. What is the relevance of the marketing concept to the non-profit organisation, and why are such organisations making more use of the techniques of marketing?

2 *Consumerism*
Discuss the notion that, in a society that has embraced the concept of free enterprise, business should be allowed to get on with its wealth-creating activities without interference from consumerists.

3 *Ethics*
Marketing has been criticised on both economic and ethical grounds. Discuss these criticisms, indicating how far you think they are justified.

4 *Quality*
How is marketing involved in the company-wide process of total quality management?

5 *Strategic marketing*
How do you view the scenario, as put forward by Sheth, that marketing should be viewed as a process of co-ordination across an organisation's functional units? How can it be implemented?

References

Brownlie, D. and Saren, M. (1992). The four Ps of the marketing concept: prescription, polemic, permanent and problematical. *European Journal of Marketing*, **26(4)**, 34–47.

Carson, R. (1962). *Silent Spring*. Houghton Mifflin Co.

DTI (1993). *Best Practice Benchmarking*. Department of Trade and Industry.

Kasturirangan, V., Moriaty, R. T. and Swartz, G. S. (1992). Segmenting customers in mature industrial markets. *Journal of Marketing*, **56(2)**, 89.

Nader, R. (1965). *Unsafe at Any Speed*. Grossman.

Packard, V. (1957). *The Hidden Persuaders*. David McKay.

Piercy, N. (1991). *Market-led Strategic Change*, p. 367. Harper Collins Publishers Ltd.

Schill, R. L. and McArthur, D. N. (1992). Redefining the strategic competitive unit: towards a new global marketing paradigm. *International Marketing Review*, **9(3)**, 5–23.

Sheth, J. N. (1992). Emerging marketing strategies in a changing macroeconomic environment: a commentary. *International Marketing Review*, **9(1)**, 57–63.

Stalk, G., Evans, P. and Schulman, L. E. (1992). Competing of capabilities: the new rules of corporate strategy. *Harvard Business Review*, **Apr**, 57–69.

Taeger, D. (1992). 3M's got it taped. *Total Quality Management*, **Dec**, 1–5.

Willigan, G. E. (1992). High performance marketing. *Harvard Business Review*, **Jul**, 104.

Further reading

Armstrong, G. and Kotler, P. (2000). Marketing and society: social responsibility and marketing ethics. *Marketing: An Introduction*, 5th edn, Chapter 16. Prentice Hall.

Blythe, J. (2001). Sustainable marketing. *Essentials of Marketing*, Chapter 12. Person Educational Ltd.

Kotler, P. and Andreasen, A. R. (1991). *Strategic Marketing for Non-Profit Organisations*. Prentice Hall.

Packard, V. (1960). *The Waste Makers*. David McKay.

Packard, V. (1964). *The Naked Society*. Longman Press.

Marketing strategy, planning and control 17

17.1 Introduction

Most companies have adopted the marketing concept over the past 25 years, in particular the notion of customer orientation. Sometimes, in their pursuit of customer satisfaction, companies neglect an aspect of marketing that refers to strategic management – a systematic approach to planning, analysis and control. Not only does such an approach facilitate customer satisfaction; it also helps to ensure the firm's survival by ensuring profitability.

Businesses that are less than totally committed to marketing can be grouped into three categories:

1 Those that make no real plans at all

2 Those that make plans based on partial, poorly collected or poorly interpreted marketing information

3 Those that make plans but do not adhere to them.

Some businesses are directed by talented leaders who have a 'feel' for the market and whose intuitive decisions lead to success. Intuition is an important ingredient of successful management, but few of us could say that our intuition is so frequently correct that we could use it as the basis for the management of a company. Markets change rapidly, and the intuitive leader constantly runs risks that are unacceptable to shareholders as well as to company employees. Moreover, if the intuitive leader is suddenly indisposed, what is to happen?

Some companies merely respond to current demand. Providing that the order book is full, they see no need for planning. When sales slow down, the policy is to put pressure on the sales force to sell more.

Planning systems that have not evolved from the origins of marketing planning are often based on the company's financial budgeting process. Available resources are allocated to functional managers on a haphazard basis. Why, for instance, the advertising manager has received too much or too little money during a given period is never queried. Still worse, there is no facility available to evaluate expenditure in terms of what it has achieved. So long as the department has not overrun its budget allocation, everybody is satisfied. Sometimes plans are made but then changed when somebody has what appears to be a better idea, and so the process continues. The net result is that none of the plans are fully developed and evaluated, and true planning is not taking place at all.

17.2 Formalised planning procedures

17.2.1 Planning is central to marketing

Many managers maintain they have a marketing orientation, but overlook one fundamental aspect – a formalised planning procedure that takes into account the firm's environment, its internal resources and its longer-term objectives. Planning is difficult in practice, but its concept is quite straightforward (see Figure 17.1).

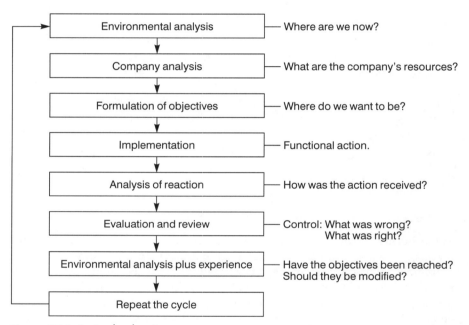

Figure 17.1 A simple planning system.

The company's commitment to planning has been assumed throughout this text, and chapters relating to marketing mix elements, for example, have constantly referred to the design and implementation of strategy. In practice, strategies are the result of careful preparation and a lot of hard work. Contained within Figure 17.1 are the combined efforts, not just of senior management, but also of various functional areas that make up the company. The planning process is continuous. Throughout a given year, information should be constantly collected and analysed, and performance should be under constant review. At given intervals, problems (a fact of business life) are assessed and decisions are made as to the most appropriate course of action.

Key point
The planning process is continuous.

Planning is at the heart of marketing, and is not an abstract or separate function within business. This chapter brings together the elements of marketing to show how they are practised concurrently and in conjunction with each other. Figure 17.1 outlines the contents of planning, strategy formulation and control. Each of these basic themes is equally important to the company. Strategy formulation is probably the most exciting activity for marketing practitioners because of its creative content, but we should not overlook the fact that control provides a means to discover whether or not the strategy has been appropriate and provides the information that allows corrective action to be taken if necessary.

Another simple view of planning can be remembered through the acronym 'MOST', which stands for:

- **M**ission – the business we are in

- **O**bjectives – that we need to accomplish

- **S**trategies – in general terms, how are we going to do it?

- **T**actics – in specific terms, how are we going to do it?

Key point
Planning is at the heart of marketing, and is not an abstract or separate function within business.

17.2.2 Terms in common use

The area of planning can be a source of confusion because of the wide range of words and titles that are used in its description. In particular, confusion arises over the meaning of the word 'strategy' and its use in the terms 'corporate strategy' and 'functional strategy'. It is valuable at this stage to clarify these terms:

- *Planning* is simply the process of decision-making that relates to the future. The term can be used at all levels of company decision-making.

- *Corporate planning* refers specifically to decision-making at the highest levels of management. Decisions made here refer to the future of the total business. Corporate planning is sometimes referred to as *strategic planning*, and some older texts refer to it as *long-range planning*. Corporate or strategic planning is not concerned with forecasting sales, devising marketing mix strategies or organising production and raw material supply to accommodate this forecast. Corporate planning involves asking: What business are we really in? Is this the right business? What are our basic objectives? Are our markets growing or declining? Are new technologies threatening our products? After analysis, strategic plans can be drawn up based on the answers to such questions.

- *Operational or functional planning* is the process that develops the corporate or strategic plan. One strategic corporate objective may be to enter a new market and achieve x per cent market share with y per cent return on investment within two years. Operational planning will indicate how this should be best achieved (for instance, by adopting a particular marketing mix strategy and financial allocation).

- The word *strategy* can be used at an operational level (product, price or advertising strategy) because it describes medium- to long-term actions.

Definition
Corporate planning refers specifically to decision-making at the highest levels of management.

- *Tactics* are actions that bring about temporary modifications to operational plans (e.g. a price change or an increase in advertising intensity necessitated by unexpected competitive action). They are essentially short-term in nature.

- *Objectives* should be 'SMART' (**S**pecific, **M**easurable, **A**chievable, **R**ealistic and **T**ime-related).

There is a hierarchy of planning as follows:

1 Corporate planning

2 Functional (e.g. marketing) planning

3 Sub-functional (e.g. sales) planning.

The above can be expanded as follows:

1 Strategic corporate planning

- Define organisational mission

- Establish strategic business units (SBUs) (see later for definition)

- Anticipate change

2 Marketing planning for SBUs

- Set marketing objectives

- Develop marketing strategy

- Make formal marketing plans

3 Operational marketing plans.

17.3 Strategic planning at the corporate level

The term 'corporate planning' has evolved in line with the increasing size of companies and numbers of multi-product, multi-market companies. Take-overs, mergers and multinational activity have created a complex and wide-ranging business environment, so that larger companies are indirectly responsible for the direction of several firms who are involved in various, often unrelated, markets. The task is to define a 'corporate mission' or 'corporate goal' and develop plans that enable this to be accomplished. The mission should be stated in marketing terms so as to encourage as wide a view of opportunities as is realistic within resource constraints.

Key point
The mission should be stated in marketing terms so as to encourage as wide a view of opportunities as is realistic within resource constraints.

Objectives are defined and communicated to individual parts of the company, whose managers develop their own plans for achieving these objectives. Such a process facilitates a marketing mission rather than a product orientation.

To illustrate marketing evolution, a company whose principal activity is the manufacture of fountain pens, for example, should perhaps consider itself to be in the gift market, or perhaps in the graphics market. In addition to adopting a marketing orientation, businesses can include a social dimension in their corporate mission statement (e.g. the achievement of goals by means of a commitment to reduce pollution). Whatever the mission, it should serve to generate a common theme throughout the company and motivate the workforce towards a common goal.

Vignette 17.1

AT&T Corp., a company with a strategy based on research, welcomes you to 'broadband' as providers of digital television, digital telephone and high-speed cable Internet services

AT&T Corp. is one of the most well-known and successful companies in the world. The organisation is amongst the world's premier voice and data communications companies, serving consumers, businesses and government. The company has annual revenues of more than $462 billion and employs 160000 people. AT&T is a global company, and provides a range of services to customers world-wide. Its success over the years has been firmly based on a strategy of continuous research and product and service innovation.

AT&T is strong on applied research, and is backed by one of the world's most sophisticated research companies, AT&T Labs. This strong research strategy has kept the organisation in the forefront of technological developments and made it a truly world-class firm. The company runs the world's largest and most sophisticated communications network, and has one of the largest digital wireless networks in North America. AT&T is a leading provider of data and Internet services for business, and offers a range of related consultancy services.

The company has recently made a number of cable acquisitions, which will enable the company to bring its broadband video, voice and data services to customers throughout the USA. AT&T Broadband gives the customer incredible entertainment options. It allows customers to watch just the programmes they choose on the channels they want. It also enables customers to get 'hooked up' to the Internet, which they will be able to access at super-fast speeds. The recent cable acquisitions will enable the organisation to bring the fruits of its considerable research and development programmes into the home of every citizen of the United States. AT&T continues to fund research and innovations in order to improve its range of services even more. Internationally, AT&T has teamed up with the British telecommunications giant BT plc. The AT&T/BT Global Venture, which is called 'CONCERT', will enable the group to offer advanced communications services to multinational companies world-wide.

17.4 Strategic business units (SBUs)

In order to realise corporate objectives, management must break down areas of responsibilities into identifiable and manageable units. This facilitates analysis, planning and control. A method of identifying such business areas is to divide the total business into 'strategic business units' (SBUs) or operational entities to which corporate strategy is delegated. A major criterion of SBU management is that SBUs should be easily identifiable. They should represent the key business areas of the company. Although it is not always possible to delineate business areas exactly, ideally SBUs should be single businesses that can be planned independently of the company's other businesses. This suggests that they have an identifiable management with responsibility for managing and controlling resource allocation, and direct competitors can be identified. For multi-market or multi-industry organisations, SBUs may be whole companies in themselves. Single industry or 'product-line dominant' companies may be able to identify SBUs based on specific market areas.

Vignette 17.2

GlaxoSmithKline uses licensing as a strategic tool to fill a gap in its product portfolio

GlaxoSmithKline (GSK) found itself with a gap in its 'late stage' new product development portfolio within the antidepressant segment. Realising it was rather late to start an innovation programme of its own, the firm decided to acquire a 'ready-made' antidepressant product through the use of a licensing agreement. GSK is to license the USA rights to a potentially very effective antidepressant drug that is currently in late stage medical trials with Merck KGaA, the German pharmaceutical and chemicals group.

Merck is perhaps better known in Europe, and does not have such a strong presence within the USA pharmaceutical market. This in fact one of the reasons behind the licensing agreement. Both parties benefit; GSK gets a much needed new product in its portfolio, and Merck gets a deal with a company that has all the right credentials to market its new product successfully in America.

GSK will get the USA marketing rights to the antidepressant drug, known by its working code title of EMD-68843. Merck will retain the rights for Europe and some other countries. The USA is by far the biggest and most important market for such a product, accounting for some 75 per cent of the world antidepressant market. GSK already has a strong presence in the US and indeed the world antidepressant market with its drug 'Paxil/ Serotat', which is protected by patent until 2006 in most countries. However, it thought ahead strategically and realised that a new generation of antidepressant drugs was coming on line in the near future and that it needed a new product to take over from Paxil/Serotat. The deal will come as a great relief to the management of GSK, who were becoming concerned at the lack of new products waiting in the wing for this important market. Both organisations see the agreement as a natural strategic alliance, with each organisation benefiting from the other one's strengths. GSK has been encouraged by its successful agreement with Merck, and is now searching the world for other likely pharmaceutical products with which the firm can get involved using licensing.

17.5 Audit and SWOT

Having defined corporate objectives and identified SBUs, the company proceeds to the stages of planning outlined in Figure 17.1. The first stage is *environmental analysis* (sometimes called the external audit), and it is known through the acronym 'PEST' analysis (**P**olitical, **E**conomic, **S**ocio-cultural and **T**echnological analysis). Some authors cite the acronym as 'STEP', as there is no chronological sequence in the way each factor should be considered. Each of these four categories should be investigated in turn. These separate 'PEST' factors were later broadened to include legal aspects, making the acronym 'SLEPT'. Still later, environmental factors were considered as a separate category; this led to the acronym becoming 'PESTLE'. The latest factor to be included is ecological, and the acronym has now become 'STEEPLE'. However, it is felt that the introduction of so many extra factors unnecessarily complicates what is a sound tool of analysis, and for most situations 'PEST' analysis works well.

As well as this external audit, the company also performs an internal company analysis. In this stage the company analyses its own internal strengths and weaknesses and its external opportunities and threats (called 'SWOT' analysis). **S**trengths and **W**eaknesses are bullet points listed from an internal company perspective, and **O**pportunities and **T**hreats from an external macro-environmental viewpoint. This latter part of the analysis uses information that has already been identified from the 'PEST' analysis. With this information to hand, planners can consider the strengths and opportunities of their SBUs, situate them in their respective environments, and then formulate plans designed to realise corporate objectives.

Key point
Strengths and Weaknesses are bullet points listed from an internal company perspective, and **O**pportunities and Threats from an external macro-environmental viewpoint.

17.6 Portfolio analysis

17.6.1 Boston Consulting Group (BCG) matrix

A popular approach to planning, called *portfolio analysis*, was pioneered in the USA by the Boston Consulting Group, and is sometimes referred to as the *Boston Box*. This method identifies the company's SBUs and places these on a matrix that considers 'market growth' and 'relative market share' (see Figure 17.2).

Four business types can be distinguished:

1 *Stars* are SBUs that have a promising future. Significant investments of cash are necessary to develop their full potential. If managed correctly, they will develop into a valuable source of revenue as the market evolves.

2 *Cash cows* have achieved a high market share in a mature market. They deserve the company's fullest attention, because the cash they generate can be invested in newer market areas with high growth potential.

3 *Question marks* (or *problem children* or *wildcats*, as they are sometimes called) pose a problem for management. Whilst market growth prospects are good, question-mark SBUs have a low relative market share. If they are to be moved to the left (i.e. increase relative market share), substantial investment may be required. Based on available marketing information, management must decide whether such investment could be better employed in supporting other SBUs.

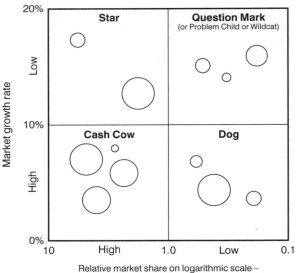

Figure 17.2 The BCG portfolio analysis matrix.

4 *Dogs* show no growth potential, and their relative market share is low. Although they may not necessarily be a drain on the company's resources, they are unable to make a positive contribution to profits.

The BCG model was originally designed for multi-industry companies. Thus, SBUs as depicted in Figure 17.2 were likely to be for competing companies. BCG analysis is now more commonly used by individual companies where SBUs relate to individual product lines. The size of each circle represents the value of sales.

The major object of business is to optimise performance so that corporate objectives or strategy can be realised. Little can be done by a single company to change market growth rate, which is defined by the position on the vertical axis. The options are, therefore, to eliminate SBUs from the 'portfolio', or to move them from the right to the left along the horizontal axis (i.e. increase their market share). Of course increased sales will increase the size of the SBUs themselves.

Let us suppose that the SBUs in Figure 17.2 are the 12 individual companies that make up a large organisation. These are the 'corporate portfolio' (it would be called the 'product portfolio' for a smaller company). The upper left quadrant reveals one small star and one large star, although three large cash cows with a high relative market share are in evidence below this, complemented by a small cash cow. The company should protect its cash cows and attempt to improve the star situation so that a new generation of cash cows can be developed. The company might have problems when attempting to move the most promising question marks from the right-hand to the left-hand quadrant. As far as the dogs are concerned, they should be examined individually to decide whether they should be kept and improved (perhaps in the interests of ensuring a more comprehensive portfolio) or sold off.

The accuracy of any model is only as good as the information on which it is based. A BCG matrix-type model requires a great deal of accurate market and company information before the model can be used as a meaningful management tool. In addition to presenting strategic alternatives, a well-prepared BCG matrix is valuable because it compels objective consideration of the elements of the portfolio in relation to each other. However, its most significant criticism is that it is too simplistic because variables used do not take into account the circumstances of growth or market share. For example, Pringle knitwear only has a small share of the overall knitwear market, but it is a leader in the luxury knitwear market. Similarly, market growth may be high, but such growth may attract competitors who might affect profit margins.

17.6.2 The General Electric (GE) matrix

General Electric of America's matrix overcomes some of the criticisms of the BCG matrix by using industry attractiveness and competitive position as its parameters. It was developed with management consultants McKinsey, and is sometimes referred to as the GE/McKinsey business screen. This matrix contains nine boxes, and offers a wider strategic choice than the BCG matrix by using broader market and company factors. It uses 'business strength' on the horizontal axis and 'industry attractiveness' on the vertical axis. It is graphically represented in Figure 17.3.

Key point
General Electric of America's matrix overcomes some of the criticisms of the BCG matrix by using industry attractiveness and competitive position as its parameters.

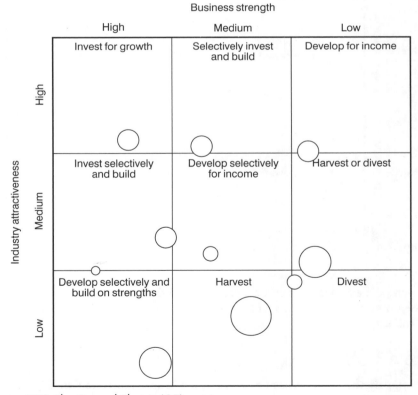

Figure 17.3 The General Electric (GE) matrix.

Each of the boxes suggests a strategy that is appropriate for the SBUs that it contains.

17.6.3 The Shell Directional Policy matrix

This matrix was developed by Shell Chemicals, and was designed to cope with a dynamic market place. The requirement was that each strategy should be evaluated against potential contingencies. Figure 17.4 shows how the vertical axis looks at measures of the company's competitive capability (e.g. market growth, the industry situation and environmental issues), and the horizontal axis examines prospects for sector profitability from an industry point of view.

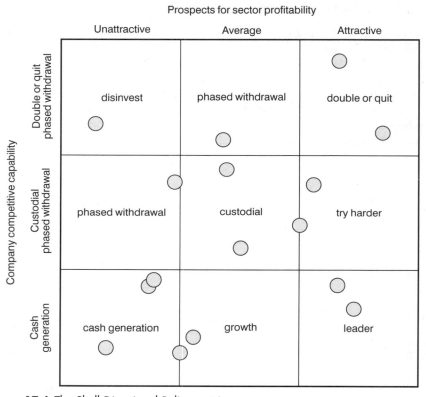

Figure 17.4 The Shell Directional Policy matrix.

Each of the SBUs is given between one and five stars along each axis. This is then quantified, and the result places each SBU at an appropriate point in the matrix.

17.6.4 Ansoff's matrix

Ansoff's matrix was described in Chapter 4 and illustrated in Figure 4.3 (Ansoff, 1957). It is a useful starting point for a strategic review of a

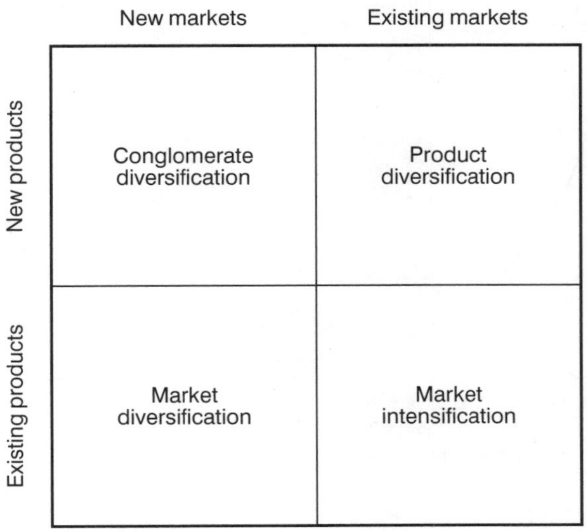

	New markets	Existing markets
New products	Conglomerate diversification	Product diversification
Existing products	Market diversification	Market intensification

Figure 17.5 Strategic alternatives.

company's position and a precursor to marketing action. Whether the matrix is used at a corporate or operational level, the act of examining each of the quadrants shown in Figure 17.5 focuses attention on where the company is and where it could (or should) be.

17.6.5 Hofer's product/market evolution approach

Marketing strategies for each stage of the product life cycle were outlined in Chapter 12. The PLC concept can also be used for corporate planning as shown in Figure 17.6. Products or companies can be arranged in terms of their competitive position in the relevant stage of the product or market life cycle.

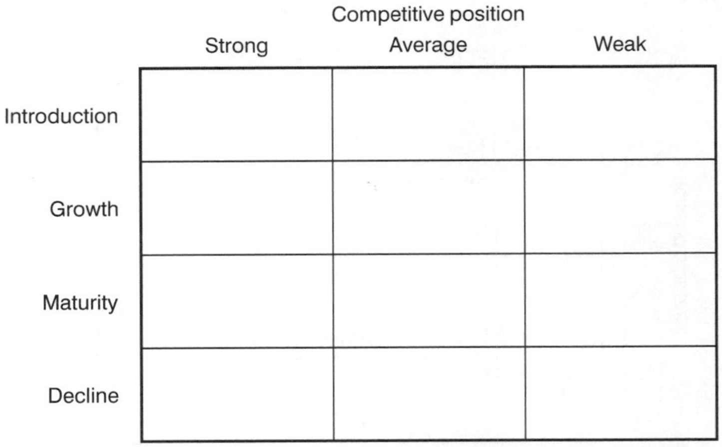

	Competitive position		
	Strong	Average	Weak
Introduction			
Growth			
Maturity			
Decline			

Figure 17.6 An adaptation of C. W. Hofer's product/market evolution portfolio matrix.

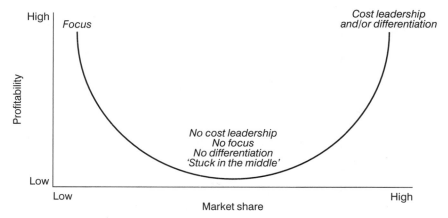

Figure 17.7 Porter's generic strategies.

17.6.6 Industry/market evolution

Porter proposed that the strategies for success are not necessarily financial coupled with high market share, as shown in Figure 17.7:

● *Focus* means the company consolidates its efforts on a small range of products in a market niche

● *Differentiation* means to establish a USP or other feature that the competition cannot match

● *Cost leadership* means the lowest price in the market

● *Stuck in the middle* describes companies at the bottom of the curve.

In 1985 Porter further developed his ideas based on evolutionary stages and whether the company was a leader or follower, as shown in Figure 17.8:

	Growth (emerging industry)	Maturity (and transition to maturity)	Decline
Leader	Keep ahead of the field	Cost leadership; raise barriers to entry; deter competitors	Redefine scope; divest peripheral activities; encourage departures
Follower	Imitation at lower cost; joint ventures	Differentiation; focus	Differentiation; look for new opportunities

(Strategic position)

Figure 17.8 Strategic position in industry life cycle.

The strategy that should be adopted depends upon whether the company is a leader or a follower. The individual evolutionary stages are explained as follows:

- *Growth* or emerging industry is characterised by conservatism amongst buyers over the attributes of new products, and the fact that they might become dated in either function or style.

- *Maturity* and transition to maturity can mean reduced profit margins as competitors come in and sales begin to slow. Buyers are more confident as they are familiar with the product, and manufacturing emphasis is on features and intangible factors like image. Attempts should be made to serve specialist market segments.

- *Decline* indicates that the market has become saturated. Alternative products might appear that supplant traditional products, and this is when companies should look for alternative products.

17.6.7 Industry maturity/competitive position matrix

Management consultants Arthur D. Little developed a matrix that looked at life-cycle stages for the industry under review, and considered where individual companies fitted into each stage under criteria ranging from 'dominant' to 'weak'. This idea is illustrated in Figure 17.9.

	Embryonic	Growth	Maturity	Ageing
Dominant				
Strong				
Favourable				
Tentative				
Weak				

Figure 17.9 Industry maturity/competitive position matrix.

17.6.8 Product (or market) life-cycle matrix

Barksdale and Harris developed a model that combined the BCG matrix with the product life-cycle concept in an attempt to overcome the problem in the BCG matrix that ignores the position of the industry in relation to its stage of development (Barksdale and Harris, 1982). The resultant matrix is described in Figure 17.10.

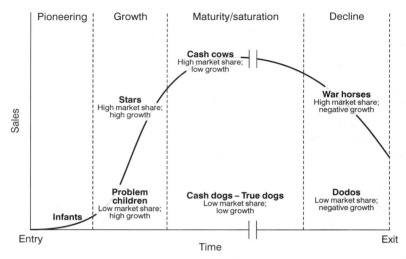

Figure 17.10 Barksdale and Harris BCG/PLC combined portfolio.

- *Infants* are in a situation where R&D costs are being recovered with high promotional expenditure in term of educating the market.

- *Stars* have high promotional costs, but good future potential once the product/service has been accepted by the market.

- *Problem children* (or wildcats or question marks) are in a high growth situation, but have low market share. They are costly to maintain, and market action should be taken to move them to star and, ultimately, cash cow positions.

- *Cash cows* earn money in a high market share/low growth situation. Promotional costs are lower as the market is familiar with the product/service.

- *Cash dogs* with a low market share are to the maturity side of the box in a saturated market and have a flat cash flow. *True dogs* have a low market share towards the saturation side of the box with a negative cash flow.

- *War horses* are in a declining market but still have a relatively high market share, probably as a result of competitors exiting from the market. This contributes to a positive cash flow.

- *Dodos* are in a declining market with a low market share and a negative cash flow. They should be deleted, but might still be there because management hope that they will stage a revival.

Key point
All planning begins with an analysis of the company's widest environment and proceeds to analyse the company's marketing environment through the marketing information system.

In concluding this insight into corporate planning through the medium of portfolio analysis, we should refer again to the planning stages illustrated in Figure 17.1. All planning begins with an analysis of the company's widest environment and proceeds to analyse the company's marketing environment through the marketing information system. The information gathered and resultant analyses are the base on which strategic corporate objectives can be formulated. These indicate the basic direction that the company wishes to follow. Corporate objectives are then communicated to operational management for implementation. Later planning stages are similar at both corporate and operational levels, and are now considered in more detail in terms of marketing planning.

Vignette 17.3

Cable and Wireless changes strategy as it is threatened with expulsion from the Caribbean

Cable and Wireless (C&W), the UK telecommunications giant, has had to reconsider its strategic decision to pull out of operations on the island of St Lucia. The company had enjoyed virtual monopoly status on the island, but the authorities in St Lucia wanted to renegotiate the terms of Cable and Wireless's contract in an attempt to open the market up to greater competition. Cable and Wireless was having none of it, and decided to withdraw from operations on the island. However, the leaders of the five eastern Caribbean states, including St Lucia, have said that the company may be forced to leave the Caribbean in general if it pulls out of St Lucia.

C&W has exclusive control of telecom services in eight English-speaking Caribbean countries. The governments of these countries are negotiating with the company to end its exclusive licensing agreements prematurely and allow greater competition within the market. C&G thought it had the moral high ground; after all, its exclusive license agreements still had some time to run and it did not see why it should make any concessions.

C&W argued that it did not have time to put new arrangements in place before the government of St Lucia wanted the changes to take place. The company therefore threatened to leave St Lucia altogether, in the hope that this threat would make the authorities climb down. In fact the strategy 'backfired', and it is now the company that has had to climb down.

17.7 Marketing planning at an operational level

17.7.1 TOWS matrix

The success of marketing planning at this level depends on a judicious deployment of the marketing mix. Before a mix strategy can be developed, operational management must carefully consider the company's position in the market again, with particular emphasis on 'SWOT' analysis. A useful tool here is 'TOWS' analysis, which facilitates the formulation of strategies. A number of stages are considered:

1 Evaluate the influence of environmental factors (STEEPLE issues) on the company

2 Make a diagnosis about the future

Product: refrigerators

	Strengths 1. Brand name 2. UK sales force 3. Good after sales 4. Competitive price	Weaknesses 1. International markets 2. UK specified products 3. Logistics
Opportunities 1. EU market 2. Disposable income 3. Second homes 4. Cheaper transport	Use existing brand name and after sales support to market to EU countries (S1, S3, W1, O1)	Established manufacturing plant in potential EU entrant country to market new low capacity range (W1, W2, W3, O1, O3, O4, T4)
Threats 1. Far East imports 2. Currency variations 3. New low-cost countries entering EU	Establish depots in EU and recruit sales force using UK trainers (S2, S3, S4, W1, W3, O1)	Source components in Far East for new ultra-low cost range of additional home freezers (S1, S3, S4, O3, T1, T3)

Figure 17.11 The application of TOWS analysis.

3 Assess the company's strengths and weaknesses in relation to operations management, finance and marketing

4 Develop strategic options.

An application of 'TOWS' is best illustrated through the use of a simple example, as shown in Figure 17.11.

17.7.2 Procedure for marketing planning

Figure 17.12 outlines a basic marketing planning routine, and this encapsulates the whole activity that comprises marketing in a strategic framework. The strategic planning process should have now taken place, and an individual plan is required for each SBU or product line.

According to Abell, in essence the marketing plan should include the following (Abell, 1979):

1 Analysis

2 Setting objectives

3 Forecasting

4 Budgeting

5 Organisation

6 Target selection

7 Developing the mix

8 Control.

These are now discussed separately in the context of marketing planning at an operational level.

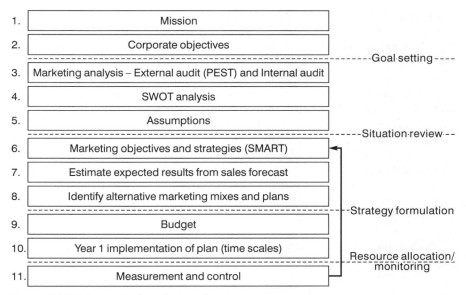

Figure 17.12 A model of marketing planning.

17.7.3 Analysis

We rely on marketing research to provide a detailed picture of the market and profiles of potential consumers. Information is needed about competitive activity, patterns of distribution, prices, products and trends. We must also ask potential consumers where they buy, how they buy, and what they consider to be problems with current supplies/suppliers. In particular, we need to know the market size. Within a company, costs must be analysed and production and distribution capabilities assessed.

17.7.4 Setting objectives

Based on marketing research/analysis and knowledge of its internal capabilities, the company must decide on its objectives – i.e. the market position the company will seek. The objectives of a marketing plan must be realistic, attainable and specific so that they can be easily communicated throughout the company. 'To increase sales' or 'to increase brand awareness' is meaningless. More specific (SMART) objectives provide a focus for marketing effort and permit subsequent evaluations of such effort. For example, a useful objective would be 'to increase sales by x per cent in market y during period z'.

17.7.5 Forecasting

Forecasting is concerned with future activity, and this distinguishes it from much of marketing research and marketing control, which are based on analyses of past events. The precise location of forecasting as a stage in the marketing plan will vary according to the type of product (new or existing) and the objectives that have been set (purely marketing based, e.g. increasing brand awareness, or financially based, e.g. reducing costs or increasing sales). An existing product can be adapted to a different market, so it is likely (because of ignorance of the market) that forecasting will precede the objective-setting stage in this case. If we were dealing with an existing product and a known market, analysis would have provided sufficient information to permit the setting of objectives. Specific estimation of buyer intentions (i.e. sales forecasting) can then follow.

The total market potential is estimated, then the information is refined into a specific company sales forecast. Whatever specific forecasting techniques are used, the net result is the company's best estimate of its expected participation in a given market during a given period (usually one year). The sales forecast (combined with marketing objectives) thus becomes the basis of planning throughout the company.

Key point
Production, human resources and financial decisions, as well as appropriate marketing mix strategies, can only be based on anticipated sales.

Production, human resources and financial decisions, as well as appropriate marketing mix strategies, can only be based on anticipated sales. It is emphasised that forecasts are estimates rather than predictions. Accurate sales forecasting is fraught with difficulties, as discussed in Chapter 14.

17.7.6 Budgeting

When the company has forecast future sales, it can allocate resources on the basis of anticipated revenue. Marketing objectives can influence resource allocation. Procter and Gamble is well known as a company that achieves high market share by aggressive advertising. This requires a high advertising expenditure during the product's introduction and growth stages, which could not be justified on purely financial grounds. The option to inject funds into the marketing budget is also important when, for example (using BCG terminology), the company wishes to transform a 'question mark' SBU into a 'star'. In general, when considering costs of production, distribution and marketing, expenditure should not exceed expected revenue. Sometimes finance will not allocate a set amount of money to marketing, but will require a certain level of forecast profit. The amount of money that is available for marketing will then be the amount of profit forecast in excess of company requirements.

How money is then apportioned to individual elements of the marketing mix is the responsibility of marketing. One technique for arriving at the optimum profit level is to forecast the effect of different levels of expenditure on different marketing mix elements. For example, operating a high service level will incur high costs, but these may be more than offset by increased sales. There will be a point at which further investment in the level of service is superfluous and other mix elements assume greater importance. The relationship between marketing and sales is called the 'sales response function'.

Given unlimited funding, there is little that a marketing manager could not achieve. Budgeting emphasises the 'realistic' nature of marketing. Financial resources are always limited and in demand elsewhere in the company. There is pressure on the marketing manager to transform financial resources into profitable results.

17.7.7 Organisation

This is a vital element of the marketing plan. Too often, extra responsibilities are given to employees without due consideration of how this will affect their overall performance. Similarly, personnel are sometimes 'misplaced' in terms of experience and expertise. As well as numbers and types of personnel, the company must consider the relationships between departments that might be overstaffed, whilst others might be under pressure coping with their workload.

17.7.8 Target selection

This involves defining the market segments to be approached (see Chapter 5). It might be that a demographically based segmentation strategy is appropriate, or perhaps behavioural variables such as benefits sought or usage rate might be better.

17.7.9 The marketing mix

When the first five planning stages described in Figure 17.11 have been thoroughly and carefully executed, specific marketing strategies can be developed. Each market segment should have its own marketing mix. The marketing mix strategy is the means for achieving company objectives in a specific marketing situation. It is developed within the framework of financial and company resources that are available.

17.7.10 Control

The effectiveness of a marketing mix strategy must be monitored, and after a predetermined period of time it must be evaluated and reviewed. This is the 'control' process.

Before considering control in more detail in the next section, the following observations can be made:

Key point
The effectiveness of a marketing mix strategy must be monitored, and after a predetermined period of time it must be evaluated and reviewed.

- Goals and objectives only assume value when they are translated into action

- We should be aware the planning is not an end in itself, only a means to an end – the 'end' being the provision of customer satisfaction by a means which provides the company with a profit

- Only if a company makes profits can its customers be served and employment maintained.

Vignette 17.4

Marks and Spencer plc changes its mind on European expansion strategy

Marks and Spencer plc, the beleaguered UK high street clothing and food store chain, is having a rethink about its long-term strategy for European expansion. The firm currently has 38 stores on the continent, of which 18 are in France, nine are in Spain and the rest are in Germany, Belgium, Luxembourg and The Netherlands. The company has always been keen to have a significant presence throughout Europe, and had a vision of turning the company into a truly pan-European retailing chain. However, that vision has had to be revised because their European operations are significantly underperforming.

The company has been facing problems for some time in both its UK and overseas operations. Falling profits has meant the firm has decided to close 20 per cent of its European stores in a first wave of closures. More closures may follow if the medicine does not do the trick. UK redundancies, including five senior staff from the company's head office, indicate that the firm has still not got to grips with the fundamental problems that caused its dramatic commercial decline in the late 1990s and through to 2001. The company employs 3500 continental staff, and many of these will lose their jobs. In terms of the continental closures the stores in the Benelux countries are likely to be the first to close, as these have been the poorest performers. The German stores in cities such as Hamburg and Cologne have seen a fall in trading but are still profitable.

In 1997 the continental side of the business made a profit of £38 million, which changed to a loss of £6.1 million in 2000. In 2001 things seem to be getting worse, with losses of about £10 million reported for the first six months alone. Management thought the Marks and Spencer concept would work in a regiocentric manner across the whole of Western Europe, but this does not seem to be the case. The format worked reasonably well in France and Germany, but less well elsewhere in Europe. Future strategy seems to be to concentrate more on solving the UK side of the business and restoring the business there, rather than looking to Europe for expansion.

17.8 Marketing control

Figure 17.1 portrayed a simple planning system that can be applied at strategic and operational levels. Whilst we make a distinction between these planning levels, the process itself is essentially the same for each. Implicit in successful planning is the need to look back with the light of experience so that performance can be evaluated and improved. We know from everyday experiences that plans do not always work out. Control systems enable us to find out what has gone wrong, and, more importantly, why practice has deviated from the plan.

Key point
Control systems enable us to find out what has gone wrong, and, more importantly, why practice has deviated from the plan.

People can be given independence when plans are being implemented, but responsibility must be borne by all levels of management and operational personnel. It acts as a powerful stimulus, because success can contribute to their personal future. In contrast, control tends to have a negative connotation. People are less inclined to respond positively to requests for information and analysis of their performance for control purposes.

Whilst it is clear that control procedures are vital to the success of marketing plans, we should not lose sight of the fact that plans are implemented by people. From an organisational point of view, control (if it is to be effective) should be approached with thought and sensitivity. Senior management is ultimately responsible for the fortunes of marketing plans. Logically, managers are also responsible for organising control procedures. These should be set up with the human factor as the starting point. They should be aware of the 'law of diminishing returns' as it applies to the usefulness and efficiency of gathering information. Managers should try to establish a priority of information needs and ascertain the minimum rather than the maximum requirement.

This will mean greater, not less, efficiency. At the functional level, marketing personnel tend to see their vital role as 'doing' rather than accounting for their activities.

The aims of control are often misunderstood. Often, the word is seen as being synonymous with coercion and allocation of blame. Clearly, these are not the objectives. The analogy of a rocket launch and a space programme is often used to illustrate marketing control. A rocket is launched with a clear objective or mission. During its flight, for a variety of reasons, numerous modifications may be made to ensure that the craft stays on course. The analogous function of marketing control is to identify changes in the marketing situation before they become serious problems, and to initiate corrective action. This is referred to as 'driving control'. Management must also ensure that targets are reached satisfactorily. This is done when a particular activity has been completed, and only then can evaluation and recommendations be made. This is 'results control'. Marketing is essentially concerned with results, so it is very important. Unfortunately, what marketing management considers to be driving control may appear to marketing staff (e.g. salespeople) to be results control and take on a punitive connotation. This behavioural observation highlights the sensitive nature of marketing control management.

Key point
The aims of control are often misunderstood.

Having taken these critical human or organisational factors into account, there are a series of elements that must be included in any control system (see Figure 17.13). In addition to these essential elements, the system should be designed to maximise communication and minimise noise – the distortion that can occur when messages are passed through a system via a series of 'human filters' (as in the game 'Chinese Whispers').

Marketing control is essential because it:

1 Enables running or 'driving' corrections and modifications to be made in response to problems which, if not detected at an early stage, could have serious consequences for the marketing plan

2 Provides information that can be used to review at regular intervals (e.g. bi-annually) how effectively objectives have been implemented. Deviations caused by internal or external forces can be identified and corrected

3 Provokes analysis that, in turn, causes opportunities to be identified

4 Acts as a motivating force at all levels of operational activity.

Put succinctly, control serves to minimise misdirected marketing effort.

17.9 Execution of control systems

We can now examine the execution of control in more detail. Figure 17.13 outlines the basic steps in the control process. Just as planning must have

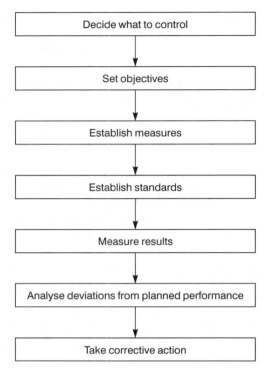

Figure 17.13 Steps in the control process.

objectives in order to be meaningful, control systems must also set objectives and establish how these are to be achieved.

What to control (the parameters) is the foundation of the control process. Typically, sales, costs and profits are the major preoccupations of management. These are central indicators of the firm's efficiency. Marketing activity extends beyond these basic criteria, and each of the marketing functions has individual objectives that must be subject to control.

When the parameters of control have been established, *control objectives* can be defined. Usually they are defined in terms of financial, as well as functional, performance. If planning objectives have been well defined, the control process can also use these. The sales manager's target must be achieved within a given budget and there are sub-objectives that must be controlled and included in the 'sales plan' – e.g. an optimum call-frequency-to-sales ratio. Other functional objectives can be identified in a similar manner.

Measures of success must be incorporated into the control process. The sales objectives may be to achieve a certain level of sales force efficiency (e.g. the quality of their contribution to marketing information or their ability to obtain new accounts). Success can be measured in terms of cross-references to other sources of information, or the contribution to annual sales turnover.

Objectives are rarely achieved in absolute terms. Standards must be established that refer to the 'real life' environment in which objectives are implemented. A *standard* may refer to upper and lower limits for a particular budget, or to a required level of brand awareness.

Key point
Measures of success must be incorporated into the control process.

Once the preceding steps have established, a framework for control, *measurement of results* can begin. Management must decide how often and at what level this should be undertaken – considerations of cost and time allocation are crucial in such decisions. The measurement procedures should be such that their costs do not exceed the value of their contribution to the company. Management should also take steps to ensure that activities associated with data collection for 'measurement' reasons do not detract from the efficiency of operational activities; on the other hand, measurement should be conducted often enough to detect early warning signals of deviations from the plan.

In *analysing results*, there is a danger that wrong conclusions may be drawn. Analysis may reveal shortcomings in performance, but care should be taken to be sure that the original objectives were realistic. In addition to simply comparing results with what was planned, emphasis should be placed on the identification of changes, either internal or external, and new information that genuinely affects the ability of those concerned to meet objectives. Analysis should be sufficiently detailed to uncover individual factors that affect the performance of a basically sound plan. Sometimes one product can be the cause of poor profitability of an otherwise sound product line. The necessary action in such a case could be to remove this product, rather than alter the whole product line. The ability of a firm to take appropriate corrective action depends on the efficiency of the analysis process.

Key point
The ability of a firm to take appropriate corrective action depends on the efficiency of the analysis process.

The *marketing audit* provides systematic appraisal of the company's activities at the corporate level. The purpose of the marketing audit is to consider the company in its entirety, and its objectives are:

1 To consider the marketing environment in both macro and micro terms to identify changes and tendencies that might affect the firm's future activities

2 To re-examine corporate strategy in the light of the above. What new or revised objectives should be communicated to operational marketing management?

To consider the efficiency of marketing at an operational level, it should be appreciated that the marketing audit is not concerned with measuring results. Rather, it is concerned with examining objectives and how well the company is equipped to fulfil them. The marketing audit at this level encompasses all marketing functions as well as marketing's organisational structure. It is particularly important that organisation is not overlooked, because the efficiency of any plan relies on the skill and the proper deployment of and relationships between the people who carry out that plan.

Companies that carry out a full-scale marketing audit display a high level of commitment to marketing orientation. They recognise that, in order to provide customer satisfaction, the company must endeavour to optimise efficiency at all levels. Control systems are the means by which efficiency can be assessed.

Key point
Control systems are the means by which efficiency can be assessed.

17.10 Summary

✓ Strategy, planning and control embrace all marketing activities. At the corporate level, marketing information systems (Chapter 13) and the marketing environment (Chapter 3) link with this topic. At the operational level, functional marketing mix areas (Chapters 7–12) are involved. Financial analysis is referred to at various points in the text, but is elsewhere more concerned with using these techniques in the execution rather than the formulation and control of marketing tactics and plans.

✓ The control process is concerned with all marketing activity. As well as being a continuous process that permits 'fine tuning' of plans whilst they are being implemented, it involves a review of activity after it has taken place. Usually this is an annual event that allows a company to look objectively at the total value of its efforts. Such a review should occur at both corporate and operational levels.

✓ At the operational level, the company is concerned with the marketing plan. When considering what to control, sales, costs and profits are of particular significance. Again, we must address the reality that marketing costs must not exceed the profits that sales provide. It is logical to suppose that if each functional activity efficiently achieves its objectives, then the net result for the firm would be overall success. However, this is not necessarily true. Often objectives are achieved at cost levels that are disproportionate to the value of the achievement. Annual control of the marketing plan allows the company to consider whether or not its financial resources are being optimised across the marketing mix. In a competitive environment, cost control is usually the key to profitability. Some management systems consider each functional area as a separate profit (or loss) centre with its own accounting procedures. This ensures functional managers are close to financial reality.

Questions

1 A significant proportion of marketing effort is devoted to satisfying the demands of control systems. How would you justify such a claim on a company's financial and human resources?

2 Differentiate between *corporate goals* and *operational*, or *functional*, marketing objectives. How are these planning activities related?

3 What is the relationship between strategic marketing planning and overall corporate planning?

References

Abell, D. (1979). *Strategic Market Planning: Problems and Analytical Perspectives*, Chapters 4 and 5. Prentice Hall.

Ansoff, I. (1957). Strategies for diversification. *Harvard Business Review*, **Sep**, 38.

Barksdale, H. C. and Harris, C. E. (Jr) (1982). Portfolio analysis and the product life cycle. *Journal of Long Range Planning*, **15**, 6.

Porter, M. (1985). *Competitive Advantage*. The Free Press.

Further reading

Armstrong, G. and Kotler, P. (2000). Strategic planning and the marketing process. *Marketing: An Introduction*, 5th edn, Chapter 2. Prentice Hall.

Blythe, J. (2001). Marketing planning, implementation and control. *Essentials of Marketing*, Chapter 10. Person Educational Ltd.

Davies, M. (1998). Marketing planning, the environment and competitive strategy. *Understanding Marketing*, Chapter 2. Prentice Hall.

Dibb, S., Simkin, L., Pride, W. M. and Ferrell, O. C. (1994). *Marketing Concepts and Strategies*, 2nd European edn. Houghton Mifflin.

Hofer, C. W. and Schendel, D. (1978). *Strategy Formulation: Analytical Concepts*. West Publishing Company.

Hussey, D. E. and Langham, M. J. (1979). *Corporate Planning – The Human Factor*. Pergamon Press.

Keegan, W. J. and Green, M. S. (2000). Leading, organising and controlling the global marketing effort. *Global Marketing*, 2nd edn, Chapter 16. Prentice Hall.

Kotler, P. (1988). *Marketing Management, Analysis, Planning, Implementation and Control*, 6th edn, p. 65. Prentice Hall.

Lancaster, G. A. and Massingham, L. C. (1994). *Essentials of Marketing* (in particular, Part 5). McGraw Hill.

Lancaster, G. A. and Reynolds, P. L. (1998). Marketing planning. *Marketing*, Chapter 15. Macmillan Press.

MacDonald, M. (1999). *Marketing Plans: How to Prepare Them, How to Use Them*, fourth edition. Butterworth-Heinemann.

Patel, P. and Younger, M. (1978). A frame of reference for strategy development. *Long Range Planning*, **Apr**, 6–12.

Plamer, A. (2000). Developing a sustainable competitive advantage. *Principles of Marketing*, Chapter 11, Oxford University Press.

Robinson, S. J. (1978). The directional policy matrix – tools for strategic planning. *Long Range Planning*, **Jun**, 8–15.

Stapleton, J. (1982). *How to Prepare a Marketing Plan*. Gower.

Steiner, G. A. (1979). *Strategic Planning (What Every Manager Must Know)*. The Free Press.

The use of Internet technology in marketing

18

18.1 Introduction

Today, technology is all around us and influences every area of our lives. This is particularly true of computer-based technology. In this chapter we shall be looking at developments such as the World Wide Web, the Internet, e-commerce in general, databases and their application such as data mining and data fusion, and the way these new developments and techniques have changed the face of marketing practice over the last 10 years. The Internet (or simply the Net) is a vast and continually growing web of computer networks that links computers around the world. The World Wide Web (or simply the Web) is a development of the Internet where the accessing of information is user friendly. The term 'electronic commerce' is a general term for the buying and selling process that is supported by electronic means. Advances in technology are having a tremendous impact on all areas of business, including marketing. This chapter cannot make readers experts in the subject of electronic commerce, because there has been an explosion of information on the subject and it would take many books to do justice to this. However, by reading this chapter it is possible nonetheless to be able to appreciate the main issues involved with the use of electronic commerce. It is important to understand what some of these key technological advances are and how they are affecting the marketing firm and impacting on marketing activities. It is also important to have some understanding of the main trends and how the continual development of technology is likely to affect marketing firms in the future.

As we enter the twenty-first century, we enter a millennium of advanced technology. People living in this century are going to see staggering advances in the application and development of technology, which at present they would scarcely recognise or believe possible. The life cycle of many products is moving ever faster as technological advances supersede existing product types and forms. Some people cannot cope; some firms cannot cope. However, we must do more than cope if, as marketing professionals, we can hope to capitalise on and fully exploit the tremendous business opportunities that this new technology brings. It is no good the firm's management hiding their heads in the sand like an ostrich and pretending that the technological revolution is not happening. Denial will get them nowhere at all. In this penultimate

Definition
The term 'electronic commerce' is a general term for the buying and selling process that is supported by electronic means.

chapter we are going to be examining and discussing some of the more important developments and advances in computer-based technology that are of interest to the marketing firm. In particular we will be examining the use of the Internet and the World Wide Web, which has formed the platform for the new e-marketing revolution.

We can now begin to analyse and assess some of the more salient technological developments that are taking place with respect to marketing and business in general. Here this discussion focuses on the impact, applications and implications of these technologies with regard to marketing practices and processes, rather than an analysis of the technologies themselves. Finally, it is important to note that many of the technological developments that follow are interrelated. So, for example, the development of databases and the growth of e-commerce are both underpinned by advances in the technologies of computing such as 'data mining' and 'data fusion'. These topics and others will be covered in greater depth later in the chapter.

18.2 The importance of electronic commerce

Business in general, and certainly marketing in particular, has become more and more affected by and dependent upon technology. Furthermore, technological progress itself is altering and accelerating. Technology seems to be developing at an exponential rate. The rate of development increases because scientists and technologists learn from what has happened in the past; in a sense, they are 'standing on the shoulders of giants'. For example, the digital computer was developed in a laboratory in Manchester University, England, and since then other people have developed the basic technology into what we can see today. We shall examine some of the more salient of these changes and advances in technology as they affect the marketer in more detail in this chapter. Suffice it to say, at this stage, that advances in technology are now beginning basically to change the nature of marketing and other business and commercial activities, so much so that many consider that in as little as 10 years the process of marketing will have changed beyond recognition. Some experts go so far as to say that the traditional marketing model or 'paradigm' is no longer applicable in the world of the Internet, and that a new model is called for. Certainly, at the very least, the modern-day marketer needs to be familiar with the key advances in technology that are at this time impacting on the marketing process. A summary of the reasons for this, which captures the importance of technological advances, is listed below:

Key point
Certainly, at the very least, the modern-day marketer needs to be familiar with the key advances in technology that are at this time impacting on the marketing process.

- Advances in technology enable the marketing process to be carried out not only more effectively but also more efficiently; computer-aided questionnaire design for marketing research is a case in point. The computerisation of measuring instruments for advertising research is another good example. Advances in technology allow the marketing professional to do more things, and to do tasks better.

- New technology increasingly facilitates the ease with which information, so vital to effective marketing planning and decision-making, can be collected, analysed and used. Marketing information systems and the ability to 'tap' into internal and external databases has revolutionised the planning process in marketing in terms of detail and speed. Data mining and data fusion are techniques that allow marketing research professionals to 'engineer' information from a wide variety of sources, and even create virtual consumer models from such information.

- Competitive success is increasingly based on the application of advances in technology. Take mobile telephones, for example. It is no longer enough to produce a product that is capable of making a telephone call; today people want telephones that can send text messages, answer e-mails, play computer games and perform a host of other functions.

- Developments in business-related technology often contribute to the growth of the international company and a move towards the global market and consumer. Smaller firms in particular benefit from Internet-based business technologies, as these reduce their size disadvantage. Electronic commerce has no geographic boundaries; it is just as easy for companies in the UK to interact with consumers in New Zealand as it is for them to interact with consumers in the next town. Many firms, in order to both differentiate their products and reduce their costs, are increasingly using computer-based technology. Just-In-Time ordering and stock-holding systems save firms millions in inventory and logistics costs compared with the more traditional way of doing things in the past. Computers have facilitated the use of these new systems and processes.

- Some of the developments in business-related computer technology allow the marketer to be much more customer focused and marketing oriented, with, for example, much faster and more flexible responses to customer needs. The use of database marketing and data mining has improved the accuracy and efficiency of many marketing operations, particularly marketing communications such as direct mail.

The examples given above demonstrate that marketing management must not only be aware of but must also understand the advances in technology that are taking place, otherwise they will not be able to do their job. Some marketing firms may even contribute to these changes; for example, Napster.com has pioneered the marketing of music on the Internet, and many other e-marketing firms are likely to follow its lead in one way or another. Amazon.com leads the way in the marketing of books and compact discs (CDs) on the Internet, and is one of the most high profile names in the whole of e-marketing. Napster.com and Amazon.com are two examples of how the marketing firms making use of the new technology are themselves contributing to the development of the Internet as a mainstream commercial medium. These companies are rather like Proctor and Gamble Limited as it was back in the 1950s and 1960s, when it pioneered many of the fast-moving consumer goods marketing techniques used today, especially in the field of branding and sales promotions.

Key point
Marketing is all about staying ahead of the competition.

Moreover, the marketer must also be aware of and be prepared for future advances in technology. Marketing is all about staying ahead of the competition. This in turn means that the marketer must also have the required skills to use the new technologies of today and tomorrow to help assist the marketing process. Similarly, those organisations whose management and marketers are unaware of or unable to use advances in technology will become increasingly uncompetitive. Marketing managers of the future will need an understanding of the use of technology within the discipline. They may not need to be technical experts (after all, these are available as staff), but they must be able to appreciate how they can factor in the use of new technology into all aspects of their marketing plans and operations.

Key point
Marketing managers of the future will need an understanding of the use of technology within the discipline.

Vignette 18.1

The 'I Love You' computer bug sweeps through international business corporations and costs business nearly £2 billion

People found it hard to resist. When they came to work in the morning and opened up their e-mail, they saw three tantalising little words that were both beguiling and intriguing. The three little words were 'I Love You'. Many people thought that they must have a secret romantic admirer trying to contact them. The message was in fact a 'sugar trap' to make users open the e-mail message. As soon as they did, they were hit by one of the most vicious and powerful computer viruses ever recorded. The romantic little message has turned out to be one of the most expensive business disasters in history, with the total cost of the damage done by the bug currently running at around £2 billion.

The 'I Love You' bug has swept through the computer systems of some of the world's largest corporations, causing havoc and leaving chaos in its wake. The virus has affected around 45 million computer users ranging from large international corporations such as The Ford Motor Corporation to government departments such as the British Parliament, and a plethora of small to medium-sized enterprises and of course individual users.

The bug was even more devastating than the notorious 'Melissa' virus that preceded it because of the way it was able to copy itself and infect so many other users in such a short period of time. The 'I Love You' bug worked by flattering people into opening the message and then replicating itself by spreading to stored e-mail addresses. Instead of reading a romantic message from some one in the office who 'fancied' them, computer users found their computer files destroyed. The episode now ranks alongside such well-known natural disasters as the Exxon Valdez oil spill. The big insurance companies such as Lloyds of London will be expected to pay for some of the losses.

Not since the Industrial Revolution has the marketing firm been affected so much, down to the very core of its business, by changes in the technological environment. Those firms that are not fully aware of technological advances and developments will fall behind in the commercial race and will probably cease trading. There is a significant change in the technological environment of marketing firms; this is not a minor technological change, but a huge 'step' change in the way marketing firms do business (Figure 18.1). If they do not

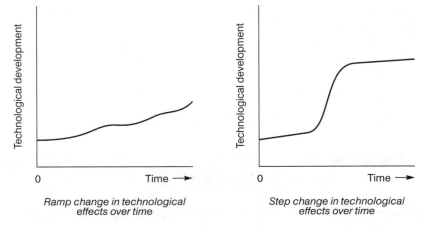

Figure 18.1 Graphs showing examples of ramp and step changes in the effects or impact of technological development.

react and adapt to the new environmental factors, there is a danger that they will become, like the dinosaur, extinct. It is a cliché, but one that is highly applicable in today's rapidly changing technological environment.

18.3 Database marketing

18.3.1 Database marketing defined

The world of sales and marketing is changing all the time. The Internet, e-commerce, the continuing rise of direct marketing and the increasing marketing emphasis on customer retention over customer acquisition are only a few of the salient factors affecting the way firms carry out business in the modern world. Firms have to move very fast, keep up with the latest developments and trends, and invest in the most relevant software and systems to stay ahead of the competition. 'Database marketing' is two words: the first word implies that data is organised and stored in a computer system; the second word implies that firms use this data in their marketing and sales programmes.

Definition
Database marketing is a marketing and sales system that continually gathers, refines and utilises information and data that then drives relevant marketing and sales communications programmes.

Database marketing is a marketing and sales system that continually gathers, refines and utilises information and data that then drives relevant marketing and sales communications programmes. Examples of this are sales calls, direct mail pieces, and advertising to selected companies in order to acquire new customers, retain customers, generate more business from existing customers, and create long-term loyalty. Database marketing is much more than just a data retrieval system. While 'direct marketing' describes a collection of marketing communication tactics (such as direct mail, telemarketing, response advertising, etc.), database marketing describes a way of organising a company's total marketing and sales process. It is very broad, and can have an impact from market research and product development all the way through customer service. Information about customers that is accurate and available to everyone can truly transform a company's market capacity.

18.3.2 What does database marketing allow you to do?

Database marketing is all about focusing and targeting. Databases take the 'guess' out of marketing programmes. They do not necessarily provide perfect accuracy, but they do allow for significant improvements in both accuracy and efficiency if used properly. Many companies do a sort of 'hit-or-miss' marketing, for want of a better phrase. That means that management often makes decisions based on intuition or instinct rather than on hard facts based on clear 'scientific' evidence. Hence instead for predicting their target audience based on hard facts, they make their best 'guesses' about whom their target audience is and what their audience wants. This process of 'best guessing' can be very expensive in terms of wasted direct mail shots and other forms of communication, and wasted time and effort. As already mentioned, database marketing lets us work more intelligently and provides the tools to make more accurate assessments. It lets us take the information we already have in our customer or sales-lead databases, analyse it to find the patterns in it such as purchasing associations and relationships, and use the information gained from this analysis to produce and instigate better marketing and sales programmes. 'Running better marketing and sales programmes' simply means targeting specific groups with specific messages about products that are important to them rather than giving them irrelevant and uninteresting information. If we are able to target the right industries with the right messages about the right products, less sales and marketing resources will be spent marketing to companies and/or individuals that are never going to buy. Hence there will be more resources to spend on the prospects that are most likely to buy, thereby increasing the return on marketing and sales investment. Basically, the proper use of databases gives the marketing professional the tools to do a more accurate and professional job. It improves the effectiveness of marketing campaigns and saves time and money. It allows for the more effective allocation and utilisation of valuable marketing resources. Database marketing is sometimes referred to as precision marketing. Directing a marketing programme from a well constructed and managed database is analogous to shooting a rifle at a target using an advanced precision telescopic sight rather than a conventional sight.

Key point
Database marketing is sometimes referred to as precision marketing.

18.3.3 Basic principles of database marketing

Below are some illustrations of the possible applications and basic principles of database marketing. They are not intended to be exhaustive or definitive, but they do serve to illustrate the main principles. Applications include:

First of all, finding out what characteristics the company's best customers have in common so the next programmes can be targeted to prospects that have those same characteristics. See exactly which market segments buy from the firm; although the marketing department might think that it already knows the best market segments, analysis may reveal market segments to which a significant amount of product has been sold without it realising. This process may enable the firm to improve its segmentation of the market by refocusing and redefining existing segments, or may highlight totally unexpected new segments.

- Ascertaining whether different market segments buy different products from the company. This information will allow more effective expenditure of marketing and sales resources by marketing each of the firm's products to the best potential industries, individual firms or individual people. Learn which market segments bring the most revenue and which ones bring the highest average revenue. This is what differentiated marketing is all about – dividing the total market into segments and then having a slightly different marketing strategy for each segment.

- Finding out what types of industries, firms or individuals respond to what types of marketing communications so a decision can be made regarding where to spend the advertising and marketing resources the next time. Find out which market segments not only respond to the company's programmes but also actually buy, and which buy from it repeatedly. Again, these might have very different demographic profiles or be different in some other way that may be commercially exploitable, and this might lead to a decision to modify targeting tactics and only market to the segments that buy repeatedly or at least reasonably frequently.

- Calculating the average lifetime value of customers. This can be done using discounted cash flow procedures. This information can be used to find out which customers are not living up to their potential, and to devise marketing and sales programmes to encourage them to buy more. Identify new customers and create programmes that will encourage them to buy again. Reward the most frequent buyers and the buyers that bring in the highest revenue. The concept of 'lifetime' value is central to the idea of customer retention and long-term relationship marketing, and this subject is covered in more detail in Chapter 19.

18.3.4 Data mining

Definition
Database marketing is a process that enables marketers to develop, test, implement, measure and modify marketing programmes and strategies more accurately and efficiently than non-database methods.

Database marketing is a process that enables marketers to develop, test, implement, measure and modify marketing programmes and strategies more accurately and efficiently than non-database methods. By applying data mining techniques, marketers can fully harvest data about customers' buying patterns and behaviour, and gain a greater understanding of customer motivations. Data mining and customer relationship management (CRM) software allows users to analyse large databases to solve business decision problems. Data mining, as the name suggests, involves 'interrogating' a database in order to discover interesting and hopefully commercially exploitable associations, patterns or relationships in the data. Modern data analysis software such as SPSS allows the user to manipulate, group and correlate data variables and sets.

18.3.5 Basic principles of data mining

In order to implement successful database marketing solutions, management needs to know how to carry out certain basic tasks, some of which are listed below. The list is again not intended to be prescriptive and certainly not exhaustive. However, once more it does serve to illustrate some of the basic principles. Tasks include:

- Identifying and gathering relevant data about customers and prospects to construct the database in the first place.

- Using data warehousing techniques, which are systems of data storage and organising, to transform raw data into powerful, accessible marketing information. This adds value to the data collected by putting it in a format so that it can be retrieved and analysed effectively.

- Applying statistical techniques to customer and prospect databases to analyse behaviour and attempt to establish patterns, associations or relationships in the data that may be commercially exploitable.

- Establishing meaningful market segments that are measurable, reachable, viable and hence commercially valuable.

- Scoring individuals in terms of the probability of their response. This will involve prioritising prospects in terms of the probability of purchase and long-term commercial value.

Data mining is, in some ways, an extension of statistical analysis. Like statistics, data mining is not a business solution; it is just a technology. CRM, on the other hand, involves turning information in a database into business decisions. For example, consider a catalogue retailer who needs to decide who to send a new catalogue to. The information incorporated into the customer relationship management process is the historical database of previous mailings and the features associated with the (potential) customers, such as age, postcode, their response in the past, etc. The software can use these data to build a model of customer behaviour that can be used to predict which customers are likely to respond to the new catalogue – rather like building a 'virtual customer'. By using this information, a marketing manager can target the customers who are likely to respond. It provides much greater accuracy, and saves time and money.

Key point
Data mining is, in some ways, an extension of statistical analysis.

18.3.6 Data fusion

Data fusion is in many ways similar to data mining. Again, as the name implies, data is obtained from a range of different sources and put together, rather like a jigsaw puzzle, to form a complete profile of an individual. For example, a customer may fill in a loyalty card form at a supermarket, which means a lot of his personal information is now on a company database. He may also apply for a bank account or credit facilities with the same or related company (supermarkets such as J. Sainsbury Ltd offer bank and credit facilities to its customers), filling in another form and giving further personal details. These data may be merged and integrated with data held about him on other personal databases, for example those run by Equifax Ltd or Experian Ltd, which supply personal data (including financial data such as credit history) to firms.

Data from all these sources will be 'fused' together, cleaned using a 'filtering system', and will basically form a complete picture of the customer as a person and as a consumer. Sometimes data will be fused together from fragments held on different databases on different people. These people may share similar characteristics and form part of the same market segment. There may be associations between key variables that link a particular consumer to a particular segment. If customers have the right value on one or two of these variables, they are then treated as if they have the characteristics of the 'virtual consumer' built up from the fused data fragments. Using these techniques, firms can attribute a probability that certain customers will behave in a certain way as modelled by their virtual consumer profile. Data fusion is a formal framework in which are expressed means and tools for the alliance of data originating from different sources. It aims at obtaining information of greater quality; the exact definition of 'greater quality' will depend upon the application.

It has been suggested that the terms merging, integration and combination should be used in a much broader sense than fusion, with combination being even broader than merging (see Wald, 1998). These terms define any process that implies a mathematical operation performed on at least two sets of information. These definitions are used very loosely intentionally, and offer space for various interpretations.

Another domain pertains to data fusion: data assimilation or optimal control. Data assimilation deals with the inclusion of measured data into numerical models for the forecasting or analysis of the behaviour of a system. A well-known example of a mathematical technique used in data assimilation is the Kalman filtering system. Data assimilation is used daily for weather forecasting.

Definition
Data assimilation deals with the inclusion of measured data into numerical models for the forecasting or analysis of the behaviour of a system.

Filtering

People have been filtering things for virtually our entire history. Water filtering is a simple example; impurities can be filtered from the water just by using our hands to skim dirt and leaves off the top. Another example is filtering out noise from our surroundings. If we paid attention to all the little noises around us we would go mad. We learn to ignore superfluous sounds (traffic, appliances, etc.) and focus on important sounds, like the voices of people we are speaking with.

There are many examples in engineering where filtering is desirable. Radio communications signals are often corrupted with noise. A good filtering algorithm can remove the noise from electromagnetic signals while still retaining the useful information. Another example is voltages. Many countries require in-home filtering of line voltages in order to power personal computers and peripherals. Without filtering, the power fluctuations would drastically shorten the useful life span of the devices. Kalman filtering is a relatively recent (1960) development in filtering, although it has its roots as far back as Gauss (1795) (see Bos, 1976; Benham, 1974; Agostinelli, 1978). Kalman

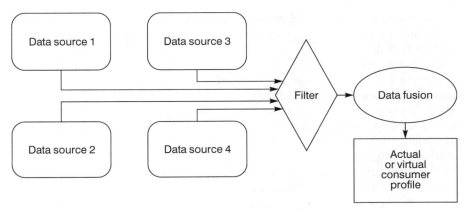

Figure 18.2 Schematic flow chart representing the data fusion process.

filtering has been applied in areas as diverse as aerospace, marine navigation, nuclear power plant instrumentation, demographic modelling, manufacturing, and many others, including data fusion (see Anderson and Moore, 1979; Sorenson, 1985).

The data fusion process is illustrated in Figure 18.2.

18.4 The Internet

The Internet is not a fad or short-term trend; it is a major technological development that is here to stay and will continually evolve. This is the beginning of the next business revolution, and will affect the way we live, work and possibly play for the rest of our lives. The technology involved in setting up the Internet has demonstrated to management that it will significantly change the way people interact with each other, particularly so in the sphere of business. The Internet crosses the boundaries of geography, politics, race, sex, religion, time zones and culture. Technology of any kind helps to make possible, and hopefully improve, the way we work. Without it many of the things we do – and often take for granted – would be at best difficult and sometimes impossible. For example, much of advertising relies on communications technology; effective distribution and logistics relies on transport technologies; an marketing research and analysis increasingly relies upon computing technology. Admittedly, this reliance on and use of technology in marketing is not new, but the extent to which it is used and the way in which it is used today is new. Think for a moment how different our lives would be without, say, the calculator, e-mail or even television. What would our lives be like without the technology to telephone a relative, or deliver electricity and power to our homes and offices? Less noticeably, but in context perhaps no less significantly, technology also affects and helps to aid marketing and the marketing process – so much so that some areas of marketing and marketing techniques are almost totally underpinned by technology and its application. An obvious example is the use

Key point
The Internet crosses the boundaries of geography, politics, race, sex, religion, time zones and culture.

of e-marketing. Some of these new marketing activities, such as database marketing, data fusion, electronic data 'warehousing' and data analysis, simply could not be done without the new technology.

E-business, based on Internet technology and the variations that have been developed from the original Internet concept such as the Intranet and the Extranet, connects and links employees, customers, suppliers and partners. The Internet has reduced the planet into a 'global village', accelerated the pace of technology, opened up tremendous possibilities for marketers, and altered the way they think about doing business. It has started the new revolution in marketing, some say the most important revolution since the invention of commercial advertising – the 'e-commerce revolution'. It is the revolution people can no longer ignore. Some experts believe that the new revolution will rebuild the existing economy and change the way business is conducted, while others say the likely effect of the new technology is 'overblown' and that many people will stop using it once the initial novelty has worn off. Certainly the financial community seems to blow hot and cold over the perceived commercial prospects of 'high tech' companies and their stocks. Worries about the prospects of such new companies have led to the downturn in the US equity markets, which is starting to spread to other stock markets throughout the world.

18.5 World Wide Web

According to many experts on the subject, and publications such as the *Financial Times*, the World Wide Web market will reach a staggering £1 trillion by 2003. The World Wide Web has unique features that differentiate it from other forms of business communications. Because the Web is so different from the more traditional media, such as television and radio, its use is revolutionising the manner in which some marketing activities are carried out. In fact, they could not be carried out at all without the use of Web-based technology.

Key point
Some writers see the Web as an innovation that will totally transform the whole marketing concept.

Some writers see the Web as an innovation that will totally transform the whole marketing concept. Many argue that for firms' marketing activities to be successful using the new technology a totally new model of marketing is required for the Web-based society in which these firms will be doing business. In the USA, more than two-thirds of firms are setting up computer-based systems such as Intranet and/or Extranet facilities. As in many other technological innovations, the USA seems to be leading the way and acting as a driving force for the diffusion of the new technology, and the new marketing methods that go with it, across the world. These are tools that have the potential to increase profits by cutting costs, by improving productivity, efficiency and communications, and by reducing paper work. E-commerce helps to improve all areas of business – bringing in new customers, improving service levels, creating growth potential, tracking customers, data mining of databases, better targeting of marketing communications, reducing distribution costs and speeding up growth.

The so-called E-commerce revolution, of which the World Wide Web is at the very epicentre, has been hailed as one of the most important developments ever to occur in the world of business. These developments will affect every area of firms' business operations, but especially marketing. Some experts are calling the new developments in marketing a 'paradigm shift'. This means that the new technology is not simply resulting in marketing firms doing basically the same thing but with more up-to-date technology; it means that we have to change the whole way we think about doing marketing – we need a new model or 'paradigm'.

Vignette 18.2

Sun Microsystems Inc. uses Java Technology to enable the Co-operative Bank to offer an on-line Internet banking service

The Co-operative Bank plc is one of the most 'upmarket' high street banks in the UK. Customers are typically busy people, often professionals, who tend to travel a great deal and hence need access to their bank accounts at all times of the day and from wherever they happen to be in the world at the time. Like most other retail banks, the Co-operative wanted to be able to offer secure Internet banking to its customers and it searched for a provider that could supply this.

The business challenge facing the bank was to develop a strongly customer-orientated Internet banking facility that integrates the flexibility of on-line services with the necessary security that its customers expected. The bank needed a banking service that would provide all of the banking functions including basic transactions, transferring money, paying bills, changing standing orders and ordering statements. All of this needed to be done in a secure manner to gain the confidence of the customer.

The solution to the bank's demands came from Sun Microsystems Inc., who were able to offer:

● Flexible yet secure solutions

● Differentiated service through Java software based interface

● Fast development and deployment.

The whole of the bank's on-line Internet banking system depended on Sun's Java technology platform. This was chosen for its reliability and versatility; especially the fact that it would work on any Java-enabled device. This supported the bank's philosophy that customers should be able to access their accounts and carry out transactions at any time, anywhere. The Java-based system was also very secure.

The bank now uses the Internet for all of its main lines of activity. The bank's home pages are regarded as advanced and 'state of the art' within the industry. They are regularly updated and refreshed, and attracted over half a million visitors in the first six months of operation. The bank's long-term strategic position is that in 25 years' time Internet banking will be the normal form of banking for the majority of the population, and the Co-operative bank intends to one of the leaders – if not the leader – in this field of retail banking. Management sees that it has taken 25 years for the majority of customers to use ATM machines, and feels that it will take about the same amount of time for the massive change in consumer behaviour to occur so that the majority of customers bank on-line.

18.6 The World Wide Web: new model for electronic marketing

Definition
The World Wide Web is a form of 'hypermedia computer-mediated environment' (HCME) that is networked on a global scale.

The World Wide Web is a form of 'hypermedia computer-mediated environment' (HCME) that is networked on a global scale. This is a bit of a mouthful, but basically an HCME is a networked system that allows the users of the system to interact in some way with the system. Both the sender and the receiver of the message can supply information to and interact with each other, with other users, and with the system itself. This makes the World Wide Web very different from other systems used in marketing, and in particular in marketing communications, at the present time. The telephone and other media allow for certain amount of interaction. For example, people can telephone the local radio channel and be heard by listeners participating in the programme. However the interactivity provided by the World Wide Web goes much further than this. As mentioned earlier, users can not only interact with the sender of the commercial message but also with other users of the system, and can contribute material to the system itself. It is this person interaction and machine interaction that differentiates the Web from other commercial media and has led to its widespread use and adoption as a marketing media (see Hoffman and Novak, 1994).

Let us consider for a moment the standard one-way simple model of marketing communication. The models illustrated in Figures 18.3 and 18.4 have already been discussed in depth in Chapter 7, but here we are discussing them in a slightly different context. The conventional simple model of marketing communications has been developed and discussed by a number of writers, including Lasswell (1948) and Katz and Lazarfield (1955). The model is one where the sender, in this case the marketing firm, encodes and transmits a message to multiple receivers – i.e. the target audience. In these models no interaction takes place between the sender and receiver, although there is a feedback loop whereby the sender can evaluate the effectiveness of the communication using research.

18.6.1 Models of communication

Models of the communications process may be verbal, non-verbal or mathematical. Regardless of form, they share three basic elements: *sender*, *message* and *receiver*. The message may be sent to one receiver or, as is more common in marketing communications, to multiple receivers simultaneously.

In its simplest form, the communications process can be modelled as shown in Figure 18.3. The above model is similar to Figure 7.1, except that it incorporates multiple receivers. The sender (source) is a person or group having a thought to share with some other person or group (the receiver or destination). In marketing, receivers are present and prospective consumers of the company's product. The message is a symbolic expression of the sender's thoughts. The message may take the form of the printed or the spoken word, a magazine advertisement or television commercial being examples. Figure 18.3 shows a simplified model, which underlies many such models of mass

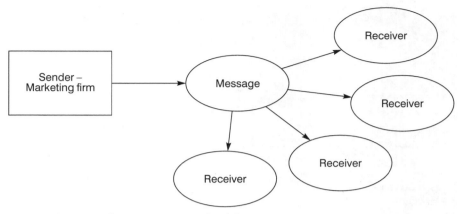

Figure 18.3 A simple communications model.

communications such as those of Lasswell (1948) and Katz and Lazarsfield (1955). The main feature of this model is the 'one-to-many' communication where the firm transmits a message to consumers. The communications may be static, such as a poster, or dynamic, such as a video recording. A dynamic element can be added to the basic model (see Bornman and van Solms, 1993). Note that no interaction between consumers and firms is present in this model. This is typical of all contemporary models of mass media effects, which are all basically variations on this particular theme (see, for example, the work of Kotler, 1994).

Figure 18.4 shows a slightly more complex model. This model introduces *encoding*, *decoding*, *channel* and *feedback* elements. Encoding is the process, controlled by the sender, of putting thought into symbolic form. The encoding process might use music, visual art or a psychological message containing sadness, guilt etc. Similarly, decoding is the process of transforming message symbols back into thought, but is controlled by the receiver. Both encoding and decoding are mental processes. The message itself is the manifestation of the encoding process, and is the instrument used in sharing thought with a receiver. The channel is the path through which the message moves from the sender to the receiver. The feedback element recognises the two-way nature of the communications process; in reality, individuals are both senders and receivers and interact with each other continually. Feedback allows the sender of the original message to monitor how accurately the message is being received. Thus, the feedback mechanism gives the sender some measure of

Definition
Encoding is the process, controlled by the sender, of putting thought into symbolic form.

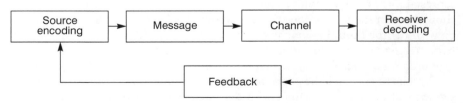

Figure 18.4 A more detailed model of the communication process.

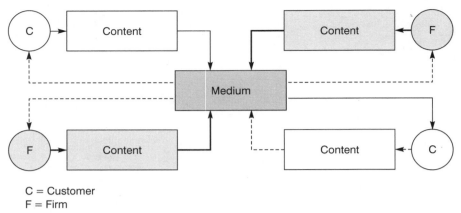

C = Customer
F = Firm

Figure 18.5 A communications model for an HCME such as the World Wide Web (based on the work of Hoffman and Novak, 1995).

control in the communication process. In marketing, it is sometimes acknowledged that the customers originally intended do not receive an advertising message. Based on market feedback, the message can be re-examined and perhaps corrected. This model was discussed in detail in Chapter 7, and readers are referred back to that section for a more detailed explanation.

The key feature of all the conventional simple models of mass media communications is that there is no interaction taking place between the sender and the receivers of the message. Hoffman and Novak (1995) constructed a new model of communication that is more suitable for a hypermedia computer-mediated environment (HCME) such as the World Wide Web. In this model customers/receivers can actually interact with the medium, and both marketing firms and the receivers of the message can provide actual content. In this mediated model Hoffman and Novak show that the primary relationships are not between the sender and receiver so much as with the HCME itself, with which they interact (Figure 18.5). Hence in this new model information or content is not simply transmitted from sender to receiver, but mediated environments are actually created by all parties using the system and then experienced by them.

Figure 18.5 is also based on traditional models of mass communication, although the model incorporates a feedback view of interactivity between the firm and customers and between customers and customers. Interactivity is the feature that really differentiates Figure 18.5 from the two previous figures; it represents a 'many-to-many' communications model. Hoffman and Novak show through their work (on which this model is based) that interactivity can be with the medium, i.e. machine interactivity, and through the medium, i.e. person interactivity. This model is based upon an earlier mediated model proposed by Steuer (1992), which is shown below in Figure 18.6.

This illustrates that the main form of communication is not between the sender and receiver, but rather with the 'mediated environment', with which both interact. Because of the interaction, the sender is also a receiver and the

Figure 18.6 A mediated communications model (based on the work of Steuer, 1992).

receiver is also a sender. Hence in this model information is not simply transmitted from a sender to receiver, as in Figures 18.3 and 18.4, but instead 'mediated environments' are created, which are then experienced by both parties. That is, the sender and receivers actually become part of a simulated, virtual world, and actually participate, contribute to and interact in this world.

18.7 E-commerce: opportunities

As we have seen, one of the most important areas affected by advances in technology has been business, with the growth of electronic commerce – sometimes referred to as electronic marketing (or e-marketing) or more generically as e-business or e-commerce. E-commerce is a collective term to describe a variety of commercial transactions that make use of the technologies of electronic processing and data transmission. The majority of these are based on the Internet and its hybrids such as the Extranet and Intranet.

Electronic commerce can be defined as:

> the use of electronic technologies and systems so as to facilitate and enhance transactions between different parts of the value chain.

This definition focuses on the fact that all electronic commerce is designed to improve the business transaction processes. E-commerce would not have grown to the extent it has and will continue to do had it not provided potential improvements to the marketing process. Often these potential improvements, as already stated, will be in the form of cost reductions for the marketer, but much more important are those improvements that can be passed on to the customer. Put another way, the growth of e-commerce would not have been possible without the growth of the e-customer – for example, it will be some time before e-commerce becomes a major mass force in carrying out business transactions in developing countries such as India. That is because the majority of the rural population in India does not even have electricity, gas or the telephone yet. Even if such people could make use of cyber café or Internet facilities provided by local authorities, most would not have an acceptable credit card in order to facilitate such commercial transactions anyway.

The marketing concept states that marketing is about identifying and satisfying customer needs and wants more efficiently and more effectively than the competition. If customers did not want to become e-commerce customers, the technology would have never have been adopted by so many people in the first place. Finally, the definition above points to the fact that e-commerce and the technologies that underpin it can and do relate to the total value chain,

Definition
E-commerce is a collective term to describe a variety of commercial transactions that make use of the technologies of electronic processing and data transmission.

including not only customers but also intermediaries, suppliers and other external agencies such as, for example, advertising and market research companies. In fact, the ability to link and co-ordinate all the members of the so called 'value chain' is one of the primary reasons for the growth of e-commerce. E-commerce is the extension of Internet technology to on-line marketing or on-line shopping, 24 hours a day, seven days a week, with the whole world as a marketplace. A theatre or restaurant can use e-commerce applications to book tickets on-line for a film, drama or concert, or to book a table. Schools, colleges and universities can use e-commerce applications for marketing and on-line admissions. Restaurants and hotels also use this application for home delivery of ordered menu. E-commerce can be used to sell on-line any products and services within towns, cities or states, nationally or globally. Amazon.com is utilising e-commerce facilities for selling books, cassettes and compact discs worth £ millions. It is possible to sell paintings and handicrafts on-line. Businesses can sell grocery, footwear, leather products, textiles, accessories, jewellery or any industrial products using e-commerce technologies.

Definition
E-commerce is the extension of Internet technology to on-line marketing or on-line shopping, 24 hours a day, seven days a week, with the whole world as a marketplace.

Vignette 18.3

Selling produce direct to the customer on-line may be the way forward for beleaguered British farmers

According to the National Farmers' Union in the UK, the nation's farmers have seen their incomes drop by 75 per cent on average over the last two years. The foot and mouth crisis of 2001 has added to their troubles. Just as many farmers were recovering from the BSE (mad cow disease) debacle and thinking things could not get any worse, they did. However, every cloud has a silver lining, as they say – at least for some. Customers are becoming increasingly worried about the problems in British farming, especially in terms of the methods used to raise livestock. Both BSE and the more recent foot and mouth outbreak has led many consumers to question the wisdom of intensive farming methods. Many consumers are prepared to pay more money for food they know has been produced in more traditional ways. After the foot and mouth crisis, the way that livestock farming is carried out in the UK is bound to alter. For many farmers the way forward may be to sell their produce direct to customers on-line and cut out the supermarkets altogether. There is evidence that this method of purchasing is growing in popularity with the public.

Many farmers have turned away from intensive agriculture and used the Internet to save their business. Many now sell high-quality speciality food, from meat to organically grown fruit and vegetables, direct to their customers on their website. All the food on offer has been produced naturally without the use of chemicals and drugs. For example, all the animals have been fed on natural feeds and are slaughtered at a local abattoir. The meat is carefully prepared by a qualified butcher and packed to keep it fresh and in good condition in transit. Customers have to purchase in reasonable quantities to make the operation cost effective, and the minimum acceptable order works out at about one-quarter of a lamb. Selling on-line cuts out the supermarkets and seems to be the way forward for British farming. The biggest UK portal for speciality food, featuring some 270 producers, is http://www.Fooduk.com.

E-commerce can facilitate small businesses to market their goods globally with minimum cost without travelling overseas; this is allowing small and medium-sized enterprises to market their products and services internationally without being disadvantaged by their size. E-commerce can save enormous expense, time and effort on marketing, accounting, financing and billing. There is no need to print catalogues or price lists. Leading publishers of newspapers, magazines and books are doing lucrative business on the Internet. Electronic commerce is serious business and is attracting money; out of total on-line business, retailing accounts only for approximately10–15 per cent, while the rest is made up of business-to-business commerce.

18.7.1 E-commerce challenges

The main challenge to the unlimited prospect of e-commerce is infrastructure and security. There is the threat of unauthorised access to confidential information stored on the Intranet and Extranet. Many potential e-commerce customers hold back from ordering over the Internet, not because they cannot use the technology or do not like what they see on the Web page, but because they have fears about security. This worry is usually particularly acute regarding giving credit card details over the Internet. Unless the problem of security can be solved, it is likely to inhibit the growth of e-marketing amongst the significant security-conscious segment of the market. The company's database system has to be protected from the outside world, while at the same time allowing legitimate users access to the data they require. Most data requires some kind of conversion for it to be read from another system. Incompatible data formats can be a stumbling block. Businesses want to provide easy access to information, but need to secure corporate networks. It is a known fact that hackers can surmount any barrier. There has to be adequate security against the potential hazards of opening business information to the world. Industrial espionage and the inappropriate use of private commercial data is a big problem. Computer fraud and computer crime is very big business. We can see even from the limited list of applications discussed above that the range of industries and markets now affected by e-commerce is diverse, and moreover the list is growing all the time. From its original business-to-business market usage, the effect of e-commerce and the technologies that underpin it are becoming more and more widespread. Clearly, e-commerce and new technology is having significant effects on marketing and markets.

18.7.2 The Intranet

An Intranet is an electronic system of internal communication throughout an organisation. Similar to the Internet but operating within an organisational system, the Intranet facilites rapid and effective internal systems of communication. The Intranet is similar to an internal management information system that is open to all approved users within the firm. The use of the Intranet is good for achieving internal marketing within an organisation. People feel they are included and that they matter. It helps to create the right internal culture, and makes people feel they are valued and part of the team.

Definition
An Intranet is an electronic system of internal communication throughout an organisation.

Intranets may, for example, allow employees to access information from other parts of the company, although obviously some of this may be restricted. This allows greater management of communication and can be used to advantage for relaying, say, information on important developments from outside an organisation, such as competitor actions etc. The Intranet may also be used to advantage for internal promotional material such as company newsletters.

The Intranet is a secure internal network that uses technologies developed for the Internet, World Wide Web and browsers to allow the sharing of information and knowledge among employees of a single company. It connects different departments within an organisation. It interconnects all departments across all branches within the country and around the world. Companies start publishing information on their homepage or websites, which are accessed by employees around the world. The same information is circulated all around the organisation, irrespective of location, distance, time or hierarchy. It increases transparency within an organisation, and confidence and morale among employees. It can empower employees, cut down hierarchies and change the fundamentals of business processes. Any employee can talk and communicate with any other employee irrespective of hierarchies. It cuts down the time and cost of finding and spreading information. It is no longer necessary to print and circulate copies of new information to employees; the information can be updated instead. It also reduces cost and facilitates training. Employees can learn on the job, what and when they need to learn, without leaving their work desks. The Intranet not only reduces cost and effort, but also stimulates co-ordination between various departments and branches of the organisation and, in time, communication. It results in more efficiency, more profits and faster growth.

Definition
The Intranet is a secure internal network that uses technologies developed for the Internet, World Wide Web and browsers to allow the sharing of information and knowledge among employees of a single company.

18.7.3 E-mail

Direct e-mailing can be an effective tool for marketing a firm's products, services and website. Firms have to persuade readers to read the messages, and then follow them up by contacting receivers again. E-mails should be interesting; it may be a good point always to offer receivers something such as a special offer or discount to make the message valuable and increase the likelihood that it will be read. Write what is necessary, or thank them for doing business with the company or for visiting the site. Readers can also be informed about interesting websites that the company has identified or articles that may interest them – anything that indicates that they have not been forgotten. The marketer may have a good list of customers and potential customers who have e-mail addresses, and this is the starting point. E-mail can be an effective tool to transmit the firm's marketing message as well as to handle routine communications with the firm's clients. Many of the larger firms have given selected clients access to the firm's e-mail system to speed up the flow of communication, and to foster contact and utilise electronic invoicing. Communications with clients can also be made through organisations such as CompuServe, Lexis Counsel Connect and America On Line. On-line services are also a good source of business information on prospective and existing clients. Where communications are confidential, documents can be encrypted to ensure that the wrong party does not read them.

18.7.4 Extranet

Many firms want to be able to communicate confidentially with a selected group of other firms and individuals that help them to achieve their business objectives and in a sense help them to run their business. As a group, these other organisations are often referred to in the marketing literature as the 'task environment'. The technology developed for the Internet has been developed further to form what has become known as the Extranet. The Internet has been used as a model to form variations on the basic application of the technology. This has taken the form of Intranets and Extranets, resulting in significant opportunities for increased efficiencies and profits within the value chain. The Extranet potential is limited only by the business strategies and methods used by firms to make use of it. Extranets are a natural evolution, taking advantage of the basic Internet infrastructure and previous Internet investments to focus communications to exchange information and share applications with business partners, suppliers and customers. The Extranet is similar to the Internet except that it links downstream and upstream business 'partners' such as agents, distributors, suppliers etc. – i.e. other firms in the task environment.

Key point
Extranet potential is limited only by the business strategies and methods used by firms to make use of it.

Examples of Extranet applications include:

- Providing a way of using high volumes of data using electronic data interchange (EDI)

- Sharing product catalogues and inventory levels exclusively with partners

- Collaborating with other companies on joint development efforts

- Sharing news of common interest exclusively with partner companies

- Making 'partner' organisations part of the team (i.e. relationship marketing)

- Providing project management tools for companies and collaborating third parties – everyone involved in the project can be kept informed as to what everyone else is doing

- Sharing ideas and information with select groups such as suppliers, agents and other intermediaries

- On-line training for re-sellers such as agents or dealers.

This list is not intended to be exhaustive, but merely indicates the kind of things this technology can be used for.

The Extranet has helped to facilitate the application of the concepts of relationship marketing and internal marketing within firms. The marketing firm may be depending on other independent firms to help it to achieve its own business success. These other independent organisations may be suppliers, logistics specialists, manufacturers making product components, subcontractors and others. The marketing firm wants all of these other 'business partners' to feel that they are valued and are an intrinsic part of the business team. These relationships are mutually beneficial relationships where the participants are engaged in a sort of win–win situation – that is, every member of the team is benefiting in some way by being part of the network. Not only does the Extranet bring the various business collaborators and partners together by allowing them to share information, but also the sharing of such information is often vital to the functioning of the business relationship. In project management situations, for example, it is absolutely paramount that each team member of the project is aware of what is going on elsewhere and of what other teams are doing. The fact that staff members from each of the organisations are able to share information and participate and contribute across ordinary organisational boundaries also makes them feel more important, valued and part of the team. Hence the Extranet contributes towards the achievement of internal team spirit, and the feeling of belonging to the network of organisations in the value chain – i.e. it facilitates an internal marketing outcome.

18.8 Principles of successful Internet marketing

The increasing growth of the Internet as a commercial medium is good news for business because it provides such enormous commercial opportunities. The Internet offers unique opportunities for companies and customers to communicate with each other via a mass medium on a new mediated environment. Business firms and customers are now in positions to build relationships with one another both effectively and cost-efficiently. They can learn on an individual basis how to satisfy needs and wants of their customers by using Internet technologies. At the same time the new medium also challenges business, because the Web and its relationship-marketing business model may conflict with more established marketing methods. A hypermedia computer-mediated environment (HCME), which is what the Internet and the World Wide Web actually is, is very different from the conventional marketing media and methods of carrying out the marketing task.

Key point
A hypermedia computer-mediated environment (HCME), which is what the Internet and the World Wide Web actually is, is very different from the conventional marketing media and methods of carrying out the marketing task.

Firms will need to redefine their businesses in terms of organisational structure, production, marketing, communications, sales, after sales services, and overall strategic planning processes. Successful web strategies can only be achieved by embracing the medium proactively and from a complete organisational point of view. It should be part of overall and comprehensive corporate strategies formulated by the top management. Internet marketing strategies should be integrated within the entire organisation, and it should not be viewed as simply an additional marketing and advertising channel. It has opened immense opportunities for business people to reach global sourcing. The Internet will be the most cost-effective business place. It is estimated that the value of shopping transactions completed on the Internet world-wide in the year 2001 will be US$ 1000 billion. It is projected that there will be over 250 million Internet users by 2005, and one billion users by 2010. There are also new Internet connection products now available, and one that can connect every home television to the Internet. It is not very difficult to sell products and services over the Internet. However, firms must consider seriously the following points when thinking about using the Internet to market their goods and/or services:

- What is the firm's site, and what is in it? Are the contents correct for the type of business being run? Is the amount and type of information on the site correct and suitable for the type of potential customer it is hoped to attract?

- How big is the company's Internet budget, and is the organisation fit for Web traffic? Is the firm taking the Internet venture seriously, and does it have all the necessary facilities in place to handle both the volume and type of Internet traffic expected? Are there support lines, and have product return strategies been worked out? Are there people who can answer enquiries both on-line and off-line?

- What purpose does the website have, and is the website justified? Is the firm clear as to what the objectives for the website are? Is it to provide information and educate? Is it merely a backup for other more 'mainline' marketing communications tools such as conventional media advertising?

  What value does your website add to your customers? Is it informative, interesting or valuable from an operational point of view? For example can your industrial customers re-order their industrial consumables from your website?

  What do your website customers know about the Internet? How often do they use the Internet? What do they want to know from your site and what Internet connection do they have?

  What goals and objectives do you set for your website and how are you going to measure, control, and act on these metrics? How are you going to track truncations and enquiries etc? What kind of analysis are you going to employ in the evaluation process?

18.8.1 How to persuade visitors to return to the site

It is important not only to attract visitors to the site once, but also to make them come back often. That is why it is necessary to keep web content up to date and change it regularly. It should be updated or 'refreshed' with information and articles. Visitors should be given reasons to come back – for example, regular articles, newsletters or even a story. It should be remembered that web content and web promotion is not a one-time affair but an ongoing process to market and build relationships. Your website should be a place of 'community atmosphere'. Internet web content should have definite project goals. Internet sites should not be launched due to internal excitement, but as a result of a website intention and corporate marketing plan.

Vignette 18.4

Universal Serial Bus (USB) will connect the world of gadgets without the need for a personal computer (PC)

A number of firms are developing USB technologies that will enable different electronic gadgets to be connected without the need for a PC to act as a 'middleman'. USBs can be found in most desktops and notebooks. This enables them to be used as hubs for connecting gadgets such as printers or cameras. At present such devices cannot connect with one another directly, but need the PC to act as a sort of middleman. The USB 'on-the-go' technology, as it has become known, will eliminate the need for a PC to act as facilitator and go-between.

At present we have a situation where the PC is the host machine and in effect devices connecting to the PC are 'subordinates'. With the new USB 'on-the-go' technology, other devices can act either as 'hosts' or as 'slaves'. Such devices will be able to interact with one another directly, and determine which device is to act as host according to the particular situation.

Such developments are obviously of great interest to marketing firms working within the computer applications and related industries. Experts expect that the new technology will be widely used by the manufacturers of products such as digital cameras and cell phones etc. Such gadgets are selling well, despite the recent down turn in the PC market itself.

18.9 Basic principles in website construction

Think of a website as being analogous to a television programme. It has to have some of the same qualities, creativity and interest, to be intriguing, beguiling and so forth. Web surfers have similar characteristics to television channel surfers, but the difference is that there are hundreds of millions of channels on the Internet, so an individual website has to stand out if it is to be noticed. There is so much material on the Internet that most of it just passes us by. Try a little exercise: what method does your most popular website currently use to capture the attention of web surfers? What stimulates your interest, while providing information about products or services? There are no definitive rules, although the following general principles should prove useful.

A firm's website must consider the following elements:

- How can the firm ensure that visitors will come back and visit again?

- How can it promote word-of-mouth communication?

- How does the website communicate with potential customers?

- Does the firm use traditional marketing methods on the Internet?

- How does the company use Internet-based technologies to increase sales?

- How can the firm attract people to its website?

- How can the customers' interest be retained long enough to sell the company's products or services?

Key point
A commercial website has a single objective: to stimulate its visitors into taking some form of desired action, such as placing an order.

A commercial website has a single objective: to stimulate its visitors into taking some form of desired action, such as placing an order. This key motive is behind every element of a commercial website design and content. Firms should start with the idea that they have one chance to reach their customers. Customers will never return to a site unless the marketing firm makes it worth their while, and they will not buy unless they are encouraged to do so.

18.10 Improving web sales

A business website may get a lot of visits or 'hits', but are these visitors buying anything? Attracting visitors to a site is half the battle, but visitors do not always mean sales; on the contrary, the majority of people visiting a site will buy nothing. Many of these will simply be having a look around or 'surfing' the Web. Also, attracting attention in today's loud, crowded business culture is difficult. No business should bother attracting lots of visitors to its site if it does not know what to do with them once they are there. Instead, it needs to turn all those Web surfers into dedicated Web buyers if the site is to be commercially viable. The following points are important.

18.10.1 Provide the possibility for communicating with people

Look around any particular website. Can you tell that it involves human beings in any way? Could it just as easily be a front-end for a database or search engine? Many e-commerce sites are unwelcoming, and need to do substantially more to make visitors 'feel at home' and welcome them to the site. That is no surprise: their focus is on the sale, not the customer. However, the key thing to remember is that the Web is a communication tool directed at human beings. Marketing firms have to give customers what they want, and this means a user-friendly and attractive website, which reassures them and allows them to contact people from the marketing firm if necessary. The key is to create opportunities for visitors to interact with actual human beings – or at least to get the sense that there is someone behind all those bits and bytes. A free telephone number that lets customers talk to an actual person is an invaluable addition to any website. An Internet marketing company would rather have customers telephone in their orders or call for help than have them leave the website with nothing. Even listing the address of the company's physical location will reassure customers. Consider offering live, instant customer service through the Internet, using a chat-like interface. Several companies are now offering this service at very little cost, or even for free. It adds a valuable human dimension to a medium that can sometimes appear cold and unfriendly.

Key point
Marketing firms have to give customers what they want, and this means a user-friendly and attractive website, which reassures them and allows them to contact people from the marketing firm if necessary.

18.10.2 Instil confidence in visitors

Many potential website customers are worried about carrying out transactions on the Internet for security and other reasons. We have all read horrendous newspapers stories about unethical marketing companies operating on the Web and 'fleecing' the general public. People want reassurance. Customers want to know that a site is legitimate, and that they can trust the people behind it. They also want to know who they can contact if something goes wrong. A firm will never get business if they cannot instil confidence in their customers. One idea that many successful Internet-based firms use is to include a 'Comments from our customers' page to show newcomers that others like to buy at the site. Some sites also have 'chat' facilities where customers can discuss products and related issues. Others, like Amazon.com and

Napster.com, allow visitors to post their own product reviews. If the firm's site feels like a comfortable place to visit, customers will return and will be more likely to purchase and tell other people about the site and their experience. It is useful to join a trade association, professional organisation or industry group, and abide by the rules they set. For example, franchisees can display the logo of the British Franchise Association, which tells the user of the site that the company is ethical and abides by a code of practice. The Direct Marketing Association has a similar scheme that its members can use to instil confidence in their business practices in the minds of potential customers. When the logos of such nationally or internationally recognised bodies are displayed, customers know that the firm has put its name and reputation on the line, and will not be suddenly going out of business or, worse, running off with their money. If customers distrust the privacy of a transaction, they probably will not start one.

Another important point is that e-marketing firms should create and prominently display a returns policy. If customers buy a product from a conventional retail store, they can usually take the product back and have it replaced if it turns out to be faulty. Many potential Internet customers are worried that they may not be able to do this if they purchase from a website. A clear returns policy will give customers the information needed to make informed purchasing decisions, and save the company a lot of time and effort when items are returned. Customers often leave sites because they are too slow or difficult to navigate. It may be easy to keep much of the business a company may be losing simply by making the shopping experience more convenient for users. We have all been on websites that take far too long to load, and when we eventually get on to them things do not work or it is difficult to get the information we want. People who have had that experience learn by it, and the next time they come across a slow-loading or difficult website they immediately exit.

Key point
Customers often leave sites because they are too slow or difficult to navigate.

18.10.3 Include a search option and a frequently asked questions list

Firms should provide e-mail links for users to ask questions, and should provide answers effectively and efficiently. Many sites accept only MasterCard and Visa credit cards, for example. Some users may find this inconvenient, so the firm should consider offering other payment options, such as American Express, Discover, on-line cheques, money orders, and cash-on-delivery (as companies like Gateway Computers do).

Finally, firms should try to identify the reasons customers abandon transactions on their sites. This may be a relatively simple question to answer (for example, a company may be receiving a lot of e-mail about the returns policy or some other aspect of business customers are not happy with), or it may be incredibly difficult. There are Internet consultants who will track the behaviour of customers and get an idea of when and why they are backing out of transactions. These services can be expensive, but are worth it if a company is ready to commit seriously to an e-commerce site. Alternatively, a company can carry out the tracking and analysis of customers exit behaviour in-house if it has staff with the right expertise and the time to do it.

Vignette 18.5

Southern Europe is falling behind the rest of the continent in adoption of Internet technology

Interesting research reported by Forrester Research on the Web page http://uk.internet.com shows that on-line sales in Southern European countries significantly lag behind those in Northern Europe. There are basically two reasons for this: the first is that the South has fewer people connected to the Internet, and hence there are fewer on-line customers; secondly, provision of on-line retail provision is very limited.

The research indicated that Southern Europeans have fewer places to shop on-line in their own language, and get to see fewer advertisements, promotions and media pieces about on-line shopping as a result. The area has a plethora of small retailers serving the population. These retailers do not necessarily have the skills and resources to start up an on-line service for their customers. The gap left by local retailers is likely to be filled by other retail firms using their portals to look for new business in the area. Portals will open up awareness of on-line shopping and encourage other retail 'invaders' into the area from elsewhere. The threat of losing significant amounts of business will eventually force local firms to get on-line and catch up to protect their market share. Whatever happens, it looks as if Southern Europe will stay in the on-line 'laggards' category for some time to come.

18.11 How to improve profits with current customers

A firm's existing customers are the most valuable and important assets the company has. In a sense they are the business; without customers there is no business. Many entrepreneurs feel that they should be out attracting new customers all the time, and they often do this at the expense of their existing customers. In a real sense, many firms are 'busy fools' running around trying to acquire new customers whilst all the time losing existing customers, and so they make no progress. This process is analogous to trying to fill a tub with water while the plug is out. As soon as new water is put in, the old water is forced out of the plughole (Figure 18.7).

Recently, businesses have started to calculate what they spend to get each new customer. Existing customers are more profitable and cost less to retain than it costs to attract new customers. This illustrates one of the biggest problems businesses have. Generally, when firms think of building bigger profits, they think about getting more customers. However, for bigger, quicker profits they should also market to the customers they already have. It would be good if marketing impacted on the new potential consumer and instantly persuaded him or her to buy from a firm's website, but the process is almost always more complicated. Focusing entirely on new customers can seriously deplete a company's marketing budget with little in the way of sales to show for it, and this is explained in the next section.

Existing customers

Figure 18.7 As soon as the new water (customers) goes into the tub (business), the old water (customers) is lost.

18.11.1 Steps to a successful sale

Before anyone buys from a firm's website, they have to step through at least four stages:

1 The website must get their attention (the hardest stage of all, since people are bombarded with hundreds of marketing messages every day and are very selective in what they choose to look at).

2 The prospect must be persuaded to think about the company's offer; it has to be interesting to the prospect and give some value. There has to be some unique selling proposition (USP) which is intriguing to the prospect and at least makes him or her consider the possibility of placing an order.

3 The prospect must *decide* to buy; this is one of the key stages. The material on the website must be sufficiently enticing to make the prospect decide to buy. Security and other commercial safety issues will come into play in the prospect's decision-making process here. These must be addressed for the purchase to go ahead.

4 The prospect must take *action* to buy. This is the most important stage; if the prospect does not actually place an order, then everything else has been for nothing. Even in e-marketing, there must be a way of actually 'closing' the sale with a prospect. The fundamentals are no different from traditional personal selling in this respect.

Even after customers buy, they may not come back to buy again. Studies show that many people cannot accurately remember where they bought things several weeks after the purchase. Meanwhile, current and past customers are the easiest to sell to again. All this clearly leads to the need for firms to stay in touch with the customers they already have. A lot of Internet business is based on repeat business and customer retention. For example, once someone has purchased a book on-line from Amazon.com, that same person usually purchases a book again some time in the future. Also included in this group are 'hot' prospects that have shown an interest in the business in the past. These are the most targeted and willing audiences to be found.

18.11.2 Construct a prospect list

E-marketing firms should construct lists of people who have bought from the firm in the last week, during the past month, over the past six months, and within the past year. The idea is to develop different lists so that management can send just the right offer to interest and motivate them. If it is clear that a big group buys one product or service while another group goes for a different offer, the customers can be divided up along these lines. The response rate can be doubled, tripled and quadrupled by making advertising 'zero in' on just what a customer or prospect is truly interested in buying. This is where database marketing comes into its own. A well-constructed database will allow the marketing firm to analyse the data and prioritise customers in terms of their probability to purchase, and allow effective segmentation of the firm's customer base. Any database program can be used to keep these lists organised. Most word processing programs include a basic database feature, or a more specialised program like Microsoft Access can be used.

Key point
A well-constructed database will allow the marketing firm to analyse the data and prioritise customers in terms of their probability to purchase, and allow effective segmentation of the firm's customer base.

18.11.3 Actively 'work' the prospect list

The main reason for working the in-house list of customers and 'hot' prospects is to keep the company's business in people's minds. If this is not done, customers will forget you and turn elsewhere. Today people have many choices regarding what to spend their money on, even when buying specialised products and services. If the company is based in a city of any size, there will be anywhere from a few to dozens of businesses marketing more or less the same things. There may be thousands more firms on the Internet that can take customers' credit card orders and deliver the product within a few days. If a company does not work to stay in the minds of its customers, others will. But how can the list be worked without incurring too much expense? Many e-marketing firms have found their best low-cost marketing tools for working an in-house list are postcards and e-mail. Postcards are cheaper than letters to send, and do not require the customer to open an envelope. Many people throw away enveloped direct mail without even opening it. A number of firms put a colour photograph or graphic on one side of the postcard; this adds interest and brings the communication to the customers' and prospects' attention. The other side should have the main offer in a bold, black headline, again so it can be noticed and make an impact. It should be followed with a deadline for the offer. Busy people may put off buying and soon forget about the firm's offer. The postcard offer will never be more powerful than it is right at the moment when the customer has it in his or her hands. Many firms use these simply techniques, and in principle they seem to work well and get results. Finally, the information on the card should briefly tell people how to buy from the firm, and make the process as simple as possible. It should include the firm's website, telephone number, store location if appropriate, and e-mail address. Building an e-mail list is even easier and almost free. Unlike a postcard, e-mail messages can contain just as much information as the company want to provide. Prospects' addresses must be collected – forms can be put on the website to gather e-mail addresses from prospects wanting to be sent information. A printed form can also be placed in the marketer's office or store, if he or she has one, so that customers can request to get on a list. The form that customers fill out should be kept in case there is ever a question. Some specialist Internet management firms offer a list management service for a fee.

18.11.4 Increasing the number of quality visitors to a website

1 Track the number of visits received to each page of the website at least once a month, including repeat visits. This is one way to track the effectiveness of advertising campaigns and establish what works the best. If the company has an e-commerce site, then the money generated by the site should be tracked at least once monthly. Once it is clear what works (in terms of site marketing) in a particular industry, more of it can be done. If something does not work, this is also valuable information and allows the marketer to learn from his or her mistakes.

2 Market very specifically to a target audience in order to get 'high quality' visits to the site. These are the customers that are most interested in the company's product or service, and are most likely to buy. Segmentation and targeting are of paramount importance here, and allow the company to prioritise and concentrate on marketing to those prospects that represent the highest probability of success.

3 Establish where (on the web and otherwise) the people who want the company's products like to go, and actively communicate there using Internet and non-Internet communications such as conventional direct mail, posters and advertising.

4 Register the site with as many search engines and link exchange services as possible, and re-register monthly. The site can be listed with well over 2000 search engines monthly. Specialist management companies can provide this service.

5 Exchange links with everyone who can be identified as having the same target audience. This can be a great source of 'high quality' and profitable visits. For example, if the company is targeting academics, have 'hotlinks' on other sites which may also be of interest to academics.

6 Know the purpose of the company's site. Is it to sell your product? To have people place orders? To gather data about the site's visitors? To sell advertiser's products so more ads can be placed on the company's site? To

get people to call for more information? The Web designer must understands what the company's business is about, and must effectively communicate this.

7 It is very important that prospects know who the company is and where to find it. The company's URL (site address) should be on every piece of paper that leaves it. A clear label can be added to current stationery and cards until it is reprinted; this is a cost effective way of getting the Internet details in front of prospects without wasting resources.

8 Make sure the site is a quality one. There is nothing worse than visiting a poor website that does not work properly, or one that is poorly constructed and designed. A bad site is worse than no site, as having someone come to the site and leave completely frustrated can be devastating to the achievement of the site's purpose. The site should be easy to use, attractive, and informative.

9 Include the company's URL in every print advertisement or other form of advertising media used. Print advertising can be quite effective in getting more profitable visits. People may see the website address on posters, newspaper advertising, direct mail shots, van livery and all sorts of other communications. They will then be able to visit the site and explore what is on offer.

10 Make sure the graphics communicate what the business is. The type of business and what is on offer to customers must be clearly communicated and to the point. Graphics should be chosen with a specific purpose, according to the company's overall colour scheme and page layout structures. The brand image(s) portrayed via your site should always be clear.

Vignette 18.6

DisneyWorld™ launches a multi-lingual website

In an effort to reach more international theme park customers, Walt Disney Company's Parks and Resorts On-Line Division has decided to launch multi-lingual versions of their existing DisneyWorld.com websites. Each individual language-specific site has been developed to help users plan every aspect of the Disney experience holiday perfectly. Information is available on the theme parks themselves, other resorts such as 'Down Town Disney', shopping, entertainment, dining, car hire and other aspects of holiday recreation.

Prior to these new sites, the Theme Park Division had only provided one website in English and one in Japanese. This was fine as far as it went, but many other potential customers were not getting the kind of service they wanted and indeed expected from a multinational firm such as Disney. With the number of international guests to Disney's attractions increasing, the company has worked hard to be able to provide these people with the information they need to make important decisions and in the language they feel most comfortable with – their own language.

18.12 Website management

Web design is more than just coding web pages. It is also the navigation that allows users to find what they need, the file structure that supports organised maintenance, and the planning that allows the site to fulfil its objective successfully. It has an ergonomic aspect to it in that users have to feel comfortable with it and must feel that they are competent to navigate themselves around the site and on to other related sites. There are millions of Web pages on the Internet, but many of them are unimaginative and even boring. Some do not work properly, or do not supply the user with the type of information they say they are going to, and hence waste people's time. Only a small fraction of websites account for the majority of Web visits, and even less account for the majority of Web sales. Human beings are bombarded with commercial information in all aspects of their lives virtually every day. To be able to cope with this enormous amount of information people have to be very selective. This is also true when people are on the Internet visiting websites. For a site to be successful, it has to have certain qualities. It has to work, for a start, and has to deliver the type of information the user is expecting in a way that makes navigating the site easy and enjoyable. The following are the main stages used by a firm of consultants for the design process for a commercial website:

1 At the initial consultation, the general needs of the client are determined, the purpose of the site is sketched out, and the pricing and payment terms are set.

2 The server is prepared, and any necessary domain registrations are performed.

3 The site's design proposal is prepared and presented to the client. This document outlines the file and directory structure, and provides an organised overview of the various components that will make up the site.

4 All necessary materials and data are gathered. Images are scanned, text assembled and copied, and the client's background information collected. This is a critical phase, as site design is largely on hold until it is completed.

5 The site design is initiated. Lead time is usually set at approximately two weeks, although this can vary by project.

6 The finished site is posted for final inspection, and necessary alterations are performed.

7 The site goes public, and marketing takes over.

An important consideration in the analysis of the World Wide Web as a marketing medium is that it possesses unique qualities that other marketing environments do not have. The World Wide Web is a virtual hypermedia environment, which incorporates interactivity with both people and computers. The Web does not really try to simulate a real world shopping experience, although some of the characteristics that customers would expect to see in a normal shopping expedition are built into the Web experience to make users feel familiar with the environment and comfortable with using the technology. What the Web provides is a virtual experience, and the experience of being in a mediated environment rather than a true 'real world' environment. Within this virtual environment, both experiential behaviour (such as 'surfing' the Web) and goal-directed behaviours (such as on-line shopping) compete for the user's attention (see Hoffman and Novak, 1995). The user of this virtual marketing environment must develop certain competencies and capabilities. Users are challenged by using the Web, and the concept of competency and 'flow' as the user goes from site to site or action to action on a single site is very important and needs to be factored into all Web design and operational considerations.

18.13 Summary

✓ The world of sales and marketing is changing all the time. The Internet, e-commerce, the continuing rise of direct marketing and the increasing marketing emphasis on customer retention over customer acquisition are only a few of the salient factors affecting the way firms carry out business in the modern world. Firms have to move very fast, keep up with the latest developments and trends, and invest in the most relevant software and systems to stay ahead of the competition. Business in general, and certainly marketing in particular, has become more and more affected by and dependent upon technology. Furthermore, technological progress itself is altering and accelerating. Technology seems to be developing at an ever-increasing exponential rate. The marketer must also be aware of and prepared for future advances in technology. Not since the Industrial Revolution has the marketing firm been affected so much, right to the very core of its business, by changes in the technological environment. Those firms that are not fully aware of technological advances and developments will fall behind in the commercial race, and will probably cease trading. There is a significant change in the technological environment of marketing firms; this is not a minor technological change, but a huge 'step' change in the way marketing firms do business. Marketing is all about staying ahead of the competition. This in turn means that the marketer must also have the required skills to use the new technologies of today and tomorrow to help assist the marketing process. Similarly, those organisations whose management and marketers are unaware of or unable to use advances in technology will become increasingly uncompetitive. The marketing manager of the future will need an understanding of the use of technology within the discipline. He or she may not need to be a technical expert – after all, these are available as staff – but must be able to appreciate how new technology can be factored into all aspects of their marketing plans and operations. Some writers see the Web as the innovation that will totally transform the whole marketing concept. Many argue that for firms' marketing activities to be successful using the new technology, a totally new model of marketing is required for the Web-based society in which these firms will be doing

Definition
Marketing is all about staying ahead of the competition.

business. In the USA, more than two-thirds of firms are setting up computer-based systems such as Intranet and/or Extranet facilities. As in many other technological innovations, the USA seems to be leading the way and acting as a driving force for the diffusion of the new technology and the new marketing methods that go with it.

✓ The so-called E-commerce revolution, of which the World Wide Web is at the very epicentre, has been hailed as one of the most important developments ever to occur in the world of business. These developments will affect every area of firms' business operations, but especially marketing. Some experts are calling the new developments in marketing a 'paradigm shift'. This means that the new technology is not simply resulting in marketing firms doing basically the same thing but with more up-to-date technology; it means that we have to change the whole way we think about doing marketing, and need a new model or 'paradigm'.

Questions

1 Using specific examples to illustrate the points made, distinguish between the Intranet and the Extranet and explain the use of these two systems within a marketing context.

2 Explain what is meant by the term 'hypermedia computer-mediated environment', and discuss how this environment differs from more conventional marketing communications media.

3 How can e-marketing companies reduce the perceived risk inherent in a website transaction for a new potential customer?

4 Explain the basic principles of database marketing and data fusion techniques.

5 Explain how the Internet can help smaller firms to enter the international arena and serve customers in international markets.

References

Agostinelli, C. (1978). Some aspects of the life and work of Carl Friedrich Gauss and that of other illustrious members of the Academy (in Italian). *Atti Accad. Sci. Torino Cl. Sci. Fis. Mat. Natur.*, **112**, Suppl., 69–88.

Anderson, B. and Moore, J. (1979). *Optimal Filtering*. Prentice Hall.

Benham, W. (1974). The Gauss anagram: an alternative solution. *Annals of Science*, **31**, 449–55.

Bos, H. J. M. (1976). Carl Friedrich Gauss: a biographical note (in Dutch). *Nieuw Tijdschr. Wisk.*, **64**, 234–40.

Bornman, H. and von Solms, S. H. (1993). Hypermedia, multimedia and hypertext – definitions and overview. *Electronic Library*, **11(4–5)**, 259–68.

Hoffman, D. L. and Novak, T. P. (1994). Commercialising the information superhighway: are we in for a smooth ride? *The Owen Manager*, **15(2)**, 2–7.

Hoffman, D. L. and Novak, T. P. (1995). Marketing in hypermedia computer-mediated environments: conceptual foundations. *Project 2000 Working Paper No. 1*. Owen Graduate School of Management, Vanderbilt University.

Katz, E. and Lazarsfeld, P. F. (1955). *Personal Influence*. Free Press.

Kotler, P. (1994). *Marketing Management: Analysis, Planning, Implementation and Control*, 8th edn. Prentice Hall.

Lasswell, H. D. (1948). The structure and function of communication in society. In: *The Communication of Ideas* (Bryson, D. ed.), pp. 119–147. Harper and Brothers.

Sorenson, H. (1985). *Kalman Filtering: Theory and Application*. IEEE Press.

Steuer, J. (1992). Defining virtual reality: dimensions determining telepresence. *Journal of Communication*, **42(4)**, 73–93.

Wald, L. (1998). A European proposal for terms of reference in data fusion. *International Archives of Photogrammetry and Remote Sensing*, **XXXII** (Part 7), 651–4.

Further reading

Armstrong, G. and Kotler, P. (2000). Direct and on-line marketing. *Marketing: An Introduction*, 5th edn, Chapter 14. Prentice Hall.

Blattenberg, R. C., Glazer, R. and Little, J. D. C. eds (1994). *The Marketing Information Revolution*. Harvard University Business School Press.

Hafner, K. and Lyon, M. (1996). *When Wizards Stay Up Late: The Origins of the Internet*. Simon & Shuster.

Hardaker, G. and Graham, G. (2001). *Wired Marketing: Energising Business for E-Commerce*. John Wiley and Sons.

Keegan, W. J. and Green, M. S. (2000). Global marketing communications decision II. *Global Marketing*, 2nd edn, Chapter 15. Prentice Hall.

Plamer, A. (2000). Direct marketing. *Principles of Marketing*, Chapter 20. Oxford University Press.

Customer care and customer relationship management 19

19.1 Introduction

The whole area of customer care and customer relationship management (CRM) has evolved and developed substantially over the last 20 years. This is the focus of the last chapter of this book; however, the topic is also related to the subjects covered in Chapter 18 because so much of modern customer care and customer relationship management systems is Internet-based. The subject of totally integrated customer relationship management has itself evolved out of the earlier but related topic of relationship marketing. As with the subject of e-commerce, some commentators feel that CRM is just the latest management search for the perfect business philosophy – in a sense the latest management 'fad'. Others see CRM as a significant change in the philosophy of business, one that incorporates and consolidates many of the earlier areas of new management thinking such as total quality management, internal marketing and relationship marketing. It is to the topic of relationship marketing that we will turn to first in this closing chapter. This will be followed by a brief treatment of the parallel subject of what has become known as 'internal marketing'. As we shall see, the two subjects are interrelated. Firms need to market the very concept of marketing to their own staff and others – the so-called 'internal customers'. Firms need to create the right spirit and internal culture before they can hope for success in their long-term external relationship marketing policies. The internal aspect of marketing is a little different from the external aspect. It has been shown that employees behave towards customers in very much the same way as the management behaves toward them. If employees are treated badly, they are more likely to treat customers badly; if they are treated well they are more likely to treat the firm's customers well. We will then go on to examine the nature and importance of customer care to the marketing environment of the new millennium. After all, both internal marketing and relationship marketing aim to provide a better internal and external business framework to enable the better care of customers. Finally we will look at the development and principles of complete customer relationship management (CRM) systems and examine some of the computer software applications in this area.

Key point
If employees are treated badly, they are more likely to treat customers badly; if they are treated well they are more likely to treat the firm's customers well.

414

19.2 The changing face of marketing

Like many things in this life, the world of marketing is full of uncertainties and dynamic change. Even over the last 10 years or so, the world of marketing has changed substantially. Many people who trained in marketing in the 1970s or 1980s find that their knowledge is out of date and the subject has changed considerably since that time. As discussed in the last chapter, a lot of this change has to do with the adoption of new computer-based technology such as the Internet, Extranet, Intranet, database marketing, data warehousing and the World Wide Web. Today, marketing management must at least have some appreciation of the commercial possibilities of these new marketing technologies. As stated in Chapter 18, managers do not necessarily have to be technical experts themselves because specialist technical staff can be employed for this side of the work. They do, however, need to be able to see the strategic implications and possibilities of the new technologies, and be able to advise others how the technology can be employed to gain a strategic advantage over the competition and to improve marketing performance.

Not all of the dramatic changes in marketing thinking over this period have been due to technological advances and change. Quite the contrary, in fact; many of the changes have been more philosophical in nature. The application of the new Internet-based marketing technologies may have facilitated some of these changes. Up until recently, for example, the concept of totally integrated customer relationship management systems remained just that in many firms – an idealised concept that was fine in the text books and academic papers, but extremely difficult to put into practice in the day-to-day business world. The development of sophisticated computer software products and the increase in the memory available to systems to enable them to store, manipulate and retrieve large amounts of customer data has made the 'idealised' concept a reality for at least the more progressive business firms.

The very nature and even the direction of modern marketing have altered. The basic definition of marketing as a business process concerned with satisfying customers needs and wants more effectively and efficiently than the competition remains the same. The basic marketing concept is as valid today as it has always been. However, the processes used to accomplish this have changed. On comparing a standard marketing textbook from the 1970s or even the 1980s with one from today, it is clear that there are a number of topics in the more recent version that were not even mentioned in the earlier ones. Topics such as internal marketing, relationship marketing, e-marketing, green marketing and customer relationship management (CRM) are all fairly recent additions to the marketing literature. In particular, there has been what can only be described as a complete paradigm shift in the way the management of marketing firms views its customers, looks after them, nurtures them and establishes relationships with them over the long term. Basically, the focus of marketing has shifted from the shorter-term view of customers as the next 'transaction' to seeing customers as a long-term income stream over many years – a so-called 'relationship marketing' approach.

Industrial companies have practised this relationship building and management approach for some years in their business-to-business marketing, but it

Key point
The basic definition of marketing as a business process concerned with satisfying customers needs and wants more effectively and efficiently than the competition remains the same.

is a fairly new concept in business-to-consumer marketing. Of course, the relationship marketing approach may not be appropriate in all situations.

19.3 Relationship marketing

Definition
Relationship marketing is a business concept that has developed from a growing body of literature expressing lack of satisfaction with conventional 'transactional' marketing.

Relationship marketing is a business concept that has developed from a growing body of literature expressing lack of satisfaction with conventional 'transactional' marketing. This dissatisfaction applies to all areas of marketing, but especially business-to-business and services marketing, where the shortcomings of the more conventional marketing approach were first recognised. In 1954, Peter Drucker said: 'There is only one valid definition of business: to create customers. It is the customer who determines what the business is' (Drucker, 1973). Hence customers are central to business, and the underlying theme behind relationship marketing is the acquisition, satisfaction and retention of customers. In a sense it is the marketing concept in principle, but developed into a format in which it can be applied in an operational setting rather than merely being a concept.

The concept of relationship marketing was introduced into the literature by early researchers into customer care, such as Berry (1983). The subject of marketing had been developed largely from the experience of firms and university business school researchers involved in consumer markets and based in the USA. Marketing as a subject and business discipline was developed in the USA. These principles and theories seemed to have almost universal applicability in the consumer markets of developed economies throughout the world and especially in Europe where the concept arrived from the USA and was applied by firms as an overriding business philosophy much later. Some adaptation was of course necessary because of cultural and environmental difference in different markets, and this was covered in the international marketing literature. However, the principles and practices of modern marketing developed in the crucible of the USA consumer market sector did not work quite so well in business-to-business environments or for the increasingly important service sector. As the 'first world' western economies reconstructed and developed after the war, agriculture and manufacturing became less important and provided a smaller proportion of these countries' GDP. Such countries are often described by economic commentators as being in the post-industrial phase of development. In a post-industrial economy, a lot of the jobs are of an intellectual or at least 'brain-based' type. Services become the predominant economic activity carried out by human beings. Marketers looked to the conventional wisdom in the marketing literature, and found that it no longer fitted so well in the new 'service-based' economies and some new thinking was required. In the growing business-to-business sector of the economy, too, there developed a deep dissatisfaction with the conventional 'one sale ahead' transactional marketing approach. It had been recognised in industrial markets for some time that commercial relationships between buyer and seller organisations required a more long-term 'interaction approach' rather than the short-termism of the next sale. This new thinking resulted in the development of the relationship marketing model. This has now been accepted by firms 'across the board', so to speak, and not only by firms involved in the marketing of services or involved in industrial markets.

Vignette 19.1

First Union Corporation of the USA uses MicroStrategy to create long-term relationships with its 16 million customers

The financial services sector has witnessed increased competition in recent years. It is even more important for firms in the industry to be able to retain their customers and grow further by both leveraging more business from their existing customer base and from acquisition. The majority of firms in the industry employ a relationship marketing strategy, as building and maintaining profitable relationships with customers is the key factor in commercial success. An interesting case concerning the First Union Corporation is discussed in the journal *Data Warehousing*.

The First Union Corporation, the USA financial services provider with $230 billion in assets, has a long-term strategic objective of continual growth. The organisation has developed a Web-based customer relationship management application that it hopes will give the firm a competitive advantage in developing and maintaining vital relationships with customers. The firm has used MicroStrategy DSS Suite, a leading business intelligence platform that enables First Union to interface with its data warehouse of customer information. First Union uses a network of sales and service organisations to carry out its business. Authorised members of the network 'team' can access the firm's customer database directly. The resulting sales leads are then actioned by the sales and service organisations by direct, personalised marketing programmes.

The system has been called SIGMA. It facilitates a number of business activities by authorised users, including identifying 'cross-selling' opportunities with specific customers by profiling the bank's 16 million customers and cross-tabulating demand for products and services. It also assists management in the forecasting of sales for different products and services, and allows for the planning of the efficient allocation of the firm's resources. In addition to stronger customer relationships, SIGMA is also resulting in more efficient marketing programmes. By using SIGMA to identify those customers most likely to be interested in certain products and services, the firm can then follow up identified leads with targeted and personalised marketing programmes. This projects the company as a pro-active firm with customers' financial interests at heart.

Writing on relationship marketing, Gronroos (1990) proposed a marketing strategy continuum ranging from 'transaction marketing', which was regarded as more appropriate to business-to-consumer marketing (particularly in the field of fast-moving consumer goods), through to relationship marketing. This approach was seen as more suitable for business-to-business marketing and services marketing. However, relationship marketing is now used in all markets, including consumer markets. Copulsky and Wolf (1990) used the term 'relationship marketing' to identify a type of database marketing. In their model, the database is used by marketing firms to select suitable customer targets for the promotion of products and services. The message sent to customers is tailor made to fit in with their particular needs and wants. The response is monitored and used to produce various measures, including the projected lifetime value of the customer. McKenna (1991) linked relationship marketing to the organisational structure of a business. The whole business was organised to produce a relationship marketing approach rather than it being merely a business process. To summarise at this stage, the major concern amongst practitioners with the conventional marketing approach was that it was too short term and transactional in focus. This may have worked well over the years in a predominantly business-to-consumer environment, but less so for service marketing, industrial and other forms of business-to-business marketing, where the creation and maintenance of long-term relationships with customers was crucial for long-term commercial success. The modern usage of the term 'relationship marketing' describes a situation where the creation, satisfaction and retention of customers are at the very centre of marketing strategy.

19.3.1 TQM as the starting point

In the 1970s, W. Edwards Deming, the well known expert on quality issues, formulated a now seminal theory of quality based upon his intimate knowledge of Japanese manufacturing. This concerned 14 key quality points, and revolutionised many aspects of production management. His ideas on quality have been termed 'total quality management' (TQM). However, this TQM philosophy now permeates thinking throughout entire organisations that adopt his philosophy. Total quality management is a structured system for satisfying internal and external customers and suppliers by integrating the business environment. One of the keys to implementing TQM can be found in this definition. It is the idea that TQM is a structured system. In describing TQM as a structured system, it is meant that it is a strategy derived from internal and external customer and supplier wants and needs that have been determined by management. Pinpointing internal and external requirements allows management continuously to improve, develop and maintain quality, cost, delivery and morale. TQM is a system that integrates all of this activity and information.

19.3.2 Reverse marketing

Since the 1980s, many firms have recognised that the way forward for business success is to change from an emphasis on cost and price as key marketing elements to one of providing superior service through personal interaction and the formation of long-term relationships. Hence, as discussed above, there has thus been a change from a transactional focus in marketing towards a long-term relationship approach. The traditional role of the salesperson was seen as one of initiating commercial transactions by visiting buyers with the objective of securing orders or being considered for the next tendering round. However, with the development of what is now

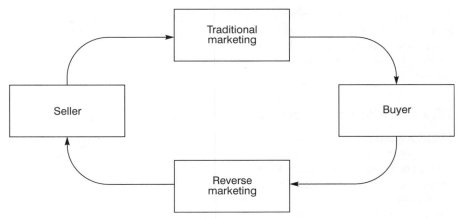

Figure 19.1 The notion of reverse marketing.

termed 'lean' manufacturing (formerly 'just in time' manufacturing, or JIT), where deliveries are very tightly scheduled and quality must presuppose zero defects, there has been a move in this commercial emphasis and it is now common for buyers actively to source their suppliers with a view to the establishment of long-term 'co-makership' partnerships. This is the idea of reverse marketing, and is illustrated in Figure 19.1.

The implication for sellers is that they must build on these partnerships in the knowledge that sales will continue so long as they supply goods of the right quality, at the right time and at an agreed price. The term used for the techniques involved in this process is 'relationship marketing'. This has also led to the modern notion of customer care, which involves a plethora of methods to ensure that such customers are permanently satisfied in terms of meeting and exceeding their expectations. TQM that is driven from the marketplace and total manufacturing quality (zero defects) are the realities of such partnership agreements. The tactics of relationship marketing mean that companies should sense changes in the marketplace, which is where the quality chain is based.

In a properly operating lean manufacturing system, demands from customers are met and operating costs are reduced through a reduction in inventories of raw materials and component parts. Holding stock is an unproductive resource that has to be financed, so lean manufacturing through its practice of reducing stocks to an absolute minimum is an efficient means of making cost savings. In such systems, relationships must be formed between customers and their suppliers. This normally means a reduction in the number of suppliers and long-term relationships being developed with a key small group of suppliers – sometimes only one. The role of the salesperson also alters from that of a 'transactional salesperson' to one of a 'relationship salesperson', who devotes more time to acting in a troubleshooting capacity, keeping the flow of supplies secure and ensuring consistent quality and acting more in a liaison capacity. The concept of relationship marketing means that marketing endeavours should be based on many customer contacts over time, rather than concentrating on singular transactions. It also involves the idea of what is called 'team selling', where non-marketing people like accountants and production personnel all form part of this relationship team which actively meets and associates with these major customers in terms of nurturing the relationship and ensuring that the partnership (termed 'partnership sourcing) works.

19.3.3 The practical effects of relationship marketing

There is a tendency for many companies to bring marketing and new product development together at earlier stages in the development process. Project teams are set up, which include people from a number of departments led by a project or product 'champion', to see through the entire development process of new products. This process can start when the idea is being tested out through techniques like brainstorming, extending to the research and design stage and so on to when the product is finally launched. Such a process means that there is a continuity of involvement by the project champion.

An adaptation of this idea is termed 'best practice benchmarking' (BPB), where multifunctional personnel co-operate in a similar way to the process described above, and the team's duty is to acquire data on products and companies in their industry that have higher performance and activity levels than those of their own companies, and from this study suggest ways in which improvements can be made. Because of the multi-functional nature of the team, it is acknowledged that the benefits that accrue from such BPB exercises should drive team members to establish better standards of performance.

19.3.4 Supply chain integration

In 1994 a study was undertaken in the UK by A. T. Kearney, Consultants. It investigated the supply chain from end-of-line manufacturers right back up the supply chain to sources of raw materials. Its conclusions were that business improvements would be possible not by simply viewing dealings between purchasers and sellers as isolated transactions each time, but by seeking to involve everybody down the supply chain. Hence came the term 'supply chain integration' (SCI).

The study stated that different supply chain relationships should be possible, with some members merely being content to act as manufacturers and fabricators and supplying to a specification (i.e. seeing their task as being good producers at the right quality and at the right time), while others might like to become more involved in end-use applications and even proffer suggestions for improvement, even though they may be towards the beginning of the supply chain. By considering the entire supply chain, new opportunities would present themselves and benefit everybody in it. This would improve overall effectiveness in the chain with regard to the elimination of waste and suggesting better ways of doing things, thus reducing overall costs.

The result would be that it would be possible to impel service standards to final customers to superior levels by concentrating the complete supply chain in this direction through mutual co-operation, rather than weakening the attempts of individual elements of the chain through conflicting objectives. The outcome would be the necessity for closer relationships between suppliers and customers. The task would not be easy, because of the problems of such integration and the task of investigating the measures of sophistication that individual members of the supply chain wanted or expected.

19.3.5 A new paradigm

Following the discussions relating to relationship marketing and SCI, it is appropriate to consider the view put forward by Christian Gronroos (1990), who argued that traditional views of marketing are unsatisfactory in a modern business environment. He emphasised the shortcomings of McCarthy's 'Four Ps', and went on to say that more 'Ps', like 'people' and 'planning', should be added as new marketing viewpoints. He states that the basic concept of supplying customer needs and wants in target markets has always had relevance, but contends that this still views the firm as supplying the solutions and not receiving its ideas from the marketplace. He therefore attempted to redefine marketing in a way that applies the principles of relationship marketing:

> Marketing is to establish, maintain and enhance long-term customer relationships at a profit so that the objectives of the parties involved are met. This is done by a mutual exchange of promises.

Definition
Marketing is to establish, maintain and enhance long-term customer relationships at a profit so that the objectives of the parties involved are met. This is done by a mutual exchange of promises.

19.4 Internal marketing

As explained earlier in the text, good internal marketing can be viewed as a pre-requisite for good, effective external marketing polices. It would be difficult to have one without the other. In a very real sense, the internal marketing is actually an intrinsic part of the relationship marketing process. However, the mass adoption of the internal marketing ethos by firms could be regarded as a 'macro' issue. The principles of internal marketing are being widely adopted by all kinds of firms as they strive to create a truly customer-orientated culture within their organisations. More than at any time before, today good marketing is seen as just as much of an internal process as an external one.

19.4.1 Internal marketing and its widespread adoption by firms

Internal marketing takes place at the interface between marketing and human resource management, and involves both of these management disciplines. The application of internal public relations has a salient role to play in the overall process of achieving an internal marketing culture, because it too embraces both of these areas of management. Management is discovering that it is all very well to talk about the firm becoming more customer-focused or marketing oriented, but how do they make this a reality? Whether the firm wishes to employ relationship-marketing policies to engage in social marketing activities or to practice 'green marketing' policies, those working for the organisation will still need the right spirit, ethos and

Definition
Marketing as a business philosophy is concerned with producing the appropriate internal company culture or 'internal spirit' that will result in the firm becoming truly marketing orientated and customer focused.

internal culture. This is where internal marketing comes into the picture. More and more firms are embracing the notion of internal marketing, and the widespread adoption of internal marketing is itself a form of 'macro' issue in marketing. The trend in marketing firms throughout the world is to pay much more attention to getting the 'spirit' or the 'culture' right before going on and attempting to improve the external marketing performance of the organisation. Internal marketing has now become an important and intrinsic part of what is considered the conventional marketing 'wisdom'. The term 'internal marketing' refers to the process of applying the general principles of marketing inside the firm. Marketing as a business philosophy is concerned with producing the appropriate internal company culture or 'internal spirit' that will result in the firm becoming truly marketing orientated and customer focused. The process of internal marketing involves much more than simply the application of internal public relations inside firms although, as discussed earlier, internal public relations is of paramount importance here.

Vignette 19.2

The Hilton Hotel Corporation appreciates the value of its staff, and uses internal marketing to retain them and make them feel valued

The Hilton Hotels Corporation is recognised internationally as a pre-eminent hospitality company. The company owns, manages or franchises 1900 hotels, resorts and vacation ownership properties. Its portfolio includes many of the world's best-known and respected hotel brands, including Hilton®, Doubletree®, Embassy Suites® and others. At the Hilton organisation, management realises that the firm's team members add value and quality to the business. In fact, it is the people working for the organisation that makes the Hilton Hotels Corporation such an international success. A hotel is an actual physical product, but a lot of the experience of visiting a hotel relates to the service offered by its staff. In terms of the 'Seven Ps' marketing mix model, certainly the people, processes and physical evidence are vital components of the marketing mix for service providers such as hotels.

We have all been to a hotel and been disappointed by the service and the attitude of staff, and as a result usually decided not to return in the future. A bad experience is usual recounted several times to family and friends, and so the hotel's poor reputation is passed on by word of mouth to many other potential future visitors. At the Hilton organisation, management realises that staff treat customers with about the same degree of respect as they themselves are treated by their own employers. If staff are not valued and treated well, they in turn will not respect or treat customers very well. Obviously this is bad for business.

The Hilton Hotel Corporation invests a lot of time and money in its staff. It takes training and staff development very seriously. It involves staff in all aspects of its marketing plans and strategy, so that everyone knows what is going on and how they can make a contribution. It rewards its staff for effort with awards and promotion. It includes its staff by allowing them access to the Extranet, which it also shares with its business partners. Management offers a comprehensive benefits package to its staff, including:

- Medical, dental and vision care coverage
- Life, accident and disability insurance
- The 'Thrift' savings plan
- The Hilton stock purchase plan
- The heart programme
- The flexible work arrangement
- Other benefits, including vacation and holiday pay plus special privileges when staff stay at Hilton hotels.

At the Hilton group, management really try to retain good staff and do everything possible to make working for The Hilton Hotel Corporation a rewarding and satisfying experience.

19.5 Customer care

High levels of customer care are essential to firms operating in the increasingly competitive market environments of today. As with the provision of telecommunications services commodities, customer service, rather than price, becomes the prime differentiator. High quality customer care is the key to achieving many of the business objectives confronting all competitive firms, such as:

- minimising churn
- attracting new customers
- improving profitability
- enhancing company image
- improving customer and employee satisfaction.

However, high quality customer care is a relative thing. With new operators and competitive forces constantly coming into play, no firm can afford to stand still. Regular customer care health checks will become an essential part of the operating strategy for existing firms, and new firms will need to ensure that they enter the market as high up the customer service ladder as possible. The cost of replacing customers is much greater than the cost of keeping them. If those lost include some of the customers firms can least afford to lose – the most profitable ones – then the impact on profitability is significant. In their book *The Loyalty Effect*, Reichheld and Teal (1996) provide data supporting this view; a 5 per cent increase in retention can lead to profit improvements of up to 85 per cent. However, they also warn of what they call the 'Satisfaction Trap', which is an interesting concept, particularly for marketing researchers involved in carrying out customer service appreciation surveys. Their research

Key point
The cost of replacing customers is much greater than the cost of keeping them.

shows that 60–80 per cent of customers who defect from firms had said in a satisfaction survey just prior to defecting that they were 'satisfied' or 'very satisfied' with the service provided by the company. Customer purchase patterns themselves seem to provide a more accurate basis for measuring satisfaction than customer surveys.

19.6 Customer relationship management

Definition

Customer relationship management has developed from a synthesis of relationship marketing, internal marketing and customer care to form a fully integrated system.

Definition

CRM creates a mutually beneficial relationship with customers.

Customer relationship management has developed from a synthesis of relationship marketing, internal marketing and customer care to form a fully integrated system. The ability of firms to actually use such a system owes a lot to the availability of the appropriate computer-based technologies; this was discussed in Chapter 18. However, customer relationship management is much more than just a Web-based customer care programme or an enhanced database marketing programme. In fact, customer relationship management (CRM) is evolving from a technology-centred scheme to a business-value enterprise as firms move from viewing customers as purely exploitable income sources to seeing them as important assets that have to be looked after and developed – in fact, the most important asset the company has. CRM is a comprehensive approach that provides total integration of every area of business that impacts on the customer – marketing, sales, customer service and field support – through the integration of people, process and technology, taking advantage of the communication possibilities of the Internet (Figure 19.2). CRM creates a mutually beneficial relationship with customers.

Society is changing at what seems to be an ever-increasing rate. There is more choice, and less time to choose and to enjoy the results of our choice. Everyone seems to have less time, even though the futurologists of only a few

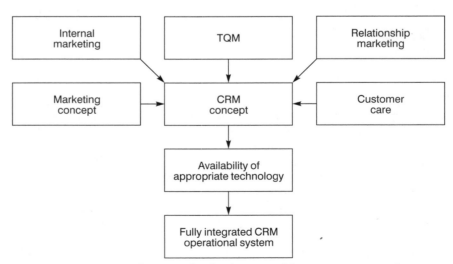

Figure 19.2 Factors contributing to the development of the CRM concept and its practical implementation.

years back stated that new technology would lead to the 'leisure society'. Customers have more products and services to choose from, and more information available to them to help them make their purchasing decisions. For example, think about the task of purchasing a new mobile telephone. The products are so sophisticated today, there are so many different models, and the information available on the capabilities of each model in magazines, on the Internet and in conventional advertising is enormous. Where do you start? Consumers wish to shop at all hours, even on a Sunday or bank holiday. Some people want to go to the supermarket in the middle of the night. People do their banking on their mobile telephone, research house purchases on the Internet, and book their air tickets through the television offers using Teletext. Seth Godin, author of the book *Permission Marketing*, said that the average consumer sees 3000 marketing messages a day, and so, to reach its audience, a message has to be relevant and well targeted (Godin, 1999). Godin and his colleagues are working to persuade some of the most important firms in the world to change the way they relate to their customers. His argument is both simple and radical: Conventional marketing communications, particularly conventional media advertising, is not as effective as it used to be. This is partly because there is much more of it for consumers to see and digest, and in part because people have learned to ignore it. Additionally, the rise of the Internet means that companies can go further than conventional communications would allow them to in the past.

Vignette 19.3

IBM solutions for Business Integration cover a broad range of technology issues and provide companies with a forward-looking approach to integrating their technology infrastructures

IBM has a range of solutions for business integration that make it easier to meet the global challenge and seize the opportunities by integrating and managing the diverse environment. The successful resolution of almost any business issue that you care to name – like managing a customer relationship, or doing e-business on the Web – depends on collaboration between different business systems. This collaboration means adapting and connecting existing systems for new business approaches with a speed and flexibility that has never been possible before. When business systems can collaborate like this, IBM calls it business integration.

In a world where many business organisations are perceived by customers as being similar, what sets an organisation apart increasingly is its level of customer service. It's also vital for profitability: it costs less to keep an existing customer than to sell to a new one. In fact, for some businesses, customer service is *the* critical element in corporate survival. From ATMs through to Web browsers, IT is the primary means of customer service delivery of today – and excellent customer service requires flexible, speedy and responsive IT systems.

Business integration is rapidly becoming one of the most important priorities in business today. This trend is due to a number of forces that are compelling companies to focus their resources:

- Globalisation of markets and brands is compelling companies with different operating units round the world to act as one integrated company, and consumers to view these organisations as single entities with consistent world-wide brands.

- E-business is attracting new Web customers from everywhere in the world, and these customers expect the same level of service as they receive through traditional channels.

- Increasingly sophisticated consumers are expecting more choice, and more ways of choosing. For instance, bank customers are now dealing through call centres, the Internet, ATMs and cash-back, as well as tellers. Furthermore, they are expecting consistent and prompt service through every route they choose.

- Increasing cost pressures are focusing attention on every part of the value chain. By making different parts of the chain work together, as in just-in-time delivery, inventory or manufacturing, costs are cut and business is moving faster.

- Competitiveness is reaching new dimensions; new competitors are entering the market (as in banking, for instance), and time-scales in a digital world are revised continually downwards.

These factors are creating a demand for co-ordinated and integrated business strategy that is only possible through the sophisticated business integration of computer systems.

There is a new group of products and services that relies on customers registering their interest in them with the company. Amazon.com encourages its customers to review books and publishes their comments on the website so both the firm and other users can read them and make use of them. A US airline invites customers to register their preferences for last minute offers via its website, and then e-mails potential customers with details of weekend breaks at their preferred resorts. Building high value, loyal, lifetime relationships is the most powerful competitive tool a firm possesses.

Management should reward staff for doing it right and make sure that they ask the customers if they are satisfied with the service they are getting, then check their purchasing behaviour to see if they remain loyal. For example, The Leadership Factor is a marketing research firm based in Huddersfield, UK, which carries out customer service satisfaction surveys for clients and monitors customer retention and loyalty. Some people take it very seriously indeed. Jeff Bezos (CEO of Amazon.com) says:

> I encourage everyone who works at Amazon to wake up terrified every morning. They should be afraid of our customers. Those are the folks who send us money. That is why our strategy is to say; heads down, focus on the customer, because the customer needs change at a slower rate.

Control of the relationship lies in the hands of customers. The marketing firm should help customers train them to meet their needs.

Customer relationship management is a major part of many companies' e-commerce strategy and their long-term relationship marketing strategy. CRM is a business and technology discipline that helps firms in the acquisition and retention of their most important and profitable customers. Ideally, CRM systems help firms provide start to finish customer care, from initial acquisition of the customer right the way through to product delivery and after care services. But CRM is rapidly evolving from being a technology-centred undertaking to a business-value endeavour. Organisations are moving away from seeing their customers as merely exploitable income sources to treating them as assets to be valued and nurtured. The value of customers is a long-term concept; lifetime value of customers is now what is important to many firms. This is an important trend that represents the use of knowledge management practices, such as the use of databases to capture and store comprehensive information about the customer, to build long-term, mutually beneficial customer relationships. Companies need a CRM strategy because it helps them understand their customer acquisition and retention goals, which is the whole basis of relationship marketing practices. CRM also helps companies retain customers and increase profitability, and a CRM strategy helps companies to co-ordinate the management of customer relationships across systems and strategic business units.

Key point
Organisations are moving away from seeing their customers as merely exploitable income sources to treating them as assets to be valued and nurtured.

Vignette 19.4

The Data Warehousing Institute in the USA finds that the majority of firms have not adopted the CRM concept

The Data Warehousing Institute supports, develops, and distributes a wide range of publications to keep its members up to date on the new techniques, events and issues in data warehousing, as well as the trends within the vendor community. The Data Warehouse Institute (TDWI) is a research organisation based in Seattle, Washington State, USA that has carried out extensive research that shows some interesting results. The firm's Industry Study 2000, entitled *Harnessing Customer Information for Strategic Advantage: Technical Challenges and Business Solutions*, surveyed 1670 business executives and IT professionals. Results indicated that although customer relationship management (CRM) has moved from theoretical concept to commercial reality in some firms, it still has a long way to go before it reaches any form of market maturity comparable to, say, the application of the total quality management concept (TQM) within business. The results of the research indicate that more than 75 per cent of the firms surveyed have not yet installed a fully integrated CRM system as a business solution. However, the majority of the firms surveyed plan to instigate such a system in 'the near future'. Amongst the 25 per cent with a CRM system in the firm, the majority were large organisations with at least $10 billion annual turnover and seemed to be concentrated in industries such as financial services, software or telecommunications.

The TDWI survey indicates that, on average, the majority of CRM strategies consist of at least six cross-functional applications, including database marketing, telephone call centres, Web marketing, direct mail programmes, filed sales and Internet self service for customers.

19.6.1 CRM computer software

CRM software can bring together data from disparate systems and business units to provide a holistic view of customers and a company's relationship with them. It can help co-ordinate customer contact and relationships across channels (retail, channel, Web) by presenting a unified message regardless of where the contact point is. CRM strategies can be a defence against being the same as every other supplier, and can allow the marketing firm to differentiate itself through superior service. For example, if the company manufactures a 'commodity type product' such as welding rods, it can differentiate itself through better customer relationship management and customer service. CRM is most effective when companies use pro-active strategies to support the whole sales process through acquisition, retention and development. Most businesses are moving to Web-based CRM, but this does not do away with the need for personal interaction that is so crucial to many companies' sales and marketing approach. Active CRM technology means that a customer contacting a website for information can be followed up immediately by a telephone call or some other form of communication. A mixture of communications can be used from the Internet, telephone, direct mail and even personal contact.

Key point
CRM projects are important, and managers must have clearly defined objectives for their programmes.

CRM projects are important, and managers must have clearly defined objectives for their programmes. Measuring the return on investment is an important first step in determining the criteria against which success of the programme will be appraised. The main quality of any set of measures must be to tell management if each project requirement was achieved. Some common CRM measures include the number of new customers, the cost of acquiring those new customers, customer satisfaction, customer attrition, the cost of promoting products, profit margins, incremental revenue, and inventory turnover. Firms need to consider ways in which Web-based CRM will enhance relationships with their customers and provide excellent service and information, whilst also allowing the relationship management teams really to utilise data available to cement and nurture the relationship with their clients. At this point, the e-communication and e-interaction between a firm and its external customers will truly be dyadic.

19.7 Summary

✓ The nature and direction of modern marketing has altered. The basic definition of marketing as a business process concerned with satisfying customers' needs and wants more effectively and efficiently than the competition remains the same, and the basic marketing concept is as valid today as it has always been. However, the processes used to achieve this have changed, and this is clearly evident when comparing a current marketing textbook with one from the 1970s or 1980s. Basically, marketing now sees a customer as a long-term income stream rather than simply as a single 'transaction'.

✓ Customer relationship management is a discipline that helps firms to acquire and retain their most important and profitable customers. Companies cannot succeed or grow unless they can serve their customers with a better value proposition than the competition – after all, this is what the marketing concept has always been about. Measuring customer loyalty can accurately measure the weaknesses in a company's value proposition and help to formulate improvements. Providing customers with ongoing value, satisfying their individual needs, and ensuring that customers get what they want when and where they want it is critical in today's dynamic and competitive market. If one company fails its customers, any number of rivals are waiting to take over. With e-commerce, any company anywhere in the world can take away customers. Retention is especially difficult with respect to commodity products when all it takes to move to another supplier is to type in a new Web address.

Questions

1 Explain the historical development of the relationship marketing concept from the end of the Second World War to the present day.

2 Compare and contrast the concept of 'reverse marketing' with the traditional marketing concept.

3 What are the main component parts of a fully integrated customer relationship management system?

4 Explain how the development of Internet-based technologies has facilitated the adoption and application of the customer relationship management (CRM) concept.

5 Discuss the contention that the customer relationship management concept is more of a step change in fundamental marketing philosophy than simply the application of computer database techniques to consumer profiles.

References

Berry, L. L. (1983). Relationship marketing. In *Emerging Perspectives on Services Marketing* (L. L. Berry *et al.*, eds), pp. 25–8. American Marketing Association.

Copulsky, J. R. and Wolf, M. J. (1990). Relationship marketing: positioning for the future. *Journal of Business Strategy*, **Jul–Aug,** 16–20.

Deming, W. E. (1993). *The New Economics for Industry, Government, Education.* Massachusetts Institute of Technology Center for Advanced Engineering Study.

Drucker, P. (1973). *Management Tasks, Responsibilities, Practices.* Harper and Row.

Godin, S. (1999). *Permission Marketing.* Simon and Schuster.

Gronroos, C. (1990). Relationship approach to marketing in service contexts: the marketing and organisational behaviour interface. *Journal of Business Research*, **20**, 3–11.

McKenna, R. (1991). *Relationship Marketing*. Century Business.

Reichheld, F. F. and Teal, T. (1996). *The Loyalty Effect: The Hidden Force Behind Growth, Profits and Lasting Value*. McGraw Hill.

Further reading

Armstrong, G. and Kotler, P. (2000). Relationship marketing in personal selling and sales promotion. *Marketing: An Introduction*, 5th edn, Chapter 13, p. 459. Prentice Hall.

Lancaster, G. A. and Reynolds, P. L. (1999). Macro issues in marketing. *Introduction to Marketing: A Step by Step Guide to All the Tools of Marketing*, Chapter 14. Kogan Page.

Plamer, A. (2000). The marketing of services. *Principles of Marketing*, Chapter 22. Oxford University Press.

Tate, S. (1999). First Union – using microstrategy to build more profitable relationships with 16 million customers. *Data Warehousing*, **8**, pp. 141–152.

Index

Above-the-line, 127–8
Accessories, 238
ACORN, 77–8
Ad hoc research, 263
Adoption process (buyer behaviour), 106
Advertising, 56, 127–37
Advertising by objectives, 134–7
After-sales, 168
Agents, 317–18
Alternative choice (selling), 166
Ansoff's matrix, 51–2, 364–5
Area sample, 266
Arthur D. Little matrix, 367
Associative segmentation, 79
Attitudes (buyer behaviour), 100
Audit (marketing), 360–1, 377,
Automatic vending, 187–8

Barksdale & Harris matrix, 367–9
Basic close (selling), 166
Batch production, 7
Bayesian decision theory, 294–8
Behavioural segmentation, 79–80
Below-the-line, 127–8
Benefit segmentation, 80
Boston consulting group (BCG) matrix, 361–3
BPB, 351
Brand:
  loyalty, 101
  management, 252–4
Brand-image school of advertising, 133–4
Break-even analysis, 222–3
British Overseas Trade Board (BOTB), 318, 330

Budgeting, 372
Business:
  analysis (new product development), 242
  format franchising, 185–6
Business-to-business (B2B), 63, 417
Buyer behaviour, 89–116
Buyer-decision process (buyer behaviour), 102–6
Buyers (DMU), 114
Buying centre, 114

C & F, 323
Cafeteria question, 280
Canned selling, 62
Cash:
  cows, 361, 368
  flow, 215
CATI, 40
Causal models (forecasting), 299
Channels, 57–9, 176–89
Checklist, 280
CIF, 323
Closing, 166–8
Cluster sample, 266
Cognitive dissonance, 105
Commercialisation (new product development), 244
Commission (sales), 171
Communication gap, 62
Communications:
  mix/process, 56–7, 119–51
  research, 258
Competitive environment, 34–6
Components, 238
Concentrated marketing, 71
Concept testing, 242

Consumer protection, 343–5
Consumerism, 334, 340–5
Control (marketing plan), 373–7
Convenience goods, 235–6
Co-operative ventures, 327
Corporate:
    identity/image, 141–2,
    planning, 259, 357–9
Cost (pricing), 219–20, 223–4
Credit, 44, 189,
Criticisms of marketing, 335–9
Cultural:
    environment, 43–6
    influences (buyer behaviour), 90–2,
        93, 325
Customer:
    care, 414–21, 423–4
    orientation, 2
    relationship management (CRM),
        414–16, 424–8
    use projections (forecasting), 293–4

DAGMAR, 129–31, 135
Darwin, Charles, 28, 180
Data:
    collection, 269–75, 287–91,
    fusion, 387–9
    mining, 386–7
Database marketing, 384–9
Deciders (DMU), 114
Decision making unit (DMU), 114–16,
    146, 149, 154
Decline (PLC), 249–50
Decoding, 120
Demand and supply, 210–11
Demographic segmentation, 75–9
Demonstration (sales), 164–5
Depth interview, 274
Development (PLC), 246
Development (product), 242–3
Dichotomous question, 280
Differentiated marketing, 70–1
Direct:
    marketing/mail/response, 142–6, 188
    segmentation, 79–80
    selling, 187
Discounting, 226–7
Discriminatory pricing, 229–30
Dissonance theory, 132
Distribution:
    channels, 57–9, 321
    research, 259

Distributive environment, 36
Distributors, 317–18
Division of labour, 10
DMU, 114–16
Dodos, 368
Dogs, 362
Door-to-door selling, 187
Double-barrelled question, 280
Double linear moving average, 301–3

Early:
    adopters, 108, 252
    majority, 108, 252
ECGD, 330
E-commerce, 380–43, 395–400
Economic environment, 38–9
Education (segmentation), 77
EEC, 38, 155
Elastic demand, 211
E-mail, 398
Encoding, 120
Entrepreneurship, 9–10
Environment, marketing, 28–46
Environmental:
    analysis, 360–1
    monitoring, 30
EPOS, 40
Ethics and marketing, 333–5
EU, 38–9, 42–3, 155
Evaluation (of salespersons), 169–70
Exclusive distribution, 178
Executive opinion (forecasting), 292–3
Exhibitions, 148–51
Experiment (marketing research), 265
Experimentation, 269–70
Exploratory research, 268
Exponential smoothing, 303–5
Exporting, 311
External audit, 360–1
Extranet, 399–400
Ex-works, 323
Eye camera, 270

Family:
    buyer behaviour, 94–6
    life cycle, 76, 94–6,
FAS, 323
Feedback, 120
Fieldwork, 263, 277–8
Filtering, 388–9
Final objection (selling), 167–8

Five Ps, 29
Flow-line production, 7–8
FMCG, 40, 104, 107, 153, 154, 212
FOB, 323
Forecasting, 40, 285–308, 371–2
Form utility, 58
Four Ps, 29, 49–50, 87, 122, 191, 233
FOW, 323
Franchising, 185–6
Free delivered, 323

Gaps, 72
Gatekeepers (DMU), 114
GE/McKinsey business screen, 363–4
Geographic:
    pricing, 227
    segmentation, 75
Global marketing, 328–9
Going-rate pricing, 225
Green marketing, 334–5
Group interview, 274
Growth (PLC), 248
Guttman's scalogram, 273

Hard sell, 105
HDTV, 40
Hierarchy of needs (buyer behaviour),
    98–9
Hofer's product/market evolution
    matrix, 365
Hoffman & Novak WWW
    communications model, 394
Hypermarkets, 180

Idea generation, 241–2
Imitative products, 240
Industrial:
    buying behaviour, 109–10
    goods, 237–9
    revolution, 1, 2, 383
    segmentation, 81–2
Industry maturity/competitive position
    matrix, 367
Inelastic demand, 211
Infants, 368
Influencers (DMU), 114
Information technology (IT), 40, 189
Innovative products, 240
Innovators, 108, 252
Installations, 238

Intensive distribution, 178
Internal marketing, 421–3
International trade/marketing, 10–11,
    39, 310–32,
Internet marketing, 380–413
Interviews (marketing research), 264,
Intra-firm environment, 29, 31–2
Intranet, 397–8
Introduction (PLC), 247
Inventory, 193, 195, 203–6
Investment (international), 327

Job:
    production, 7
    specialisation, 10–11
Joint venture, 327–8
Journey planning, 162–4
Jury method (forecasting), 292–3
Just-in-time (JIT), 59, 116, 192, 419

Keegan's five strategies for multinational
    marketing, 328–9
Kennedy's consumer rights, 342–3

Labelling, 320
Laggards, 108, 252
Lasswell's model of communication,
    120–1, 393
Late majority, 108, 252
Lean manufacturing, 59, 116, 192, 419
Learned behaviour (buyer behaviour),
    100–2
Legal environment, 41–3
Letter of credit, 323
Licensing, 327
Lifestyle:
    buyer behaviour, 93
    segmentation, 79
Likert summated ratings, 273
Line production, 7–8
Logistics, 59
Logo, 320
Loyalty status (segmentation), 80
Luxury products, 8–9

Macro-environment, 28–9
Mail order, 188
Management information system (MIS),
    261

Market:
  intelligence, 65–6, 261, 324–5
  management, 252–4
  penetration, 229
  share analysis, 219
  skimming, 227–9
Marketing:
  audit, 377
  concept, 1–5
  definition, 1–2, 5–6
  environment, 28–46
  experiment, 265
  history, 6–11
  information system (MkIS), 64–6,
    260–1, 324–5
  mix, 30, 49–51, 87, 233, 373
  myopia, 3–4
  orientation, 7, 18–23
  philosophy, 2, 4, 23–5, 29
  plan, 371
  research brief, 267–8
  research process/planning, 268–9,
    276–7
  research, 65, 257–83
  strategy, 355–79
Maturity (PLC), 248–9
Megamarkets, 180
Mental states (buyer behaviour), 103
Message source, 125–7
Middlemen, 58
Missionary selling, 63
Mixed economies, 30
Model 'T' Ford car, 7–8, 15
Modified rebuy, 114
MOSAIC, 78–9
Motivation:
  buyer behaviour, 98–9
  research, 99, 274
Moving averages, 299–303
Multi-level marketing, 197
Multinational marketing, 311, 328–9
Multiple choice question, 280
Multiples, 191–82
Multi-stage sample, 266

Negotiation, 165–6
Nested approach to segmentation, 82
New:
  product development, 239–44
  task buying, 114
Non-shop shopping, 187–9
Not-for-profit marketing, 3, 349–50,

Objective methods (forecasting),
    299–307
Observation (marketing research),
    270–1
Occasions for purchase (segmentation),
    79
Occupation (segmentation), 77
Oligopoly, 212–3
One-stop shopping, 183–4
Open-ended question, 279–80
Order processing, 193–5
Organisational buying behaviour,
    109–16
Osgood's semantical differential, 273

Packaging, 320
Paired comparisons, 273
Panel survey, 265
Pantry audit, 270
Part-time marketer, 350
Party plan (selling), 187
Penetration pricing, 229
People (in five Ps), 29
Perception (buyer behaviour), 99–100
Personal:
  interview (marketing research), 264,
    272–3,
  selling *see* Selling
PEST, 29, 37, 41–2, 318, 361
PESTLE, 29, 361
Physical distribution management
    (PDM), 57, 59–61, 191–207
Place, 57–61, 123
  utility, 58
Planning, 356–7
Political environment, 41–3
Porter's generic strategies, 366–7
Positioning, 49–50, 68, 84–6
Possession utility, 58
Postal:
  questionnaire, 264–5
  survey, 271–2
Prediction (forecasting), 286
Presentation (sales), 164–5
Prestige price, 224–5
Price, 53–5, 209–31, 322–3
Pricing research, 258
Problem children, 361
Product, 51–3, 233–55
  adoption, 251–2
  life cycle (PLC), 51, 245–51, 365

Product (*continued*)
line, 254–5
management, 252–4
mix, 254–5
research, 258
Product (international considerations), 319–20
Product/market life cycle matrix, 367–9
Production orientation, 6–9, 14–15
Profit, 216, 220–2
Project production, 7
Projective technique, 274
Promotion, 55–7, 320–1
Proximate macro-environment, 32–4
Psycho-galvanometer, 270
Psychographic segmentation, 79
Psychological pricing, 224–5
Public relations (PR), 56, 141–2, 146–7,
Puppy dog technique (selling), 167
Pyramid of influences (buyer behaviour), 102

Quality and marketing, 350–1
Question marks, 361, 368
Questionnaire design, 264–5, 271–4, 278–82,

Random sample, 265
Raw materials, 238
Recruitment (sales), 172–3
Reference groups (buyer behaviour), 93–4, 96
Relationship marketing, 416–21
Relaunched products, 240
Remuneration (sales), 170
Replacement products, 240
Report (marketing research), 278
Resale prices act, 181
Research:
brief, 267–8
process, 268–9
Retail audit, 270
Retailing, 123
Return on investment, 214
Reverse marketing, 418–20
RORO, 196
Rorschach test, 274
RPM, 180–1

SAGA, 46
Salary/commission (sales), 171
Sales:
forecasting, 40, 285–308, 371–2
journey cycle, 163
management, 169–73, 324
orientation, 15–17, 19, 333
promotion, 56, 123, 137–40
sequence, 160–8
Salesperson (role of), 157–8
Sampling, 265–6
Saturation (PLC), 249
SBU, 359–60, 361, 370
Scaling techniques, 273
Scrambled merchandising, 182
Screening, 242
Segmentation, 49–50, 73, 68–84
Selection (sales personnel), 172–3
Selective distribution, 178
Self-actualisation (buyer behaviour), 98
Self-concept (buyer behaviour), 96–8
Selling, 56, 61–4, 122–3, 153–73
Sentence completion test, 274
Sequence of effects model, 131
Service elasticity, 200–3
Services (industrial), 239
SET, 181
Sharp angle (selling), 167
Shell directional policy matrix, 364
Shopping goods, 236
Similar situation (selling), 167
Simple moving average, 299–301
Skimming (pricing), 227–9
Sleeper effect, 126–7
SLEPT, 29
SMART objectives, 358, 371
Smith, Adam, 2–3
Social:
class/influences (buyer behaviour), 90–2, 93
class (segmentation), 77
environment, 43–6,
Social/societal marketing, 333–54,
Speciality goods, 236
Sponsorship, 146–8
Starch model of advertising, 129
Stars, 361, 368
STEEPLE, 29, 37, 361, 369
STEP, 361
Stephenson's sort technique, 273
Stock levels, 193
Straight rebuy, 114

Strategic:
  business unit (SBU), 359–60, 361
  marketing, 355–79
Stratified sample, 266
Subjective methods (forecasting), 292–8
Summary question (selling), 167
Supplier environment, 33–4
Suppliers' market, 15
Supplies, 239
Supply:
  and demand, 210–11
  chain integration (SCI), 420–1
SWOT, 360–1
Systematic sample, 265
Systems approach (PDM), 197–9

Tachistoscope, 270
Tactics, 358
Target market, 55
Targeting, 49–50, 68, 69–73, 115
TEA (segmentation), 77,
Technological environment/change,
  39–41, 384
Telephone:
  interview (marketing research), 264
  marketing, 142
  survey, 272
Test marketing, 243–4
Thermometer question, 280
Thurstone's paired comparisons, 273
Time:
  series, 299
  utility, 58

Total approach (PDM), 197–9
TOWS matrix, 369–70
TQM, 350, 418–19
Traffic counter, 271
Transactional marketing, 417
Transportation, 193, 196
Trial close (selling), 166

Unaided recall, 280
Undifferentiated marketing, 70
Unique selling proposition (USP),
  132–3, 165
Unsought goods, 236–7
User/usage segmentation, 80
Users (DMU), 114
Utility products, 8–9

War horses, 368
Warehousing, 193, 195
Website:
  construction, 402–9
  management, 410–11
Wheel of retailing, 180
Wildcats, 361, 368
Winter's trend and seasonal model, 307
Word association test, 274
Word-of-mouth communication, 106
World Wide Web (WWW), 380–413,

Zone pricing, 227